Museums and the
Making of "Ourselves"

With reverence and deep respect, this book is dedicated to
His Royal Highness, *Omo N'Oba N'Edo Uku Akpolokpolo Erediauwa,* C.F.R.,
The Oba of Benin, Nigeria

Museums and the Making of "Ourselves"

The Role of Objects in National Identity

Edited by
Flora E.S. Kaplan

Leicester University Press
London and New York

Leicester University Press
A Cassell Imprint
Wellington House, 125 Strand, London, WC2R 0BB
215 Park Avenue South, New York, New York 10003

First Published in 1994
Paperback edition first published in 1996

British Library Cataloguing-in-Publication Data

A CIP catalogue record for this book is available from the British Library.

ISBN 0 7185 1775 X (hardback)

ISBN 0 7185 0039 3 (paperback)

Typeset by Mayhew Typesetting, Rhayader, Powys
Printed and bound in Great Britain by SRP Ltd, Exeter

Contents

List of Contributors

Flora E.S. Kaplan (editor and contributor) is an anthropologist, Professor, founder, and Director, the Program in Museum Studies, Graduate School of Arts and Science, New York University. She received her doctorate from the Graduate School and University Center of the City University of New York. She has done field work in Nigeria, Mexico, and the United States. From 1983 to 1985, Dr. Kaplan was a Fulbright professor at the University of Benin where she taught anthropology and art, and did research on royal women. She has published on art and cognitive systems, graffiti, pottery, and museums; her photographs have been exhibited, and she has curated exhibitions of Benin court art in the United States and Nigeria. Before coming to New York University in 1976, she taught anthropology from 1970 to 1976 at Herbert H. Lehman College, CUNY. She was formerly Curator of the Department of Africa, Oceania, and New World Art, at The Brooklyn Museum. Some recent publications include, *A Mexican Folk Pottery Tradition: Tradition and Style in Material Culture in the Valley of Puebla*; (editor) *Queens, Queen Mothers, Priestesses, and Power: Case Studies in African Gender*; *Images of Power: Art of the Royal Court of Benin, Nigeria*; and the articles in *Visual Anthropology*, "Some Uses of Photographs in Recovering Cultural History at the Royal Court of Benin, Nigeria" (1990), and "Benin Art Revisited" (1991); in *African Arts* (1993); and in *Art History*, "Iyoba, The Queen Mother of Benin: Images and Ambiguities in Gender and Sex Roles in Court Art" (1993). She has twice been elected to the United States AAM/ICOM Board.

Adrienne L. Kaeppler is Curator of Oceanic Ethnology at the National Museum of Natural History/National Museum of Man, at the Smithsonian Institution, Washington D.C. She attended the University of Wisconsin-Milwaukee and received her B.A, M.A, and Ph.D. degrees from the University of Hawai'i. From 1967–80 she was an anthropologist on the staff of the Bishop Museum in Honolulu, Hawai'i. She has taught anthropology, ethnomusicology, anthropology of dance, and art history at the University of Hawai'i, the University of Maryland, College Park, The Queen's University in Belfast, Northern Ireland, Johns Hopkins University, and the University of California, Los Angeles. She has carried out field research in Tonga, Hawai'i, Tahiti, Easter Island, the Cook Islands, the Solomon Islands, New Guinea, and Japan. Her research focusses on the interrelationships between social structure and the arts, especially dance, music, and the visual arts. She has published widely on these subjects, has recently completed a book on Hawaiian dance and ritual, and is currently working on books on cross-cultural aesthetics, the social history of early English museums, Tongan material culture, and Hawaiian art.

Margaret Anderson worked for many years in Australian museums and was the founding director of the Migration Museum in South Australia. She now teaches material culture and museum studies and public history at Monash University in Victoria. She has published widely on the practice of history in museums, on women's history, and on the history and demography of the family in Australia. She is the author of a national report on Australian museums and collections, Heritage Collections in Australia, and is currently researching a history of material life in Australia. She is president of the Museums Association of Australia and secretary of the federated professional organization, the Council of Australian Museum Associations.

Andrew Reeves has worked as a historian in museums and archives for many years and is currently director, Human Studies at the Museum of Victoria. His research has concentrated on Australian trade unionism, working-class communities, and more recently on Australian material culture. He is the author of *Badges of Labour: Banners of Pride* (with Ann Stephen), *Another Day, Another Dollar: Working Lives in Australian History*, and *A Vision of Australia: The Sydney Wharfies' Mural*. He has also published widely on Australian museology, cultural policy, and labor history. He is currently vice president of the Council of Australian Museum Associations.

Abdullah Hassan Masry was born in 1947 in Makkah, Saudi Arabia. After high school, he studied in the United States and acquired a Master of Arts in 1971 and Ph.D in 1973 from the University of Chicago. He was a lecturer at King Saud University from 1973 to 1981. Since 1980 he has served as Assistant Deputy Minister for Antiquities and Museums. He is a member of the Governing Body of the Islamic Research Center and the International Commission for the Preservation of Islamic Cultural Heritage; the Arab Archaeological Conference Association (Arab League); the King Faisal Foundation, Riyadh; the Board of Directors of Middle East Broadcasting Corporation; the High Council of Antiquities; the High Council for Religious Endowments; the King Abdulaziz Research Institute Board; the Max Van Berchem Foundation, Geneva; and the American Anthropological Association. He is the author of many reviews in professional journals, and has published *Prehistory in North East Arabia* (1974); *An Introduction to Saudi Arabian Antiquities*; *Traditions of Archaeological Research in the Near East*; *From the Beginning of Food Production up to the First States*; *The Arabian Peninsula* (UNESCO). He is also the Editor-in-Chief of *Atlal*, the Journal of Saudi Arabian Archaeology.

Luis Gerardo Morales-Moreno was born in the city of Puebla, Mexico. He received his Master's degree in history, Universidad Autónoma Metropolitana-Iztapalapa, and is a doctoral candidate at the Iberoamericana University. He is a research professor and academic coordinator for the Bachelor's Degree, Department of Ethnohistory, Escuela Nacional de Antropología e Historia, Mexico City. Morales' research examines the history of museums and its cultural significance in Mexico. He is now extending his research to the United States and South America. An historical anthology of the National History Museum is in press.

Alissandra Cummins has been the Director of the Barbados Museum and Historical Society since 1985. She has been directly involved in Caribbean museum development and training since her appointment as Deputy Director in 1983. Cummins was instrumental in the formation of the new Museums Association of the Caribbean (1989), of which she is now President. She holds a Master's Degree in Museum Studies from the University of Leicester, England. Ms. Cummins works with several Caribbean environmental and archaeological organizations including the Caribbean Conservation Association, the International Association for Caribbean Archeology (President), the Barbados National Committee of ICOM (Chair) and the Association of Caribbean Historians. She was recently appointed to the Board of the Peter Moores Barbados Trust, and now serves on the Advisory Committee of the Atlantic Slave Trade Gallery, a new exhibit being developed at Liverpool's National Museums and Galleries on Merseyside, with funding from the Peter Moores Foundation. Ms. Cummins is the author of several articles on Barbadian and Caribbean art history and is at present preparing a book on the 18th century Caribbean artist, Agostino Brunias (1730–1796).

John Dickenson is Senior Lecturer in Geography at the University of Liverpool and has held Visiting Professorships at the University of Pittsburgh and Universidade Federal de Minas Gerais. He has had research interests in Brazil since the early 1960s, initially in economic development and more recently in cultural geography and conservation. He is the author of two books and numerous papers on the economic geography and cultural landscape of Brazil. Field work for the present paper was carried out during a Visiting Professorship in Minas Gerais in 1991.

Maria Avgouli is an archaeologist, and curator at the National Museum of Greek Folk Art, in Athens. A museum educator, she organizes programs for the Center for Educational Programs, Greek Ministry of Culture. She recently completed the post-graduate Museum Studies Program at New York University, and is a candidate for the doctoral degree in archaeology, Athens University. She currently excavates in Crete.

Douglas Newton, a citizen of Great Britain, was born in Malaysia, and educated in London. His relationship with the Rockefeller Museum of Primitive Art began in 1957, continued as director, and as trustee after the museum became the Michael C. Rockefeller Wing, Metropolitan Museum of Art. Newton organized and installed the new Department of the Art of Africa, Oceania and the Americas, which he chaired at the Metropolitan from 1975, until retiring in 1990, as Curator Emeritus. He has carried out numerous expeditions in the East Sepik Province, Papua New Guinea; he has organized more than 64 exhibitions and supervised the design and publication of some dozen catalogs and books. Among his well-known exhibitions are: *Art of the Pacific Islands*, co-curated with A. Kaeppler and P. Gathercole for the National Gallery of Art, Washington, D.C.; *Mimbres Pottery*, for the American Federation of Arts; *Te Maori*, co-curated with S.M. Mead, for the American Federation of Arts; *Islands and Ancestors: Indigenous Styles of*

Southeast Asia, co-curated with J.P. Barbier, and installed at the Metropolitan Museum of Art. Newton has served in various capacities at the Australian Museum, Sydney; the National Gallery of Australia, Canberra; at the National Endowment for the Arts, and the American Federation of Arts, among others. He has organized international symposia on the Pacific in Basel and New York. He has lectured extensively in art history, most recently at Columbia University, and in museum studies, at New York University.

Madalena Braz Teixeira is a curator and Director of the Museu Nacional do Traje (Costume Museum) in Lisbon. She graduated in History and Philosophy from the Faculdade de Letras, of the Universidade Clássica de Lisboa, as well as in Museum Studies from the Instituto Português do Património Cultural. She received her Master of Arts in History of Art from the Faculdade de Ciéncias Sociais e Humanas of the Universidade Nova de Lisboa. She also studied music at the Conservatório Nacional de Lisboa, where she graduated in piano. She has taught Museum Studies at the Escola Superior de Belas Artes de Lisboa and at the Universidade Luís de Camões. She is member of ICOM, the International Council of Museums, and of the Association Museologie Nouvelle Experimentation Sociale. Madalena Braz Teixeira has published in the fields of History and the aesthetics of costume, jewelery, and related subjects. She also does research and writes about the history of museums in Portugal. A recent article, published by UNESCO in *Museum*, No. 3, 1991, is entitled "Les Musées et les femmes au Portugal: brève histoire d'une relation florissante."

Magen Broshi was born in Jerusalem in 1929. He was educated at Hebrew University, where he earned his Bachelor's and Master's degrees. He did postgraduate studies as a Fulbright student, 1959–61 at The Oriental Institute, University of Chicago. Broshi has participated in many expeditions and directed the following ones: Tel Megadim, a Phoenician coastal town (1967–69); Mount Zion Expedition, Old City of Jerusalem, inside and outside the city walls (1971–78); and The Holy Sepulchre (1976). His research and publications have focussed on archaeology, historical demography, history and topography of Jerusalem, Dead Sea Scrolls. Magen Broshi is Curator, Shrine of the Book, the Dead Sea Scrolls Wing of the Israel Museum, since 1964. He is Chair, Museum Association of Israel (1975–80); and guest lecturer, Bar Ilan University, since 1985. He was Guest Scholar, Woodrow Wilson International Center for Scholars, Smithsonian Institution, 1992.

Ekpo Eyo is Professor of Art History, University of Maryland at College Park, since 1986. Previously he was Director-General of the Nigerian National Commission for Museums and Monuments, between 1968 and 1986. Dr. Eyo is Currently President, Pan African Association on Prehistory and Related Subjects, Member of the Board of Directors of the Center for African Art, New York, and Member of the Scientific Advisory Committee of the Leakey Foundation for Research into Human Origins, Behaviour and Survival. Previously, he served as President of the Organization of Museums and Monuments in Africa (OMMSA); President, West African Archeological Association; Member of the Expert Committees that drafted UNESCO's 1970

Conventions on (a) *The Illicit Transfer of Cultural Property*, (b) *Restitution or Return of Cultural Property to their Countries of Origin* and (c) *The Preservation of World Cultural and Natural Heritages*. He received his Master's degree in Social Anthropology, Pembroke College, Cambridge University, England; Post Graduate Academic Diploma with a mark of Distinction in Prehistoric Archeology, University of London; and his Ph.D. in Archeology, University of Ibadan, Nigeria. He holds a diploma in Conservation of Museum Objects, University of London, and a diploma of the Museums Association of Great Britain and Ireland. Dr Eyo was a Regents Fellow, Smithsonian Institution, 1984. He was awarded an honorary doctoral degree from the University of Calabar, Nigeria. He is an officer of the Order of the Federal Republic of Nigeria, d'Officier dans L'Ordre des Arts et des Lettres, France, d'Officier de L'Ordre de la Valeur, Republique Unie du Cameroun and an Honorary Member of the International Council of Museums (ICOM).

George H.J. Abrams, a full-blood member of the Seneca Nation of Indians, was born on the Allegany Indian Reservation, Salamanca, New York, where he continues to maintain a home. He earned his Bachelor's and Master's in anthropology at the State University of New York, Buffalo. He pursued doctoral studies at the University of Arizona, Tucson. He is the author of 14 publications in anthropology and ethnohistory, including a monograph on the Seneca, *The Seneca People*. He was Director and Curator of Collections of the Seneca-Iroquois National Museum on the Allegany Reservation; and he served as Special Assistant to the Director, National Museum of the American Indian, Smithsonian Institution. Mr. Abrams served as a Trustee of the Museum of the American Indian-Heye Foundation, New York City, from 1977 to the end of 1989. He is currently Research-Consultant to the Christian A. Johnson Endeavor Foundation, New York. Mr. Abrams and his wife, a Cuban-American anthropologist, are the parents of a college-age daughter.

Howard D. Winters is professor of anthropology at New York University, specializing in Mesoamerica and prehistoric Midwestern North American Indians. He formerly taught at the University of Virginia and has conducted extensive archaeological excavations in Mexico, Illinois, and various parts of eastern North America. He trained at William and Mary, and received his doctorate from the University of Chicago. His numerous articles and publications have explored human ecology, the structure and organization of complex societies, long-distance procurement and trade, and the functional analysis of artifacts.

Introduction

Flora Edouwaye S. Kaplan

The revolutionary movements which are often the basis for nation-state formation frequently assert the uniqueness of one or more ethnic groups within such states. In attempting to preserve their cultural heritage, culturally and historically significant collections and sites, that were formerly the property of elites, are transferred into public hands as a national legacy. That legacy is then made available in museums for the enrichment, education and collective identity of the citzenry. Two kinds of basic resources are customarily collected, conserved and displayed in museums: objects, meaning the "things" of culture, belonging to the material world, that have been made, altered or utilized by human beings; and specimens or phenomena of the natural world. Writ large, these resources include monuments, architecture and sites, as well as living collections from nature, like arboretums, zoos, geological phenomena, gardens and their social constructions. Sometimes change is less dramatic than revolution, but is still the result of contested access to means of publicly defining self and nation, cultural and national identity and ambitions.

This book presents the histories and case studies of some of the ways in which national cultural heritage was and is still being created, transformed and shaped into collective views of the state, its regions, municipalities, constituent groups, values and ideas. *Museums and the Making of "Ourselves"* calls attention to museums as social institutions. It treats museums as a potent force in forging self consciousness, within specific historical contexts and as part of a political process of democratization. The spread of museums in the 19th century was apparently spurred by burgeoning science and capitalism in the West; and in the 20th century, by industrialization, change and the demise of colonialism.

The book chronicles some of the ways in which collections have played important roles in creating national identity and in promoting national agendas. It also provides examples in which an object or objects, themselves, stand for the nation-state, and embody the "idea" of the state for a people—for example, the Old Testament Bible for Israel (Broshi, Chapter 3), and Iroquois wampum for some North American Indians (Abrams, Chapter 5). Other collections and objects are being rediscovered and reinterpreted elsewhere (Kaeppler, Chapter 1).

In the past, the collection and public display of objects and symbols of wealth and power have proclaimed the glories of autocracies, theocracies, kingdoms and empires. Indeed, criteria of civilization and high cultures used by archaeologists presuppose some centralization of power, specialization of crafts and knowledge and impressive public displays. Aside from an innate acquisitive "instinct" often attributed to human beings, collections and displays were intended to unite a populace, to reduce conflict, and to ensure political stability and continuity. But they also served as focal points of discontent for groups seeking power. Symbols of state, power and prestige are invariably products of intensive, specialized labor, rarities and luxury goods. They were usually items acquired by long-distance trade and conquest, monopolized and controlled by those in power, or by those seeking influence and power. Ownership, consequently, was either private or restricted, in the sense of limited public access; and collections were contained within the palaces, temples, churches and residences of elites.

In egalitarian societies prestige and power are acquired individually, and symbols frequently shared and accessible to others, subject to age, sex and gender differences. Prowess, ritual and performance are means of attaining discrete recognition. Power finds expression in personal ornamentation, use of objects, redistribution of resources, objects and symbols, and control without especial use of physical force.

Museums appear to be unique public institutions that have emerged in western nation-states of democratic bent. They are spaces in which elites and competing social groups express their ideas and world views. Unlike palaces, churches, temples and noble residences, there is no hereditary or ordained monopoly of access, possession and display of symbols of power. On the contrary, museums accommodate diverse contents and ideas. And access is tolerated, and even encouraged, among a large and differentiated population, making accumulated knowledge widely available.

Elite world views underlie the collection and display of objects and symbols of wealth, knowledge and power in society. *Elite* refers to those groups who are both organized and conscious of themselves as at the top of a social hierarchy, and recognized as such by others. *State* is the term used here to distinguish those polities controlled by a centralized authority; *nation* refers to those states comprised of heterogeneous ethnic groups having a common identity imposed and based on geographic boundaries established, defended and administered by a central authority. These terms are used in the Weberian sense of actors who are legitimated (authority), and those able to impose their decisions on others by force, if necessary (power). *Democratic states* are defined here as those which allow for popular participation in the selection process, of persons and entities exercising authority and power, by known and practiced, public procedures.

To emphasize the nature of an historical process presumed to be both reflexive and ideological, 14 chapters were invited. The criteria were as follows: each author was to address what was previously an undocumented political transformation to nation-state; the focus was to be on collections and the appearance of museums; the museums were to be away from primary centers of museum developments in the industrializing west, in new and emergent nation-states. The underlying assumptions to be utilized were that museums are purveyors of ideology and of a downward spread of knowledge to the public, thereby contributing to an historical process of democratization.

The invited chapters were expected to test the working assumptions and the process; and to make possible some cross-cultural comparison on the national, as well as regional and local levels. The chapters, like all edited collections, are not representative of the universe of museums or that of any one country; and neither are they representative chronologically nor geographically. However, they are based on original research, drawn from the following geographic areas: the Pacific (Kaeppler, Newton, Anderson and Reeves); Africa (Eyo, Kaplan); the Americas (North America: Abrams, Winters; and South America: Dickenson, Morales-Moreno); the Caribbean (Cummins); the Middle East (Masry, Broshi); and Europe (Avgouli, Teixeira). These chapters anticipate further development of museological theory and method and western art historical, historical, and anthropological scholarship.

The chapters are grouped into three loosely defined categories: the first is concerned with new nations in the 20th century, seeking unity amidst diversity. Museums and museum systems are treated as instruments in defining self and nation (Kaeppler, for the Pacific; Kaplan, Nigeria; Anderson and Reeves, Australia; and Masry, Saudi Arabia). The second category deals with museums that emerged at a time of expanding scientific research and economic development in the mid- to late 19th and 20th centuries, when there was considerable growth of capitalism (Morales-Moreno, Mexico; Cummins, West Indies; Dickenson, Brazil; Avgouli, Greece). The third category embraces recent change, rising consciousnesses of gender roles, imagery, and "nationness" (Teixeira, Portugal). It also considers the roles and place of objects in defining the "self" among nations delimited territorially, and those not so defined (Newton, the Pacific, especially, New Zealand; Broshi, Israel; Eyo, Africa and Nigeria; Abrams and Winters, North American Indians).

Two of the chapters included (Eyo and Kaeppler) were first presented as part of a distinguished lecture series at New York University (1987–88), celebrating the tenth anniversary of the graduate Program in Museum Studies, Faculty of Arts and Science. A third paper was not prepared for publication (Deetz). The lecture series was made possible through the generosity of a grant from the New York Council for the Humanities, and received additional funding from the Humanities Council of New York University. The series gave public forum to ideas that guided the inception of the program 17 years ago. These ideas included the role of material culture and natural phenomena—their arrangement and use in museums—as the embodiment and reflection of the accumulated knowledge, world views and values of national elites and would-be elites. The notion was that each country uses its museums to represent and reconstitute itself anew in each generation. The lecture series also called attention to the increasing diversity today of museums, museum staff, collections and exhibits, and a broader spectrum of constituencies and cultures to be represented. In formulating my ideas for this series and later, for publication, it was encouraging to me to find some parallel ideas being advanced elsewhere, by Anderson (1983), Cohen (1980), and

Hobsbawm and Ranger (1983). Similarly, it is encouraging to find related ideas on museums, nationalism and the formation of collective identity through cultural heritage, becoming subjects of intense scrutiny and review in anthropology and political theory (Foster 1991).

By making explicit the notions that museums, collections, and exhibitions are products and agents of social and political change—that museums are themselves social institutions to be usefully studied— *Museums and the Making of "Ourselves"* will add to the growing literature on museology, and expand the institutions examined by anthropologists, historians, art historians and political scientists in their studies of change. The literature is already being expanded through a series of recent books edited by Susan Pearce for Leicester University Press, as well as others published by Athlone Press and Routledge, in England (Hooper-Greenhill, 1992, 1994; Kavanagh, 1990, 1991; Pearce, 1989, 1990, 1992). A series of pioneering papers have been edited since 1981 by Vinos Sofka for the International Committee for Museology (ICOFOM), and published in its *Working Paper Series* from 1981–90. Ground-breaking studies of material culture in anthropology have been edited by George Stocking (1985), and earlier by Thomas Schlereth (1982, 1985), in history and American civilization.

There are precursors of this thrust to be found among anthropologists, but while they were not primarily concerned with museums, they turned serious attention again towards art and material culture, beginning around the early 1970s: Adams (1969), Briggs (1977, 1980), Deetz (1965, 1967, 1977), Glassie (1969, 1975), Hardin (1970, 1977), Kaplan (1973, 1976, 1977, 1980), Muller (1966a, 1966b, 1975, 1977, 1980), Roe (1974, 1975, 1980), and Sturtevant (1967). Others, especially in archaeology, continued the ever-present search for meaning in material culture—e.g., Conkey (1978, 1984), Gathercole and Lowenthal (1985), Hodder (1981, 1982, 1989), and Renfrew (1982), among many others. Articles, chapters and books relevant to museums have, in recent years, begun to appear in increasing number (Appadurai, 1986; Karp and Lavine, 1991; Lumley, 1988; Redman, 1991; Vergo, 1989; Weiner and Schneider 1989). There is growing interest in objects, displays and exhibitions in museums, and these are becoming new subjects of anthropological attention—e.g. a new "Exhibitions Review" section has been established in the *American Anthropologist* (1991: 264).

An expanded journal (1991) of the Council for Museum Anthropology, *Museum Anthropology*, has been added to the literature. Museum practitioners, in critical pursuit of their classic goals—to collect, conserve and interpret art, technology, science, culture and history for the education and enjoyment of the public—now find themselves being asked to rethink their missions, ethics, roles and responsibilities. To do this, they must first know their own history and its uses.

Discussion

Adrienne Kaeppler examines some of the ways in which ethnic groups in a number of new Pacific Island nations view culture, objects and identity in museums and centers (Chapter 1). She draws on her fieldwork in Fiji, Hawai'i, Tonga, New Zealand and the Solomon Islands. Each has experienced dramatically different post-colonial directions. In Fiji, national identity is sometimes a violently contested issue between the indigenous Fijians and the majority population who are descendants of Indian indentured laborers brought to Fiji during the British colonial days. On another Pacific island, Easter Island, the establishment of a museum is enabling islanders to learn about their history for the first time; in Papua New Guinea, a plethora of distinct and formerly warring tribes are trying to weld themselves into a nation. Hawai'i is finding its rich cultural history as a complex chiefdom in danger of being subsumed by its identification as America's 50th state.

Archaeology in Saudi Arabia is helping to revise that country's self awareness and presentation of self today (Chapter 4). Saudi Arabia has pursued an intensive program of discovery in the last two decades, with the result that thousands of sites, ranging from rock art to urban centers, have now been identified. Abdullah Masry reviews the scope and intent of the country's research program. Much of it is of his own devising, as head of research in the country, and he gives some of the important results in Chapter 4.

Masry's program led to founding a series of regional museums that also serve as research centers. The museums house displays of archaeological materials from a hitherto, long-buried past—dating from the early paleolithic to the ethnographic present. A major National Museum at Riyadh was part of the program, as are several historical

Islamic museums founded in the 1980s. Evidently, Saudi Arabia is intensifying its own sense of "nationness" through modern scholarship, and presenting itself to the world as a nation of considerable time depth. It can claim a dynamic role in the history and prehistory of the region and the Middle East. Previously, its known past was mostly historical, and its knowledge of the provinces fragmentary. Saudi Arabia's provinces were known mainly through their relationship to other research and sites in neighboring states—in Jordan, Egypt, Syria and Iraq, rather than in relation to Arabia itself. This is a new picture of the country, recovered through research, publication and a nationwide system of museums.

Elsewhere in the world assertion of national identity has meant addressing questions of minorities and ethnic groups. Douglas Newton reflects on these issues among Pacific museums, especially in New Zealand, where an indigenous population was asked to decide how it wanted to present itself to the outside world at the Metropolitan Museum of Art, in connection with an exhibition entitled "Te Maori" (Chapter 9). Ekpo Eyo addresses the problem of loss of cultural heritage among emerging nations seeking to recover key objects in the reconstruction of their history (Chapter 12). Repatriation is considered in terms of the Nigerian experience. He details the difficulties encountered in enforcing international covenants prohibiting the illicit traffic in cultural property. Policing has not, thus far, eliminated post-colonial trafficking, expropriation and looting of objects of cultural pride from Africa and elsewhere. Eyo cites the examples of a recent case that involved the attempt to sell a clay head from the Nok culture, c. 500 B.C.–c. 200 A.D.—taken out of Nigeria and not returned to date. He cites another example that involved Ife heads, c. 12th–15th century A.D. Two have been recovered by Nigeria, one remains in England.

Eyo, as a framer of some of the UNESCO provisions for repatriation, concludes that the best hope for the future will come from greater moral and ethical behavior on the part of museum curators and directors. This kind of behavior, he emphasizes, will be hastened with professional, museological training. He fears African countries will otherwise lack the art and material culture to build truly authentic cultural identities for future generations. Abrams, making the case for Iroquois wampum (Chapter 13), and Winters (Chapter 14), come to similar conclusions with regard to North American Indian material culture. Abrams explicates some issues facing museums in sorting through the conflicting claims of factions within American Indian nations. Nowadays, such groups are found within the borders of larger, contemporary nation-states, i.e., North American Indian nations in the United States of America.

Madalena Teixeira, on Portugal (Chapter 10) and Magen Broshi, on Israel's archaeology and museums (Chapter 11), are among those who confront the question of ethnic and national identity from the perspective of older, formerly separate, cultural and regional political entities. The unification of many modern countries, despite roots in old worlds, really began as late 19th-century phenomena, and assumed their present recognizable shape in the 20th century. This is as true of modern Greece, described by Maria Avgouli (Chapter 8), as it is of Israel and Portugal.

Revolution, conflict and protest often marked responses in new worlds to lengthy periods of colonialism and life in a diaspora. The book looks at the contexts of these responses, through museums, in the chapters by Alissandra Cummins, on Barbados and the West Indies (Chapter 6), Kaplan, on Nigeria (Chapter 2), Anderson and Reeves, on Australia (Chapter 3), and Morales-Moreno, on Mexico (Chapter 5).

Museum interpretation is examined in depth by Howard Winters (Chapter 14), but is applicable to interpretation problems elsewhere. Winters is concerned with human ecology and shows how careful scholarship must be used to revise traditional museum interpretations of subsistence activities among North American Indians in both simple and complex societies. He points out that our fascination with the exotic and unique, like the Northwest Coast "potlatch" ceremonies, often obscures their real achievements in utilizing commonplace resources. Old museum dioramas emphasized hunting, fishing and warfare, which were usually male activities, and thus obscured the vital roles of women in sustenance and survival in many prehistoric and historic societies. Madalena Teixeira (Chapter 10), chronicles the wealth of art and goods flowing to Portugal in the years of state formation and the period of the discoveries, from the 12th to 15th centuries. Her chapter also reveals a largely unknown women's history of collecting. She shows how the choices made by noble women, many of whom entered cloistered life with their valuable personal possessions, helped to create the early art collections of the religious orders, churches and palaces of Portugal. Later, these collections became the basis for the nation's great museums, but their gender-based origins were obscured.

Museums have long served to house a national heritage, thereby creating a national identity that often fulfilled national ambitions. Often beginning with the private collections of elites obtained through conquest and exploitation, museums came to conserve cultural heritage and to educate the public. It is the nature of the collections, and the way in which they are used to illuminate and interpret the past, that is now generally under serious review among museum professionals. In the western world they seem to be discovering the impact of class and colonialism in museums (Ames 1986; Karp and Lavine 1991; Williams 1990); gender still gets less attention from scholars. In the developing world, professionals seem to be more concerned with using the potential of museums to educate and mobilize their populations to minimize conflict and make new choices (Gella 1992; Kaplan 1980, 1982, 1983, 1987; ICOM 1989).

Nigeria, for example, resembles other developing countries in assigning national roles to their museums. Under the initiative of Eyo, the first indigenous director-general of museums and monuments, a "museum of unity" was established in each state. The objective was to unite the various ethnic groups in a state, create mutual respect, and present a coherent picture of the local, state and national political entity to others—whether foreign or Nigerian tourists, visitors, politicians or potential investors. The Federal Republic of Nigeria, and its civilian and military governments, have all recognized the importance of museums as educational institutions and instruments of nation-building. Adults and children alike have equal opportunity to see authentic displays—scientific, historical and cultural—often created with assistance from the communities themselves; and they learn about their unique heritage as well as that of their neighbors.

Scholars and museologists who prepare exhibitions in Nigeria nowadays focus on public health programs as well as art and archaeology. The new private museums and even theme parks with historical displays are also beginning to play important roles in Nigeria. Like the animation of America's President Abraham Lincoln delivering his Gettysburg Address at Disney World, the garden of

Nigeria's past presidents and political leaders at Okada Wonderland introduces the public to the country's living history, and encourages learning in school and museum settings. Not just the past but the future is envisioned by The Didi Memorial Centre, where a modern art museum gives recognition to the country's living and leading artists, in Lagos.

Conclusions

Museums and the Making of "Ourselves" comprises a series of case studies that treat the political phenomena of museums from anthropological and museological perspectives. It calls attention to the impetus for museums arising in circumstances where knowledge is being expanded and objectified, and where changing economic and political conditions have led to competition in the form of capitalism and the democratization of social institutions.

The 14 case studies, each with their distinct emphasis, are drawn from areas that were or are presently on the periphery of the western industrialized world—the purpose being better to see the process of nation-building at work. And like all edited volumes, this book lays no claims to being truly representative of the universe of museums, geographically or chronologically. It does, however, attempt to redress the balance of what is known of the development of museums outside the major western centers; and it provides original research, much of it based on fieldwork, direct participant-observation, archival, ethno-historic and library research. The results bring into consideration a broader, worldwide view of museums—they make available a new body of original research—and they provide untapped sources for future study in a variety of fields (political, economic and social). Each author has tackled the subject with diligence and enthusiasm. Their chapters show that it is not through reification of mythical images that history is made meaningful, but through a reassessment of received wisdom, respect for diversity, and a search into the undeniable reality of the material world as human beings have found it and remade it for themselves.

References

Adams, Marie-Jeanne
  1969 System and Meaning in East Sumba Textile Design: A Study in Traditional Indonesian Art. *Southeast Asia Studies Cultural Report Series*, No. 16. New Haven: Yale University.
Anderson, Burton
  1983 *Imagined Communities: Reflections on the Origin and Spread of Nationalism.* London: Verso.
Ames, Michael
  1986 *Museums, the Public and Anthropology.* Vancouver: University of British Columbia Press.
Appadurai, Arjun, ed.
  1986 *The Social Life of Things: Commodities in Cultural Perspective.* Cambridge: Cambridge University Press.
Briggs, Charles L.
  1977 The Imagery of Unification: Symbol and Context in the Religious Art of Hispano New Mexico. Symposium, *Latin American Folk Art*, LAG. Paper presented at the 76th Annual Meeting of the American Anthropological Association, Houston, TX, December 1.
  1980 *The Wood Carvers of Córdova, New Mexico.* Knoxville: The University of Tennessee Press.
Cohen, Bernard S.
  1980 History and Anthropology: the State of Play. *Comparative Studies in Society and History* 22(1): 198–221.
Conkey, Margaret W.
  1978 Style and information in cultural evolution: Toward a predictive model for the Paleolithic. In *Social Archaeology: Beyond Subsistence and Dating*, Charles L. Redman, Mary Jane Berman, Edward V. Curtin, William T. Langhorne, Jr., Nina M. Versaggi, and Jeffrey C. Wanser, eds. New York: Academic Press. Pp. 61–85.
  1984 The Place of Material Culture Studies in Contemporary Anthropology. In *The Place of Museums in Anthropological Material Culture Studies*, R. Breunig and A.D. Dittert, eds. New York: Academic Press.
Deetz, James
  1965 *The Dynamics of Stylistic Change in Arikara Ceramics.* Illinois Studies in Anthropology, No. 4. Urbana: University of Illinois Press.
  1967 *Invitation to Archaeology*, Garden City, New York: The Natural History Press.
  1977 *In Small Things Forgotten.* New York: Doubleday.
Foster, Robert J.
  1991 Making National Cultures in the Global Ecumene. *Annual Review of Anthropology* 20: 235–260.

Gathercole, Peter and D. Lowenthal, eds.
1985 *The Politics of the Past*. London: Unwin Hyman Ltd.
Gella, Yaro T.
1992 The Use of Cultures of Nigeria as Sources of National Strength. Paper delivered at the National Institute for Strategic Planning and Policy, Bukuru, Nigeria. November 10, 1992.
Glassie, Henry
1969 *Pattern in the Material Folklife of Eastern United States*. Folklore and Folklife Monographs, No. 1., University of Pennsylvania Series. Philadelphia: University of Pennsylvania Press.
1975 *Folk Housing in Middle Virginia*. Knoxville: University of Tennessee Press.
Hardin, Margaret Friedrich
1970 Design Structure and Social Interaction: Archaeological Implications of an Ethnographic Analysis. *American Antiquity* 35: 332–349.
1977 Representational Components in Art Styles: A Comparison of Tarascan and Zuni Cases. Symposium, *Latin American Folk Art*, LAG. Paper presented at the 76th Annual Meeting of the American Anthropological Association, Houston, TX. December 1.
Hobsbawm, Eric J. and Terence Ranger, eds.
1983 *The Invention of Tradition*. Cambridge: Cambridge University Press.
Hodder, Ian, ed.
1981 *Patterns of the Past*. New York: Cambridge University Press.
1982 *Symbols in Action*. New York: Cambridge University Press.
1989 (1986) *The Meaning of Things: Material Culture and Symbolic Expression*. London: Unwin Hyman Ltd.
Hooper-Greenhill, Eilean
1992 *Museums and the Shaping of Knowledge*. London: Routledge.
Hooper-Greenhill, Eilean ed.
1994 *Museums, Media, Message*. London: Routledge.
International Council of Museums
1989 ICOM '89 Museums: Generators of a Culture. Reports and comments. 15th General Conference, 27 August–6 September 1989. The Hague: The Netherlands.
Kaplan, Flora S.
1973 Emic vs. Etic Analysis of Pottery Making in Mexico: Some Cultural Implications. Paper presented at the 72nd Annual Meeting of the American Anthropological Association, New Orleans, LA. November 30, 1973.
1976 Learning and the Transmission of Style Among Folk-Urban Potters in the Valley of Puebla, Mexico. *ACTAS, XLI International Congress of Americanists*, III, Mexico City. Pp. 243–250.
1977 Stucturalism and the Analysis of Folk Art. Symposium, *Latin American Folk Art*, LAG. Paper presented at the 76th Annual

Meeting of the American Anthropological Association, Houston, TX. December 1.

1980 *Una Tradición Alfarera: Conocimiento y Estilo*. Mexico D.F.: Instituto Nacional Indigenista.

1982 Towards a "Science" of Museology. In *Museological Working Papers*, No. 2/1981, Pp. 14–15. Paris and Stockholm: ICOM.

1983 Methodology of Museology and Training Personnel. Paper presented at ICOM London, July 1983.

1987 On Material Culture, Museums and Museology. Seminar on the Need for Museology, ICOFOM, Helsinki, Finland.

1990 (1986) Some Uses of Photographs in Recovering Cultural History at the Royal Court of Benin, Nigeria. *Visual Anthropology*, Vol. 3, Pp. 317–341.

1994 *A Mexican Folk Pottery Tradition: Cognition and Style in Material Culture in the Valley of Puebla*. Carbondale, Illinois: Southern Illinois University Press.

Kaplan, Flora S., ed.

1981 *Images of Power: Art of the Royal Court of Benin, Nigeria*. New York University.

Karp, Ivan and Steven D. Lavine, eds.

1991 *Exhibiting Cultures: The Poetics and Politics of Museum Display*. Washington, D.C.: Smithsonian Institution Press.

Kavanagh, Gaynor

1990 *History Curatorship*. Leicester: Leicester University Press.

Kavanagh, Gaynor, ed.

1991 *Museum Languages: Objects and Texts*. Leicester: Leicester University Press.

Lumley, Robert, ed.

1988 *The Museum Time Machine: Putting Cultures on Display*. London: Routledge/Comedia.

Muller, Jon

1966a An Experimental Theory of Stylistic Analysis. Unpublished Ph.D. dissertation, Department of Anthropology, Harvard University.

1966b Archaeological Analysis of Art Styles. *Tennessee Archaeologist* 23(1): 25–39.

1975 Generative Algorithms in Art. Paper presented at the 74th Meeting of the American Anthropological Association, San Francisco, CA. December 2–6.

1977 Individual Variation in Art Styles. In *The Individual in Prehistory*, James N. Hill and Joel Gunn, eds. Austin: University of Texas Press.

1980 Structural Studies of Art Styles. In *The Visual Arts: Plastic and Graphic*, Justine M. Cordwell, ed. The Hague: Mouton. Pp. 139–211.

Pearce, Susan M., ed.

1989 *Museum Studies in Material Culture*. Leicester: Leicester University Press.

Pearce, Susan M.
   1990 *Archaeology Curatorship.* Leicester: Leicester University Press.
   1992 *Museums, Objects and Collections.* Leicester: Leicester University Press.
Redman, Charles
   1991 Distinguished Lecture. In Defense of the Seventies. *American Anthropologist* 93 (2): 177–183.
Renfrew, Colin
   1982 *Towards an Archaeology of Mind: An Inaugural Lecture.* Cambridge: Cambridge University Press.
Roe, Peter
   1974 A Further Exploration of the Rowe-Chavin Seriation and Its Implications for North Coast Chronology. *Studies in Pre-Columbian Art and Archaeology* 14. Washington, D.C.: Dumbarton Oaks Research Library and Collections.
   1975 Comparing Panoan Art Styles Through Componential Analysis. Paper presented at the 74th Annual Meeting of the American Anthropological Association. San Francisco, CA., December 2–6.
   1980 Art and Residence among the Shipibo Indians: A study in Micro Acculturation. *American Anthropologist* 82(1): 42–71.
Schlereth, Thomas J., ed.
   1982 *Material Culture Studies in America: 1876–1976.* Nashville, Tennessee: American Association for State and Local History.
Schlereth, Thomas J.
   1985 *Material Culture: A Research Guide.* Lawrence: University Press of Kansas.
Schneider, Jane
   1978 Peacocks and Penguins: The Political Economy of European Cloth and Colors. *American Ethnologist* 5: 413–437.
   1987 The Anthropology of Cloth. *Annual Review of Anthropology* 16: 409–448.
Stocking, George W., Jr.
   1985 *Objects and Others: Essays on Museums and Material Culture.* History of Anthropology Series, Volume 3. Madison: University of Wisconsin Press.
Sturtevant, William C.
   1967 Seminole Men's Clothing. In *Essays on the Verbal and Visual Arts.* June Helm MacNeish, ed. Seattle: University of Washington Press. Pp. 160–174.
Vergo, Peter, ed.
   1989 *The New Museology.* London: Reaktion Books.
Weiner, Annette B. and Jane Schneider, eds.
   1989 *Cloth and Human Experience.* Washington: Smithsonian Institution Press.

Williams, B.F.
  1990 Nationalism, Traditionalism, and the Problem of Cultural In-
  authenticity. In *Nationalist Ideologies and the Production of National
  Cultures*, R.G. Fox, ed. Washington, D.C.: American Anthropological
  Association.

PART I
NEW MUSEUMS, DEFINING THE "SELF" AND NATION-STATES

1 Paradise Regained: The Role of Pacific Museums in Forging National Identity

Adrienne L. Kaeppler

When Flora Kaplan invited me to write on Pacific museums in the postcolonial era, I had very mixed feelings and many questions.[1] One might consider museums to be the epitome of a colonial institution, yet many new nations have them. Does "postcolonial" refer, I wondered, to politics or philosophy? Do Pacific Islanders want museums, or are museums a colonial hangover whose purpose is to assuage the collective conscience of colonial administrations that have destroyed the traditions that they now seek to enshrine? When objects become artifacts or art, and thus suitable to be placed in a museum, does this mean that a nation is in the process of losing its culture? Or, to take the opposite point of view, when objects become artifacts or art, does this mean that a nation has recognized its past and is educating its citizens about it?

Accepting Dr. Kaplan's invitation forced me to think more seriously about museums in other cultural systems. Here in the United States, we are in an era of rethinking how we represent other cultures, as well as our own past, to an ever-widening museum public. But does our new acceptance of social responsibility have anything to do with museums in developing countries, where such institutions are not part of their indigenous traditions? My remarks certainly do not answer these questions, but I hope they encourage further thoughts on the subject.

Museums in the Pacific are products of the overall process of social and cultural change. Traditions and social forms are important cultural elements that change slowly, while objects and technologies change more rapidly. What does one do with important artifacts that have become technologically obsolete, important tabu objects that no longer have traditional keepers, objects that are embedded in hierarchical social structure when democracy has taken over, or important religious icons when Christianity has changed the way one views the world? What sort of treasure house can assist in forging cultural, ethnic, or national identity and serve as a link to a future that recognizes its roots in the past? How can the Western concept of a museum be reinterpreted to accommodate other social realities?

To paraphrase Shakespeare's *As You Like It*, "all museums are stages, and the artifacts are merely players. They have their exits and their entrances, and each artifact in its time plays many parts." But what parts or roles should artifacts play in Pacific museums? And does this differ from island group to island group or between Polynesia, Melanesia, and Micronesia? In addition to the indigenous differences that existed in precolonial times, the colonial experiences of the Pacific include such diverse imperial traditions as those of England, France, Germany, Netherlands, Spain, Russia, Japan, Chile, Indonesia and the United States of America—in a variety of combinations.

The influence of outsiders on Pacific Island societies has been uneven, ranging from that of some areas of New Guinea, where the primary contact has been with patrol officers and possibly anthropologists, to most of those island groups that are important overseas possessions of major outside powers, such as the Society Islands and France, Irian Jaya (West New Guinea) and Indonesia, or Hawai'i, now the 50th of the U.S. States. Between these extremes are Tonga, an independent kingdom (which, although extensively influenced by England, was never completely a colony but only a Protected State); a number of newly independent states, such as the Solomon Islands, Vanuatu (formerly the New Hebrides), Fiji, Kiribati (formerly the Gilbert Islands), Tuvalu (formerly the Ellice Islands); and those islands still attached to a larger political power, such as the Cook Islands and New Zealand, or Guam and the United States.

The indigenous and evolved cultures of Pacific Island societies are extremely varied. The sociocultural systems within Polynesia, Micronesia, and Melanesia share certain core characteristics, but some societies do not easily fit into one of the major groups, such as New Caledonia, which has many elements in common with other Melanesian societies but has hereditary chiefs (which is more characteristic of Polynesia), or Fiji, which is in many ways a transitional area between Melanesia and

Polynesia. Many of the cultures of the Pacific are as different from each other as they are from other cultures in the world. For example, Melanesians (who are classified as Oceanic negroids) have similar physical characteristics to groups in Africa, but some Polynesians (who do not share these physical characteristics) have more in common with some African social structures.

In recent years the peoples of the Pacific Islands have come to feel that they have more in common with each other than with outsiders. These feelings are not trivial or manufactured but derive from real concerns as these societies face their separate futures. What these societies do have in common is the colonial experience, as varied as it may have been, and the love-hate relationship that has emerged with the colonizing power in the wake of efforts and successes toward independence. An important dilemma in independence is the necessity of interaction with other world societies in the international arena, such as meetings of the United Nations (UN) and the United Nations Educational, Scientific and Cultural Organization (UNESCO) and the maintenance of embassies and other consular activities in foreign metropolitan areas, while at the same time maintaining cultural individuality and forging national identity. Although politicians are usually not artists, performers, or sociologists, they do legislate cultural policy—and it appears that, throughout the Pacific, identity is considered to be of political as well as social value. It is not usually credited that museum workers, especially in small museums, are powerful and influential individuals. But, it is they who decide what stories are told or not told. It is their vision that is disseminated to the museum goer. It is they who can be a force in forging or discouraging national identity. Museums, as much as some people would like to deny it, *are* political.

Museums in the West are traditionally places where objects are organized and displayed to all comers. But how does this function square with Pacific traditions? In some parts of the Pacific, there were indigenous places where objects were also organized and displayed. New Guinea men's-houses, for example, were places where ritual objects were prepared, stored, and displayed to their own constituencies. On special occasions they might be displayed for the populace. They were not, however, open upon demand, and women and uninitiated men could never enter therein. In places where certain objects are associated only with certain people, based on gender, age, initiation, or other ascribed or achieved status, such as in New Guinea, the idea of a place where everyone can see a building's contents, and perhaps even touch the objects, must seem anathema. Unlike in North America, where the clients of a museum are the general public, in the Pacific world there are areas in which the concept of "the general public" does not exist and, if it did, would be destructive to a culture. If a ritual mask can only be seen by initiated men, how can it ever go into a museum in its homeland? Can or should the past be democratized or made gender free? And if so, does this signal the passing of traditional culture? If you think it does, you will be glad to hear that there are few museums in the Pacific—at least museums in the traditional sense. I am going to tell you about a few of them, traditional and nontraditional.

Bishop Museum, Honolulu, Hawai'i

Perhaps the best-known museum in the Pacific is the Bernice Pauahi Bishop Museum in Honolulu, where I worked for 14 years. *Hale Ho'ike'ike o Kamehameha*, the treasure house of the Kamehamehas, is Bishop Museum's Hawaiian name. It was begun in 1889 by Charles Reed Bishop, the banker husband of Princess Pauahi, the last of the royal line of the chiefly Kamehamehas, to honor her memory and to house the objects of her chiefly lineage. Bishop also, however, had grander ideas. He wanted his museum to "rank with museums of the world"— museums like he and his wife had visited on their trips abroad. The nucleus of the collection was the possessions of Princess Pauahi herself and the then recently deceased Princess Ruth Ke'elikolani, consisting primarily of Hawaiian material from the Kamehameha line. Almost immediately were added the Dowager Queen Emma's collection, the Emerson collection, and the collection of the Hawaiian government to form the Bishop Museum of Polynesian and Kindred Antiquities. The first curator-scientist was William T. Brigham who, with Mr. Bishop, planned and executed a "museum to instruct and delight" and almost immediately brought in objects that were not Hawaiian. Collections from Australia, New Zealand, and New Guinea were donated and purchased. Hawai'i's last queen, Lili'uokalani, rubbed shoulders with Caroline Island chiefs. Students, citizens of Hawai'i, and visitors came to pay homage, to learn, or to do research. From the beginning, it was a museum of the people of Hawai'i whatever their ethnic background, because by that time many Hawaiians had intermarried. Originally aimed at illustrating the "life habits and customs of the aboriginal inhabitants of the islands of the Pacific Ocean and of the natural history of said islands," it was not long before items of importance to other cultural groups began to find their way into the storerooms and eventually into the exhibitions. Even the thrones of the rival Kalākaua lineage became part of the Bishop Museum's collection and only recently were lent back to Iolani Palace.

Since the 1960s, exhibits about immigrant ethnic groups occupied much of the third floor of the largest gallery of the museum (Figure 1.1); and in the 1970s, the Hawai'i Immigrant Heritage Preservation Center was built on Bishop Museum's grounds in order to recognize the important cultural heritage of all of Hawai'i's people. Like other states of the United States of America, immigrants now outnumber its original inhabitants, and museums seek to display immigrant experiences, as well as the heritage of its aboriginal inhabitants. Bishop Museum, however, has always emphasized the Hawaiian element of its population, even taking an anti-U.S. stance by displaying, for example, the traditional religious importance of the island of Kaho'olawe, which the U.S. Navy uses as a bombing target.

What has the Bishop Museum done to forge identity? Well, generally speaking not much—at least not consciously. All the while I worked there, there was no policy to promote one thing or another. Bishop Museum is a metropolitan museum with a Hawaiian emphasis. Hawaiians, however, may see it differently. As the Treasure House of the Kamehamehas, housing the important cultural artifacts of Princess Pauahi, Princess Ruth Ke'elikolani, and Queen Emma, which were inherited from their illustrious ancestors, the museum has a sacred quality. Most Hawaiians, at least during my time at the Bishop Museum, were reluctant to touch the feather cloaks, the god images, and especially the *kahilis*, "feathered standards," the handles of which may include bones of the chiefs. Employing outsiders, who are not hurt by the sacred *mana* (supernatural power) of these objects, can be considered a continuation of the Polynesian tradition of bringing in outsiders, such as ceremonial attendants, nonrelatives, and even slaves, to do such necessary work as haircutting, tattooing, funeral preparation, and looking after sacred objects. What makes an object sacred is who wore it

Figure 1.1   Hawaiian Hall, Bishop Museum in the 1970s. The lower two floors exhibit objects from Hawai'i; the third floor exhibits representative objects of immigrant groups. Photograph Bishop Museum.

or used it, what prayers were said over it, and what power it attained during warfare or religious ceremonies. For the most part, these are things of the past. Hawaiians want to identify with them, but they do not want to return to their old stratified society in which authority, prestige, and power were ascribed by birth or achieved in warfare. Recent trends by so-called radical Hawaiians, who believe in Hawai'i for the Hawaiians and in an end to tourism, base their cultural identity on objects in the Bishop Museum's collection. Perhaps because the Bishop Museum takes no point of view—except that promoted by Kenneth Emory and all of us who have worked there, that Hawaiian culture is equal to any in the world—it inadvertently promotes Hawaiian identity for Hawaiians and part Hawaiians, while at the same time it promotes understanding and cultural equality among non-Hawaiian residents of the 50th state and cultural appreciation by visitors. There are no objects or exhibitions from Greece, Rome, or Egypt. The European Renaissance is an irrelevant notion. Hawai'i's identity as an island state with close ties to the Orient is the message—the same message promulgated in the political arena. Consciously or not, Bishop Museum echoes politics.

New Zealand

At the opposite end of Polynesia is Aotearoa (New Zealand) with a quite different mix of identity, politics, and museums. The four large metropolitan museums in Wellington, Auckland, Christchurch, and Dunedin have traditionally operated on the British model of displaying artifacts, preserving them, and doing research on them. They are analogous to the Bishop Museum in some ways, but Maoris have a different set of cultural traditions and a different colonial history than do the Hawaiians. Not many Maoris were really assimilated within the Western tradition of their *pakeha* (white) colonizers. Most importantly, Maoris kept alive their ceremonial traditions dealing with ancestors and the *marae* (meeting places for social, religious, and educational purposes). Parents continued to teach the lore of the ancestors and continued the carving traditions that are the important part of the *marae* buildings. If and when carvings were sold, new ones were made to replace them. It was ideas and social relations that were important. True, their older carvings were in *pakeha* museums, but as such things were inalienable in a philosophical sense, they still "belonged" to the tribal descendants of their original owners.

In this segment, I wish to express some of the thoughts of a Maori who has examined his cultural heritage in the context of New Zealand museums and academia in the wake of the "Te Maori" exhibition after its successful tour of four U.S. museums and the associated openings and cultural events. My remarks were stimulated by a paper given by Maori scholar Stephen O'Regan at the 1986 World Archaeological Congress in Southampton, England. Although not direct quotations, the next several paragraphs are based on his paper.

The "Te Maori" exhibition brought to the surface the considerable tension between the Maori and the *pakeha* academics over who should control Maori heritage—tangible and intangible. Unlike Hawai'i, which has large populations of several ethnic groups, New Zealand has a more typical colonial past in which the British came to conquer and colonize. The Maori Wars pitted relatives against each other, and quite understandably Britain won. Maoris were to be assimilated and their cultural heritage written down and preserved in museums as the remnants of a vanishing race. However, they neither vanished nor assimilated, choosing instead to retain their Maoriness and to learn how to operate by *pakeha* rules when necessary. Some became bicultural. Today Maoris verbalize their relationship with *pakehas* as "two cultures, one nation" or "two peoples, one nation."

In recent years ethnologists, curators, anthropologists, and archaeologists have found themselves under increasingly critical Maori scrutiny. People who have devoted their professional and scholarly careers to the study of various aspects of Maori culture, history, and prehistory are being challenged by a growing Maori determination that Maoris should define and interpret Maori culture. The view that the Maori people and tribal communities are the primary proprietors of Maori heritage and that the *pakehas* have only secondary rights in that heritage is gaining widespread acceptance amongst the Maori people. There is also a more stridently held position that *pakehas* and the larger New Zealand society have no rights at all in the management and decision making of and for Maori culture. Notions of "Maori sovereignty" and "cultural autonomy" are being advanced.

According to O'Regan, Maoris are beginning to ask important questions. *To whom does Maori culture belong? Who has the right of control and management of the Maori heritage? Who can speak authentically for it?* A *pakeha* response goes something like this: *Why, Maori of course, but this rich heritage surely belongs to all New Zealanders. Increased awareness and respect by us all enlarges and enriches our bicultural society. It strengthens the quality of our living together and enlarges the cultural potential of our common future. That's why* pakeha *people are learning to speak Maori, visiting* marae, *buying books on*

Figure 1.2 "Te Maori" exhibit installed at the Metropolitan Museum of Art, New York, 1984, designed by David Harvey. Photograph David Harvey.

Maori, going to Maori courses, and so on. But many Maori are opposed to the vision such a response represents. They see the increasing status of things Maori in the larger New Zealand society as merely moving their heritage further into the hands of those who have status and power, primarily *pakehas.* They see the increasing *pakeha* interest and competence in things Maori as a reflection of further *pakeha* control in education, wealth, and decision making.

The development of the "Te Maori" exhibition took three years. Its initial impact on Maori community thinking came when elders in the different tribal regions were consulted about their consenting to allow the *taonga* (treasures)—originally from the elders' areas but now in New Zealand museums—to travel to the United States (Figure 1.2). One of the effects of this consultative process was to widen the awareness of the ethnological importance of *taonga* and their enlarged status as art objects more widely in the Maori world. This awareness had previously been confined to elders with special interests and to a limited body of museum workers and scholars.

As a result of the "Te Maori" buildup, the Maori leadership was, for the first time in the current generation, being asked to focus on the Maori content of museums. Also for the first time, this leadership was having to confront the measure to which a major element of its cultural heritage was being interpreted and articulated—spoken for—by people who had little or no *mana*, or authority, in Maori terms. Museum journals of record and scholarly papers, even popular books on Maori history and culture, have largely passed the Maori world by. They have been dismissed as "*pakehas* writing letters to each other," and cultural status has been reserved for knowledge transmitted orally in the *marae* situation.

The sharpest tension arose from the book produced to accompany the exhibition (Mead 1984). As well as scholarly essays, it carried detailed descriptions of the various items in the exhibition, including extensive references to the histories and origins of the pieces. For many of the Maori leadership, it was an unpleasant shock to be identified publicly with historical and ethnological judgments, many of which they considered to be not just nonsense but academic invention. Matters reached a climax when one of Maoridom's most respected elders paused in the middle of an oration on his *marae*, tore out certain offending pages, and graphically wiped his backside with them. The trigger to his anger was not the actual description of his tribal treasure but what he considered to be a grossly incorrect treatment of the associated *whakapapa* (genealogy) and history. The primary value of the *taonga* in Maori terms derives from the *whakapapa* and history—its association with particular ancestors. These carry the spiritual links that bind Maori identity. The spiritual dimension of the objects in "Te Maori," as with all ancestral objects, is the focus of Maori concern. They comprise *wairua* (spirituality) and *mana*. These two qualities give them life in an important sense for the Maori people. Any artistic or ethnographic interest is seen as quite incidental and deriving from *pakeha* values.

Despite all their increasing familiarity with academia, many tribal leaders were plunged into shock by "Te Maori." They were well involved in the enterprise before it dawned on them that the *taonga* did not belong to them any more—that they now belonged to museum trustees. Many of them were heading off to New York before they had any idea of what was being said and written about their heritage, which formed the content of the exhibition. Questions and doubts began to be more stridently echoed by the tribes—aroused by the measure of media attention accorded to "Te Maori." The internal politics of Maoridom have begun to pressure the leadership into more stringent positions on heritage questions as a result of the "Te Maori" experience.

O'Regan concludes that the

> enormous media attention within New Zealand and the hugely enhanced public status of Maori art derived from "Te Maori" has greatly increased general Maori awareness of the Maori art heritage. This has, in turn, focussed sharper attention on the institutions and processes that manage and define that heritage. The spirit of the times demands that *pakeha* control of Maori heritage will be increasingly transferred to Maori control and that implies constraint on scholars and authors. The challenge facing the Maori leadership will be to devise constraints which quench the popular resentments at this *pakeha* domination of Maori Studies, which enforces reference to tribal authorities, and which, while constraining scholars, does not constrain sound scholarship.

Is this an example of museums gone wrong? Will museums in New Zealand use this as an opportunity to achieve a constructive role in forging a new kind of identity? And what will that identity be? Are Maoris and their heritage to be considered separate from *pakehas* and the huge population of other Pacific Islanders who make New Zealand their home? Will museums be on the forefront of cultivating new kinds of identity and educating the varied population about those identities? Should New Zealand museums not only display heritage as art but present the frustrations of the dispossessed? Should they echo the political climate, or should they be a force for change?[2]

Easter Island

An entirely different museum role is being forged at the third point of the Polynesian triangle. Rapa Nui, known in English as Easter Island, is one of the most remote places in the world. It has not been so much colonized as devastated. Most of the adult-male population was kidnapped—blackbirded—during the 19th century until few more than 100 Easter Islanders were left. Those who survived were not ritual or religious leaders—little wonder, then, that most of history is a mystery.

The present native governor of Easter Island is an archaeologist trained in the United States and married to an American linguist. Before becoming governor, Sergio Rapu was vitally interested in his past and began the museum which houses the objects and records from archaeological work carried out on the island. The whole island is in a way a museum, an archaeological site of great proportion and importance.

Most Easter Islanders know little about their past. Many of their traditions died with the kidnapped and disease-decimated ancestors. The huge stone heads are just part of the landscape (Figure 1.3). But Governor Rapu is trying to change all this. Archaeological restoration and preservation has become a priority and has progressed with support and funds from UNESCO, international organizations dealing with the preservation of monuments, and public and private funds from a variety of nations. Along with outdoor preservation, the museum is being enlarged and improved, and an effort is being made to restore for Easter Islanders an identity that was lost and forgotten. Artifacts, books, reports, historical accounts, and the like are being recovered and information based on them taught in the museum, in schools, and as island policy. In Easter Island, identity is not a political issue, it is political policy—no difficulty when the policymaker is also a political force. A happier conjunction of power, politics, knowledge, and vision could hardly be imagined. What kind of identity will arise remains to be seen. What is sure is that the museum will play a role in it.

Fiji

Yet a different situation prevails in Fiji. The Fiji Museum was founded by a voluntary society in 1904 but is now supported by the government as an independent body governed by its Board of Trustees. It plays an educational and cultural role in Fiji but deals almost exclusively with the past of indigenous Fijians. Less than half of the 725,000-person population of Fiji is ethnically Fijian. A large part of the population is Indian, brought to Fiji as indentured laborers, while a significant number of other inhabitants are Chinese and European (primarily from the United Kingdom, Australia, and New Zealand). There are also minorities from nearby Rotuma, Banaba, and Tonga, as well as other

Figure 1.3 Stone statues as part of the townscape. Hangaroa, Easter Island, 1984. Photograph Adrienne L. Kaeppler.

Pacific Islanders. In recent years, probably because of the large, vocal, and politically powerful Indian population, Fiji has dedicated itself to cultural pluralism. Unlike Hawai'i, where imported male laborers intermarried with Hawaiians, in Fiji Indian families migrated and little intermarriage has taken place. An example of the official policy of cultural pluralism can be seen in the delegation and performance sent to the Fourth Pacific Festival of Arts held in Tahiti in 1985 (Kaeppler 1988). Fiji sent a performing group that included Fijians, Indians, Chinese, Rotumans, and Banabans, each of which performed separately. This contrasted markedly with all other 22 island areas, which sent primarily indigenous performances. Hawai'i, for example, which has large populations of Japanese, Chinese, Koreans, Filipinos, Portuguese, and other Europeans, sent only a Hawaiian performing group.

Fiji's racial philosophy has been pluralistic, not homogeneous. There has never been an effort toward a "melting pot." There are few inter-racial marriages except with Europeans. Most significant, and politically contentious, is that outsiders (i.e., non-Fijians) cannot own land, thereby separating landowners from workers of the land. With a system of government based on Britain's parliamentary democracy, however, each person has a vote. Fijians have always had the majority of seats in Parliament, and therefore the prime minister has always been Fijian. Most well known, of course, is Ratu Mara, who is a very high chief in his own right and a respected, elected leader. That is, until quite recently. In the 1987 Fijian election, a coalition government dominated by Indians ousted the long-entrenched Fijian regime. This unprecedented event was followed by an even more unexpected event: a coup, in which a Fijian military man, Colonel Sitiveni Rabuka, overthrew elected Prime Minister Timoce Bavadra. There followed a state of confusion during which authority vacillated between military control and a civilian council and during which Bavadra was sent to prison and then released. After a second coup, in September 1987, Colonel Rabuka declared himself head of state, apparently supporting the political philosophy of the Taukei Movement, a group of militant Fijians who want to exclude Indians from power.

What does a coup have to do with a museum? It could have a great deal to do with it, primarily in the form of philosophy. As I noted above, Fijian political philosophy is based on racial and cultural pluralism. Indians do not join in Fijian dancing. Chinese do not live in

Figure 1.4 Fiji Museum, Suva, Fiji, 1989. Photograph Adrienne L. Kaeppler.

grass houses. Intermarriage is not encouraged. This can be contrasted with Hawai'i, for example, where a dance group will probably have more Japanese and Filipino blood than Hawaiian, but these dancers have taken on a Hawaiianness—something almost impossible in Fiji. Fiji has not encouraged the forging of a national identity and the museum echoes this stance. Exhibits in the Fiji Museum are 99% Fijian (Figure 1.4). Although there may be an occasional small exhibit of Indian or Chinese objects, there is little attempt to bring the non-Fijian experience into a sympathetic understanding of the nation's history. This is not a criticism of the Fiji Museum, which is in many ways a model institution. It was founded by the Fiji Society, which was solely interested in learning about and preserving indigenous Fijian culture, history, and prehistory.

But should this mandate have been enlarged when Fiji became an independent nation and a member of the British Commonwealth? Should the museum have been designated a place where a national identity could have been probed in a nonthreatening environment? The museum embeds the philosophy of ethnic Fijian importance in a culturally pluralistic Fiji. The Indians, however, do not have a parallel institution. If Fijians ever decide that a national identity that includes non-Fijians is desirable, then a museum would be one place to start to implement this philosophy and to educate the populace about it. The Fiji Museum could take such a position on its own but, with funds coming from a government with a different set of priorities, what would happen? If the objectives of a government and a museum are not compatible, what happens to a museum whose funds come from the government? Again, politics and museums are intertwined. Sorting out the nation and its coups may set a different direction for a museum that until now, has been focused on the past of its indigenous minority.

New Guinea

Let us move now to a different set of problems in the concept of forging national identity, to New Guinea, where the museum and various other cultural institutions have dealt with the concept in a most effective way. New Guinea is the home of some 700 linguistic and tribal groups that were traditionally politically separate and equal—and often at war with one another. Except for temporary or specific purposes, small groups of people typically under a "big man" were not amalgamated into large political groups. During the colonial era, various parts of New Guinea were dominated by Britain, Germany, and Holland, with influence from Russia and other European countries. Without going into the long, involved history, let me relate only the conclusion, which has resulted in a bilateral division of this huge island into Irian Jaya, the western half of New Guinea (which is now part of Indonesia), while the eastern half (along with some islands to the east) is the independent nation Papua New Guinea. The objective of forging a national identity out of diverse tribal groups is shared by the government, the museum, and other cultural institutions in this new nation. Although individual groups of tribes are encouraged to preserve their distinctive cultures as living entities, new institutions have been created that attempt to forge a national identity based on an amalgamation of indigenous concepts.

Outstanding in this regard are dance and theater companies, especially the National Theatre Company (formerly the National Dance and Drama Company) and the Raun Raun Theatre. These two companies have taken indigenous concepts, songs, dances, and stories from all over Papua New Guinea and woven them around literary pieces written by their own respected artists, radical thinkers, and philosophers. These works are not simply composites but are the forging of new artistic forms that are theatrical events representative of the New Guinea nation, understandable to themselves as well as to outsiders. These companies perform for important occasions in New Guinea, tour throughout the country performing for local audiences, travel to international festivals, and perform on stages in many parts of the world.

The National Museum and Art Gallery has a similar mandate. Although drawing their objects from the rich variety of local forms, exhibits are often cross-cultural in concept and design. One of the opening exhibits was on the pottery of Papua New Guinea, in which pieces of pottery from a variety of local groups were brought together to show similarities in technique, while emphasizing differences in style. The dramatic entrance pavilion features carved house posts from several areas and painted housefronts, which are a desacralized, generic representation of the housefronts of sacred men's-houses (Figure 1.5).

Fortunately, the political leaders of the new nation-state, especially then Prime Minister Michael Somare, set and implemented cultural policy and realized the potential role of a museum in disseminating this policy. They realized at the outset that "a museum can be instrumental in the effort of the nation's people to regain their identity which was lost in the colonial period," while at the same time it could "assist in the process of unifying different cultural groups into a nation" (Smidt 1979:392). Museum workers felt that, in addition to the traditional roles of a museum "to collect, store, preserve, display, and research objects which are meaningful to the community and to educate the public," the museum was also vital to preserving the cultural heritage. They felt that the "objects, presented as far as possible in their original social context, could help the people to reassert the values of their culture and its great artistic and spiritual achievements" (1979:392). In addition to the museum buildings, there is a series of small out-buildings used for craft work (Figure 1.6) and a dance ground for dance and theatrical performances. This cultural center in the urban

Figure 1.5   Entrance pavilion, National Museum and Art Gallery, Papua New Guinea, 1977. Photograph Adrienne L. Kaeppler.

Figure 1.6 Buildings for local craftspeople. National Museum and Art Gallery, 1977. Photograph Adrienne L. Kaeppler.

capital puts into practice the government's policy of unity in diversity. This national cultural center is associated with local cultural centers in Goroka, Gogodala, and Rabaul, as well as in other areas. These local institutions are devoted to preserving and reinvigorating local traditions and objects and to sustaining the diversity that the National Museum and Art Gallery forges into unity.

The history of the enlightened museum policy of New Guinea goes back to 1889 when Sir William MacGregor, the lieutenant governor of then British New Guinea, began a collection on behalf of the future nation. This collection was held in trust in Brisbane, Australia, until the New Guinea Museum became a reality. A number of temporary accommodations were used over the years, and in 1977 a modern building was finished and in operation. The museum owes its success to the involvement of politicians in cultural affairs and to the recognition that the museum's role must be viewed in the context of the government's cultural policy. Only with an enlightened cultural policy and a determination to preserve cultural heritage can a museum educate its audience in the concept of unity in diversity and thereby promote national identity. The New Guinea Museum and Art Gallery is also a model in its administration. While specialists are hired from the outside for short periods of time to work with and teach the curatorial staff about museum practices and techniques, its director and trustees are New Guineans.

New Caledonia

In a 1984 article called "Why Museums in the Pacific?," Patrice Godin, a New Caledonian, focuses on cultural identity, noting that having a museum is their right and is necessary for conserving the material proofs of their history and culture for the benefit of future generations. Starting with the traditional function of a museum, she notes that the first duty of a museum is to assemble collections, or as she calls them, "works of heritage." This is particularly important in numerous Pacific areas because many, if not most, significant cultural objects are in overseas collections. The mission of the New Caledonia Museum is to act as the instrument of cultural reappropriation—of cultural heritage alienated by colonization—by controlling exports; by refusing to permit pieces to leave the country, including all objects made before 1939; and by claiming the right of preemption, in which New Caledonia could preempt objects from France and prevent the sale of objects overseas. The second function of a Pacific museum is conservation of the assembled objects—especially difficult in the Pacific because of the diversity of materials and the problems with temperature and humidity control. The third function is scientific study, which necessitates having basic information about objects in the collection and elsewhere and setting up library, archival, film, and sound units. Scientific research into an artifact's original cultural context and meaning should be done by interviewing the makers and original owners of the object or their descendants. Training for indigenous people is a prerequisite for such research.

Godin feels that the most important function of the museum is education of the country's inhabitants—and especially its native inhabitants—in cultural identity. Their French colonizers had attempted to make them all Frenchmen and sent thousands of workers from France and other areas to New Caledonia. Godin calls for "opening up the museum to the layman, breaking down the barriers put up by the specialists, opening the door to discussion, rethinking one's ideas." Before one plans a museum, she says,

> It is important to question the validity of accepted models before undertaking the construction of a prestigious museum which is not really adapted to the cultural forms and to the particular public concerned, and which would involve huge running expenses far out of the reach of a developing nation's budget. Here the problem is not so much coping with a lack of funds, but rather organizing new methods of cultural reappropriation. Locking away objects according to the traditional method, between the four sheets of glass of a cabinet and the cabinet between the four walls of a building, is perhaps not the best solution.

Although such walls are part and parcel of conservation and it would be difficult to do without them, Godin feels that postcolonial museums should not be based strictly on this concept. Rather, galleries need to have adjustable and mobile props, divisions, and glass-cabinet units that facilitate frequent changes in presentation. Museums should become places where teaching laboratories are combined with cultural-expression workshops for dance, music, basket making, sculpture, drawing, and so forth. These educational programs, perhaps accompanied by exhibitions, should be formulated with the cooperation of known specialists and instructors for schools, with that of the unions at work, and with that of the traditional authorities in the villages.

Godin concludes that the term "reappropriation" must be taken in its strongest sense: that of controlling cultural objects, displaying them to their best possible advantage. Decolonizing a museum means opening it up to as many people as possible. This does not imply "selling it to the masses" but simply entails giving everyone the possibility of taking what interests him to help develop his own aptitudes. In this sense, the museum is a wager, and this wager is a totally political issue. Finally, Godin restates the purpose of her article, which began as "why have museums in the Pacific?" and instead asks "for whom?"

Vanuatu

A different set of priorities is in place at the Vanuatu Cultural Centre in Port Vila, Vanuatu (formerly the New Hebrides); the center was begun in 1961. There is little emphasis here on a building or on the display of objects in their cultural context. When I visited the museum in 1984, I was rather surprised at the cavalier treatment of the quite extraordinary objects on display. Most objects were not in cases, including such fragile items as sculptures made of tree fern and earth colors. Objects can be touched, and labels were at a minimum, if they existed at all. Echoing cultural tradition, objects are not important. They are made, used, and left to be destroyed by natural causes. The collections included some 2,000 objects, most of which were in storage, a substantial library, and an archive of films, 600 hours of tapes, and some 4,000 photographs. In addition to the expatriate director and a librarian, the staff included 17 *ni-Vanuatu* (indigenous researchers), all based in their region of origin. These researchers were equipped with video cameras and tape recorders with which they recorded local events, cultural ceremonies, and the like. Objects and crafts were sent to Port Vila for display by the museum and for sale by the craft shop immediately next door to the museum.

Although many traditions were destroyed or changed during the colonial period and especially by Christianity, many still exist and others are being revived. The museum encourages these activities and, in conjunction with government policymakers, supports cultural festivals and revivals. Festivals and traditional events, costumes, and crafts are filmed and documented for future generations. An arts festival in Malekula in 1984 was based on the theme "To Learn Who We Are" and documented the processes and products that make up the tangible and intangible heritage of the population of the island. The Minister of Culture, local traditional leaders, and museum staff plan and work together to set policy and priorities to preserve, revive, and develop cultural identity. National identity is not really an issue, for although there are myriad separate, localized traditions, these traditions have a basic similarity, and each is respected by its neighbor. Vanuatu already has a national or collective identity, and few outsiders are in residence. During the colonial condominium government, administered jointly by Great Britain and France, the indigenes felt no allegiance to either power. After independence in 1980, there was no difficulty in shifting power and policy back to their own people. Cultural traditions are their own and are not promoted for tourists' consumption. During floor shows at the tourist hotels, for example, they do not even attempt to present Vanuatu dancing. Instead, they perform Polynesian dances borrowed from their Polynesian neighbors.

Museums and Cultural-Center Complexes

This brings me then to the question of what museums in the Pacific should be like. Is the traditional conceptualization of a museum at all relevant for Pacific nations? Or is the enlarged concept of a cultural center more appropriate? Museums themselves are cultural artifacts, and how they will manifest themselves in specific places is part of the culture and history of that place. In islands with large populations of non-indigenous peoples, such as in Hawai'i, New Zealand, Fiji, New Caledonia, and Tahiti, more traditional museums, centered on a building with exhibitions and storerooms, may be relevant and needed to restore confidence in one's background and identity. In areas with mainly indigenous people, such as in Vanuatu, Tonga, or New Guinea, cultural centers that include a treasure house for objects may be more appropriate. The idea of a cultural center is much more inclusive than that of a museum. In most Pacific areas, objects are not given the importance they have in Western society. Objects are created from memory and exist as processes in the minds of artists. Objects are part of a socially constructed reality. They are forms that arise from oral traditions and artistic memory and that are the more basic part of culture. In many areas, objects are made, used, and destroyed, and that destruction is part of their function and life cycle. For example, New Ireland *tatanua* masks are less important than the performance of the ritual in which they are worn. Museums change this relationship and inhibit social and cultural reproduction by saving objects, thereby making it unnecessary to reproduce them. In this way, museums can be considered a barrier to cultural preservation. In some areas, it may be more relevant to represent the aesthetic and philosophical systems rather than the objects wrenched from these systems. New objects are as good as old ones if they are part of the system being reproduced. What is needed are places (i.e., cultural centers) to present these systems of processes and the products thereby generated, or simply the equipment for recording the events or rituals as in Vanuatu, and a place in which to store the videotapes. A treasure house may house and preserve objects, but objects are simply one type of thing that can be saved and should exist alongside archives for films, tapes, photographs, and books. What is crucial is the preservation of knowledge—much of which exists only in the minds of the elders—for with knowledge all things can be reproduced. This is not to deny the usefulness of traditional museums or treasure houses because everyone knows that things and knowledge change over time.

In some areas, such as in Tonga, presentation is an important cultural concept, but the act of presentation is often more culturally important than the object presented. In a ritual in which European-cloth grave decorations are presented along with more traditional barkcloth and mats, what would a museum save? They would surely save the barkcloth and mats and let the European cloth disintegrate. But, is not the preservation of values, traditions, and processes just as important as the objects? Cultural centers recognize this more fully than do museums. Pacific cultural centers may be in the forefront of the museum movement—not only forging national or cultural identity but leading the way for cultural rather than object, preservation.

In this attempt to examine the role of Pacific museums in forging national identity, I have simply questioned and probed what such roles are or could be in several museums and cultural centers. I suggest that this would be a good topic on which to do research in conjunction with research on political and cultural policy. In the postcolonial era, paradise may be regained, but it may be a different paradise. Politicians and museum workers must decide which Eden is desirable and which apple must be eaten to attain it.

Notes

1. This chapter was first given as a lecture at New York University on November 5, 1987, and was the first lecture in the series "Museums and National Identity: The Importance of Objects in the Formation of the Nation-State," in honor of the 10th anniversary of the Museum Studies Program of the Graduate School of Arts and Science at New York University. The lecture was accompanied by slides, but the text as printed here is essentially as it was given on that occasion.
2. Since 1987 there have been considerable changes in the involvement of Maori leaders and students in museums at all levels. In addition, Maori elders and others interested in cultural conservation invited 16 museum curators from overseas to New Zealand to take part in a conference to learn proper Maori protocol and appreciation for their *taonga*. It was a successful event—uniting Maori, *pakeha*, and curators from overseas in the most remarkable way. The proceedings included talks given by the curators about the histories of the collections in overseas museums (see Lindsay 1991).

References

Godin, Patrice
    1984 Why Museums in the Pacific? *Pacific 2000*. Noumea, New Caledonia.
Kaeppler, Adrienne L.
    1988 Pacific Festivals and the Promotion of Identity, Politics, and Tourism. In *The Impact of Tourism on Traditional Music*. A. L. Kaeppler and O. Lewin, eds. Jamaica: Government Printer for ICTM. Pp. 121–38.
Lindsay, Mark, ed.
    1991 *Taonga Maori*. Wellington: Department of Internal Affairs.
Mead, Sidney Moko, ed.
    1984 *Te Maori: Maori Art from New Zealand Collections*. New York: Harry N. Abrams, Inc.

O'Regan, Stephen
  1986 Maori Control of Maori Heritage. Paper presented at the World
       Archaeological Congress, Southampton, England.
Smidt, Dirk
  1979 Establishing Museums in Developing Countries: The Case of Papua
       New Guinea. In *Exploring the Visual Art of Oceania*. Sidney M. Mead,
       ed. Honolulu: University Press of Hawaii. Pp. 392–404.

2 Nigerian Museums: Envisaging Culture as National Identity

Flora Edouwaye S. Kaplan

Nigerian museums are a 20th century phenomenon. They are the product of a passion for preserving indigenous art and cultural history among some expatriates in the British colonial service and some traditional rulers, especially, the Oba of Benin, and the Oni of Ife, who founded local museums on their palace grounds before World War II. After independence in 1960, the fledgling system of less than a dozen existing museums scattered about the country, assumed a new role under its first Nigerian director-general, Dr. Ekpo Eyo. He saw art and archaeology as a means of creating a vision of national identity, fostering unity through new museums, as new states were founded. The present director-general, Dr. Yaro T. Gella, advocates a strong role for culture in political and economic national development, providing examples of uniquely African systems that have "worked" over the millennia. For him, culture is both "the fruit of a people's history and a determinant of history," being the ideas, values, and systems that give meaning and order to life (1992a: 9–10). Thus, museums which shelter culture in its material forms continue to be pivotal places for envisaging collective identity and national goals.

What is today the largest and most extensive museum system in Africa, is administered through the National Commission for Museums and Monuments (NCMM), established by federal Decree No. 77 of 1979, replacing the former Antiquities Commission and Department of Antiquities. The NCMM aims to unite and educate the country's diverse peoples, nearly 90 million strong (1992 National Census). Nigeria, the most populous and powerful country in Black Africa, has more than 250 ethnic groups, of which the three largest are: the Yoruba in the south and west, the Igbo in the east, and the Hausa-Fulani in the north. The predominantly Muslim north has smaller groups of Nupe, Tiv, and Kanuri among others; there are significant numbers of Efiks, Ibibios, and Eastern Ijaw in the east; and among the smaller but notable groups in the south and west there are numerous Edo-speaking Benins, the Western Ijaw, and smaller groups of Igbo, Yoruba and others in the area, particularly in Edo and Niger States.

The country's ethnic diversity has led many people to question whether or not Nigeria is or can be truly a nation in the face of apparent "tribalism," with its conflicting values and seemingly inevitable, instability. Dr. Gella, an historian and historiographer, who was professor of history at Ahmadu Bello University, dismisses this question. Nigeria's cultural pluralism does not support a thesis of the inevitability of instability or of Africa's failure to catch up with the West. He points to countries like America, Britain, and Australia, among the world's most powerful "nations," as models for Nigeria. They are places where great cultural and racial diversity are linked and given meaning by their respective histories. Nigeria's ethnic groups, too, are indissolubly linked by their common colonial and precolonial experiences. In a recent, major speech on national strengths, Gella observed that national neglect of culture in development arises from a failure to distinguish between the "forms" of culture and its essence. Whereas the forms, the very stuff of museum displays, consist of the "things" of culture as well as ephemerae, created and performed— masquerades, festivals, initiations, music, dance, and oral tradition—the "essence" of a people's culture lies in its ideas and values. But it is well to remember ideas and values persist amidst changing forms, being embedded in a people's material culture.

Dr. Gella offers this perspective on Nigeria's national museums: "With 50 years of history behind museum services in Nigeria and with about 30 stations [museums] and about 100 declared monuments, the NCMM is a large organization with skilled manpower to provide the required services" . . . although it lacks adequate resources to do so. His objective now is to involve all levels of government and private organizations in creating and supporting better museums:

> It is my intention to turn the museums in the country into living museums; a place which will take visitors into a delightful journey into the past, [a] living past and not a dead one. A place where people can enter

into meaningful and comprehensible communication with the past and draw inspirations and exciting experiences from such a journey. It is our desire to create an environment in the museum that makes one feel at home away from home. (Dr. Yaro T. Gella, 1992b)

Pride, not simply nostalgia for what is ancient and traditional, is needed to offset the violence of the colonial experience. "African" cultural components can be made part of decisions for national economic and political development, taking into account what is indigenous and useful, and discarding what is not. For example, traditional institutions of leadership have long successfully regulated relations between those exercising authority and influence, and those governed. African judicial processes have traditionally stressed equity and reconciliation vs confrontation and the assignment of blame, embodied in the "winner-takes-all" approach of imported, Western legal systems (Gella 1992a:27). Although African institutions enjoy wide-spread support in Nigeria, they have generally been ignored at the national level in favor of adopting Western models. Museums can play an active and vital role in changing this practice by raising historical and national consciousness, interpreting displays in broad contexts, and educating the public to the history of indigenous polities.

Beginnings

Foremost among the expatriates who contributed to the beginnings of the national museums is Kenneth C. Murray, who came to Nigeria in the 1920s as an artist and education officer. Having dropped out of Oxford, he found his life's calling in Nigeria (Willett 1973). Murray's efforts were directed to salvaging the rapidly changing artistic works of the people he encountered. This became virtually an "obsession" with him. In the process he founded a number of museums in various parts of the country that constitute the nucleus of the present-day system: the national museums at Esie (1948), Ife (1948), Lagos (1956), and Oron (1959). Under the British, Nigeria was divided into regions: North, West, and Eastern, with the capital in Lagos. With the exception of Lagos, the emphasis of the museums then, was local.

In 1943 Murray then persuaded the British colonial administration to set up an Antiquities Survey. As its head, he set out to locate antiquities and indigenous cultural artifacts, and to staunch their flow out of the country. He also influenced the British to establish the Department of Antiquities (Act No. 17 of 1953), and served as its first director until 1957 (and again, later, from 1963–1967). An advisory Antiquities Commission set up at the same time had, as its first chair, the distinguished Nigerian scholar, Dr. Kenneth Onwuka Dike. About this time it became mandatory to obtain an export permit for any Nigerian antiquity or work of art being sent abroad.

Murray retired at age 55, but he continued to live in Nigeria. On April 22, 1972, he was killed in a car crash while on Antiquities Commission business in Nigeria (Willett 1973). Widely acknowledged in the country for his role in contributing to the establishment of museums, collections, sites, and monuments now preserved in the country, Kenneth C. Murray was called the "father of Nigerian antiquities," during his lifetime.

Bernard Fagg, another British expatriate, played an important role in the discovery of unknown and very early cultures in Nigeria. In the beginning, Fagg was appointed to the administrative service in 1939. After serving in East Africa during the second world war, he returned to Nigeria in 1943. Fagg was then appointed a district officer, and later, an assistant surveyor and government archaeologist, based in Jos. It was there he recognized that the Nok finds being made in the Jos tin mines represented early cultures. He collected these materials, and established the museum at Jos, which was opened to the public in 1952. At Jos, Fagg began training indigenous technicians, conservators, and archaeologists. (Nigeria's first, outside professionally trained, archaeologist, Alhaji Liman Ciroma, took his degree at the University of Birmingham, in England; he later entered government service and went on to become a permanent secretary and head of federal service.) The second director of the Department of Antiquities (1957–1963), Fagg's service extended into the early years of independence, after which he returned to England to become a curator at the Pitt-Rivers Museum, Oxford University.

The first Nigerian to become director-general of the NCMM (1980–1986), was Dr. Ekpo Eyo, an archaeologist, educated in Nigeria at the University of Ibadan, and afterwards at Cambridge. He was also director of the Department of Antiquities (1967–1979), where he began as an assistant in the early 1950s. Eyo excavated at Rop, Ife, Owo, and conducted ethnographic surveys at Owo and in the Niger Delta. As head of the NCMM Eyo was responsible for setting national goals. He originated the concept of a "museum of unity" which was to guide the structure and content of post independence museums in Nigeria. With the creation of states in the 1970s, each national museum established in each state of the federation was to adopt the same format: local cultures were featured on the ground floor; statewide displays occupied the first floor; and dominant national cultures were installed on the second floor. The overall effect was to integrate the three political tiers. After Eyo, Dr. A.M. Obayemi became director-general (1987–1991). His interests were in furthering archaeology and tourism.

The Antiquities Act No. 17 of 1953 had broadly defined an "antiquity" in much the same way it still is: any object of archaeological interest; any relic of early European settlement or colonization; any work of art, or craft, including any statue, modelled clay figure, figure cast or wrought in metal, or any carving, housepost, door, ancestral figure, religious mask or other object, if such work of craft is of indigenous origin, if it was made or fashioned before 1918; and if the object was otherwise of historical, artistic, or scientific interest; and any work if it is or has been used at any time in the performance and for the purpose of any traditional African ceremony.

Later steps taken to control illegal activities include federal Decree No. 9 of 1974, making it illegal for any unauthorized person to buy or sell Nigerian antiquities. The commission was charged to examine each piece and issue or withhold an export permit. It was also directed to educate and lecture to the police and customs officers on the prevention of illicit exportation of antiquities to protect cultural and artistic heritage. NCMM governance is relevant to these duties.

Structure and Function of the NCMM

The NCMM is responsible for establishing and administrating all Nigerian museums, antiquities, and monuments. It consists, at the moment, of three departments: Administration and Finance, Museums and Monuments, and Research and Training. Presently, each is headed as follows: Dr. Yaro T. Gella, Director-General, Dr. Charles K. Gonyok, Director of Museums and Monuments, and Dr. L. I. Izuakor, Director of Research and Training. While essentially following the mandates contained in the NCMM 1979 Decree, revisions presently under consideration assign duties to the Honourable Minister for Information and Culture, enlarge the number of commission members on the basis of merit and nationwide representation, and institute other organizational changes (Dr. Yaro T. Gella 1992b).

The Decree No. 77 of 1979 that established the NCMM, dissolved the former Antiquities Commission and the Federal Department of Antiquities. It made new provisions for the declaration and violation of national monuments. Antiquities were expanded to include arts and crafts, architecture, natural history, and educational services. The Nigerian 1979 Constitution granted state and local governments the powers to establish museums. The NCMM, however, has the authority to approve all privately run museums, to control all archaeological sites and excavations in Nigeria, and to oversee university museums.

The government plans to found a national museum in each of the present 30 states of the Federal Republic of Nigeria. Among those longest run by the commission are some of the country's best known, most started in colonial days: the National Museum, Lagos (1956), the country's major national museum and the present headquarters of the NCMM (a new national museum headquarters is scheduled for Abuja, the new federal capital). Others in order of founding are: the National Museum, Benin (opened in 1944; and reopened as a new facility in 1973); the National Museum, Esie (Esie House of Images, 1948); the National Museum, Jos (1952), the first public museum in the country; and the National Museum, Ife, at Ile-Ife (1954); the National Museum, Owo (1957–1958; reopened in 1983); the National Museum, Oron (1959; reopened 1977); the Gidan Makama National Museum, Kano (1960); and a local Kanta Museum, Argungu. Later, the National Museum, Kaduna was opened (1975), as was the National War Museum, Umuahia (1985). Each is discussed briefly here (in chronological order, except Lagos).

The NCMM opened many museums in the 1980s: the National War Museum, Umuahia, Imo State; the Colonial History Museum, Aba; and the National Museum, Port Harcourt. New buildings were built at Calabar, Enugu, Ibadan, Maiduguri, Sokoto; and additions begun to the National Museum, Lagos.

Figure 2.1 Members of the British Crown's "Punitive Expedition" against the Kingdom of Benin, shown amidst the art taken from shrines and private quarters of the Oba's Palace, 1897. Photograph by R.K. Granville, 1897. Courtesy of the Pitt-Rivers Museum, Oxford.

Figure 2.2   The Oba of Benin Akenzua II, shown holding the coral regalia of his grandfather, Oba Ovonramnwen, the last Oba of the independent Kingdom of Benin, exiled in 1897. His coral crown, shirt, and other things were returned to the reigning oba by the British in 1938. Photograph by S.O. Alonge, 1938. Collection Flora E.S. Kaplan.

Figure 2.3 Entrance, National Museum, Lagos. At right, a bronze statue by the distinguished Nigerian sculptor, Ben Enwonwu, is mounted on the cut-stone wall of the museum, 1992. Photograph Flora E.S. Kaplan.

National Museum, Lagos

The main museum of the country, the National Museum, Lagos, was built in 1956–1957 (Figure 2.3). It serves as the headquarters of the NCMM and houses many of the finest works of the 250 ethnic groups in the country. Approximately 1% of its more than 0.5 million objects are actually on view.

Besides the main building, stores, galleries, and special exhibition gallery, there is a small, separate museum dedicated to the political history of the country entitled, Nigerian Governments: Yesterday and Today. There is a Technology Gallery that displays the progression of tools and metalworking in Nigeria from the Stone Age on, from gathering and hunting to farming communities. It includes a full-scale model of a fifth-century iron smelting foundry; and lost-wax casting is illustrated and explained, with examples from Igbo Ukwu and Benin. There is a Crafts Village compound, and a Museum Kitchen. Administrative offices for the director-general, a library, meeting rooms, and various staff offices, at present, complete the Lagos museum complex. The country's national museum will eventually be built at Abuja.

The Lagos National Museum is rich in ethnographic collections. Its stores hold more than 40,000 ethnographic objects and even more excavated and recovered archaeological materials. There are musical instruments, various clothing, face and helmet masks, weapons, orna-ments, horse trappings, armor, pipes, and sculptures. There are thousands of carved wood, twin-cult figures, *ibeji*, and *Sango* cult objects, masquerade dress, *Epa* head masks, *Ifa* divination objects, and musical instruments—all from the Yoruba. There is also a complete beaded ceremonial set of clothing that belonged to a late Yoruba *oba*. The spectacular crown has 16 birds at the top; it was made for Oba Abimbolu Afonlade II, of Ode Remo, a town near Shaagmu, Ogun State, Nigeria. All these items are kept for study, loan, and exhibition.

The Crafts Village on the grounds of the Lagos National Museum is a series of traditional African houses, each devoted to a different craft. Beadworkers make hats and ornaments for sale; hairdressers do braiding and weaving in a variety of styles for women; goldsmiths create jewelry; and women show and sell examples of their skills at weaving, and tie-dyeing, stencilling, doing batik, and *ikat* cloths. Yoruba wood-carvers offer sculptures, combs, and carvings for sale and to-order, for example, screens, a pair of wood doors, house posts, and other items.

The Museum Kitchen is a popular eating place at the Lagos National Museum. It offers special luncheons and traditional music, and features regional dishes, daily and weekly. The cooks use only traditional methods of preparing meats, whether cow or goat, and in preparing the many varieties of "soups" (stews) eaten in Nigeria. Fish and vegetable soups are very popular. Mortars and pestles are used to pound yams. Palm wine and other native and popular drinks are served. Office workers, museum staff, African and European visitors mingle and eat at tables, in a communal setting (Figure 2.4).

National Museum, Benin

The National Museum, Benin had its beginnings locally, in 1944, in rooms set aside for the Iwebo Society, in the Oba's Palace. During these early days, Oba Akenzua II assembled various works within the palace, where they were placed under the care of a local historian, and member of the Iwebo, Chief Jacob U. Egharevba.[1] The public's interest and desire for greater access soon led to a museum being established outside the palace. The first museum was in one room of the Benin Tax Office Building; it was later moved elsewhere on the old palace grounds, to the colonial Post Office Building. The latter building was where Kenneth Murray wanted a public museum to be administrated by the Benin Native Authority, as far back as 1946.

In 1958, the colonial government began assembling existing antiquities in Nigeria for museum display, using funds set aside as early as 1946 and 1947, to buy back Benin art from abroad. At that time most antiquities from Benin were in public and private collections in Europe and North America. A museum opened in 1960 and included objects from excavations in Benin, carried out by the Department of Antiquities. The present Benin museum took shape under the impetus of the then military governor, Colonel S. Osaigbovo Ogbemudia. He alone, among the new governors in the 1970s, responded to Dr. Ekpo Eyo's call for the states to become involved in creation of a museum of unity. Governor Ogbemudia made state funds available to purchase additional Benin objects for display and he initiated construction. A new circular building of modern design was begun, and grounds laid out in the commercial hub of Benin City, at Ring Road (Figure 2.5). The National Museum, Benin was opened to the public at ceremonies held on June 15, 1973. Oba Akenzua II attended the opening, as did the chief justice; the chairman of the Antiquities Commission, Dr. S. O. Biobaku; and the director of the federal Department of Antiquities, Dr. Ekpo Eyo. The head of station was Mr. Aghama Omoruyi, an artist and longtime member of the Department of Antiquities. Omoruyi was a native of Benin, related to the royal family, and served in the station from 1973 to 1990, when he retired.

Figure 2.4   Interior of the Museum Kitchen, National Museum, Lagos. Carved, wooden house posts from various ethnic groups (Yoruba, front center shown) support the circular roof, open to the sky. The Museum Kitchen features a different ethnic group's cooking each week, for a varied menu throughout the year, 1992. Photograph Flora E.S. Kaplan.

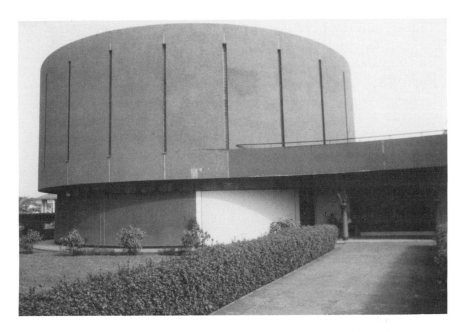

Figure 2.5 National Museum, Benin. Benin City, Edo State, Nigeria, 1985. Photograph Flora E.S. Kaplan.

Visitors to the Benin museum are guided through the local history of the Edo-speaking peoples of Benin and its empire with objects, photographs, labels, and dioramas on the ground floor. Outstanding works of art are highlighted: a bronze *Oduduwa* head; a pendant mask with serpents coming out of its nostrils; a bronze sculpture of a horn blower with an *erere*, which is sounded at the annual ceremonies and the sacrifices for the coral beads and *oba's* regalia. There are fine ivory carvings; wood staffs; brass *aquamaniles* (ewers) used by the *oba* for ritual handwashing, cast in the form of leopards. A semicircular royal ancestral altar, like those used at the Royal Court of Benin, has been reconstructed in the museum. The appropriate paraphernalia in bronze are displayed: ancestral heads, bells, celts, and offerings are placed on the altar.

The first floor of the museum (above the ground floor) is devoted to other parts of Edo State. There is pottery used particularly by women in worshipping *Olokun*, the god of the sea and bringer of wealth, who blesses women with children. There are masks for *eho ekpo* (the yearly agricultural cycle) and for the *Ekpo* cults. There is a complete costume on display, made by Lawrence of Ogiriga; the headdress was carved by Okeleke. It represents *Odogu*, the mother who appears in the dance-play called *Okakagbe*, among the Ishan people.

From the Niger Delta region there are headdresses, the *emedjo*, a headdress with a human figure; there is a fish headdress, a crocodile headdress with its forefeet stretched out at either side. There are displays of musical instruments, such as the *akpata* (Benin harp), *asologun* (linguaphone), and many types of flutes, drums, and rattles from various ethnic groups in the state. Utilitarian objects are also shown: combs, containers, wooden food-platters, palm-wine servers, and other items of daily use. Motifs of serpents, mudfish, and humans, some with mudfish legs, are found in Benin and Ife antiquities, and appear in modern Yoruba art.

The second floor of the Benin museum is dedicated to the major ethnic groups of the country and to the main ethnic groups in the state: the Edos, Urhobos, Igbos, and the Itsekiri and Ijaw peoples. The overall organization of the museum literally illustrates the theme of national unity. As visitors move from the ground, to the first, to the second floors of the building, they are gradually exposed to a widening horizon of cultures—from local and state, to national levels—within a single building that seems to embrace all of Nigeria.

The first museum in Benin, in 1944, was a manifestation of local ethnic pride by Oba Akenzua II, and by an unprepossessing scholar-historian, Chief Jacob U. Egharevba. Similar qualities of local pride and historical sensibilities were to be met, later, in another local innovator from Benin, Military Governor S. O. Ogbemudia, the first governor to provide funds to build a modern museum of unity, 1973.

National Museum, Esie

The National Museum, Esie, southeast of Ilorin, Kwara State, founded in 1948, contains more than 1,000 soapstone sculptures discovered on farmlands near the town of Esie. These carvings comprise the largest such collection in Africa; they range in height from 14 cm to one meter. According to local tradition, the figures represent foreign visitors to Esie, turned to stone by *Olorun*, the supreme deity, for having quarreled with and having maliciously acted toward the king of Esie. The existence of the stone sculptures has been known for some time. Leo V.

Frobenius collected three heads of the Esie style in 1912; and H. G. Ramsey, school inspector of the Protestant Church Missionary Society, is said to have discovered (really rediscovered) the soapstone figures in 1933. The source of the soapstone carvings, however, is a subject of controversy. Some scholars believe it to be Ife, others that closer examination points to Nupe influence from the north. The present controversy has yet to be resolved (Dr. Yaro T. Gella 1992b).

National Museum, Jos

The museum at Jos, in the capital of Plateau State, in north-central Nigeria, was the country's first public museum. The foundation stone was laid on September 23, 1949, and the museum was built at a cost of 10,000 pounds sterling, using direct labor. It was officially opened by the British governor on April 26, 1952. It was the first museum to use dressed stone on its facade, a technique used a few years after at Lagos (see Figure 2.1), and now a hallmark at most national museums. In its first year alone, nearly 65,000 people visited the Jos museum. The main museum contains archaeological and ethnographic collections; it also has one of the finest collections of Arabic manuscripts in Nigeria.

The Jos museum was, for a long time, the headquarters for the Department of Antiquities and its main research station. It serves today as the archaeological research center for the NCMM. When it opened in 1952, the Jos museum complex covered 11 acres; now it covers some 80 acres, in addition to the 120 acres allotted for the Museum of Traditional Nigerian Architecture (MOTNA).

Jos is recognized as the home of some of the earliest cultures in Nigeria, dating back more than 2,000 years. The city of Jos is located in the center of alluvial mining areas that are part of the Jos Plateau and the neighboring lowlands. There, on the plateau in 1903, European prospectors discovered tin and used new technology and heavy equipment to extract and process the lode deposits. Archaeological discoveries made during mining operations in the 1920s and 1930s led to the national recognition of Jos's importance: for example, in 1928, the well-fired pottery head of a monkey was washed out of tin-bearing gravels in the Nok Valley and was taken to the incipient museum at Jos; in 1943, the famed *Jema'a Head* was found 25 feet below alluvial deposits at Tsauni in the hills above Jema'a. It, too, was taken to Jos. Bernard Fagg

Figure 2.6   Detail of label giving names of birds exhibited in English, Latin, and Hausa languages. Zoological Park, National Museum, Jos, Nigeria, 1982. Photograph Flora E.S. Kaplan.

and Kenneth C. Murray well understood the significance of these finds and actively pursued their study; today these collections are among the most valued in Nigeria. Thus, the beginnings of the Jos museum complex are intimately associated with the tin mining operations in the area.

Over the next 40 years, after the museum opened, a series of smaller museums was opened as part of the national complex. This includes: the Zoological Park (1955) (Figure 2.6), the Craft Center (1959), the Pottery Museum (1963), the Museum of Traditional Nigerian Architecture (MOTNA) (1976) (Figure 2.7), the Tin Museum (1977), and the Bauchi Light Railway Museum. There is also a Bilingual Training Center for the Preservation of Natural and Cultural Heritage, jointly sponsored by the federal government of Nigeria and the United Nations Educational, Scientific and Cultural Organization (UNESCO). Organized at Jos in 1963 for Africa south of the Sahara, the center offers courses in museology and conservation in French and English. The Institute for Museum Studies has three schools: field archaeology, museology, and

Figure 2.7   Moses Abun, (late) head of station at the National Museum, Jos, checks the condition of traditional houses used by students at the UNESCO Training Center, Nigeria, 1982. Photograph Flora E.S. Kaplan.

museum studies. By March 1993, it is anticipated that PREMA in Rome will also have a location in this complex (Dr. Yaro T. Gella 1992b). The Jos museum houses one of the commission's two research libraries, the other being in Lagos. Eventually, each state museum will have its own library.

The Tin Museum (1977) at Jos shows European methods of extraction, as well as indigenous methods of obtaining alluvial deposits and refining tin. Tin mining predates European contact in northern Nigeria: first tin ore and then straw tin were traded with the Arabs across the desert up until the 16th century. Tin was important in brass manufacture at Benin, Bida, and Ile-Ife.

The Bauchi Light Railway, linking Jos and Zaria with the coast's main line, reached Jos in July 1914 and operated until 1957. The museum's collections include two locomotives, three carriages, and track and lineside equipment. Some of the earliest mechanized vehicles on the Jos Plateau are exhibited here: a Bedford kitcar, an Albion lorry, and a traction engine.

The Zoological Park of the Jos museum was opened in 1955, mainly for children. At first, it housed few dangerous animals. It now contains lions, hyenas (spotted and striped), baboons, mandrills, various monkeys, and a group of active chimpanzees. Boa constrictors and pythons are kept in viewing pits. There are crocodiles, deer fox, and porcupines, and such birds as eagles and vultures (see Figure 2.6). Overall, there are 250 specimens in the zoo's collection, many of which are kept in buildings of traditional design and in areas that blend into the landscape. The Zoological Society was formed in 1960, and the commission manages the zoo's daily affairs.

The Pottery Museum (1963) at Jos contains about 300 pieces collected between 1957 and 1962 by Sylvia Leith-Ross, a former education officer in southern Nigeria. The pottery compound was designed by the University of Gdansk Professor Z. R. Dmochowski, the chief architect for the Department of Antiquities and a specialist in tropical architecture. Many species of shrubs and trees from throughout Africa are planted in the courtyards of the Pottery Museum. The museum's three fishponds are stocked with many varieties of tropical fish.

The Craft Center of the Jos museum complex began with a 1,500 pound sterling donation from an American, Mrs. Spruyt. A museum workshop was built, and kilns were added in 1963; the pottery which has been produced here since 1964, is for sale. Michael Cardew, founder of a workshop at Abuja, trained Kofi Athey, a potter at Jos, who has since achieved international recognition. The pottery-making equipment was donated by UNESCO. Other craft workshops on the grounds of the Jos museum include weavers, leather workers, and brass workers from various parts of Nigeria. Two Buji blacksmiths and a woman potter from the Jarawa village of Fobur, southeast of Jos, have worked there. All of the crafts made at the museum are for sale.

Perhaps the most spectacular museum in the complex at Jos is MOTNA. Epitomizing a national endeavor on a grand scale, it is an open-air, 120-acre museum that now holds and will eventually contain more outstanding examples of indigenous architecture from all parts of Nigeria. The reproduced buildings utilize the basic materials actually used in the original structures: earth, loam, timber, grass, and so forth—all of which are susceptible to destruction by weather and insects. Therefore, MOTNA has the important task of preserving and presenting these indigenous achievements of the past. At MOTNA, local techniques, as well as local materials, and local workmen are used to replicate the structures.

The idea for this open-air museum originated with Dmochowski. Work began on MOTNA in 1973, and the first phase was completed in 1978. Alhaji Baba Galadima assumed supervision of the project in 1976. The northern sector was begun first, along with some buildings from the west and east of Nigeria. MOTNA represents a kind of miniature architectural map of the country, linked on the ground by a network of footpaths.

Among the notable buildings and sites at MOTNA are the following, discussed briefly here: Rukuba Compound was built by Rukuba craftsmen from the Rukuba Hills, about 30km northeast of Jos, during the dry season of 1975–1976. From eastern Nigeria are the village living quarters of the Igbo man, a small, enclosed compound represented by the *Nwaokator Omili's* House, Nimo; Chief Ekwunife's Compound—*Ifite-Nibo*, "*Nkpo Enu*"—from Nibo, near Awaka; Chief Ogbua's Compound, the *Onitsha-Umuaroli*; and a type of Igbo compound, called *iba*, that services the religious, social, and domestic needs of its inhabitants. An *ogwa* (colonnaded portico), decorated with elaborate geometrical bas-reliefs in loam, has some carved wooden doors for which the Igbo are famous. The Mbari House, *Owerri*, is an outstanding example of a well-known type of mud-sculptured architecture. Its stepped walls contain dozens of human and animal mythological figures.

An Ife shrine, *Ile Orisa Ikire*, is a gabled building with a veranda that has to be repainted each year in traditional blue-grey, red, and white colors, with animals and symbols used to celebrate annual festivals. The *Afin Akure*, another Yoruba building, is the royal residence of the *afin*, a traditional ruler. There is a series of courtyards, surrounded by small rooms, and a roofed veranda that is used for secular and religious purposes. The veranda posts and the doors are finely carved in typical Yoruba style.

From northern Nigeria there are several structures: the Pategi Compound, reminiscent of the ancient Nupe Emirate of Pategi, on the southern bank of the Niger River in Kwara State; and Tiv Compound, the Abuja Palace, and the Katsina Palace are among the other gems of the collection. The Emir of Pategi sent builders to do the work at Jos and sent the carved house posts. The *katamba* (circular entrance building) of the emir's palace is spectacular for its high-shaped, thatched roof, supported by a ring of more than 90 carved posts, each different from the next. A Nupe man spent two years at the museum just carving these posts. The doors at opposite ends of the *katamba* are high enough to allow a man on horseback to enter. The Katsina Palace was completed in 1976.

The Tiv Compound, Benue State, was completed by Tiv craftsmen in 1976. There is a reception house, or *ate*, furnished with clay platforms, a wood reclining chair, and a drum; two sleeping houses; a large oval sleeping house; a cooking house; and three granaries.

The Abuja Palace, Niger State, was built at MOTNA in 1975–1976. When the emir visited Jos, he chose to stay in the replica rather than go to a hotel. The large, circular building has a reception hall and a domed, thatched roof, and it houses a number of circular rooms for members of the family, attendants, and children.

The Katsina Palace, built at MOTNA in 1978–1979, is a replica of the oldest part of the emir's palace. At the southern end of the building, the location of the former throne room is marked as a reminder of the Fulani ancestry of the emirs of Katsina. The emir's armory is located in an enclosed courtyard; it includes an entrance room, the council chamber of the emir and his chiefs, and a reception room. The emir's master builders carried out most of the work at MOTNA.

More recent northern structures at Jos include the Mosque at Ilorin, with its many arches supporting the 48 bays of its roof. The floor plan of this building resembles that of most mosques throughout the Islamic world, with its prayer niche, or *mihrab*, facing toward Mecca. Construction of the mosque began in 1982. It was designed and built by Babban Gwani Mikaila for Emir Abdulkarim. The complex of buildings has sculptured arches in the main hall that enclose six principal spaces. The structure illustrates two basic components of Hausa architecture: the *azara* and the *tubali*. The *azara* are timber lengths cut from Deleb palm trees to reinforce the loam structure; the *tubali* are cone-shaped sun-dried bricks, the basic units used to build wall courses.

The City Walls of Kano, Kano State, are perhaps the most monumental project undertaken at MOTNA. The walls form one entire boundary of the museum. They are made up of millions of *tubali*; and the crest and roof structure of the gate make use of the *azara* technique. The walls at MOTNA are about half the length of the actual walls, based on a survey of the remaining sections in the area of *Kofar Duka Wuya*; and they include the iron gate. Sketches made in 1903 and recent photographs were used to reconstruct the geometric crest of the walls, now rarely found in place at Kano or at other fortifications in Nigeria.

The *Bight of Benin* at Jos is a Benin nobleman's house, made of red clay from the area. The steep, thatched roof is crowned with two sculptures: the bronze *Bird of Disaster* and a European soldier. A long bronze python is suspended on the roof above the doorway, and there is a sunken patio, or *pluvium*, inside. The building itself serves as one of the museum complex's restaurants, with traditional food and drink offered to visitors.

Ethnographic galleries at the Jos museum feature works by local and state ethnic groups, such as Mumuye ritual carvings; Dakakari funerary pottery sculptures in the shape of horsemen, elephants, and other animals; and brass work from Bida, an ancient Nupe capital. Northern gourd containers—stained, scorched, engraved, and decorated—are well represented in the collections. Objects on display from ethnic groups in other parts of Nigeria are, for example, Yoruba *Gelede* masks, Ibibio *Ekpo* masks, and Ijaw men's society masks, as well as Igbo and Yoruba carvings of doors, house posts, and sculptures, most of which are not more than 70 to 100 years old. Objects of daily and ceremonial life have been collected: musical instruments, agricultural tools, and hunting gear. There are also metal weapons, horse trappings, and pottery.

The Jos local community has participated in programs involving the museum since July 1972. Public lectures, films showing Nigerian history and culture, demonstrations of wood carving, and archaeological site visits are arranged. There are musical performances, modern-art exhibits, and sales at the museum. There have been educational programs for children offered since November, 1974. These activities were stimulated by a local organization in 1972, like the Nigerian National Museum Society, Lagos, started in July, 1969.

National Museum, Ife

In 1910, Leo V. Frobenius, a German ethnologist then in Africa, came across some Ife heads, which he likened to the classical world's god or goddess of the sea. He tried to buy them, but was frustrated by Charles Partridge, a British district officer. Frobenius did, however, manage to carry away several terra-cotta heads, now in the Museum für Volkerkunde, Berlin, Germany. An Ife head of *Olokun*, the god of the sea, first described by Frobenius, is now known only from a copy. The whereabouts of the original is still unknown. The old copy, on loan from Ife, may be seen at the National Museum, Lagos.

The long history of the Ife museum itself (founded 1954) began in the dry season of 1938–1939. A man digging a house foundation in Wunmonije Compound uncovered some clay sculptures and 18 exceptional cast-bronze and copper heads near the palace of the *oni* of Ife. The *oni* himself kept most of the finds, but three heads were sold. Two have since been returned to Nigeria; one remains in the British Museum. The heads found in the Wunmonije Compound are unique in Africa for their naturalism, technical skill, and sophisticated style. Life-size, the heads are thought to represent dead *onis* (kings) in the prime of life. They include a rare and exquisite copper casting of Oni Obalufon and a terra-cotta head of the "Usurper," Lajuwa (Eyo and Willett 1980: plates 41, 49). Other outstanding pieces remained in the *oni* of Ife's palace.

From 1938 on, the *oni* took an active role in collecting the metal and terra-cotta works of art being discovered in and around the city, whenever houses were being built and lands were being cleared and planted. The *oni* also brought many works previously kept in local shrines and sacred groves into the palace for safekeeping.

The first Ife museum, completed in 1948, was located on the grounds of the *oni*'s palace. The *oni* had donated the land for the museum, along with his collections, but construction problems delayed the opening until 1954. Archaeologists pursued the accidental discoveries of 1938–1939 with scientific excavations that began in 1949. Bernard Fagg, his brother William, and John Godwin worked at the site of Abiri, to which they returned in 1953, excavating at the sacred groves of Osangangan, Obamakin, Olokun Walode, and others. Frank Willett excavated a shrine at Ita Yemoo in 1957–1958. Another shrine was uncovered at Ita Yemoo during the second season, 1962–1963, where the first radio-carbon and thermoluminescence dates for Ife were obtained. Among the other Ife sites excavated are: Igbo Obameri and Oduduwa College, by Oliver Meyers in 1964; Odo Ogbe Street in Ile-Ife by Ekpo Eyo in 1969; and the site of Lafogido, also in 1969. The Lafogido site revealed a rectangular pottery pavement, with a series of 14 globular pots inserted around the edge of what was probably a royal burial. The pots had animal-head lids: an elephant, a mythical beast (possibly a hippopotamus), and a ram (Eyo and Willett 1980: plates 55, 56). The *oni*, because of the royal burial site, halted excavations at Lafogido. Later, Peter Garlake excavated at Ife, 1971–1972, at the sites of Obalara's Land and Woye Asiri.

National Museum, Owo

The Owo museum, on the grounds of the palace of the *Olowu* of Owo, was originally built to house the palace antiquities. The Owo collections were made in 1957–1958, and include recently excavated archaeological objects. In all, there are more than 10,000 pieces.

Owo, about 80 miles southeast of Ife, is an important traditional center for the Eastern Yoruba. Owo is said to have been founded by *Ojugbelu*, the youngest son of the high god, *Oduduwa*, founder of the Yoruba city of Ile-Ife. In 1969, Eyo excavated at the site of Igbo 'Laja, near the palace of the *Olowu*, about a quarter mile from the center of the city. The recovered objects show strong stylistic affinities among Owo, Ife, and Benin.

National Museum, Oron

The Oron National Museum was founded in 1959 and, like the Owo museum, predates independence. Most of the approximately 800 known ancestral figures, or *ekpu*, of the Oron people are housed in the museum. The *ekpu*, held in trust by the museum, are on loan from the Oron people, who still worship them. The collection includes Igbo house posts, drums, and a Cross River monolith. The museum was severely damaged during the Nigerian Civil War (1966–1970), and was reopened in 1977. Today, its collections number between 2,000 and 4,000 ethnographic objects. There is also a Craft Village. Keith Nicklin, a British ethnographer, then with the Nigerian Antiquities Department, prepared an excellent *Guide to the National Museum, Oron*, based on his intensive fieldwork, when the museum reopened. Most of the detailed information on Oron that follows is drawn from his guide. Nicklin later became director of the Horniman Museum, London.

The importance of the *ekpu* carvings was recognized by Murray as early as 1938; and he took steps to repair and preserve them when he began the Antiquities Survey in 1943. By 1948 when the cult was in decline, a collection was made for the first museum which was opened in 1959. Approximately three hundred *ekpu* figures were collected by the Oron Clan Council and the British district officer. The collection was removed for safekeeping from the museum during the war. Many were destroyed, scattered, stolen, or sold abroad in that period. At the end of the Civil War, the Department of Antiquities was able to retrieve about 100 of them.

The Oron museum, like those instituted or rebuilt during Eyo's tenure as the commission's director-general, focused on local cultures at the same time as it included cultures throughout the states and major national ethnic groups. The famed skin-covered masks produced by some schools of artists in Cross River, in the 1940s and 1950s, were documented by Kenneth Murray when he collected samples of their work. Keith Nicklin and Ekpo Eyo both collected masks and made similar records and photographs in the 1970s. Few such masks are now made; and only three modern artists are said to achieve high-quality masks: Thomas Ochagwu Ogwogwo of Ezekwe, Ogoja; Patrick Adeh Achong of Odajie-Mbube, Ogoja; and Nwa Nkwa of Urua Inyang, Abak, in the Annang-Ibibio area. The masks are used by age sets, dance groups, and associations of hunters and warriors. (Similar skin masks are still made and used in some parts of western Cameroon, among the Widekum near Mamfe and among the Bangwa at Fontem).

A number of major Cross River stone monoliths are installed on the grounds of the National Museum, Lagos. These monoliths are well known. The various sculptures have conical torsos with protruding navels, arms carved in low relief, and distinctly human features that bear tribal marks and beards. They are large sculptures, some as tall as two meters. Known locally as *akwanshi* or *atal*, more than 300 have been found in Middle Cross River. The sculptures are believed to have been carved as memorials for deceased chiefs, or *ntoons*, among the Nta group. Their dating is uncertain, but the monoliths were made at least as early as the 16th century and continued to be made until the 19th century. They have been found mostly among small groups of Ejagham peoples, such as the Ekajuk, Abanyom, Nnam, Nselle, and Nta.

The Cross River area is also important for having yielded late Stone Age finds that include pottery dating back more than 5,000 years. These data include objects found at sites near Afikpo on the Cross River and at Nsukka in eastern Nigeria. There are many such sites that await excavation in the area.

The National Museum, Oron takes an active role also in incorporating modern Nigerian artists of the area into the museum complex. Cement sculptures by S. J. Skpan of Ikot Obio Offong, Uyo, were made for the museum grounds, as was a carved tree stump in the shape of a traditional Cross River monolith, by Alphant Chukwu of Utu Etim Ekpo, Abak. The museum restaurant is decorated with a mural, *Girl From Fattening Room*, by the Annang-Ibibio artist, Imeh Fabian of Ikot Esse, Ikot Ekpene. Thus, traditional themes are incorporated into modern works commissioned from Abak artists by the museum, underscoring the roles of living peoples.

The Gidan Makama National Museum, Kano

The Gidan Makama or National Museum, Kano is an architectural jewel in the old city. It was the residence of the *makama*, a traditional title holder responsible for administering small provincial districts of the Kano Emirate. The Gidan Makama was probably built by the same master builder who erected the famed Zaria Mosque and the City Walls of Kano.

At MOTNA, in Jos, the Zaria Mosque and the City Walls of Kano have been rebuilt as part of the permanent exhibition of indigenous buildings of distinction. The Gidan Makama was completed restored at Kano by the NCMM, which runs it. The display has been expanded to show other examples of traditional architecture from the Kano Emirate. Local crafts, as well as the emir's regalia, are shown.

Kanta Museum, Argungu

Among the first museums run by the Department of Antiquities under the British, the Kanta Museum at Argungu, Kebbi State, is the only local museum still under the national commission's jurisdiction. The museum is the former residence of the Emir of Argungu. He used it until 1935, when a new palace was constructed. The museum collections focus on occupational artifacts and tools used by local peoples for hunting, fishing, and warfare. Argungu is the site of the most important annual fishing festival in Nigeria.

National Museum, Kaduna

The concept of a craft village was first introduced at the Kaduna Museum, founded in 1975. Visitors to the Kaduna museum are encouraged to observe and acquire the works produced by modern potters, weavers, smiths, and wood-carvers and to utilize the services of hairdressers. Their crafts generate much needed revenue and allow the public to partake of living cultural heritage.

Displays at the museum include evidence of human prehistory, finds made in East Africa more than 2 million years ago. The earliest human skeleton found in Nigeria, at Iwo Eleru, however, is about 11,000 years old. Late Stone Age finds are common in the country; the period lasted from about 12,000 B.C. to 2,000 years ago in West Africa.

Archaeological displays in this museum trace the history of iron smelting in West Africa back about 2,500 years ago, to the Nok culture. Thus, it seems, that the Iron Age apparently followed the

Stone Age in West Africa, without passing through a Bronze Age, which came much later. Lost-wax casting, widely used from about the ninth century A.D., is illustrated at Kaduna. The 13th century overland trade route to West Africa from North Africa and coastal trade with Europe from the 15th century on made increasing quantities of copper alloy available for bronze casting. Benin, Asante (Ashante), and Dahomey produced many fine works of art in bronze and gold, using the lost-wax method.

The Ethnography Gallery of the Kaduna museum presents masquerades and rituals used in connection with deities and the ancestors. Some are performed at death, others at puberty, still others at marriage, naming, curing, and similar occasions. Most are performed at critical points in a person's life cycle and in the community's agricultural cycle. *Mmo* society masks, probably from Onitsha, may represent water spirits or maiden spirits; some masks of the *Ekpo* society present disease-ravaged faces. The gallery includes many local ethnic groups. There are Yoruba *orisha* (figures); *ikega* or *ikenga* sculptures, associated with the hand or arm; and Igbo sculptures that are used throughout southern Nigeria. Ancestral figures from the northern local Mumuye peoples are also on view.

Ethnographic textile exhibits present weaving techniques and looms—some used by men (horizontal) some by women (vertical). Looms are used to make head cloths, wrappers, and other cloths as bride wealth. There is also a large collection of armor and weapons which, from the 16th century, were mostly a local affair, as a result of several states emerging and competing among themselves in Hausaland. Nineteenth century revolutionary Islamic movements in West Africa, like the Sokoto *jihad*, led to large scale indigenous production of arms and armor (Dr. Yaro T. Gella 1992b). Among these items is a coat of iron chain mail of German manufacture, with charms and amulets attached for protection. The "Koran Writing" exhibit shows the copy boards used by Nigerian Muslim *mallams* (teachers). There are various musical instruments used to accompany singing, dancing, communal labor, storytelling, and many other activities. They include rattles, pot drums, zithers, horns, double gongs, clappers, xylophones, harps, banjos, and violins. These instruments are made of diverse materials, often in combinations of wood, bronze, brass, ivory, glass, clay, skin, leather, bone, horn, clay, and iron.

On display at Kaduna is a collection of clay and brass smoking pipes that were used for both tobacco and hemp. Only knee-shaped pipes, or bent bowl, are displayed at Kaduna. Tubular ones were used in East and South Africa. European pipes were introduced into West Africa in about the mid-17th century, when tobacco was already known. The earliest Europeans visiting West Africa in the 15th century already reported seeing pipes being smoked.

Currency came into use with European contact in the 15th century. The Portuguese and Dutch traded in pepper, ivory, and slaves. They developed and used special-purpose currency—manillas, cowrie shells, currency hoes, rods, and bars of copper, brass, and iron. Tobacco, gin, palm oil, cloths, shirts, animals, beads, salt, tin, silver, rings, and ornaments were also used in exchanges. In southeastern Nigeria, manillas were widely used; in the western and northern parts, cowrie shells. Iron bars and currency hoes were widely used, and copper and brass rods were frequently used in the southeast. Bracelets and anklets were used not only for ornamentation but for burial and bride wealth.

National War Museum, Umuahia

Among the most recent national museums is the War Museum at Umuahia, Imo State, opened in 1985. It emphasizes national unity and the role of the armed forces themselves as instruments of collective nation building. General Olusegun Obasanjo, a former head of state, conceived the museum as a memorial to those who died in the Nigerian Civil War. Important historic events are presented in the form of dioramas in the museum. Two of them are the "Jihad War of 1830," and the "Peace Treaty with Biafra" (1970). The latter was the event that ended Nigeria's bitter Civil War. Other exhibits show modern and traditional weapons, many of which could as well be considered works of art: staffs, clubs, axes, knives, and swords in wood, bronze, iron, and ivory. The weapons and artifacts are maintained and cleaned under the supervision of a designated military attaché who sees to their safe use and demonstration. The on-site staff is comprised of approximately 60 people, including the principal curator, senior curator, head of research, head of administration, an education officer, as well as security personnel, grounds keepers, and others.

Other Private Museums

In 1989, Okada Wonderland, a commercial recreational facility, inspired by Disney World, was opened at Okada village, Edo State. Built by Chief G. O. Igbinedion, the Esama of Benin, it includes a kind of open-air museum or gallery for the public, replete with near-life-size original statues of past and present political leaders and military rulers of Nigeria. Named the "Garden of Fame and Heroes," it is both a patriotic park and an overview of the country's political history, with national figures from a wide ethnic spectrum presented to a diverse public without charge (Figure 2.8). It joins a growing, if modest, number of facilities opened to the public on private initiative. All collections of "historic interest," broadly defined by law, however, come under the supervision of the NCMM.

The Didi Museum, a nonprofit, professionally run museum on Victoria Island, in Lagos, is the country's first, private, and leading modern art museum. The founder, Chief Newton Chuka Jibunoh and his wife, Elizabeth, the director of the museum, actively collect, display, and promote modern Nigerian artists. Traditional works are also on view, but the major thrust of the Didi Museum is to educate the public in art, especially modern and contemporary art, through exhibitions, lectures, and classes. It is the first such museum in the country (Figures 2.9 and 2.10); and it is part of the Didi Memorial Centre, dedicated to Edith Jibunoh, the late sister of Chief Jibunoh. Many of the artists exhibited at the museum have made international reputations, like Ben Osawe, and Ben Enwonwu, who studied art initially with Kenneth Murray; and along with others like Erabor Emokpae, gave international expression to their national "voices" at the Festival of Arts and Culture of West Africa (FESTAC '77). The work of these and other, younger, modern artists and sculptors are more surely finding an audience in the country, in its museums, and in exhibitions in Nigeria and abroad.

Conclusions

The present Nigerian system of museums has its roots in the decades just before World War II, among some uncommon British expatriates in

Figure 2.8   Visitor at the Okada Wonderland, Garden of Fame and Heroes, Okada, Nigeria, 1990. Photograph Flora E.S. Kaplan.

Figure 2.9 The Didi Museum, Victoria Island, Lagos, Nigeria. The country's first private modern art museum. Photograph courtesy of the Didi Museum.

the colonial service, a few enlightened traditional rulers, and an emerging group of indigenous museum professionals, historians, and archaeologists, first trained locally, then abroad. To western notions of institutional recovery, preservation and display of art and culture history, these people brought different yet shared concerns for the country's rich cultural heritage that was already rapidly disappearing—sometimes being abandoned and denigrated—sometimes destroyed—and sometimes stolen and sent abroad. Many of those who worked to salvage these works had deep feelings for the country and people. Most particularly, Kenneth Murray and Bernard Fagg, along with other expatriates were prodigious in their efforts to preserve Nigeria's cultural history and art. Most important, perhaps, was the solid group of trained, indigenous professionals within the country, who were prepared to lead the burgeoning national museums after independence and a rending civil war that ended in 1970. Dr. Ekpo Eyo's innovative approach and clear

Figure 2.10 Exhibition of sculpture by Greg Agbonkonkon, 1987 (L to R) Greg Agbonkonkon, Obi Ufala Okagbue (the Obi of Onitsha), Professor Jibril Aminu, and Chief Newton Jibunoh (founder, Didi Museum).

vision of the museums' role in those crucial years was carried forward with a strong NCMM staff. Dr. Ade Obayemi later focused on archaeology and tourism in a national agenda. The present director-general, Dr. Yaro T. Gella, sees culture and history which underlie Nigeria's large and complex system of museums, historic sites and monuments as yielding indigenous models for national political and economic development.

The impetus to increase self-awareness, national unity and identity, so urgent in the early decades following independence, spurred expansion of Nigeria's modern museum system. It remains integral to the role of the national museums. From salvage efforts, to envisaging national unity, museums will now be tested to yield working Afro-centric models for public education and national development.

Note

1. Egharevba's early efforts in collecting and writing down local history and oral tradition among Benin elders resulted, in 1933, in his most important work, privately printed at first, *A Short History of Benin*, as well as other writings. Although later historians have questioned the accuracy of his history in some respects, the volume has been a major resource for all those who have worked in Benin. Similarly, R.E. Bradbury's *Benin Studies* (1973), a compilation of some ten articles, including sections from his doctoral thesis, and especially his anthropological field notes and detailed diaries kept at the University of Birmingham, England, have been heavily used by virtually all ethnographers of Benin, since Bradbury's untimely death at age 40, in 1969.

References

Egharevba, Jacob U.
  1960 *A Short History of Benin*. 3rd edition. Ibadan: Ibadan University Press.
Eyo, Ekpo and Frank Willett
  1980 *Treasures of Ancient Nigeria*. New York: Knopf.
Gella, Yaro T.
  1992a The Use of Cultures of Nigeria as Sources of National Strength. Paper delivered at the National Institute for Strategic Planning and Policy, Bikuru, Nigeria. November 10, 1992.
  1992b Personal Communication, Letter, November 24, 1992.

Nicklin, Keith
    1977 *Guide to the National Museum, Oron.* Lagos: National Commission for
        Museums and Monuments.
Willett, Frank, ed.
    1973 Kenneth Murray Through the Eyes of his Friends, *African Arts*,
        VI(4). Pp. 2, 5, 7, 74–78, 90–93.

3 Contested Identities: Museums and the Nation in Australia

Margaret Anderson and Andrew Reeves

The day was typically Australian. The heat, which was not excessive, was softened by a gentle breeze, and the bright rays of the morning sun beating down upon the metallic fittings of the assembled gunboats, and the tint of the restless waters around them, produced a scene of loveliness and dazzling brilliancy. What a contrast to that historic morn, with its countless craft, merchantmen, and steamboats crowding in the harbour to join in the reception, make with that on which, over a century ago, Captain Arthur Phillip, founder and first Governor of New South Wales, sailed into Port Jackson in the "Sirius", followed by her consorts! [Commonwealth of Australia 1904:21]

In this way, the official record of the inaugural celebrations of the Commonwealth of Australia described the scene on Sydney Harbor on January 1, 1901, as the first governor-general of Australia, the Earl of Hopetown, arrived from Britain to take up his position as titular head of the newly federated nation. As chief site of the ceremonies associated with this momentous event, Sydney had left nothing to chance. No fewer than six committees of worthy citizens had planned the series of events which were to make up the celebration, and the organizers were well pleased with their efforts. Over successive days, Sydneysiders and an estimated 70,000 visitors participated in a range of ceremonial occasions on a scale never before attempted. Apart from the formal ceremonies, which included the swearing in of the governor-general and the proclamation of the Commonwealth of Australia, there were two huge processions, military parades, a state banquet, and a carefully staged reenactment of Captain James Cook's first landing on Australian shores. The streets were decorated with an elaborate series of triumphal arches, and buildings in the central city were festooned with garlands and flags.

Strangely, the celebration did not extend to holding an exhibition, although the separate Australian colonies had been enthusiastic participants in the many international and intercolonial exhibitions so popular after 1851. The severe economic recession of the 1890s and the prolonged and bitter industrial struggles that accompanied it may have sapped the energy of even these enthusiastic nationalists, for Australia attempted no international exhibitions after Melbourne's extravagant performance in 1888 (Davison 1988a). Nor did the momentous occasion of federation give rise to any new institutions dedicated to recording and preserving examples of Australia's natural and cultural heritage, although at their annual meeting in 1902 the Australian Library Association had called for the establishment of a national museum of Australia, to be housed in the nation's new capital when this city's site was determined (McShane 1991). This call was to be repeated on many occasions in successive decades, but no such museum has been built. Some 90 years after this first suggestion, Australians are still waiting for their national museum. How did this happen? Why have successive Australian governments held such scant interest in their own environment and history when many smaller and less wealthy nations have embraced theirs with such pride? The answer lies partly in Australia's colonial origins and partly—in the 20th century—in a specific construction of the nation and national identity that all but precluded the need for a general, nonmilitary-history museum and that consistently undervalued indigenous flora and fauna.

The commonwealth government's reluctance to fund a national museum would have surprised many colonial Australians, whose zeal in this regard had been extraordinary. As early as 1821, some 33 years after European settlement, a group of scientific men in New South Wales had established the Philosophical Society, one of the aims of which was to establish a museum of natural history (Strahan 1979:7). The society was short-lived, but its collection was preserved, and by 1827 the colonial press was calling on the government to found an Australian museum. An anonymous writer argued: the "earlier that such an institution is formed, the better it will be for posterity" (*Sydney Gazette*, June 29, 1827). Six months later, another anonymous writer (perhaps the same one) repeated the call in another journal, suggesting that the establishment of a natural-history museum, could not but raise [Australia] in the estimation of the world at large, while it would excite her to further efforts to maintain and increase that good opinion and respect which such a measure would produce. [qt. in Strahan 1979:8]

Despite desultory discussion, nothing concrete was forthcoming, which the *Sydney Gazette* called a "disgrace" (June 28, 1828). Whether in response to this criticism or after reassurance that Lord Charles Bathurst, secretary of state for the colonies, endorsed the idea, the attorney general finally agreed to allow the Philosophical Society's collection to be housed in a former postal office off Macquarie Street in Sydney and provided a salary for carpenter-and-joiner turned-zoologist William Holmes to care for the collection and escort visitors around the museum.

Although Lord Bathurst had specifically referred in correspondence to the desirability of founding a "Public Museum" (Strahan 1979:8), it is clear from early press references that the "public" envisaged stopped short of including the *hoi polloi* of Sydney, the majority of whom were still either convicts or ex-convicts. A small notice in the *Sydney Gazette* on February 6, 1830, advised,

The public are not generally aware that a beautiful Collection of Australian Curiosities, the property of Government, is deposited in the Old Post Office. This Museum is under the Superintendence of Mr. Holmes, who, between the hours of ten and three, politely shows the same to any respectable individuals who may think fit to call.

But a mere three years later, the Colonial Museum (renamed the Australian Museum in 1834) had dwindled sadly. Holmes, who had accidentally shot himself while on a collecting trip to Moreton Bay, had not been replaced, and there was some public controversy over the continued funding of a museum. The semiofficial *Sydney Gazette* was consistently supportive, but its opposition newspaper, the *Sydney Monitor*, adopted a more populist stance, attacking the museum as part of an overall campaign against the nonelected government's rule through patronage and privilege. Proprietor William Charles Wentworth, Australian born although English educated and son of a wealthy surgeon and ex-convict, dismissed on July 20, 1833 all government expenditures on science in round terms.

Zoology and Mineralogy, and Astronomy, and Botany, and the other sciences, are all very good things, but we have no great opinion of an infantile people being taxed to promote them. . . . We might as well give salaries to painters, sculptors, and chemists, as to botanists, astronomers, and Museum collectors.

Specific as this early controversy was to early Sydney, it nevertheless contained several elements that were to recur throughout the next century of museum growth in Australia and that, in some respects, still dog museums today. All of Australia's early museums were founded and endowed by the government at the instigation of wealthy men, first with an interest in science and later with pretensions to art and culture. Although these men often supported their institutions strenuously, their support was only rarely financial: endowments on the scale of American museum practice are largely unknown in Australia. As government institutions, museums were and remain at the mercy of the public purse, with all its competing priorities, and in new colonies such competition was great indeed. Colonial governments, which were struggling to establish cities, roads, and later schools, seldom had much to spare for museums, which most people continued to see as peripheral to the twin tasks of commercial development and nation building. As a result, attempts to bolster museum funding, from colonial times to the present, have stressed their economic and cultural and scientific benefits, be they museums of art, history, or science (Smith 1945:86–87). In the late 19th century, this led in some institutions to an intellectual alliance between museums, agriculture, and manufacturing industry: in the late 20th century, the association is with tourism—increasingly an "industry" also. In neither case has it been a tactic much attended by success: poverty has been another recurring theme in Australian museum history.

Debate over the "public" nature of museums has also recurred. In the sense that they were established as public institutions, museums in Australia were "born modern": no revolutions, either intellectual or political, were required to break down their doors. But they were unquestionably also creatures of their times and of the class of their creators—open to the public, free to all, and yet until the beginning of the 20th century open only during the hours when most people were at work. Toward the end of the 19th century, there was a protracted debate over Sunday openings in Victoria, with the Science Museum defying

Parliament on several occasions to gauge public demand. Although thousands thronged to the galleries on each occasion, "Sabbatarianism" was still too strong for a conservative legislature and the museum was instructed to remain closed. To emphasize the class dimensions of the debate, the emergent Labour party in Victoria included Sunday opening for museums and galleries in their election platform, one of the very few occasions on which museums have featured in any significant way in party politics (*Argus*, May 4, 1883:7; Perry 1972:20–23). However, the major point remains. Museums ostensibly created for the benefit of the public, even later in the 19th century, for the supposed benefit of the people, have rarely been truly *of* the people—an especially important issue in Australian museums at present (Bennett 1988).

When Australia was settled by Europeans at the close of the 18th century, interest in scientific exploration and classification was at its height. Not surprisingly, some of the first "exports" from Australia were specimens of native flora and fauna, dispatched to major museums and wealthy private collectors in Britain and Europe, often with the assistance of the colonial authorities. Although there was widespread interest in such Australian curiosities, it did not occur to these early administrators that the nation they were founding might one day regret this wholesale export of their scientific heritage. Indeed, such an opinion was hardly to be expected since they had no separate national consciousness *per se*. For at least the first 60 years of settlement, Australian scientists cheerfully and uncritically dispatched the most interesting specimens to the country most of them still called home (Hale 1956:vii, 2–3; Strahan 1979:1–3). Change came with the first stirrings of a separate Australian consciousness in the middle years of the 19th century, as Australia moved toward responsible government. At about the same time, the Australian Museum, and then its newly founded sister institutions in Victoria and South Australia, began both to collect in earnest and to classify their specimens themselves. Classification until this point had only been undertaken in Britain and Europe, which meant that most of the early type specimens of Australian flora and fauna were held (and continue to be held) by foreign museums.

However, interest in, even fascination for, Australian flora and fauna amongst early Australian scientists did not necessarily mean that they particularly valued their environment or sought to preserve it. Their taxonomic models continued to be drawn from Britain and Europe, and their arrangement of specimens in exhibitions reflected inherited assumptions about the order of nature. In the hierarchical arrangement of species and subspecies that characterized 19th-century taxonomy, Australian animals hovered near the bottom of the evolutionary scale as examples of isolated, primitive survivals. Like many of their fellow settlers, their writings also suggest that most scientists accepted the inevitability of change, as Western "civilization" "tamed" the "savage" landscape and saw their own role merely as preservers of the *record* of what had been. In their third annual report in 1857, the board of the South Australian Institute (later the South Australian Museum) expressed their mission in these terms:

> it is highly desirable, and, indeed, almost a national duty, to preserve for posterity the forms and semblances of the various singular and beautiful birds, reptiles, and insects now inhabiting Australia, ere they shall have finally disappeared before the footsteps of the white man. [Hale 1956:10]

If 19th-century curators mourned the passing of these animals, their feelings are not reflected in the records of their institutions (Figure 3.1). As late as 1954, Sir Russel Grimwade, chairman of the trustees of the National Museum of Victoria, could write in a preface to the official history of this museum,

> There are both duties and obligations upon those of a civilised people who, for their own or their country's advantage, enter a strange and almost empty land. . . . Australians today are apt to forget that at the time of first entry their land produced no orthodox food and its soils had never been cultivated and that abundance of foods produced within its boundaries today all have their origins overseas. . . .
>
> The thoughtful man in a new country like this . . . becomes aware of his obligations to his successors and realises that his coming to a new land may cause permanent changes in his environment. In no other country has the natural equilibrium achieved by countless centuries of isolation been so violently upset as in Australia. . . . In no other country, therefore, does the responsibility of preserving a knowledge of the past rest quite so heavily upon its people. [Pescott 1954:ix–x]

Although some groups had begun agitating for the preservation of the Australian environment in the early 20th century, there were, no doubt, still many who agreed with Grimwade in the 1950s, accepting the

Figure 3.1 Transferral of the collections of the National Museum of Victoria from the University of Melbourne to its new premises at Russell Street in the center of the city, 1899. Museum of Victoria Collection.

19th-century image of presettlement Australia as a "strange and almost empty land."

However great the loss of important scientific material in the first decades after the European invasion, worldwide fascination for "Antipodean Curiosities" encouraged the development of museums in Australia and ensured that active collecting of native flora and fauna specimens would take place. No such interest developed in the material culture of Australian Aborigines. Nor did Australia's infant museums show much interest in exploring their customs and beliefs. There was an export trade of sorts, which flourished in a small way around the middle decades of the 19th century, and some important collections of Aboriginal artifacts found their way to both Britain and Germany in particular (Plomley 1962), but this trade did not stimulate the zoologists and biologists in Australian museums to make equivalent collections of their own, despite some apparent early encouragement. One of those who suggested the importance of building such collections was Dr. George Bennett, later curator of the Australian Museum. After a visit in 1832, he suggested that the museum should collect examples of "native weapons" and physical remains alongside their systematic collections of flora and fauna, and his justification reflects the almost-universal assumption of the time that the Australian Aborigines were doomed to extinction before the onslaught of European civilization.

> Native weapons, utensils and other specimens of the arts, . . . as well as the skulls of different tribes, and accurate drawings of their peculiar cast of features, would be a desirable addition. At the present time, such might be procured without difficulty, but it is equally certain, as well as much to be regretted, that the tribes in the settled parts of the Colony are fast decreasing, and many, if not all, will, at no distant period, be known but by name. Here, in a public museum, the remains of the arts, etc, as existing among them, may be preserved as lasting memorials of the former races inhabiting the lands, when they had ceased to exist. [Bennett 1834:68–69]

Curiously, Bennett collected very little of this material himself when he became curator: Jim Specht, the current curator of the Australian ethnology collection at the Australian Museum, points out that Bennett's first catalog of the collection, published in 1837, listed only 25 Aboriginal items, and Aboriginal collections remained a low priority for the institution until the 1920s (Specht, 1979:141–142). Tragically, even this meager early collection, along with several private collections, was destroyed by fire after the 1879 International Exhibition in Sydney.

There was a similar disinterest in Victoria, despite some equivalent early feeling that Aboriginal material should be collected. In 1857, only three years after the National Museum's foundation, the assistant registrar-general of Victoria published a lengthy description of the museum in his *Facts and Figures: Or, Notes of Progress, Statistical and General.* After describing the galleries one by one, William Archer observed "one prominent defect which we should be glad to see remedied at once." His comments, following, bear a remarkable similarity to those of Bennett, 20 years earlier.

> We allude to the total absence of Victorian Aboriginal relics. Whole tribes . . . have ceased to exist; others are fast decaying, and their implements of hunting and of war will become more and more difficult to procure with every passing year. All that tangibly relates to the Aboriginal natives of the land we now inhabit should find a place for perpetual preservation here. We would not only save their boomerangs, spears, and waddies, but even collect the skulls of their deceased men, women, and children; and, if possible, preserve their very bodies as mummies. [1858:28]

Circumscribed as they were, the views of men like Archer and Bennett on appropriate categories of Aboriginal material for museums to collect were widely shared. Lacking the analytical framework that was to develop within anthropology in the 20th century, 19th-century scientists were principally interested in the physical characteristics of the indigenous population, a preoccupation that was strengthened in the later 19th century as social Darwinism found wide acceptance. Although they would not have countenanced treating the remains of Europeans as public exhibits, they had no such qualms where Aboriginal physical remains were concerned. Poor Truganninni, the reputed "last" Aboriginal Tasmanian, went to great lengths to prevent her body's desecration after death, to no avail. Her skeleton was articulated by the National Museum of Victoria (who were still proud of the quality of the job in the 1950s), and thereafter casts were traded all over the world. In 1912, the National Museum traded one of theirs with the Museum of Natural History in New York City in exchange for a cast of the skull of a *Tyrannosaurus* (Pescott 1954:102–108). These casts were not returned to the appropriate Aboriginal custodians in Tasmania until recently.

There was scant interest in Aboriginal material culture, however. Apart from weaponry, which was also traded in the marketplace (although largely as trophies), museums collected little. Aboriginal material culture was widely dismissed as "crude" and sparse (Sutton 1991:37). Lacking the decoration that characterized Maori objects, for example, Aboriginal artifacts excited no admiration and little interest. As social Darwinism gained increasing credence, such material was used to support the hierarchical theories of race that placed Australian Aborigines firmly at the bottom of the evolutionary ladder. Not surprisingly, when early European explorers "discovered" some of the complex rock paintings in northwestern Australia in the 1840s, they concluded that they could not have been "executed by a self-taught savage" (Grey 1841, qt. in Jones 1991:46). Pervasive assumptions about the "primitive" and unchanging nature of Aboriginal society also led early scientists to assume that the material culture of one group differed only marginally from that of another (Figures 3.2 and 3.3). It was not until the 1890s in South Australia and the first decade of the 20th century in Victoria that systematic collecting of Aboriginal cultural heritage began in earnest, by which time early ethnographers, preoccupied with their search for "traditional" cultures, had to seek their material in North and Central Australia far from European coastal expansion. It was to be many more years before Aboriginal art began to be appreciated on its own terms (Jones 1991:168–176; Sutton 1991:33–48). As a result, contemporary Australian museums hold only small and scattered relics associated with the major coastal concentrations of Aboriginal occupation, which bore the brunt of first contact with Europeans (Specht 1979), and their collections of early contact material are also sparse. 19th-century museums collected Aboriginal relics and remains within the framework of Western biological paradigms and in the service of Western science. The public they envisaged for their museums certainly did not include Aborigines. While Aborigines were both subject and object of early collecting enterprise, it simply never occurred to anyone that they should be partners. Nor would it have occurred even to early ethnographers that their heirs might be called upon to reflect a specific Aboriginal identity or that their collections might be found lacking by a revitalized Aboriginal culture. Ironically, some of the most comprehensive collections of cultural material were gathered by missionaries, who also

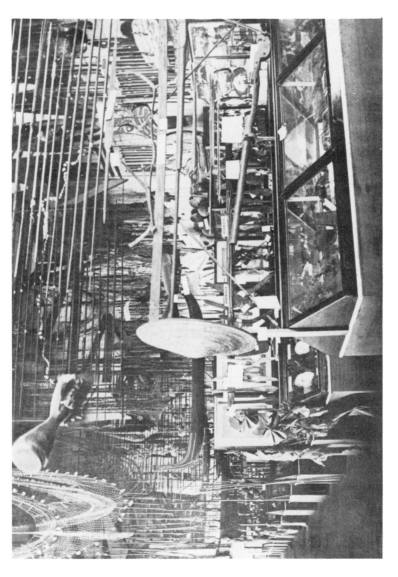

Figure 3.2 Ethnographic Court at Sydney's Garden Palace Exhibition, 1879–1880. Almost the entire ethnographical collection of the museum was displayed at this exhibition and subsequently lost when the Garden Palace was destroyed by fire in 1882. Australian Museum Collection.

Figure 3.3 Diorama depicting Aborigines of the Yarra Yarra Tribe. This diorama was erected in the National Museum of Victoria in 1939 and in more recent years has been on display, in amended form, in the Aboriginal Keeping Place at Shepparton in central Victoria. Museum of Victoria Collection.

preserved examples of early sacred material, even while they discouraged its use (Jones 1991:150).

The late 19th century saw two other major additions to the museum scene in Australia: the establishment of museums of art (progressively from the 1860s) and museums of science and technology in Melbourne and Sydney. Although apparently very different institutions with vastly different objectives, there was still a measure of commonality between them. Supporters of both argued their importance for the development of industry in Australia. Art museums stressed their dual role of "improving" and "guiding" public taste while raising standards of design; technology museums followed those in Britain and the United States in asserting the need for a mechanically literate and quiescent working class (Davison 1988b; Kusamitsu 1980; Perry 1972:2–3; Smith 1945:86–89). The separate development of art museums in Australia and their interaction with an emerging Australian nationalism in the later years of the 19th century, deserves a paper of its own. We cannot do it justice here. Suffice it to say that early institutions differed markedly in their interest in acquiring contemporary Anglo-Australian art, although they were all in agreement about the irrelevance of traditional Aboriginal art until the 1960s (Jones 1991:175–176). The two science and technology museums flowered briefly in the late 19th century, the Science Museum of Victoria in particular developing an active program of exhibitions and lectures, before languishing for most of this century in the wake of the separate expansion of technical education (Perry 1972:46–50). From active interpreters of contemporary ideas and practice, they dwindled into increasingly dated museums of the history of technology, until the aggressive scientism of the 1980s gave them new relevance.

By the end of the 19th century, each of the six Australian colonies supported its own separate museum system. Even tiny Tasmania had two major museums, combination natural-history and art museums, which remain single institutions to this day. Small wonder perhaps that the fledgling Australian government preferred not to meddle. Each of these institutions had developed along individual, if broadly similar, lines, with almost no reference to their fellows. In fact, the strongest impression gained from a study of their institutional histories and correspondence records is of their separation from each other. In almost every case, there were probably stronger links with museums overseas, above all with the British Museum, than with other institutions in Australia. Distance was only part of the equation: there was also a strong element of competition between institutions, which reflected broader intracolonial rivalry. We have already pointed to the rival national aspirations of the *Australian* Museum and the *National* Museum in Victoria, but this paled into insignificance beside the jockeying for position by art museums. The National Gallery of Victoria was followed by the National Art Gallery of New South Wales (1874), the National Gallery of South Australia (1879), and the National Art Gallery of Queensland (1895), titles that long outlasted federation (McCulloch 1984:392). This pattern was to continue well into the 20th century, regardless of the new commonwealth, as a 1933 report sponsored by the Carnegie Corporation pointed out (Markham and Richards 1933:7). Interstate jealousy continues to bedevil the museum movement in Australia and is undoubtedly one reason it has proved so difficult to develop a united museum lobby. Federation forged a single political entity: colonial identities, colonial rivalries, lingered longer.

Calls for a National Museum

During the preparations for the opening of Australia's new national capital in 1927, a commonwealth cabinet paper prepared by the Minister for Home Affairs and Territories observed,

> Suggestions have been made from time to time that a National Museum should be established at Canberra to serve as a repository not only for articles of ethnographic interest, but also for articles of historical interest and articles Australian in character and of considerable intrinsic value, such as collections of precious stones. [Commonwealth of Australia 1927]

The minister's grab bag of possible collections and artifacts accurately reflects both the uncertainty with which the commonwealth considered the issue of a national museum and the tentative, generally unsuccessful steps that had been made in its direction. The issue of a national museum had been raised at a conference of the Australian Library Association as early as 1902, while the winning design for a new national capital (Canberra), that of American architect Walter Burley Griffin, included a museum as one of a range of national institutions the capital would house. But it was not until after the First World War, with its blood sacrifice and its influence upon the industrialization of the Australian economy, that the idea of a national museum became a possible metaphor for Australian nationalism.

With the exception of the proposed Australian War Memorial, itself a direct creation of war, there were three other proposals in the 1920s that all shared a common heritage and impulse. The proposals for a national museum of Australian zoology (1924), a national museum of ethnology (1927), and an Australian national museum (1928) all reflected 19th-century concerns, such as the importance of significant teaching collections, based upon comparative taxonomy and informed by a belief in Western civilization and the inevitability of social progress. Their proponents sought to confirm the virtues of postwar Australia and in the process demonstrated a heightened awareness of the emergence of a national tradition based in part upon the replacement of old cultures and old natural regimes:

> Prior to the passing of the [Zoological Museum] Act, the Federal Government had expressed regret that the Australian Nation possessed neither a collection of specimens of the unique and fast disappearing fauna of Australia, nor a museum in which such specimens could be preserved for future generations. [Commonwealth of Australia 1933]
>
> Unfortunately many Australian tribes have already disappeared, and it is now for ever impossible to discover anything about them. Many more are approaching extinction or are rapidly losing all memory of their former customs and even language. Whatever studies are to be made of the Australian natives must be completed within the next few years. [*Oceania* 1930:4]

These were the words of concerned men who wished to confirm the health of a nation that had passed through four years of war and that was finding social stability and economic prosperity—elusive qualities in the years before the Great Depression. Yet despite their concern for the preservation of collections, to the apparent neglect of living cultures or species, these advocates of the 1920s were the first to introduce a genuinely national dimension to claims for an Australian museum, and their efforts gained a wide measure of support. The reasons advanced during these interwar years for a national museum echoed the arguments in favor of establishing colonial museums 70 to 80 years previously: the need to represent Australia's unique flora and fauna and a perception of the intellectual and scientific benefits accruing from the maintenance of effective teaching collections in the fields of art, natural history, technology, and applied science. The renowned biologist turned anthropologist and director of Victoria's National Museum, Sir Baldwin Spencer, added a further dimension to the debate in 1923 when he proposed the establishment of a central museum, jointly endowed by the commonwealth and the state governments, to hold Australia's collections, accumulating from the increasingly frequent scientific expeditions (of both Australian and foreign origin) instead of such collections being lost to institutions overseas. There are well-documented instances of earlier concern regarding the loss of important individual specimens to overseas, particularly to British museums. But Spencer's argument reflects the beginning of a perception of Australia's need for representative collections of its natural, ethnographic, and social history, representative by virtue of their completeness not only in terms of taxonomy but also in terms of their acknowledgment of previously neglected disciplines. These were, however, arguments that would languish for another half century, until reviewed by the members of the Pigott Commission of Inquiry on Museums during 1974–1975.

The first of the national museums mooted during the 1920s, and the only one for which a building was actually constructed, was the National Museum of Australian Zoology. It was established following the commonwealth government's acceptance of an offer from noted orthopedist Dr. Colin McKenzie to transfer his impressive collection of Australian fauna to the commonwealth on the condition that the government establish a museum of Australian zoology. His experience in children's orthopedics and in treating war wounds had convinced McKenzie of the importance of applying lessons from the study of Australian fauna to broader aspects of medical science and comparative anatomy. Indeed, the collection offered to the commonwealth formed the basis of the laboratory and museum that McKenzie had established at his Melbourne home in 1919 (the Australian Institute of Anatomical Research). Negotiations were conducted at a high level, resulting in 1924 in an agreement between McKenzie and the federal government formalizing the establishment of the National Museum of Australian

Zoology. The agreement appointed McKenzie as director with an annual salary and identified Canberra as the site for the museum. In the meantime, McKenzie would manage its initial development from his Melbourne home. Private correspondence with the prime minister, S. M. Bruce, confirmed these arrangements.

Site development in Canberra was slow, indeed nonexistent, until January 1928, when the federal cabinet agreed to transfer the embryonic museum from the Department of Home Affairs and Territories to the Department of Health, to commence an urgent building program and to consider a change of name. In the meantime, McKenzie had gathered a small staff of six, including himself as director. Within this small hierarchy, a histologist, a scientific artist, and an osteologist took precedence over the museum's single curator. Despite the start of construction of the building in Canberra, the transfer of the National Museum of Australian Zoology to the new department effectively marked the end of this particular attempt to establish a national museum. The removal of the staff and collections to the renamed Institute of Anatomy in Canberra coincided with Australia's slide into severe economic depression. Drastic budget cuts effectively stripped it of any substantial museum function. Instead, the institute emphasized its research potential, especially in the field of anatomy and later in dietary research in a desperate struggle to survive.

The institute, prior to the collapse of the intended zoological museum, had augmented McKenzie's original donation with a number of significant ethnographic collections. While among these were relatively large collections of social and artistic materials accumulated by anthropologists or forwarded to the museum by representatives of Australia's colonial administration in Papua New Guinea, the critical link between McKenzie's primary interests and Australian ethnography appear to have been the extensive collections of Australian Aboriginal skeletal material that McKenzie commissioned or purchased for osteological and anatomical study. During 1927, his relatively proscribed interest in ethnographic material was overtaken by a proposal for another national museum, this time ethnological.

During the 1920s, the focus of ethnographic research (as distinct from collecting) began to shift from museums to Australian universities. The influence of university anthropologists, particularly those in the Department of Anthropology at the University of Sydney, was enhanced by the activities of the Australian National Research Council (ANRC). Begun in 1919 by the Australian and New Zealand Association for the Advancement of Science (ANZAAS) as a means of encouraging applied research, ANRC interest in anthropology was stimulated in 1927 by an offer from the New York-based Rockefeller Foundation to provide research funding for anthropological studies in Australia and the Pacific. The "professionalization" of Australian anthropology was closely linked to Australia's increasing role as a regional colonial power. For Australia, the fruits of victory after World War I included administration of Germany's Pacific territories, the most important of these being the former colony of New Guinea with its series of islands running from the Bismarck Archipelago north of New Guinea to the northern Solomon Islands (including Bougainville Island) to the east. Problems of colonial administration demanded the assistance of the social sciences in the "government and education of native peoples" and here, as elsewhere, anthropology became preeminent. The emerging disciplines of anthropology and colonial administration marched hand in hand. In the words of Australia's first professional journal of anthropology, *Oceania*, such an alliance provided anthropology with a practical value to match its theoretical concerns.

> There is a steadily, if slowly, growing recognition all over the world that the satisfactory control, in administration and education, of what are called backward peoples, requires a thorough understanding of their culture, their social and economic organisation, their laws and customs and their special ways of thought and that the attainment of such an understanding is made possible only by the systematic researches of the specialist.
>
> It is not intended that *Oceania* shall include in its pages discussions of the actual problem of administration. This is not properly the field for the scientists. But our policy will be guided by the desire to make anthropology of service in supplying the systematic knowledge that is necessary for the proper solution of those problems. [*Oceania* 1930:2]

Professor A. R. Radcliffe-Brown, foundation professor of anthropology at the University of Sydney, began lobbying federal politicians in 1927 for a national museum of ethnology. In pressing for a national collection, Radcliffe-Brown argued that the opportunity for

> making such a collection . . . would pass rapidly, and Australian students of anthropology would probably be forced to rely for their studies upon

the specimens which had been allowed to go so freely to the Museums of Europe and America. [Radcliffe-Brown 1927]

Apparent success quickly followed. On September 6, 1927, the federal cabinet agreed in principle to a national museum in Canberra but deferred any consideration of necessary buildings to a later date. The cabinet's endorsement of a general national museum represented the third museum proposal advanced during the 1920s, and it shared considerable common ground and support with the proposed ethnological museum. If Radcliffe-Brown provided the spur, the commonwealth's subsequent actions reflect their broader interests. Although deferring any building program, the government considered committing resources to the acquisition and storage of "articles of the greatest interest to Australia [which] should not be allowed to pass" (Commonwealth of Australia 1928/30). Material mentioned in support of this proposal not only included ethnographic artifacts from Australia and Papua New Guinea but a Cobb and Co. coach, opals, fossils, coins, tokens, paper money, and items relating to the early years of the federal capital. The ANRC lent further support at the start of 1928 in an attempt to force the pace. In addition to "heartily endorsing" the proposed museum, the ANRC later urged the commonwealth to acquire the ethnographic collections assembled by researchers working under its aegis. Many were at that time held at the Australian Museum in Sydney, where "their proper care is becoming a serious problem" (Commonwealth of Australia 1928/30).

By then, mid-1928, the commonwealth was faced with three options: the National Museum of Australian Zoology, soon to move from Melbourne to Canberra; a proposed national museum of ethnology; and its own, more broadly based, national museum. Clearly, some rationalization was required. Senator George Pearce, vice president of the executive council and minister with general overview of museum proposals, turned to Dr. A. C. D. (David) Rivett for advice in May 1928. Following a distinguished research and academic career, David Rivett had the previous year been appointed chief executive officer of the Council for Scientific and Industrial Research (CSIR). At the time of Pearce's approach, Rivett had commenced the drive that would make the CSIR a scientific organization of world standing but still found time to turn his imaginative mind to the matter of a national museum. Rivett's initial observations, written barely three weeks after receiving Pearce's query, make salutary reading more than 60 years later: he urged upon Pearce the need to avoid random acquisition, suggesting instead the need to "look fully into the matter of available collections in the Commonwealth and give a comparative estimate of their scientific and monetary value." Even more significantly, he continued,

> there can be no doubt that a Museum at Canberra, to be completely successful as a national institution, ought to establish close relations with the State Museums from which a considerable amount of admirable material might be obtained. It would be well worth while to associate the leading people in these Museums in an advisory capacity with the National Museum project right from the beginning. Otherwise, they might become very critical and quite the opposite of helpful. [Commonwealth of Australia 1928]

More than half a century later, such advice was ignored, to the cost of the National Museum of Australia.

Rivett developed his theme during July and August. Emphasizing that "mere competition . . . must be carefully avoided," Rivett suggested that state museum directors, university scientists, and the CSIR combine efforts to draft a scheme for the development of a national museum (Commonwealth of Australia 1928/30). The cabinet went part of the way. Rivett was instructed to meet Sydney and Melbourne curators to discuss his plans. He pressed ahead, and eight weeks later, together with J. A. Kershaw of the National Museum of Victoria and Dr. C. Anderson of the Australian Museum, had produced a 10-page report on the options for a national museum in Canberra (Rivett 1928). This report was enthusiastic yet cautious, arguing for staged development and concentrating initially upon anthropology, supplemented by systematic collections development in the principal areas of zoology, botany, and geology. Indeed, the report spoke of a commonwealth museum of natural history. While recognizing the obvious isolation and limitations of Canberra in 1928, the committee nevertheless urged the government to take a long-range view, arguing that

> there is every possibility that Canberra will become a great centre of intellectual work in all the sciences and that in the course of time the need for a Museum to cover all branches of natural history will be imperative.

Even though the need today may be slight, it is most desirable that systematic plans for the future should be made at this stage in order to ensure effective and rapid development when the right time comes. [Rivett 1928:2]

Despite its adherence to the classical formula of natural sciences supported by anthropology, this report did contain initiatives that plotted a new direction for a national museum: in particular, the report's emphasis upon training and recommendation that representatives of Australia's state museums sit on the board of the proposed commonwealth museum (to maximize cooperation and avoid overlap) deserves attention.

After some months of delay, this report in mid-1929 was circulated nationally. In the meantime, a tone of urgency had been adopted by the ANRC. While Radcliffe-Brown was still campaigning for a national museum of ethnology, in the eyes of the ANRC his proposal and the government's national museum plan were increasingly assimilated. They just wanted action, even if it took the occupation of the soon-to-be completed Institute of Anatomy building for a national museum to accomplish it. Between July and September, responses to Rivett's report were received from more than 15 state governments, state museums, and scientific bodies—all were favorable; each state government supported the proposal, and only western Australia's response could be described as tentative (they were concerned about ruling out financial contributions from the states and about duplication of effort). Generally, though, most comments supported the establishment of a national museum, often urging the extension of the concept rather than seeking to inhibit it.

Rivett clearly believed the development of a national museum to be a long-term project, however, neither he nor the project's other supporters were given time. In January 1929, before the general release of his report, the prices of Australia's major export commodities had begun to plummet. Gold exports were increased to pay for imports. By November, Australia's financial position was critical. Budget restrictions were imposed, and public-works programs were among the first casualties of the depression. So, too, was the proposed national museum. It was left to the Royal Society of Queensland, replying favorably to Rivett's proposal in April 1930, to write the national museum's epitaph.

The Society endorses the suggestions as a whole but recognises that under existing circumstances a postponement of activities must occur, and trusts that the postponement will be only temporary. [Commonwealth 1930]

The Role of History

Almost absent from the state museums and these schemes for a national museum was a role for Australia's own history. A ragtag collection of historical relics had found its way into most of the natural-history museums from the later years of the 19th century, but such artifacts sat uneasily beside the growing collections of natural-history and ethnology specimens and were generally viewed as a nuisance. They were almost exclusively relics associated with early explorers and prominent landowning families, who from the early years of the century had begun to consider perpetuating their significance through public collections (Anderson 1991b:132). This was about to change. In 1914, the United Kingdom declared war on Germany; Australia, like the rest of the empire, was automatically at war. There followed an extraordinary period, during which defeat in battle at Gallipoli in the Dardanelles and the subsequent appalling slaughter of the war in the Middle East and in France was reconstructed by a government and a people into the ultimate triumph of "Australian manhood" and the birth of a truly Australian national identity (White 1981). Here at last was a "history" for Australia in its own right.

Tradition had it that the official war historian, C. E. W. Bean, conceived the idea of a national war memorial and museum while surveying the carnage of battle in France in 1917 (McKernan 1991:9). Michael McKernan, official historian of the Australian War Memorial and longtime member of its staff, insists that Bean's concept, which never wavered, was for a memorial to the fallen and a museum that would reflect the terrible cost of war. Not for Bean the militaristic Hall of Warriors and the glorification of militarism (1991:xi–xii). To a degree, Bean's vision prevailed—but only to a degree.

The continued close identification of the Australian War Memorial with the services and with the powerful Returned Services League (RSL) has meant that alternative histories of the war years—peace movement, anticonscription, debates, and more recently anti-Vietnam

War moratoriums—have found virtually no place in its exhibitions, while women's activities, either at home or in the forces, have only recently forged a beachhead. Absent also is the questioning of war, or any attempt at a balanced account of the less acceptable acts of war, which Australians visiting the War Memorial could be forgiven for assuming were committed only by the other side. All of this is consistent with a *memorial*, but it presents many more difficulties for a *museum*. Be that as it may, the principal significance of the Australian War Memorial to this discussion lies less with its interpretative bias than with the fact that for half of this century it has effectively precluded the development of a more general national history museum.

For those who established the War Memorial, as for the politicians who funded it, there can be little doubt that "history" effectively meant war history. Writing in 1918 to the Department of Defence of Australia, as they struggled to collect the relics of war, Bean and his colleagues reminded their co-patriots of the significance of the events taking place: "a nation is built upon pride of race and now that Australia is making history of her own she requires every possible relic associated with this to help educate her children in that national spirit" (Webber 1986:165). Here was history in the service of patriotism indeed. When the War Memorial finally opened in Canberra in 1941, in the middle of a war, and as Australia faced the real possibility of invasion for the first time, similar points were made. Australian Labour party Prime Minister John Curtin, ironically a former conscientious objector who served a brief period in gaol during World War I, nevertheless rose nobly to the occasion and praised the siting of the War Memorial opposite Parliament House in Canberra:

> the Parliament of a free people . . . cannot but be inspired and strengthened in the performance of its great duty by the ever present opportunity to contemplate the story . . . of the great deeds that helped to make the nation. [qt. in McKernan 1991:6]

Both *The Age* in Melbourne and the *Sydney Morning Herald* reported the event in detail the following day, and each emphasized Curtin's reference to the War Memorial as a "sanctuary of Australian traditions." In paraphrasing Curtin's speech, the *Herald* added, on November 12, 1941:

> The memorial would stand as a permanent factor in assuring the continuity of the Anzac tradition. In years to come it would give inspiration to Australians to study the history of their country and to know of the deeds which had kept her freedom unimpaired.

The impressive opening ceremony underlined the national significance of the institution. Although wartime curtailed attendance, both state and federal politicians featured prominently, as did the heads of the services and the official representatives of foreign countries. Invitations were sent out in the name of the "Board of Management and Ministers of State"—an endorsement unparalleled in Australian museum history (McKernan 1991:6). With the advent of the War Memorial, Australia had a "national" museum that even if it was hardly the museum envisaged by Baldwin Spencer or A. R. Radcliffe-Brown, served to content the Australian government for another 30 years. When S. S. Markham and Professor H. C. Richards reported in 1933 to the British Museums Association and to the Carnegie Corporation of New York on museums and art galleries in Australia, their brief allusion to commonwealth initiatives glossed over the wreckage of hopes for a national museum.

After referring over-optimistically to the future of the Institute of Anatomy as a museum in Canberra they noted, "The Federal government has further allowed a site here for a projected general national museum and doubtless, as soon as funds permit, the buildings will be erected" (Markham and Richards 1933:2). However, with federal resources in this area committed to the War Memorial, the concept of a national museum failed to survive the Great Depression. The possibility of such a museum was raised sporadically over succeeding decades—generally prompted, as was the case at the 1939 ANZAAS conference, by the need to store and conserve growing but eclectic collections commissioned or acquired by the commonwealth.

The 30 years following the opening of the Australian War Memorial in 1941 were, by and large, a barren time for the concept of a national museum. There was some hint of change in the mid-1960s, when the commonwealth government commissioned the Inquiry into a National Art Gallery (subsequently opened in 1982); but the real breakthrough coincided with the election in 1972 of a Federal Labour party (or Democratic Socialist party) government. In three turbulent years in office, two successive administrations, led by Gough Whitlam, transformed Australia's cultural landscape—a transformation in which museums were slow to participate. The consequences remain influential today.

In the period following World War II, Australian cultural life underwent something of a renaissance as the federal government finally accepted a limited role as patron of the arts. Australian opera and ballet companies emerged tentatively onto the international stage, and the Australia Council for the Arts began to encourage contemporary Australian art. In the universities, Australian history broke away at last from imperial history and was taught alongside the staple British history. Australian historiography developed rapidly during the 1950s and 1960s, and during the 1970s along with the rest of the world embraced the "new" social history and feminist scholarship (Rickard 1988:251–264).

Such historical ferment largely passed the major museums by, although the 1960s saw a sudden mushrooming of historical museums at the local, community level (Davison 1988b:66; Pigott 1975:21). All government-funded museums continued to accept historical materials but the first historian was not appointed to manage these collections until 1970, when the Western Australia Museum decided to expand its collecting and exhibiting policies to include the recent past. (Archaeology, of course, had won acceptance in museums much earlier.) In 1974, when the Federal Labour party government appointed a select committee to study the state of museums in Australia, the Western Australia Museum was alone in its recognition of the value of Australian material history. Grasping this opportunity, the report by the Pigott Commission of Inquiry on Museums outlined its proposal for a national museum of history, a "Museums of Australia" which would attempt a synthesis of Australia's Aboriginal, postsettlement, and environmental history (Figure 3.4). In recommending a new national museum, the authors of the Pigott Report did not seem to be aware of earlier attempts to interest the federal government in building a national institution, although it was careful to acknowledge existing national collections and the existence of a "specialist war museum." The report's rationale derived instead from the significant expansion in Australian historiography in the then recent decades.

Virtually every nation has its national museum but here the argument for a national museum is particularly powerful. For the nation covers a whole

Figure 3.4 Artist's impression of the proposed national museum of Australia on Lake Burly Griffith, Canberra. From the *Plan for the Development of the Museum of Australia*, published by the museum's interim council in 1982.

continent. ... A new national museum will illuminate new fields of knowledge and also link traditional fields in revealing ways. Australia's natural history and human history is unusual, and today the knowledge of many facets of that history is unfolding in existing ways. A new national museum will naturally chart a course quite different to that followed by other national museums in Europe or the Americas or by those earlier Australian museums which were founded during a different educational and scientific climate. ...

We believe that a decision to establish a comprehensive museum with a national responsibility or charter is long overdue. We are confident that a decision to do this would be widely supported by Australians. [Pigott 1975:70]

In suggesting a museum with a focus on Aboriginal history rather than anthropology, on the Australian environment, and on 20th-century, rather than 19th-century history (1975:71–73), Pigott's vision was both innovative and judicious. All were themes that accorded well with historiographical scholarship of the time but that the older museums had not addressed, and it was hoped that a clearly differentiated national approach might defuse any potential state-federal rivalry. A focus on the 20th century, including in particular Australia's postwar migration drive, also suggested for the first time that museums might be amenable to differing versions of the past. While feminists might regret the absence of any reference to women's history in the report (it was, after all, written during the International Women's Year), there was much to commend in the Pigott Commission's vision.

Within five or six years, the nucleus of the Museum of Australia was established in Canberra, although it was to be some years more before collecting began in earnest. In the meantime, however, the initiative of the Western Australia Museum and almost certainly the comments of the Pigott Report itself had borne fruit elsewhere, as successive state governments scurried to redress their neglect of the past. Hobart appointed a curator of history to oversee both the history and the decorative-arts collections. In Adelaide, the History Trust of South Australia opened a political-history museum in the first Parliament House building and began planning a museum of migration history. In Sydney, the Museum of Applied Arts and Science appointed a group of contract historians, who completed a series of historical exhibitions in the wonderful Hyde Park Convict Barracks in the center of the city, before moving on to a major redevelopment in a former industrial complex (the Powerhouse). Finally, in the mid-1980s the Museum of Victoria, formed by a somewhat fraught amalgamation of the National Museum of Victoria and the Science Museum, also created a permanent history department. The vacuum observed by Pigott was no more within a decade.

Although the older museums often viewed these newly arrived historians as interlopers, there was a certain youthful enthusiasm common to many of the first attempts at public history in museums. Most of the curators compensated for their lack of seniority with a strong commitment to the ideals of the "new social history" (Anderson and Reeves 1985), and their early exhibitions reflected a determined attempt to engage the past in new ways (Anderson 1991b:133–134; Bennett 1988:76–78). Not all of the more radical exhibition proposals actually made it past the censors, either internal or external (Anderson 1991b:133–134), but a fair number of critical exhibitions were attempted at this time. At the old Parliament House in Adelaide, exhibitions challenged community perceptions of the gay community and encouraged public debate on contentious political issues. At the Migration Museum, visitors encountered anything but an affirmative version of Australia's early migration history. The Migration Museum also worked cooperatively from the first with members of an advisory committee drawn from South Australia's ethnic communities and later established an access gallery for such groups to present their own exhibitions, with assistance from the museum. While in the early days there was some pressure from more conservative communities to document only the "success" stories of migration, the overwhelming consensus from the groups involved in oral history programs, or in some of the early craft programs, was for an honest examination of the migration experience, and such community support was to prove an important source of strength for the museum. For a relatively radical experiment in museum terms and in an area fraught with potential conflict, the Migration Museum has attracted remarkably little controversy, although it undoubtedly helped to have had a supportive Labour party state government at the time of opening.

The Role of Women

If the "new" social-history exhibitions assisted in transforming the public face of museums in the 1980s, the advent of historians ushered in an even more profound challenge to what might be called the institutional culture of museums, since the vast majority of museum historians in Australia were women. Although their numbers have not even equalized (let alone reversed) the gender balance of museum staff, the male-female ratio has certainly shifted. Not so the dominant institutional ethos and style, which remains overwhelmingly masculine. Not all of these women are active feminists, committed to changing the orientation of their institutions; but a large number, perhaps a majority, have a strong commitment to change: witness the fact that one of the largest and fastest growing special-interest sections in the museum professionals' organization at present is the women's. The challenge they face is immense.

When the small committees of educated, privileged, scientific gentlemen first established museums in Australia, there was no question of their employing women. Although there were a number of educated women with an intense interest in science, particularly botany, and although some of these women contributed substantially to collecting in the early years of settlement (Hasluck 1955:173–180), their status was always that of the amateur. In 19th-century Australia, as elsewhere in the English-speaking world at the time, "ladies" did not work. Nor was their intellectual ability often accorded much respect: scholarly women were little understood and frequently ridiculed (Anderson 1983:101–113). Writing in the 1830s about the need for the Australian Museum to include more information in its labeling, Dr. George Bennett, later curator, displayed an attitude toward women that was fairly typical in its combination of amused tolerance and condescension. He argued that the "popular, colonial and native names" should be displayed with objects, "as well as the scientific (or hard names as the ladies call them)" (Bennett 1834:69–70). Some 20 years later, the same class of men set out their requirements for professors at the newly established University of Melbourne, an institution that was also to furnish both the first and the second (strictly honorary) directors of the National Museum of Victoria. These men, they decreed, should possess "such habits and manners as to stamp on their future pupils the character of loyal, well-bred, English gentlemen" (Pescott 1954:22–23). Professor Frederick McCoy, who was duly appointed, had ample opportunity to stamp his character on the museum since he acted as director for more than 40 years.

It is not clear when the first woman managed to negotiate a toehold on the payroll of an Australian museum, although the Science Museum of Victoria certainly employed two women in the 1880s, when they were charged with preparing a range of models of acclimatized fruits for the "Colonial and Indian Exhibition" of 1886 (Science Museum 1886:20). However, their numbers remained small, not least because public-service regulations from the end of the 19th century forced women to resign upon marriage (Deacon 1989:145–150). The career of at least one well-qualified and promising anthropologist, Elsie Bramel, who was employed by the Australian Museum in the 1920s and 1930s, was cut short in this way (Strahan 1979:70). The achievements of her less-qualified colleague and husband are still remembered by historians of Australian anthropology; Elsie Bramel's contribution, however, like that of other female anthropologists of this period, is less known (Jones 1991:159). The absence of women from departments of ethnography has had long-term implications for the gender balance of Aboriginal collections. A recent survey of the Aboriginal collections of the major state and federal museums revealed that between 75% and 80% of all objects relate to the material-culture of men rather than of women. If we include the science and technology collections in museums along with other historical materials, the same is true of those collections (Anderson 1991a:46–47).

The work cultures that evolved in these male scientific institutions were also overwhelmingly masculine. "Smoke socials" were the order of the day at the Australian Museum until the 1960s, when a new director introduced the novel idea of social events for the entire staff, which by then included women (Strahan 1979:81). At the Australian War Memorial a built-in masculinity was bolstered by its staff-recruitment and promotion policies, which positively discriminated in favor of applicants with war service (McKernan 1991:198). Not surprisingly the War Memorial remained, until recently, deeply suspicious of women, even where they consented to employ them, and barely accorded women a presence in the exhibition galleries. It is ironic that the first guide to the memorial was in fact written by a woman history graduate (after the male professor whom they approached proved unavailable). She completed the 108-page manuscript in under two months, but the staff at the museum were unimpressed. As the chief clerk later confided to C. E. W. Bean, "Looking back now I can see that it was not a fair thing to give the job to her, or, for that matter, to any woman to do" (1991:20). Although one woman, the famous Matron Vivian Bullwinkel, heroic survivor of a Japanese massacre and prisoner-of-war camp during World War II, was actually appointed to the Board of Trustees in the 1960s, the board was not anxious to repeat the experiment. As General Sir Thomas Daly, chairman of the board in the early 1970s, commented: "while they provided grace and dignity to the meetings they added little of substance to the discussions" (qt. in McKernan 1991:286). Women were tolerated as volunteer guides. As there was no money to pay for guides in the 1970s, the director approached the Army Officers' Wives' Association. But decision making remained firmly out of reach. The consternation, therefore, when in 1985 Dame Beryl Bearepaire was appointed to chair the Board of Trustees was substantial. The RSL immediately formed a watch-dog committee to ensure that the memorial remained true to its "origin, tradition and objects" (1991:333).

It can, of course, be argued that the War Memorial is an extreme case, hardly typical of other museums; but that is only partly true. All state and federal museums in Australia advertise themselves as equal-opportunity employers, yet there is scant evidence that these policies influence practice over many, at least when it comes to the senior-management level. Here, depending on definitions, between 80% and 90% of positions are currently held by men. The balance is somewhat better in art museums than in science and history museums. All-inclusive social events notwithstanding, work cultures also continue to be strongly gendered, although there are clearly conflicting pressures operating here. The sheer number of women employed in museums, and especially their increasing presence at the middle-management level, suggests the likelihood of change in the near future, but this cannot be assumed. Australia is no exception to the worldwide trend in museums that increasingly emphasises management skills and training in senior positions, especially as so many modern museums face pressure to increase their proportion of off-budget revenue. While management skill is undoubtedly important, the assessment of competency in this area is still highly dependent on male models of authority and interaction. Gender-based critiques of management training and models have yet to influence the majority of management-training courses available to museum workers, nor have they been debated within the museum profession in Australia to any extent, although there is a limited debate about managerialism *per se* (Griffin 1987–1988). In the meantime, there is a tendency for female managers in Australia to be required to conform to the dominant mode—if they want to join the men at the top. Other informal work-culture practices continue to disadvantage, or even exclude, women. One ritual common in middle- and senior-management circles is the weekly drinks session in the boardroom or the director's office after hours—fine, so long as someone else can collect the kids from school or childcare. The cumulative influence of these pressures tends to be all the more significant for remaining unacknowledged.

While direct expression of hostility to women or open disparagement, is less common these days, it has not entirely disappeared. One historian at a major state museum was enraged recently to be told by a male colleague that the social-history programs she proposed in labor history and multicultural history were only "girls' stuff," presumably for no other reason than that they were put forward by a woman. Feminist historians, whose assault on labor history has been particularly trenchant (Damousi 1992), would be somewhat bemused by this judgement. It may be sobering evidence that the "backlash" is also in museums (Faludi 1991), but it is just as likely that this incident is more accurately described as evidence of continuing hostility to women. Perhaps the last word on the masculinity of museums in Australia might be left to a journalist, Michael Duffy, whose lengthy article entitled "The Missionary Position" in the *Independent Monthly* for July 1992 was in fact about the Australian Museum. At one point, he paused in his musings to offer the comment: "Incidentally, Tacon, like almost everyone else named in this article, has a doctorate and a beard." Not strictly accurate, but it helped to underline the impression of the unworldly scientist. The image was confirmed in the concluding sentence. "We are all of us environmentalists these days, of course, but most of us would rather leave the actual details of nature to the men with beards" (1992:10).

Women's public presence in museums varies greatly. Some museums, like the Powerhouse in Sydney or the Migration Museum in Adelaide, have made conscious attempts to incorporate women's history and culture in their exhibition programming. As a result, the Powerhouse features a major, permanent exhibition, which explores the history of women's domestic work and attempts to place it within an explicit historical and cultural framework (White 1990). Outside these historical displays women are far less visible. At the Migration Museum, introductory displays reflect on the early history of the site as an asylum for destitute women and children, while both the didactic exhibitions dealing with migration history and the changing exhibition program, have consistently attempted to maintain a presence for women. A recent exhibition at this museum, interrogating the significance of sports in Australian culture, examines many of the sporting stereotypes that underpin popular assumptions about an Australian identity, including its often-blatant sexism. In some of the older museums, however, especially those with a strong natural-history tradition, female curators have found it more difficult to overcome long-established indifference, or even direct hostility, as we saw above. The compromises struck can be interesting cultural documents in themselves, for those schooled to decode them. The Museum of Victoria opened a historical exhibition in 1985 to coincide with the sesquicentenary of permanent European settlement. Although a female curator was eventually appointed to oversee this exhibition, she was unable to make major revisions to the exhibition structure she had inherited, which initially included no reference to women's history at all. After lengthy negotiation, she was able to incorporate two small sections, one dealing with the women's-suffrage movement and one with an early women's industrial campaign. Both, essentially political subjects, can of course be incorporated relatively easily within dominant masculine historiographic constructions. The introductory text to this section of the exhibition might be variously interpreted as a bold challenge or a rather forlorn attempt to redress the balance.

> Women have mostly been left out of history. Their participation in the past has been ignored. They have been hidden from view.
>
> Yet women are central to the past—to the making of history. Not only are the famous women part of our history, but also the vast numbers of those who worked in the home and in the paid workforce.
>
> The relationship between public and private life, paid and unpaid work, has not been recognised. A biased picture of Victoria's past has emerged.

As a cry from the wilderness, this was perhaps an important statement, although those reading it may have been puzzled that such sentiments did not appear to inform the remainder of the exhibition.

Unfortunately, it was far from a manifesto for the future. Some years later, the same museum was host to an exhibition prepared by the Overseas Telecommunications Corporation (OTC), a government-owned, telecommunications authority. The OTC identification with the exhibition extended to their staffing an information desk within the display gallery for several months. In the exhibition, which was shown in a large, centrally located gallery, the visitor was treated to a host of images of men—as learned scientists, as workers in technical workshops, as providers of the benefits of technology to Australians. Women were cast almost exclusively as beneficiaries, as consumers of radio and television. Only once did they appear as workers, and here the exhibitors clearly faced a dilemma. They resorted to a comment on fashion.

> Take a look at what the ladies at OTC Head Office were wearing in 1972. The mini skirt was a popular choice amongst staff, as was the flared polyester slack-suit, paired with the ultimate fashion accessory—the cork wedgie. Also note the attractive, 'Marcia Brady' hair styles . . . on several of the staff—*de rigeur* for the fashion-conscious 70s woman.

The work these women did was never mentioned, although their peripheral role in organizational culture was established all too clearly. Needless to say, if there were any female scientists working in OTC in 1990–1991, they did not feature in this exhibition, nor did the exhibition raise any questions about their absence. In its strong, repeated images of clever, resourceful men and passive, consuming women, the display functioned above all to reinforce conservative stereotypes.

Meanwhile, in a different gallery within the same museum, an exhibition developed by women from the Aboriginal Studies Department attempted to capture something of the lives of Aboriginal women through photographs. In both image and text, this exhibition sought to challenge stereotypes, emphasizing the pivotal role of women within Aboriginal society (Heap and Allen, 1989). Different sections of the museum simply did not connect with each other. But nor was there a policy in place that would help to ensure that avowed commitments to balance and equity of access were implemented in practice. Of equal relevance in the case of the OTC exhibition is the responsibility of the host institution to scrutinize material supplied by outside exhibitors. Failure to do this leaves little distinction between the museum and the advertising billboard. The Museum of Victoria is by no means alone when it comes to conflict between avowed aims and actual practice. Yet as Julia Clark argues, the perception is often that women are now fairly represented in exhibition programs, if not too much to the fore. She refers to a recent experience in preparing a photographic exhibition for the Hobart City Council, in which several of those involved commented, "the girls have really taken over in this exhibition." A subsequent count of images revealed, purely by chance, a precisely equal distribution, although this was clearly not the impression left with some of those involved, so used are we to exhibitions in which women have only a token presence (Clark 1992:2).

Part of the difficulty for women curators anxious to ensure that their own museums reflect principles of equal representation lies with the focus of the institutions themselves. Although each of the major state museums has established general departments of history in the past decade or so, many of the other museums (either created or proposed) are of a more specialist nature, in which male interests are paramount. They include a railway museum in Adelaide; the Stockman's Hall of Fame in outback Queensland; the Bradman Cricketing Museum in country New South Wales; the Australian National Maritime Museum in Sydney; the Earth Exchange (a revamped mining museum) also in Sydney; Scienceworks, a revised science and technology museum in Melbourne; and the proposed National Aviation Museum in country Victoria. There has also been discussion from time to time about the concept of a women's museum somewhere in Australia, but this has not attracted serious attention. It is obvious that the masculine bias inherent in the endorsement of these museum projects presents major structural difficulties for the public exhibition of women's history. Although women history curators in particular have made genuine and sustained attempts to ensure a presence for women in their galleries, museums of mining, cricket, or maritime history are not immediately sympathetic bases. Women can certainly be "added" to the mix, but it is rare that the conceptual basis of the institution is questioned sufficiently to allow a successful accommodation. Unless more accessible museum projects begin to attract support, it is difficult to see a more equitable place for women's public history in Australia in the lead-up to the centenary of Australian nationhood in 2001.

Art museums have also engaged in international debates concerning art and gender but, again, with inconsistent results. Hence, although the Queensland Art Gallery initiated and toured a major exhibition entitled "Women Artists" in 1990 and other museums have followed with either similar "compensatory" projects (Hamond and Peers 1992) or shows highlighting the work of individual women artists, these initiatives do not always have an impact on general exhibition programs. This observation was brought home to us particularly powerfully recently by a popular blockbuster entitled "Rubens and the Italian Renaissance" a touring exhibition curated by the Australian National Gallery. This high-profile exhibition was heavily promoted, and the crowds have been consistent. Gender does not feature openly in the catalog and wall texts of the exhibition, but it recurs powerfully in image after image. Some of the most confrontational for modern women have been those that are prominent in advertising and in the plethora of products accompanying these exhibitions. The painting chosen for the cover of the calendar and one of two posters, for example, is Rubens' *Leda and the Swan*, a highly erotic painting, which nevertheless stretches the credulity of the viewer (not to mention the subject) somewhat in its depiction of a languid, young, naked woman, being "seduced" by a swan. The catalog hints at, but cannot quite confront openly, this apparent preoccupation of Rubens and other Renaissance painters (and patrons) with erotic "seductions" (Australian National Gallery 1992:86, 114). Although the text in the catalog concentrates above all on a technical reading of pictures like *Leda and the Swan*, the wider erotic implications have not been lost on consumers and sponsors: *Leda and the Swan* was selected as the visual focus of a large advertisement for Southern Pacific Hotels, run in the weekend arts section of *The Age* (Melbourne) during the exhibition. With the heading "Four Ways to look at Rubens," the advertisement promised different combinations of the special night away, with "champagne and chocolates on arrival, breakfast for two, a late check-out, and tickets to Rubens (August 1, 1992, Saturday Extra). The implications are unmistakable. This reproduction of *Leda* is too reduced in size for one to see the swan clearly, yet the general impression of languid female arousal suits the hotels' purpose admirably.

However, it was the exhibition's treatment of images of rape that we found most extraordinary. Neither the ancient Romans, who devised the myths inspiring so many of the pictures in this exhibition, nor the artists themselves were particularly squeamish about rape perpetrated by gods, which in mythology at least was always assumed to confer honor on the mortal selected. But the exhibition text avoids the term at all costs, which leads to some patent absurdities. The display label attached to Rubens' *Mars and Rhea Silvia*, for example, carries euphemism to a new height: "This picture shows Mars, god of war, *abruptly descending on* the mortal Rhea Silvia, to leave her pregnant with Romulus and Remus" [our emphasis]. As the text continues, rape is transformed smoothly into "seduction" and finally into "love":

> Seated in front of the shrine of the goddess to whom she has vowed her chastity, Rhea confronts the powerful figure of the god who is determined to seduce her. By depicting Mars in armour, Rubens can illustrate how the war-god is to be disarmed both literally and metaphorically by love.

The violence inherent in the encounter is in this way negated and the rape itself subtly legitimated. But there is more in the catalog entry, for here Curator David Jaffe introduces still another dimension designed to excuse the act. Rhea's avowed commitment to chastity notwithstanding, Jaffe suggests that her "apprehension seems to be modified by at least a hint of desire"—surely the age-old defense of the rapist here appropriated, perhaps unconsciously, by the art historian (Australian National Gallery 1992:118). Despite long and careful study, we have been unable to detect this "hint of desire" that Jaffe appears to find so reassuring: Rubens seems to us to have painted a woman in fear and distress. But even if Rubens did intend to present a dedicated virgin suddenly charged with desire on seeing Mars "abruptly descending," we might have expected the catalog essay to subject such an interpretation to analysis, allowing the reader to begin at least a partial deconstruction of the masculine worldview that informs the image. Instead, the masculinist vision is reinforced, as the authoritative figure of the curator directs the viewer into his preferred reading of the picture. In fairness to the Australian National Gallery, we should point out that the institution as a whole has done a great deal over the years to raise the profile of Australian art, including women's art; but in common with other museums, specific policy commitments do not always influence general-exhibition programs.

As with many relatively "new" nations, Australia since federation has been preoccupied with defining a specific national identity (White 1981).

It is an obsession that occasionally seeks direct public expression through museums, although it is rarely entirely absent from the subtext of less-focused exhibitions. The most recent such attempt is an exhibition of Australian portraits entitled "Uncommon Australians— Towards a National Portrait Gallery," a touring exhibition that has drawn on the collections of many museums and libraries around the country. Described by one critic as an "exercise in patriotic myth-making" (Neville 1992), "Portraits" has also attracted the ire of feminist art historians. Margaret Plant argued in a letter to *The Age* on May 30, 1992, shortly after its Melbourne opening:

> A "brittle Australia" is indeed in evidence, but there needs to be a firmer statement that foregrounds the exhibition's distortion of history. Can it be that the 19th Century was entirely the achievement of males and one woman, Mrs Elizabeth Macarthur? The primary exhibiting gallery indicates just this: in the second gallery representing the 20th century more women are permitted. . . . Our aviators, Biggles boys together, adorn the poster image of the exhibition, already on the walls of many of our educational institutions. . . . Leaving aside the aesthetic questions that too many paintings and photographs give rise to, we have an exhibition that is poor history, apparently ignorant not only of the obligation to aspire to equal representation, but also to consider social history and the history of everyday life.

Convenor-patron Marilyn Darling was swift to respond; her letter in reply was accompanied by a portrait, *Mrs Darling and Her Children* by John Linnell. The response is notable not only for its apparent unconsciousness of irony but for its profound ignorance of Australian historiography of the past two decades.

> As the female member [note the singular] of the convenor patrons/curator team, I can assure her [Plant] that this exhibition was not put together by male chauvinists. With the three women members of our consultative committee who provided long lists of suitable subjects, we made a conscious effort to increase the proportion of women in the exhibition. History was against us. In fact, we did succeed rather more than we are credited with by Margaret Plant. The first room in the exhibition contains three women, not one, from last century. The wife of Abel Tasman and the wife of Governor Darling are there and indeed that says it all—that was the social history of the day. No women explorers, magistrates nor governmental heads; the hand was too busy rocking the cradle and

providing the stalwart domestic qualities expected in this new and strange land. . . . Our exhibition has 39 women subjects and artists among 116 portraits and as this spans all of Australia's history, it is an appropriate achievable representation.

Regarding Margaret Plant's assertion that as well as "distorting history," we are "apparently ignorant . . . of the obligation to aspire to equal representation." I do agree with her sentiments in relation to the present and the future. But the male/female ratio in our exhibition is realistic—history cannot be rewritten. [*The Age*, June 2, 1992]

Clearly Darling is no historian. Yet this exhibition was informed by a strong, if extremely dated, historicism, which directed the selection of evidence according to unquestioned assumptions about the past and women's dress. Not surprisingly, those women who might have been considered "uncommon" by the exhibitors' definition—women like Lady Jane Franklin, a very scholarly governor's wife, who unlike Darling's ancestor produced no brood of children and was, therefore, not "too busy rocking the cradle"; Caroline Chisolm, who set up schemes to help immigrant women; or early feminist writer Catherine Helen Spence—find no place in this exhibition: their lives clearly did not reflect the stereotypes that this exhibition was determined to enforce on 19th-century women's history and 20th-century viewers. As a result, the "Biggles boys" emerge unchallenged, and "history" finds itself harnessed, once again, to a conservative-heritage agenda.

Identity

The making of public meaning is a highly charged political process in any community. Women are not alone in demanding improved access to public space through museums. During the 1980s, the right of the white Anglo-Saxon men who manage museums to continue to showcase their own history and culture to the exclusion of other more complex readings began to be challenged. Increasingly, museums are sites of contested identity. In recent years, museums in Australia have begun in earnest to accommodate these different cultural views. "Cultural diversity" has become something of a buzzword in the 1990s, as museums vie with each other to introduce multicultural-collecting policies, community-access galleries, and appropriate community advisory groups. The public culture of museums has changed as a result, especially in areas reflecting Aboriginality and ethnicity, although the extent of this transformation is open to debate. As the discussion of gender issues above suggests, it is more often self-consciously proclaimed than actively implemented.

The acquisition and exhibition of Australian Aboriginal culture and material has been for more than a century a principal activity of many Australian museums, so much so that during the 1920s interest in this material provided a driving force for the establishment of a national museum. More recently, the relationships among museums, Aboriginal communities, and Aboriginal cultural heritage have begun to change. The interpretation of Aboriginal culture can no longer be understood as the preserve of European anthropologists. Such emerging disciplines as Aboriginal history and the claim by Aborigines to the right to manage their own culture and heritage have demanded a re-evaluation of the relationship between museums and Aboriginal communities. In this changing relationship, two points need to be emphasized. Firstly, museums are now involved in debates relating to culture, race, gender, and society. Museums must acknowledge this and actively participate if their claims to social relevance are to be valid. Secondly, such a debate cannot be defined simply in the language of consumption—that is, of audience access to or perception of exhibitions, objects, or works of art. The debate has been and continues to be conducted in terms of what is collected, who owns such cultural material, on whose behalf it is held, and the consequent role of community organizations and groups in developing the theoretical framework for public exhibitions and programs (CAMA 1993; Sculthorpe 1992).

The first results of these debates concerning culture and management are now evident. From being the objects of study and research by European anthropologists, Aboriginal people now occupy an increasingly strategic role in the research, collections development, and management of their cultural heritage. In the process, anthropology has begun to be redefined, and Aboriginal history is emerging as a discipline in its own right. In a national context, such changes are occurring at an uneven pace and not, at times, without resistance.

When considered in the broader context of such parallel political events as the long-running Aboriginal campaign for land rights, it is evident that museums' "ownership" of Aboriginal cultural heritage has been challenged and considerably diminished. Concepts of custodianship and community consultation rather than ownership now mark the language of many museums. In recognition of this changing relationship, the Council of Australian Museum Associations, together with Aboriginal museum staff and Aboriginal communities, has now embarked upon a major process to redefine the nature of the relationship between Australian museums, Aboriginal communities, and Aboriginal cultural heritage, a process in which questions of custodianship, ownership, interpretation, access, and use of such cultural material are being reconsidered. The influence of such initiatives can now be identified in such areas as Aboriginal use of collections and research materials, equivalent changes in the language and style of exhibitions, and changes in the language and focus of related publications.

Within Australia, alternative models for future management and access now exist, ranging from Aboriginal management of collections within existing museums to the rise of independent Aboriginal cultural centers and "keeping places." Each of these options is still evolving. Ultimately, effective solutions may be found in an amalgam of more than one of these alternatives. But whatever the mix, it seems clear that museums cannot continue to appropriate Aboriginal history and culture or present an essentially European cultural agenda.

Contemporary development in Aboriginal cultural heritage and multiculturalism, in particular, indicate that the relationships between museums and the communities that sustain and support them are being renegotiated, a process having a profound influence upon the development of broad national strategies in cultural heritage, as well as upon the development of a national museum. Within the ferment of change that has gripped Australian museums during the 1980s, the National Museum of Australia has been at once a beneficiary and a victim. Lacking the wider intellectual and strategic support so evident in the late 1920s, the embryonic National Museum has not yet created an effective and acknowledged role for itself within the general fields of museology and cultural heritage. With David Rivett's admonitions of the 1920s regarding state representation and cooperation forgotten or ignored, tensions between state museums and bureaucracies and the commonwealth government heightened. Rejecting the notion of yet another monolithic institution duplicating the work of existing museums, state governments argued for the allocation of resources to what had begun to be called the "dispersed national collection," found primarily in state museums (Anderson 1991a:38–42). Some of those seeking recognition of the "dispersed national collection," hoped to undermine the concept of a national museum. Others saw the potential for a collaborative approach by all museums, including the National Museum. As Robert Edwards, chairman of the Council of the National Museum, argued,

> In identifying a role for the National Museum it would be both unwise and indeed impossible to attempt to duplicate the existing National Collection by the development of a Canberra-based equivalent. On the other hand there is wisdom in the Commonwealth accepting responsibility for some of those initial tasks that cannot be undertaken by the States. . . . The Commonwealth can be a vital factor in ensuring wider access to the collections located across Australia. [Edwards 1991:85]

The ultimate fate of the National Museum of Australia remains unresolved. Debate concerning the character of the museum and its role in interpreting Australian history and culture has again shifted. Such issues as collaboration with state museums, in both research and exhibition programs, now appear to have greater emphasis than before. The recent cultural-policy *Discussion Paper*, released by the commonwealth government in April 1992, refers specifically to cooperative and devolved national strategies in this area (Commonwealth of Australia 1992:23). However, despite the commonwealth government's continued assurances of the significance of a national museum of Australia, its development has been repeatedly shelved and its future is unclear. Continued commonwealth-state tension, combined with federal indifference, has undermined earlier visions of a national museum. And yet cultural certainties, which marred early visions, linger. In the 1992 *Discussion Paper*, the commonwealth government suggested that a national museum would "'explain,' at a national level . . . what it means to be Australian" (1992:23). If the intention were to explore, rather than "to explain," the many contested readings of "what it means to be Australian," we would feel more optimistic about its future relevance; otherwise the museum will remain much the way it was envisaged by one of Canberra's first historians:

> That visionary future, representing the consummation of so much of what Canberra stands for, is already dimly in view. . . . [But] beyond this one dare not prophesy. For there will be edifices dwarfing the present

structures; great cathedrals and public halls, museums and art galleries—and no rabbits, no hares and no sheep, but all the glories that belong to a new chapter in the history of Australia and of our civilisation. [Denning 1938:109–110]

References

Anderson, M.
>   1983 "Helpmeet for Man": Women in Mid-Nineteenth-Century Western Australia. In *Exploring Women's Past: Essays in Social History*. P. Crawford, ed. Melbourne: Sisters Publishing Ltd.
>   1991a *Heritage Collections in Australia: Report to the Heritage Collections Working Group of the Cultural Ministers' Council*. Melbourne: National Centre for Australian Studies, Monash University.
>   1991b Selling the Past: History in Museums in the 1990s. In *Packaging the Past? Public Histories*. J. Rickard and P. Spearritt, eds. Melbourne: Melbourne University Press.

Anderson, M. and A. Reeves
>   1985 Directions in Australian Museums. In *Papers of the Committee to Review Australian Studies in Tertiary Education*. Vol. 3. Canberra: Government Printer.

Archer, W. H.
>   1858 *Facts and Figures: Or, Notes of Progress, Statistical and General*. Melbourne: Fairfax & Co.

Australian National Gallery
>   1992 *Rubens and the Italian Renaissance*. Canberra: Australian National Gallery.

Bennett, G.
>   1834 Wanderings in New South Wales, Batavia, Pedia Coast, Singapore, and China. London.

Bennett, T.
>   1988 Museums and "The People." In *The Museum Time Machine: Putting Cultures on Display*. R. Lumley, ed. Pp. 63–85. London: Routledge.

Council of Australian Museum Associations (CAMA)
>   1993 *Policies for Museums in Australia and Aboriginal and Torres Strait Islander Peoples: A Statement of Principles*. Issued in May 1993.

Clark, J.
>   1992 Girls' Stuff. Paper presented to the Western Australian Branch of the Museums Association of Australia, Perth. August 1992.

Commonwealth of Australia
>   1904 *The Inaugural Celebrations of the Commonwealth of Australia*. Sydney: Government Printer.
>   1927 Cabinet Memoranda, Mss. Australian Archives File A6006/1927/12/31.

1928/30 Correspondence Series (including correspondence between A. C. D. Rivett, Australian National Museum, the Research Council, S. M. Bruce, the Royal Society of Queensland, and the Vice President of the Executive Council). Australian Archives File AJ 120/6.

1933 *Commonwealth Year Book* 26. Canberra: Government Printer.

1975 Museums in Australia: Report of the Committee of Inquiry on Museums and National Collections Including the Report of the Planning Committee on the Gallery of Aboriginal Australia. (Pigott Report). Canberra: Government Printer.

1992 *The Role of the Commonwealth in Australia's Cultural Development—A Discussion Paper*. Canberra: Government Printer.

Damousi, J.

1992 The Gendering of Labour History. Eighth Roger Joyce Memorial Lecture, University of Melbourne.

Darling, M.

1992 History Cannot Be Rewritten. *The Age*, June 2, 1992.

Davison, G.

1988a Festivals of Nationhood: The International Exhibitions. In *Australian Cultural History*. S. L. Goldberg and F. B. Smith, eds. Cambridge: University Press

1988b The Use and Abuse of Australian History. *Australian Historical Studies* 23: 55–76.

Deacon, D.

1989 *Managing Gender: The State, the New Middle Class and Women Workers, 1830–1930*. Melbourne: Oxford University Press.

Denning, W.

1938 *Capital City*. Sydney: Publicist Publishing.

Duffy, M.

1992 The Missionary Position. *Independent Monthly*. July 1992, p. 10.

Edwards, R.

1991 Defining National Collections. In *Australian Museums: Collecting and Presenting Australia*. D. F. McMichael, ed. Canberra: Council of Australian Museum Associations.

Faludi, S.

1991 *Backlash: The Undeclared War Against Women*. London: Chatto & Windus.

Griffin, D.

1987–1988 Managing in the Museum Organisation, I: Leadership and Communication. *International Journal of Museum Management and Curatorship* 6:387–398; II: Conflict, Tasks Responsibilities. 7:11–23.

Hale, H. M.

1956 *The First Hundred Years of the South Australian Museum, 1856–1956*. Adelaide: South Australian Museum.

Hamond, V., and J. Peers
   1992 *Completing the Picture: Women Artists and the Heidelberg Era.*
      Melbourne: Artmoves.
Hasluck, A.
   1955 *Portrait with Background: A Life of Georgiana Molloy.* Melbourne:
      Oxford University Press.
Heap, V., and N. Allen
   1989 *Daughters of the Dreaming.* Melbourne: Museum of Victoria.
Jones, P.
   1991 Perceptions of Aboriginal Art: A History. In *Dreamings: The Art of
      Aboriginal Australia.* P. Sutton, ed. Ringwood: Penguin.
Kusamitsu, T.
   1980 Great Exhibitions Before 1851. *History Workshop Journal* 9:70–89.
Markham, S. S., and H. C. Richards
   1933 *A Report on the Museums and Art Galleries of Australia to the Carnegie
      Corporation of New York.* London: Museums Association.
McCulloch, A.
   1984 *Encyclopedia of Australian Art.* Vol. 1. Melbourne: Hutchinson.
McKernan, M.
   1991 *Here Is Their Spirit: A History of the Australian War Memorial,
      1917–1990.* St. Lucia: University of Queensland Press.
McShane, I.
   1991 A History of the History of the National Museum of Australia,
      Canberra. Ms. on file, National Museum of Australia, Canberra.
Neville, G.
   1992 Review of Uncommon Australians—Towards a National Portrait
      Gallery. *The Age,* May 27, 1992.
Oceania
   1930 1:91–98.
Perry, W.
   1974 *The Science Museum of Victoria: A History of Its First Hundred Years.*
      Melbourne: Science Museum of Victoria.
Pescott, R. T. M.
   1954 *Collections of a Century: The History of the First 100 Years of the National
      Museum of Victoria.* Melbourne: National Museum of Victoria.
Pigott
   1975 *Museums in Australia.* See Commonwealth of Australia, 1975.
Plant, M.
   1992 Only ONE Woman in That Century. *The Age,* May 30, 1992.
Radcliffe-Brown, A. R.
   1927 The Need of a National Museum of Ethnology. Australian Archives
      File AJ 120/6.
Rickard, J.
   1988 *Australia: A Cultural History.* London: Longman.

Rivett, A. C. D.
  1928 Report of a Committee to Advise on the General Question of a
       National Museum at Canberra. Australian Archives File AJ 120/6.
Sculthorpe, G.
  1992 Interpreting Aboriginal History in a Museum Context. *Museums
       Australia Journal*, 2–3:49–56.
Smith, B.
  1945 *Place, Taste and Tradition: A Study of Australian Art Since 1788*.
       Sydney: Ure Smith.
Specht, J. R.
  1979 Anthropology. In Ron Strahan *Rare and Curious Specimens: An
       Illustrated History of the Australian Museum, 1827–1979*. Sydney:
       Australian Museum, Pp. 141–50.
Strahan, R.
  1979 *Rare and Curious Specimens: An Illustrated History of the Australian
       Museum*. Sydney: Australian Museum.
Sutton, P.
  1991 *Dreamings: The Art of Aboriginal Australia*. Ringwood: Penguin.
Webber, K
  1986 Constructing Australia's Past: The Development of Historical
       Collections, 1888–1938. In *Council of Australian Museum Association
       Conference Proceedings*. P. Summerfield, ed. Perth: Council of Australian
       Museum Associations. Pp. 155–174.
White, R.
  1981 *Inventing Australia: Images and Identity, 1688–1980*. Sydney: George
       Allen and Unwin.
White, R.
  1990 'Everyday Life in Australia': Social History Exhibits, Museum of
       Applied Arts and Sciences (The Powerhouse), Sydney. *Australian
       Historical Studies*, 24(95): 293–4.

4 Archaeology and the Establishment of Museums in Saudi Arabia

Abdullah H. Masry

The land surface of Saudi Arabia is roughly equivalent to the whole of western Europe. Therefore, the scale of research operations necessary and the challenge of excavations in singularly harsh, often inhospitable terrain make the task of archaeology and the role of museums in the communities they serve complex. The Department of Antiquities and Museums, Kingdom of Saudi Arabia, has aimed to serve the needs of their communities in undertaking construction of a network of museums in several important cities over the past two decades. This network includes a National Archaeological and Ethnographical Museum in the capital city of Riyadh, budgeted at about 1 billion Saudi riyals (U.S. equivalent is $340 million), and a series of regional and site museums in the provinces. Museums have been built in the Northern Province, at Taima, and at al-Riyadh; in the Eastern Province, at Hofuf; and in the Southern Province, at Wadi, at a total cost of about 200 million Saudi riyals. Additional regional museums are planned at Dammam, Jeddah, as well as other major cities. Two Islamic museums will be installed in the holy cities of Makkah and Medina at an estimated cost of 500 million Saudi riyals.

The concept behind the system of Saudi museums is to preserve and present the archaeological, historical, and cultural heritage of the country. Their program is to conserve, investigate, and interpret their holdings to the public at the regional and local or grassroots level. The government aims to:

1. Conserve and protect sites of enduring interest
2. Provide facilities for the recording and investigation of sites
3. Act as a collection center for artifacts, providing storage, documentation, and conservation facilities

4. Investigate and record local culture and tradition
5. Act as a collection center for artifacts of local traditional culture
6. Make available to the public the local archaeology, history, and traditional cultures through exhibitions and other educational activities
7. Act as an expression of the Department of Antiquities and Museums' contribution to the local community along with the department's work in preserving the kingdom's rich cultural heritage

In this chapter I trace the recent, intensive activities of the Saudi government to recover, analyze, and interpret its ancient past, historic sites, monuments, and contemporary cultures. I consider, as well, the history and context of the modern nation-state of Saudi Arabia, which creates and unites itself through a policy of broad research, excavation, restoration and the establishment of museums.

Overview

The Kingdom of Saudi Arabia has initiated a vigorous archaeological policy that, in establishing both short- and long-term objectives, finds much of its physical expression in the country's museums. In the early 1960s the Department of Antiquities and Museums was set up, which was and remains part of the Ministry of Education. Comprehensive antiquities laws were introduced to provide standards and guidelines for the department's operations. At the same time, a consultative body was founded, the High Council for Antiquities. The primary purposes of the council are to set policies and to establish programs consonant with the need for protection, research, and preservation of the country's cultural heritage in accordance with the antiquities laws.

Beginning in the late 1960s, Arabian archaeology has affected the wider context of study of ancient Near Eastern history as a whole. That initial research of the late 1960s and early 1970s drew on and was largely dependent upon interregional comparisons based on archaeological investigations beyond Saudi Arabia. The inevitable result was a rather fragmented picture. The distinct regions within Arabia were each seen in relation to their nearest neighbors and better-known areas (e.g., Jordan, Palestine, Egypt, Syria, and Iraq), rather than in relation to Saudi Arabia or the Arabian Peninsula as an entity. Some of the results of archaeology in Saudi Arabia are national museums across the country.

Beginnings: 19th- and 20th-Century Visitors and Scholars

Antiquarian interest in the ancient monuments of the Kingdom of Saudi Arabia started with Moslem and European travelers' accounts from the 18th and 19th centuries and from the brief reports provided by the much earlier Arab geographers and historians, such as al-Hamdani and Yagut al-Hawmawi. Saudi Arabian archaeology, however, is a 20th-century phenomenon. In this century, several European and American antiquarians were active in Saudi Arabia, notably, the French Dominican Archaeological Mission of A. J. F. Jaussen and R. Savignac. They carried out three expeditions in 1907, 1909, and 1910, and they conducted an exhaustive examination of the monuments and inscriptions surviving aboveground at or in the neighborhood of the oasis of Tabuk, Madain Saleh, and al-Ula. I should also mention here Bernard Moritz's visit to al-Qurrayah in the north in 1906 and to Hijaz in 1914. American scholar Alois Musil carried out a series of important explorations in the northern Hijaz and the Najd, which greatly contributed to our knowledge of the ethnography and archaeology of northern Arabia. The explorations of St. John Philby in 1922, Henry Field, G. Ryckmans, as well as traditional local historians and antiquarians, such as Hamad al-Jassir and Abdulrehman al-Ansari.

In the 1960s, there were intermittent expeditions under the auspices of the then newly founded Department of Antiquities and Museums. These included the expeditions of Winnet and Reed in 1962 and 1972 respectively, the two former directors of the American School of Oriental Research in Jerusalem, then part of Jordan. They worked in the northwestern and northern regions of the kingdom, recording archaeological and epigraphical sites. Father Albert Jamme of Catholic University, Washington, D.C., in the United States traveled and worked mostly in Yemen and southern Arabia in 1967. He published several articles and books on the ancient inscriptions of Arabia. The British team of Parr, Ryckmans, and Dayton covered the central and northwestern regions in 1968–1969 (Parr 1970–1972). T. G. Bibby's book, *Looking for Dilmun* (1971), referred to the Eastern Province of Saudi Arabia, specifically dealt with in his earlier publication *Preliminary Survey in East Arabia* (1968). These scholars and their published works on the one hand showed the way; on the other hand, they demonstrated the need for a controlled and systematic approach to the kingdom's archaeology.

Government Surveys

It was to satisfy this need for well-researched archaeology that the government-sponsored Comprehensive Archaeological Survey was initiated in 1976. The aim was to document the archaeological remains of the entire kingdom. The program is ongoing, and the results are duly reported in *Atlal, The Journal of Saudi Arabian Archaeology*, an annual publication of the Department of Antiquities and Museums entirely dedicated to Arabian archaeology.

The survey thus far has resulted in the discovery of thousands of sites throughout the kingdom. In addition to the Comprehensive Archaeological Survey, which is generalized in scope, specialized subject surveys have also been carried out, and ancient trade routes and Islamic pilgrim caravanserai were, as a result, firmly identified. Thus, the route known as *Darb Zubaydha*, the former pilgrimage and trade route to and from Makkah, was exhaustively documented over six successive seasons; each way station on the route was pinpointed, mapped, and recorded. The results of this work are now being used for selective restoration and improvement, including actual reactivation of some of the water reservoirs and basins for the benefit of the contemporary transhumant population. Coastal Syrian and Egyptian pilgrim routes along the Red Sea and its littoral have also been surveyed, and several early Islamic town sites have been discovered (Figure 4.1).

Three successive seasons were devoted to the investigation of ancient mining sites in Arabia. Specialists from the Colorado School of Mines were involved in the investigation and documentation of forts and worked alongside local Saudi archaeological staff. The three expeditions, working within three fairly restricted areas in the Arabian Shield, northwest Hijaz, as well as areas in the southwestern region, located a large number of ancient gold, silver, and copper mines, as well as

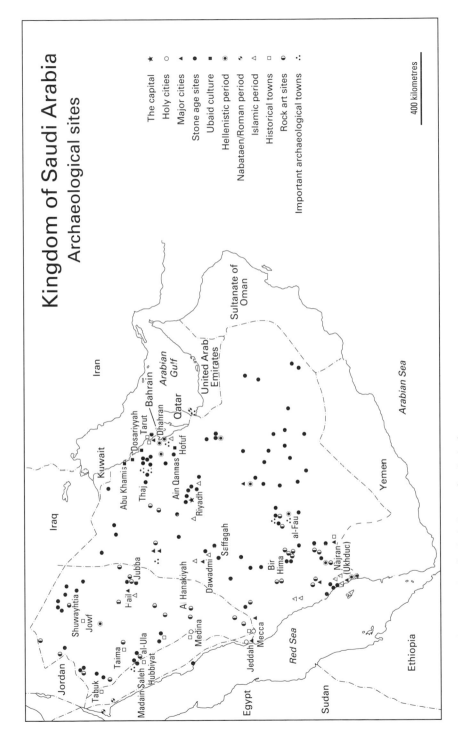

Figure 4.1 Arabia, its archaeological sites and principal museums.

semiprecious stone quarries. Another specialized survey, focusing on rock art and epigraphy, was initiated in 1985, and in four seasons over 1,000 rock art and epigraphic sites were recorded from the northern half of the country alone.

It should be noted that both the comprehensive and the specialized archaeological surveys were planned from the outset as part of the preparation for future, systematic, large-scale excavations. Limited test excavations were carried out as part of the ground-survey work. Several important prehistoric sites were excavated on a "rescue operation" basis (*Atlal* passim). In addition, early large-scale archaeological excavations took place as part of the permanent field-training program of King Saud University in Riyadh. A good example of these excavations is the late 1000 B.C. city of Al-Faw; another is the early-century Islamic town-site of Ar-Rabbadha, near the holy city of Al-Medina (Ansary 1982).

Apart from these excavations, several other large-scale excavations of potentially important sites were started in 1985: Madain Saleh and Taima in northwestern Saudi Arabia, the Dhahran tomb fields in the Eastern Province, and the third-millennium B.C. Neolithic site of Thummamah in the Central Province. Also, the second to first millennium B.C. sites of Sihi and Ukhdud in the southern region were part of the initial efforts. Excavations at early Paleolithic sites such as Dawadmi in the Central Province, and at Shuhaythia in the north of the kingdom dated early man's settlements in the Arabian Peninsula to nearly 1 million years ago.

Perspective

Arabian archaeology makes it clear, thus far, that the kingdom has always played a central role throughout history with respect to the many cultures in adjacent lands. The success of these efforts is due chiefly to the generous support of King Fahad's government. It has enabled the directorate to launch and maintain a program of research, restoration, and preservation of monuments and to establish a network of national, regional, and local museums. In addition, it made possible the participation of prominent archaeologists and interested institutions from many different parts of the world, for example, Harvard University, Southwest Texas University, University of Missouri,

University of California, the Institute of Archaeology, London, and the Centre National Recherches Scientifiques, Paris.

Our present understanding of the archaeology of Saudi Arabia, based on the results of the surveys and initial excavations, posits a general framework of cultural and chronological sequences, from early human to well-developed prehistoric cultures, as well as early agricultural and literate settlements that appear to date from around 6000–5000 B.C.

Saudi Arabia is abundantly represented in the early Neolithic phase by a vast number of sites found on the borders of the great Arabian deserts. These clearly suggest a very different environment and climate from today's extremely dry and hot conditions. During a critical period from 3000 to 2000 B.C., Saudi Arabia saw the emergence of the peculiar pattern of settled-nomadic settlements that have been an enduring characteristic of the peninsula. This has puzzled and intrigued historians and scholars from the 14th century social historian and philosopher Ibn al-Khaldun to contemporary analysts. From the late 3000–2000 B.C. period, well-developed urban centers were found throughout greater Arabia, exhibiting fully developed literary and religious traditions and political structures.

Several thousand early Arabic inscriptions, such as Thamudic, Musnad al-Janubi, Nabataean, and others were located during the epigraphic survey. Recently the department's rock art specialists and epigraphers have discovered new evidence suggesting the possibility of independent evolution and development of writing systems within the Arabian Peninsula—contrary to the currently prevailing views. The Islamic period ushers in another archaeological record that witnesses another cultural tradition, which was to assert itself over a vast area. Nevertheless, archaeological renaissance has modified this picture, too, showing the great significance of the Arabian heartland. The archaeological records and our continuing explorations afford ample data on divergent networks of cultural relations over time.

Historic Sites, Monuments, and Museums

In the mid-1970s, the Department of Antiquities and Museums inaugurated the Museum of Archaeology and Ethnography at Riyadh

(Figure 4.2). Here, for the first time, a coherent chronology for the overall history and archaeology of Saudi Arabia was laid down. Its time scale ranges from the Lower Paleolithic in the west, nearly 1 million years ago, to the high cultures of the third and second millennia in the Eastern Province, and impacts the Arabian Gulf and the centers of population and civilization which grew up in the desert oases and on the coast; and culminates in the Revelation of Islam, established in the Western Province cities in the seventh century A.D. The collection of artifacts assembled in the new national museum from all these periods, provides an overview of Arabia's past for visitors and students alike.

Historic sites have not been neglected. The department has undertaken extensive conservation and restoration of historic buildings: the old capital of Najd, Dirriyha, located about 20 km north of Riyadh; the King Abdul Aziz Palace and the Qasr al-Masmak, in Riyadh (described in more detail below); the Mosque of Ibrahim, in Hasa, Eastern Province; and Bait Nasif, in Jeddah. Numerous other watchtowers, castles, forts, and mosques throughout the kingdom have been restored and preserved in the last 15 years. The government generously allocated funds for the restoration and preservation of buildings and monuments as part of its five-year plan, 1985–1990. It is estimated that 180 million Saudi riyals were allocated for the restoration and conservation of old buildings, castles, and other historic monuments, an amount that is three times what was spent for the same purposes during the preceding five-year plan, 1980–1985.

The current rapid development and the expansion of towns and cities in the kingdom threaten to disturb archaeological sites. To protect them, the Department of Antiquities and Museums has launched a program of fencing around sites located near towns or cities. Over 46 million Saudi riyals has been spent in recent years to protect 185 sites, and some 295,000 meters of fencing have been erected.

The Department of Antiquities has a well-developed publications section for the archaeology and history of Arabia. They publish *Atlal*, but in addition, there are provisions for monographs and special publications, as well as posters depicting Saudi Arabia's antiquities which are distributed throughout the kingdom and internationally.

All research, publications, excavations, and restoration programs are

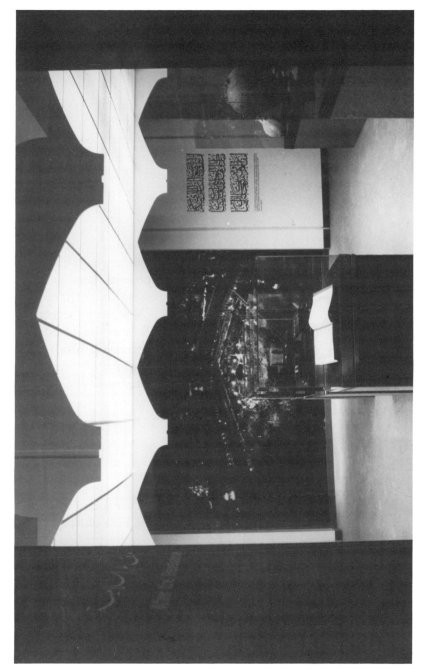

Figure 4.2 Interior, the Museum of Archaeology and Ethnography, Riyadh.

government sponsored, with budgets that are unequaled in most other countries during the last 15 years, reflecting a major national commitment. Thus, 1 billion Saudi riyals were spent for archaeological research under the first five-year plan, 1965–1970.

Museums have been constructed in a number of large cities. A network of local museums is located at Taima (Figure 4.3), al-Ula, Doamt and Jundal, Hofuf, Wadi Dawasir, Najran, Jizan and Qasim, these having cost about 200 million Saudi riyals. Each local museum reflects its region and controls all archaeological activities and preservation and restoration projects in its area. Additional regional museums at Dammam, Jeddah, and other major cities are planned, as are two Islamic museums to be installed in the holy cities of Makkah and Medina, at an estimated cost of about 500 million riyals.

To demonstrate more clearly the work of the Department of Antiquities and Museums and to give a sense of the magnitude and impact of its responsibilities, I describe two projects here in some detail and reveal the results of Saudi Arabian policy. One of these was carried out at the great northern city of Taima. A museum serves not only the historic site of Taima, itself, but all other historical and archaeological sites within a 200-km radius. I concentrate here on the Taima site within the city walls where the Department of Antiquities and Museums carried out an important series of excavations in 1979–1980.

Taima: City and Site

Regional museums follow a basic model based on two spatial plans, the choice depending upon the physical environment. All the museums have common areas that include reception, storage, conservation, laboratories, photographic services, cataloging facilities, and a library. The exhibition areas relate the region to the history and archaeology of the Kingdom of Saudi Arabia as a whole. Each museum also presents its own local history and archaeology, using materials drawn from the various sites, with support from texts, graphics, and audiovisual materials. The Taima museum, in the northwest of the kingdom, includes the following:

Figure 4.3 Excavations at Qasr al-Hama, Taima.

1. Taima about 1000 B.C.
2. Taima as a center of the Medianites
3. The Emergence of the Arabs, in northern Arabia
4. Statuary from excavated sites
5. North Arabian languages
6. Excavations at Qasr al-Hama
7. Excavations of Qasr Radam
8. The Nabataeans in northern Arabia
9. Trade and tribal confederations in pre-Islamic Arabia
10. The Qasr al-Ablaq
11. Taima in Byzantine and Sasanid times
12. Taima in early Islamic times
13. The Caliphate in Northern Arabia
14. The Ottomans in Arabia
15. The Unification of the Kingdom

Taima is the largest archaeological site in the kingdom (Figure 4.3). It had retained some of its importance as a caravan and provisioning center during the Umayyad Caliphate, which ruled from Damascus (41–132/ 661–753), based on communications between Syria and the holy cities. The Pilgrimage added a new significance to the pre-Islamic caravan routes of Arabia and must have affected Taima.

The Museum at Taima, in addition to providing a historical profile of the city and its surrounding region, also presents its natural history, flora, fauna, and environment (Figure 4.4). Other parts of the museum are devoted to Taima's ethnography. As one of the most important sites of considerable time depth, this museum provides an in-depth view of the kingdom's unique cultural richness.

Taima is arid by any standard and has summer temperatures of 120 degrees Farenheit or more. The Taima oasis forms a natural basin for the collection of water draining from a wide surrounding area. The local water table is near the surface, rendering irrigation and agriculture possible.

Bi'r Haddaj was and continues to be the source of irrigation water for the whole oasis except for outlying gardens and settlements. The channels fan out into a complex network of walled gardens, from a system of 60 draw-wheel frames and camel draws around the rim of the well, which measures over 50 feet across and 6 fathoms in depth.

Figure 4.4 Taima Museum.

A noteworthy feature of the irrigation system is its great antiquity, probably dating from the early first millennium B.C. The other wells in use are also ancient, having mostly been discovered and recently restored to use. Qasr Radam is one example (with a camel draw), although it is now abandoned again. A second great ancient well, known as Wajjaj, stands in the southern part of the ruins but now appears to be dry; this suggests that the water table has lowered substantially since antiquity.

Traditionally, the people of Taima have subsisted entirely upon the products of their own agriculture, together with the livestock and firewood traded with the Badu in exchange for their agricultural surplus of dates, wheat, and barley. Agriculture has been based of course upon the date palm, which produces dates of excellent quality. These famous dates are harvested during December, when there would be an influx of Badu from the surrounding area. Camels were used for ploughing fields for wheat and barley, the main cereal crops, as well as for drawing water from Bi'r Haddaj. Grain and fruit of high quality, including citrus, were grown in the oasis.

In addition to the historical material, the Taima Museum shows how the environment of north Arabia has affected the life of humans, animals, and plants. The earliest "buildings" in the Taima area are attributed to the late Neolithic (4000–2000 B.C.). These consist of stone circles, the remains of dwellings of seasonal, semisedentary desert people who practiced simple agriculture and pastoralism.

In Neolithic times, the rainfall in the deserts of northern Arabia was probably somewhat greater than it is today. However, the exceptional aridity of the Taima region demanded considerable adaptation by plants to enable them to survive in their natural state. The fact that the Taima oasis forms a natural basin suggests that some irrigation agriculture has always been possible. The date palm has been the most important factor in ensuring the survival and prosperity of the oasis itself.

The Taima Museum examines the various uses of plants by the historic Badu, nomadic desert dwellers. Similarly, the Badu integrated animals and birds of the region into their lives; these, too, have had to cope with extremes of daytime heat and nighttime cold and have adapted and survived in often complex and fascinating ways. The museum presents Badu life-style, material culture, and traditional social, economic, and political organization. Similarly, the life of the people of the oasis and their interdependence with the settled Badu are considered.

For a brief period, about 2,500 years ago, Taima became the capital of a great empire. Its position commanding the growing trade route from southwest Arabia to Mesopotamia, and its religious significance as a major center of the cult of Salm or Sin, the Moon-god, led the Babylonian Emperor Nabonidus to establish his court here for 10 years (from about 553 B.C., shortly before the fall of his empire, to the Persians).

The clearest evidence for the Babylonian occupation comes from the excavations at Qasr al-Hamra, an outlying area at the northwest extremity of the ancient city. Here a complex of rooms, containing a small sanctuary, was uncovered. Of the cult objects associated with this sanctuary, the two most important are a stone cube or basin with carved religious scenes on the two sides; and a broken stela, with another carved religious scene and part of an Aramaic inscription, relating to a religious dedication of an Arabian tribe. The style of the carvings and the iconographic detail—a winged sun disc, a crescent moon, a rayed star and so on—are clearly Mesopotamian in origin, though the frontal bull's head suggests southwest Arabian influence but provides further testimony to the presence of the Moon-Cult at Taima.

The remains of Taima's brief Babylonian heyday are scattered over a large area today. Many of the impressive remains probably date from this period in the sixth century B.C.: much of the great city wall, many of the extensive ruins in the southern compounds, and perhaps even the great well of Bi'r Haddaj, which provides Taima's irrigation water to this day.

The great circuit wall of Taima encloses an area of about 8 square km. Most of the city walls may have been the work of Nabonidus, who evidently greatly extended the city. These walls may have played a part in the diversion and control of flood water, as well as in fortification. The famous central well of Taima, Bi'r Haddaj, on which agriculture in the oasis depends today as it did in ancient times, may date to the Babylonian period or even farther back in time. "I hied myself afar from my city of Babylon on the road to Tema', Dadanu, Padakku, Khibra, Iadihu and as far as Iatribu; ten years I went about amongst them and to my city of Babylon I went not in" (Harran Inscription H2). Thus, spoke Nabonidus (Nabuna'id), last king of a resurgent Babylonian dynasty which, in 612 B.C., had supplanted Assyria as the great imperial power of western Asia. Nabonidus came to Taima and northwest Arabia (ca. 553 B.C.) as conqueror, after the kingdoms of Judah, Moab, and Edom to the north had all fallen to Babylonian conquest. He chose Taima as his capital for his 10-year sojourn in Arabia.

It is possible that general strategic considerations may also have brought Nabonidus to Arabia in an effort to consolidate the western part of his empire in expectation of an imminent Persian attack on Babylonia. When it actually came in 539 B.C., the Persian triumph was complete. Northwest Arabia during the late sixth and fifth centuries probably came under indirect Persian rule. They went on to conquer Egypt, and had a strong interest in a peaceful northwest Arabia.

Taima, however, was important long before Nabonidus' day. Toward the end of the second millennium B.C., a remarkable transformation took place in the society of northwest Arabia, a region often known as Midian. The city of Taima has its origin in this period, when urban life, the mining and smelting of copper, and the use of runoff water for irrigation signaled a late Bronze Age, sedentary, oasis culture called Midianite.

At Taima, the remains of this earlier period have largely been covered by the great city of the first millennium B.C., but all the remains at another site in northwest Arabia, Qurayyah, appear to date to this period. Qurayyah seems to have been the major center and source of pottery used to date Midianite sites.

Taima remained an important caravan city and, in the later pre-Islamic period, was a renowned center for the pre-Islamic tribes of the region. Its stronghold of Qasr al-Ablaq was celebrated in poetry and its princes were praised for their steadfastness and loyalty.

During the Islamic period, Taima became an important stop on the desert road from Syria. Throughout the centuries, agriculture flourished and the quality of its dates was famed. The great ancient city wall still controls and diverts the flash-flood waters carried by the seven wadis which converge upon Taima; and the ancient wells and irrigation channels are still central to the local agriculture.

One of the most famous and best preserved ancient buildings in Taima is Qasr Radam, which dates back to at least the mid-first millennium B.C., possibly contemporary with Nabonidus or even earlier.

Subsequent occupations include the Nabataean-Hellenistic period and the Islamic period. Some time after 1798/1800, after the English traveler Doughty's visit to Taima, the eastern corner of the Qasr was demolished for irrigation purposes.

The Midianites are not mentioned in the sources relating to Arabia in the first millennium B.C. The most important of these, the Assyrian records of 738–638 B.C., make frequent reference to the tribes of northern and northwestern Arabia, routinely described as "Arabs." The term "Arab" is first used in the Assyrian records of 853 B.C., with the mention of a certain Gindibu' and 1,000 camel riders from the "land of Aribi," who came to the aid of the Aramaean Kingdom of Damascus in its fight against the Assyrians at the Battle of Qarqar on the Orontes.

Taima was possibly the center of the tribe of Sumu'il and figures prominently in this period as an important center. One of the gates of Nineveh was named after the "men of Sumu'il, the men of Te-e-me." A merchant from Taima bearing the Akkadian name Am-me-ni-il is mentioned in the reign of Assurbanipal, in the late seventh century.

In the fifth and fourth centuries B.C., Taima continued to be an important local caravan center between the Hijaz and Dumat al-Jandal, and between the Gulf, eastern Arabia, and Palestine. Hence, it is not surprising to find some evidence of Nabataean occupation in the city.

The Nabataeans, established at their capital, Petra, from the third century B.C., were paramount in northwest Arabia from the second century B.C. to A.D. 106, when their kingdom was incorporated into the Roman Empire. Of nomadic origins in the region, their growing control of the overland trade made them prosperous and powerful, and they became a partially sedentary, centralized monarchic state. They were masters of hydrological techniques, and many sites testify to their agricultural sophistication. They founded another great center at Mada'in Salih, on the al-'Ula–Palestine route, and also occupied Dumat al-Jandal.

The whole of the former Nabataean Kingdom seems to have become part of the Roman "Provincia Arabia", during the second century A.D. By the third century, however, Rome had withdrawn from such outposts as al-'Ula and Dumat al-Jandal where, unlike Taima, there is evidence of legionaries having been posted.

Nomadic Arabs moved into and away from southwestern Arabia during these centuries; some moved through the peninsula and others went on into Syria and Iraq. The "southern" and "northern" Arab tribes, who traced their lineage to Qahtan and 'Adnan, respectively, organized themselves into powerful confederations: the Thamudenoi in the second century A.D.; the Tanukh and the Lakhmids from the third to the seventh centuries; the Saracenoi in the fourth; Salih and then Kinda in the fifth; and Ghasson in the sixth century. These nomadic and seminomadic tribes spoke the early Arabic dialects of Arabia and produced the famous poets whose work, originating in oral tradition, formed the earliest body of Arabic literature.

At Taima, one monument in particular is associated with this period: Qasr al-Ablaq, supposed to be the stronghold of the Taimanite prince, Al-Samaw'al bin 'Adiya, circa A.D. 535. The construction known today as Qasr al-Ablaq undoubtedly goes back to more ancient times, perhaps 1,000 years earlier, but it may have been in use at this time.

The Taima vicinity was probably visited by Muslim expeditions during the campaigns to take northern Himaz and Dumat al-Jandal. This was during the time of the Prophet and the war of the "riddah," but there is little record of it. Immediately following the fall of Khaibar to the Muslims in A.D. 628, the tribe of Ghatafan embraced Islam; and Jewish communities such as those at Taima, Wadi al-Qura (Al-'Ula), and Fadak submitted to the Muslims and were granted terms.

Qasr al-Masmak Site and Museums

Lying in the heart of the capital city, Riyadh, Qasr al-Masmak occupies a special place in the history of Saudi Arabia. It was the capture of this fortress in A.D. 1902 which enabled King 'Abd al-'Aziz ibn 'Abd al-Rahman Al Faisal Al Saud to embark upon the process of unification that culminated 30 years later in the creation of the modern Kingdom of Saudi Arabia.

The restoration of Qasr al-Masmak illustrates the kingdom's concern for presenting the evidence of its past at a time of immense material development and profound change. The Masmak stands at the heart of present-day Riyadh: its historical importance is outlined here. Masmak was meticulously restored by the Riyadh municipality and then handed for safekeeping to the Department of Antiquities and Museums. The department determined that the fortress should serve as a museum of the city, based on several related themes, including the history of the fortress itself and its role in city government, the surrounding lands, the interplay between the city and the oasis, and in the traditional society. Masmak fortress was a potent manifestation of the way of life of the people before contemporary prosperity (Figures 4.5, 4.6). The al-Masmak now enters a new phase as a monument to the proud and enduring heritage of central Arabia.

The public areas of the al-Masmak fortress, converted into a museum area, are comprised of exhibitions, texts, and audiovisual presentations on al-Masmak's history and its relationship to Riyadh and the surrounding countryside and include:

1. The principal majlis (reception hall)
2. The main courtyard
3. The Masmak and its history
4. Al-Diriyya and Riyadh, capitals of the Najd
5. Riyadh, the Old City
6. Traditional agriculture and food supplies
7. The unification of the Kingdom of Saudi Arabia
8. The capture of the Qasr al-Masmak
9. The Qasr al-Masmak as a defensive structure

The modern Saudi state traces its origins to the years circa A.D. 1744, when Muhammad ibn Saud, ruler of al-Dir'iyya, agreed to accept as his creed the Unitarian reformism of Shaikh Muhammad ibn 'Abd al-Wahab, born nearby at al-'Ayaina, and to act as its political arm. The Shaikh's mission was to purify Islam in its Arabian heartland and to propagate the doctrine among Muslims at large. In this he was spectacularly successful, with his influence spreading over much of the peninsula and beyond, reaching to Iraq in the north and to Oman in the south.

Riyadh itself became an important town relatively recently. Originally an area of ancient agricultural settlements, it is said to have been founded as a town in 1746, when a certain Daham ibn Dawwas built a circuit wall around several existing hamlets. Riyadh became the capital

Figure 4.5 Qasr al-Masmak, Riyadh.

Figure 4.6 Aerial view of the Qasr al-Masmak, Riyadh.

of the Saudi state in late 1824, as a successor to al-Dir'iyya, the original capital which is now under restoration by the Department of Antiquities and Museums. It was then under Imam Turki, the title *imam* having been the one by which its rulers were originally known. Riyadh assumed the outlines in the early 19th century that it kept for the next century and more.

Imam Turki's son, the Imam Faisal ibn Turki, also known as Faisal the Great, presided sternly over the Saudi state from June 1834 until the end of 1838 and again from July 1843 until December 1865. The first documentary evidence for the layout of Riyadh and the site of Qasr al-Masmak comes from his reign and is contained in the British traveler Palgrave's account of his visit to Riyadh in 1862.

Qasr al-Masmak stands near the site of the original house of Amir Abdullah ibn Faisal Al Saud, eldest son of Imam Faisal ibn Turki. Amir Abdullah lived in this house until the death of Imam Faisal in 1865, when he himself became ruler. On his accession, Amir Abdullah is thought to have built his ruling palace and seat of government there, on the site of Qasr al-Masmak, opposite his house.

During the latter part of the 19th century, unrest in the country resulted in the al-Rashid rulers of the northern city of Hail, seizing power in the Najdi heartland and taking control of Riyadh itself. After the death of Imam Abdullah, on November 27, 1889, Faisal's youngest son, 'Abd al-Rahman, father of King 'Abd al-'Aziz, rebelled against al-Rashid. However, in 1891 his last attempt to capture Riyadh and rid it of the al-Rashidi garrison ended in failure, and he and his family went into exile. Ibn Rashid ordered the destruction of the city walls.

In 1902, Qasr al-Masmak dominated the skyline of Riyadh. It served as a well-fortified seat of government and as garrison quarters for Ibn Rashid's governor. It was conspicuously fortified—both for practical reasons of defense and to serve as a symbol of the governor's authority.

On January 15, 1902, 'Abd al-'Aziz ibn 'Abd al-Rahman ibn Faisal Al Saud, with his band of loyal followers, infiltrated Riyadh by night and stormed the gateway of Qasr al-Masmak at dawn. In doing so, they made history.

The principal courtyard today is directly adjacent to the main gateway and contains the staircase giving access to the Qasr's defensive features over the gate and along the front of the fortress. It is, hence, probably the area through which King 'Abd al-'Aziz and his men ran when they stormed the upper level of the fortress. The northwest tower, which rises above this courtyard, was probably the one from which the proclamation of the restoration of the rule of the Al-Saud over their patrimony was made in the dawn of January 16, 1902, heralding the recovery of Riyadh.

For a short time after the capture, the Amir 'Abd al-'Aziz must have used Qasr al-Masmak as his headquarters and seat of government. However, until 1911, he was heavily engaged in campaigns to assert his authority. When after that he turned his mind to the development of Riyadh, he preferred to build his own seat of government on the site of the "old palace" of his grandfather Imam Faisal ibn Turki. He used Qasr al-Masmak henceforth as an arsenal, storehouse, and prison.

Qasr al-Masmak provided facilities for the holding of audiences; storage and treasury for tribute, stores, provisions, weapons, and ammunition; and residential accommodation for the garrison. The garrison at the time of the capture in 1902 is said to have numbered some 80 men. The principal reception hall, or *majlis* (*diwaniyya*), was situated directly adjacent to the main gateway. A large courtyard for the assembly of the garrison or large numbers of citizens was provided outside the majlis, with access immediately from the L-shaped entrance.

The remainder of the fortress was constructed along the lines of a traditional Najdi courtyard house, repeated several times. Such houses consist of rooms, sometimes interconnected, all opening onto a central courtyard, two or more sides of which are surrounded by a shaded arcade. All of these buildings, as well as the upper floor, now function as part of the al-Masmak museum.

Qasr al-Masmak Fortress is a fine example of Arabian military architecture, having been based on traditions of defensive features developed throughout the long history of military works in the Middle East as a whole, where sun-dried mud brick was employed. Among such features are the rectangular floor plan with a circular corner tower, the high curtain walls, the loopholes, the machicolations, the postern gate, the bent entrance, the battlement walkways, and the crenellations. These are demonstrated with extensive use of audiovisual techniques at the historic site today.

Qasr al-Masmak is important not only as a historical monument of the first quality but also as a splendid example of architectural and building techniques that are, in many ways, characteristic of central Arabia and that, inevitably, are being replaced by modern methods and materials. However, the practices of traditional building systems and the skills of the craftsmen engaged in the building of the Qasr Fortress and in its maintenance are recorded in the al-Masmak today, in its new role as a major museum. They describe the planning and construction techniques involved.

The Research Potential

The foregoing projects, Taima and Qasr al-Masmak, sponsored by the directorate general, Department of Archaeology and Museums, since the early 1970s have been successful chiefly due to the generous commitment of King Fahad's government. This support has enabled the directorate to launch and maintain a program of research, restoration, and preservation of monuments, and to establish a network of national, regional, and local museums. In addition, it made possible the participation of prominent archaeologists and interested institutions from different parts of the world. At least as important, it has made possible the development of a whole new generation of Saudi Arabian archaeologists and specialists who are taking responsibility for uncovering and preserving their country's past (Figures 4.7–4.10).

The work of the Department of Antiquities and Museums has amply demonstrated the important part Arabia has played in the development of human culture from remote times to the present day. Saudi Arabia, far from being an empty page in human history, is now being revealed as among one of the most significant repositories of the collective past, contributing to rather than simply deriving from or being peripheral to the great centers of civilization with which it is closely linked by geography and shared experience.

An Afterword: Research Potential in Saudi Arabia

Knowledge of the prehistory[1] of Arabia has undergone an extremely significant increase in information in recent years. While modern

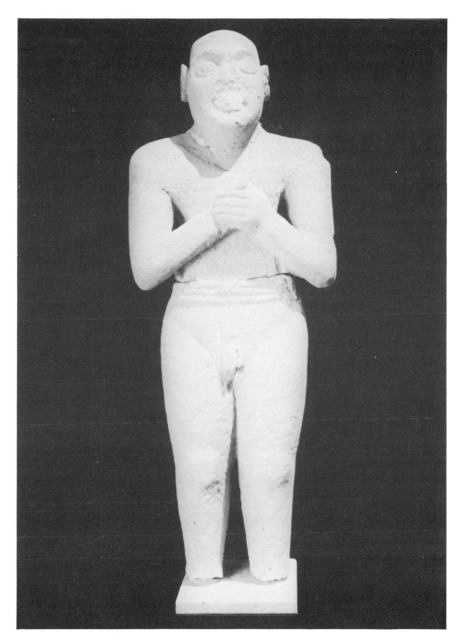

Figure 4.7 A standing limestone figure of a worshipper in Early Dynastic II style, c. 2700 B.C. from Tarut Island, eastern Saudi Arabia.

Figure 4.8   Bronze lioness-head, life size, originally part of an altar, from Najran, c. third century B.C.

Figure 4.9 Kufic milestone from Zubaidah.

Figure 4.10   A detail of a finely carved and painted door from Qasim, central Saudi Arabia.

political boundaries are strictly irrelevant to discussion of prehistory, they have to be kept in mind because different countries have different paths of priority in furthering this research, and resultant patterns should not be allowed to influence the overall picture. In the case of the Yaman (including the Hadramawt), the sum total of knowledge up to about 30 years ago came from the reports of such travelers as Ahmad Fakhry, who journeyed in 1947 in Sirwah, Marib, Raghwan, and the Jawf of the Yaman (Fakhry 1948; Fakhry and Ryckmans 1952). Systematic study may be said to have commenced with the sites' registers, compiled by G. L. Harding in 1960. In the Gulf area, work commenced in Bahrain in the 1950s largely as the result of a Danish initiative; in the United Arab Emirates, Kuwait and Oman, a comprehensive approach awaited a modern department of antiquities, like the one now in operation for several decades.

Nevertheless, even by the early 1970s, enough material had become available to attempt a synthesis, such as that of McClure (1971). It showed the need for more detailed analysis of specific areas and problem-oriented research. I undertook basic collection and analysis of data and interpretation of fundamental issues of interregional interaction (1974). My work combined survey and excavation techniques and employed the multidisciplinary approach developed by R. J. Braidwood and his school earlier, at Chicago, in the context of excavating urban and pre-urban farming communities in Iraq and Kurdistan.

The new era in archaeological research in Arabia took place through the efforts of national departments of antiquities in various countries. In Saudi Arabia a systematic archaeological survey program was begun by the Department of Antiquities with the assistance of specialists from institutions in America, Europe, and the Middle East (see *Atlal*, volumes 1–9). Within the context of the profitable results of surface reconnaissance, coupled with limited soundings, a more accurate conception of the kingdom's prehistory resulted than had hitherto been in view. The accumulation of such vast data also had the effect of posing new questions, as well as highlighting important research problems that had formerly not been so clearly comprehended. For example, the survey results clearly outlined the settlement patterns of Stone Age periods preceding the last glacial retreat as distinct from those of the periods later than about 9000 B.C. These in turn could then be correlated with the probable formation and subsequent advances of the great deserts within the peninsula (i.e., the Nafud and the Empty Quarter).

Work as recent as 1985 at al-Shuwaihitiyah, near the Wadi Sirhan in northern Arabia, tends to confirm earlier suggestions made in the course of the survey that it relates culturally to the much older Oldowan phase (ca. 1 million years B.P.). This may also have a parallel with the material from an exposed dike in Wadi Tathlith in the Southwestern Province. This could be significant on geographical grounds if one wished to postulate a cultural connection with the Oldowan sites in East Africa. The Middle Palaeolithic would be envisaged as running from about 70,000 to 30,000 B.P., and a similar range of sites is involved. The Upper Paleolithic, 30,000 to 8,000 B.P. is attested also in finds from the Rub' al-Khali. With the Early Neolithic, 8,000 to 5,000 B.P., more varied types of evidence come into play, including more advanced lithic technologies, megalithic architectural structures, and rock art. The ensuing Neolithic and Chalcolithic periods bring one into the sphere of maximum utility of radiocarbon datings, these being available now for several sites in eastern Arabia, central Arabia, and the southwest of the peninsula.

While the main concern here is the critical periods that spanned the beginnings of food production to the first ancient states appearing in a literate historical context, it is necessary to place this in the framework of the whole preneolithic development, also taking into account the geoarchaeological background. Two chronological tables are provided for the convenience of the nonspecialist reader. These reconstructions represent a plausible overview of the chronological sequence, but because this sequence remains problematic in many particulars, the tables should not be regarded as definitive. Table 4.1 places the phenomenon of early man in Arabia and his culture in geological time. Table 4.2 poses a preliminary analysis of the Neolithic to Chalcolithic-Bronze Age to Iron Age development in the peninsula. Typical and major sites I refer to by name (Figure 4.11). To provide a consistent account, I attempt to describe the present scientific position. However, particularly with regard to chronological classification of lithics, it is necessary to go into a few details of the recent history of research.

A multigroup classification of lithics was proposed by Kapel, who diagnosed Acheulian (Lower Paleolithic) hand axes, basing his arguments on finds from Qatar (Kapel 1967) and from the vicinity of

Table 4.1 Early man in Arabia and his culture in geological time.

Geological Age	Culture	Estimated dates B.P.	Examples	Notes
MIOCENE		17–15 million years	Dryopithecines at Sarrar, NE Arabia	
PLIOCENE				
PLEISTOCENE	Lower Paleolithic	500,000–70,000	Jabrin, Dawadmi, Wadi Tathlith, Shuwaihitiyah	bifaces, etc.; Argon dates obtained c. 280,000 at Dawad Cf. Oldowan
	Middle Paleolithic	70,000–30,000	Bir Hima, Abu Arish, Uwairid	Cf. Shanidar
	Upper Paleolithic	30,000–12,000	Afif, Muwahy, Bir Hima	disc cores, small bifaces, etc.
HOLOCENE	Prepottery Neolithic	12,000–8,000	Rub' al-Khali sites, Sulayyil, 'Ain Qannas	arrowheads etc., earliest structures
	Neolithic	6,000–4,000	Abu Khamis, Dowsariyah, Ain Qannas, Sihi, Rajajil, Jubbah, Thumamah	abundant C-14 corroboration of dates

Table 4.2 Relative chronologies of geological periods and cultures in Saudi Arabia.

ABSOLUTE (Years B.C.)	AGES	GEOLOGICAL	CULTURAL	PALEO-CLIMATE	PALEO-GEOGRAPHY
1000	QUATERNARY	HOLOCENE (Recent)	Iron Age	Hyper Arid Hot	Deserts
2000			Bronze Age		
3000		POST PLEISTOCENE		Intense Winds	
6000			Chalcolithic		
			Neolithic	Wet (Sub Pluvial)	
			Mesolithic		Rivers Streams (Wadis) Lakes, Ponds
10,000		PLEISTOCENE	Upper / Middle / Lower — PALEOLITHIC	Hyper Arid Hot (Pluvial) / Arid (Warm) / Wet (Pluvial)	
1,000,000	TERTIARY	Pliocene			
1,500,000		Miocene / Oligocene / Eocene / Paleocene			
20,000,000		Cretaceous			

Source: Based on McClure, 1971.

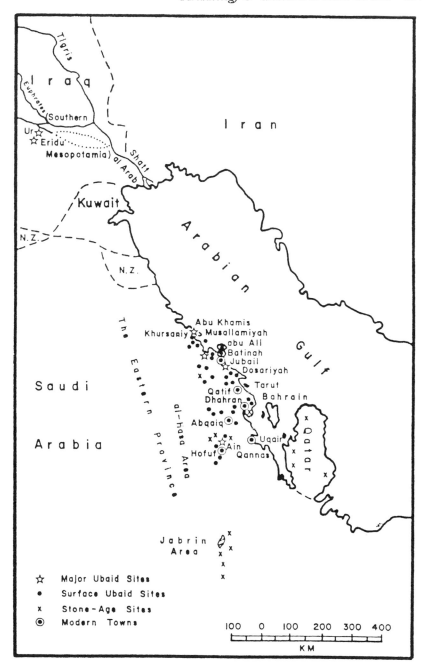

Figure 4.11 Prehistoric sites (Ubaid and earlier) in Eastern Province, Saudi Arabia.

Thaj (Kapel 1973). This material belonged to a so-called A-Group, which was supposed also to have Mousterian affinities. It stood in distinction to the C- and D-Groups, of similar suggested age, and to a later B-Group, which in turn involved a basic blade industry incorporating modified projectile points and other examples of sophistication pointing to the prepottery Neolithic. Examples from the Eastern Province (e.g., Ain Qannas) of Saudi Arabia facilitate dating to around 5000 B.C. (Masry 1974:222–224). Parallels from the prepottery Neolithic in Palestine and Syria were readily available. Technologically, Kapel's classification represents definable types, but the question of dating is complicated by the mixture of artifacts from different cultural horizons, reflected also in the coexistence of different technologies. Thus, more recent research has led to considerable modifications. Tixier (1980) has suggested recategorization of the A-Group materials to the Ubaid Neolithic. This ties in with earlier work in Qatar (Smith 1978:36) and stems in part from radiocarbon dating of hand-axe materials from Khor Rurui (Qatar) to the fifth millennium B.C. (Inizan 1980:51).

Some of the problems and perspectives can be approached from the point of view of the broad results of the Saudi Arabian survey effort, with regard to the older lithic material. In total, 110 sites were identified as Acheulian, it being occasionally possible to distinguish between upper and lower phases. Distinguished from these in turn were a further 195 sites diagnosed as Mousterian, and to these must be related a few which were included simply under the rubric Middle Paleolithic. One site was recognizably different and tentatively identified as Oldowan; this point will be returned to later. Associated with the Mousterian-type technology were nine Levallois sites, and one diagnosed as Kebaran. What emerges is the existence of extensive and varied spectra of Paleolithic sites and material.

Looking forward on the chronological scale, one finds, in simple statistical terms, much less that relates clearly to the Upper Paleolithic, Mesolithic, and immediately pre-Neolithic periods. It is not yet possible to propose a solution to this problem, but its complexity suggests a number of factors, including the problem of specific fossil indices for cultural linkage and the question of changes in population groups. This problem can only be solved with more detailed analysis of the cataloged materials. The critical nature of the subject is illustrated by the reinterpretation of Kapel's A-Group data. The cautious approach is to keep separate the cultural-technological diagnostics based on recognized type sites on one hand, and on the other hand to work within the chronological framework based on the classic evolutionary approach. Therefore, the trend in Saudi Arabia has been to stress the need for use of absolute physical dating methods wherever feasible, as has been the case with the important Acheulian site of Saffaqah-Dawadmi, where Potassium-Argon methods were employed with successful results, substantiating the date anticipated on the basis of technological type analysis.

To conclude the statistical overview of site identification, 117 sites were identified as Neolithic; 66, Chalcolithic. However, before moving on to a more detailed discussion, something must be said of the southern areas of the Arabian Peninsula which form part of this landmass and the progress of research in the present-day states in that region.

In the Yaman, emphasis has traditionally been focused on the classic urban civilization based on sites in the wadis surrounding the central desert regions. Several major expeditions have taken place and have been supplemented by a multitude of miscellaneous discoveries. These show the potential while leaving many important questions unanswered, both with regard to the chronology of the early urban phases and the nature of the earlier prehistoric developments. As I have shown elsewhere, these are key issues for understanding the fundamental basis of Arabian prehistory (1973). The first systematic excavation in the Yaman was at Hureidha in the Hadramawt (Caton Thompson 1944).

The achievements of the American Foundation for the Study of Man Expedition, associated with Wendell Phillips, W. F. Albright, F. P. Albright, and R. Le Baron Bowen are conveniently summarized by Van Beek (1968). Work was done in Wadi Bayhan, Sohar, and Marib. Excavations at Timnac and Hajar Bin Humaid identified 16 occupation levels and provided some basis for chronology. Flintknapping sites have been noted from the Yaman central desert (Sayhad) regions eastward to Oman (Pullar 1974), taking in more than 100 sites in the Hadramawt (Van Beek 1968). Similar material has been recorded in Oman in association with the typical beehive tombs at Qubur Juhhal, Amlah, and Miskin (de Cardi, et al. 1976). In spite of the scattered and disparate nature of the evidence, it is clear that it has a crucial relevance for the rest of Arabia. It seems advisable to think in terms of a proto-urban phase and to attempt to anticipate the potential relevance of this as a conceptual tool.

The early initiative in Bahrain and the rest of the Gulf was largely due to the Danish Archaeological Expedition, the work of which is described in some detail by Bibby (1971); and a more recent overview, citing the latest research, is provided by Rice (1985). Earlier, during the latter part of the 19th and early 20th centuries, the Island of Bahrain was the focus of Sumerologists who were preoccupied with the question of identifying ancient Dilmun—the Paradise Land of the ancient Sumerians (see Cornwall 1946; and Rice 1985).

The work of the Danish expedition was initially concentrated on Ra's al-Qalcah and the tumuli fields. They were able to establish sequences associated with known sequences in Iraq and identifiable in Saudi Arabia, which they also examined along the coastal areas. Later, they extended their work in Oman, with important results at Umm al-Nar, Hafit, and Buraimi (see Kuml volumes for 1962, 1965–1970; see also the *Journal of Oman Studies* generally). For the United Arab Emirates the work of H. Takriti should be mentioned, as well as the discoveries of S. Cleuzious at Hili near al-Ain. The Ubaid period has been definitively identified at Qatar (al-Daasa, Ra's Abaruk, Khor) (see Inizan 1980; Oates 1978:39) and at al-Markh on Bahrain (Roaf 1974, 1976). In general, the Mesopotamian Early Dynastic I to III is well represented in the Gulf. It is the period in which a distinctive East Arabian-Gulf culture emerges, although the later period (Barbar) in Bahrain, also has its parallels on the east Arabian littoral (Tarut, Dhahran tomb fields, Khobar middens, Umm al-Nussi) (Figure 4.11).

With regard to the earliest periods, we can state that physical evidence for the actual presence of the earliest types of man in Arabia is mainly of a cultural rather than of a direct nature. However, fossil evidence for precultural hominoids has been identified in the vicinity of Sarrar in eastern Arabia, in the context of rich fauna dating to the dam formation (Lower Miocene, 17-15 million years B.P.). These involve fragments of Dryopithecine hominoid fossils (Andrews et al. 1978; Hamilton et al. 1978). Little can be said about this apart from the obvious comment that parallels could be adduced on either side of the peninsula. More promising is the major accumulation of the considerably later evidence from the Ubaid phases and the tumuli phenomena in eastern Arabia and the Arabian Gulf countries. The multitude and frequently good state of preservation of the tumuli open major possibilities for archaeological study of population dynamics and human osteology in the Gulf area for comparison with similar data from lower Mesopotamia and western Iran (ancient Elam and Persia).

Cultural ecology and Pleistocene archaeology are two other themes of research. One interesting example is Kahman (site no. 216–208, of survey) along the southern shores of the Red Sea in Saudi Arabia. At this site, a coralline terrace some 2 m above the present sea level contains Mousterian tools (due to the existence of a complex fringing-reef system extending several kilometers inland and to the attested fluctuations in sea level linked to polar glaciation). The same phenomenon can be observed in the Farasan Islands. For Bahrain, a pioneering study of geoarchaeology has been made by Larsen (1983), who cites also material relating to the east Arabian littoral. While some of the basis for his inquiry necessarily involves geological or geophysical issues that are not yet completely understood, such as fluctuation in water levels, there can be no doubt about the fruitfulness of this line of inquiry. In this connection, an important study was done by Dayton on the historical significance of even small climatic changes, where the evidence of this complex issue is carefully reviewed (1975; see also Dayton 1979).

Focusing now on still more specific issues, the results summarized above show the need for cataloging and seriating the materials, such as is possible only with more evidence from excavations at stratified sites.

In Saudi Arabia, while the survey effort included specialized fields such as ancient mines and rock art, the main emphasis from 1982 onward was directed towards systematic excavation of selected sites (Masry 1983). Although excavation commenced earlier in most of the Arabian Peninsula states, there is still a need for generalized survey and constant reappraisal. The immediate historical progress of the subject is stressed because it is important to remember that, with few exceptions (as in Bahrain and Qaryat al-Faw in Saudi Arabia), archaeological excavation is still at a fairly early stage.

Before looking at specific type sites of the major periods and making a brief treatment of the relevance of rock art in relation to the question of nomadism, as well as the discussion of the major periods of early urbanism, I give a diachronic account as far as it is possible within the limitations of present knowledge.

Despite the increasing use of physical-science dating techniques for Arabian sites, the basic chronological framework is still essentially dependent on external parallels, primarily with Syria, Iraq, and the Nile Valley, as well as Iran and the Indus Valley. Within this system one would distinguish first the Lower Paleolithic, from about 3 million years B.P. to about 70,000 B.P. Such dating is now supported and further defined by the Potassium-Argon dating from Dawadmi and elsewhere in Saudi Arabia, as mentioned above. Most significant for Dawadmi (Whalen et al. 1983) is that it provides an Arabian typesite for Paleolithic with numerous parallels to Acheulian and similar cultures.

With regard to the Neolithic, cultural complexity may be the keynote. The first group to be investigated was that of the Ubaid sites on the Gulf littoral and inner islands. These sites now total about 40 within Saudi Arabia (Masry 1974) and relate to other sites in Bahrain and Qatar, as described above. With regard to this culture, two distinctive types of pottery must be distinguished, one with black paint on greenish paste slip, and another of chaff-tempered handmade red pottery. This pottery, particularly the former, proves a relationship with the early culture of Mesopotamia from which the name is derived. The range and number of sites show that the culture was entrenched in eastern Arabia. In this context, one must keep in mind that its influences were also present elsewhere, for example in Cyro-Cilesia and as far afield as Cyprus (Braidwood 1960).

Apart from the pottery, features of the complex are grinding stones, plastered walls, domesticated cattle and caprids, domesticated cereals, and a lithic repertoire of tanged-barbed arrowheads, tabular flints (tile flints), and scrapers with fine pressure retouch. Some sites in the eastern littoral exhibit this repertoire with the absence of pottery. However, caution must be exercised against indiscriminate lumping. For example, it could be noted that the important Neolithic site of Thummamah in central Arabia belongs to a later phase and should be dated on available evidence to the third or second millennium B.C. Thummamah exhibits a lithic technology of advanced type in conjunction with well-built circular dwellings of a substantial nature and evidence of agriculture or incipient agriculture (e.g., querns). However, from the Southwestern Province also there now seems to be evidence of agriculture, based on several radiocarbon determinations; these are from sites contemporaneous with the later Ubaid: Sihi and Muwassam near the modern port and fishing center of Jizan (classical Arabic Jazan). The samples come from shell middens, which in turn are associated with a specific pottery type, characterized by outturned rims, ring bases, and spouts (Zarins et al. 1981). Taking the evidence into account, it seems that the Neolithic complex in Arabia involves multiple economic systems, including hunting and gathering, pastoralism, farming, and sedentism. This is substantiated by the rock art evidence, where the hunting and pastoral aspects come to the fore.

Rock Art Sites

The phenomenon of prehistoric rock art is widespread in Arabia. Following the standard site-description definitions advocated by the United Nations Educational, Scientific, and Cultural Organization (UNESCO) associated Center for Rock Art Documentation, at Valcomonica, Italy, a total of some 2,000 significant rock-art sites should be distinguished in Arabia, most of which include multiple panels and phases and involve carvings or etchings in high or low relief, although a few painted rock art sites have also been discovered.

This phenomenon of ancient art expression provides invaluable cultural evidence, thus meriting the special attention that has been given to it. As a result, about a quarter of the sites have now been registered and numbered in the field in a preliminary detailed manner. Relative dating can be achieved on three grounds of analysis: the extent to which the patination has reverted back to the original oxidized color of the rock; the type of lithics used in pecking; and the subject matter of the art. It is also potentially significant when particular types of art occur regularly in conjunction with particular types of lithic scatter. Taking these factors into account, the oldest rock art, as exemplified at Kilwa and in the vicinity of the Romano-Nabataean site of Rawwafa, goes back to the horizon of the Upper Paleolithic, depicting ibex, wild buffalo, and other indistinct animals in a style that is markedly different from the later Neolithic-Chalcolithic depictions of herds of domesticated long-horned cattle in a nomadic pastoral context.

Examples of the latter are widespread in Saudi Arabia and occur in the western Hisma and Jabal Lawz, centering on the area of Bajda, at Jubba on the southern fringe of the Nafud, at Hanakiyah and in the

Jabal Qara in the Southwestern Province, where Bir Hima is the main site. One eagerly anticipates the finding of cattle bones in an archaeological context to provide further evidence to substantiate and crystalize views on this culture—or cultures.

The phenomenon of rock art extends to the Yaman, as well as from Qatar to Oman. Identical factors and conditions appear to have obtained there. At this point, it is convenient to refer again to the problem of the east Arabian tomb fields. Their particular importance rests on various factors. They exhibit typological diversity, facilitating reconstruction of cultural interrelations between the different areas where they occur in eastern Arabia, Bahrain, Qatar, the United Arab Emirates, Oman and the Yaman. Particularly with regard to the excavated evidence from the Dhahran tomb fields, these tumuli provide a link between the Chalcolithic and the later, well-substantiated urban phases. Within the context of the continued use of the tumuli tomb network, within a circumscribed area, albeit with modifications in structure, a continuity over two millennia is discernable. This finding also involves the role of the finds in demonstrating the far-flung cultural contacts of the east Arabia littoral with south Arabia, Egypt, and the Levant, Mesopotamia, the Indus Valley, and Central Asia.

Although it has been demonstrated in relation to Bahrain that the tumuli complexes could have arisen from a local population (Fröhlich and Ibrahim 1985), and the same would obviously apply to east Arabia, the precise relation to urban centers is not yet clear.

For the earliest period of urbanization, the relevant sites for discussion are Qurayyah and Taima. At these sites, the presence of a characteristically designed painted pottery enables comparison with sites in Palestine, dating to the 13th and 12th centuries B.C. (Parr 1970–1972). This was the forerunner of the urban phenomenon best known in Arabia from the first millennium B.C. In this period, one has historical documentation in sources from both inside and outside Arabia, as well as a wealth of direct archaeological evidence from large, walled cities. These cities include, to name the main examples, Thaj in eastern Arabia; Najran and Qaryat al-Faw in the southwest; Dumat al-Jandal (called Adummatu in the Assyrian sources) in the north; and in the west, Taima, al-Hijr (Mada'in Salih), and Qurayyah. It is becoming increasingly clear that these are only examples and that there were other large and small urban centers and villages going back to the second millennium B.C., such as that at Zubaydah (Parr and Qazdar 1980) and persisting into the first millennium B.C. Settlements at Padakku (Fadak), Khaibar, and Iatribu (Iathrib) are mentioned in Assyrian inscriptions from the first half of the first millennium B.C.

Finally, while the basic chronology is straightforward, details remain unclear. For the Hasaean civilization based on Thaj in eastern Arabia, but also taking into account the areas of present-day Ra's al-Zur, Dammam, and Abqaiq, Potts (1983) has proposed a chronological system divided into early, middle, and late phases. While inherently probable, and deriving to some extent from archaeological evidence, the significance of the tripartite division is not confined to the history of Thaj but rather relates to contemporary cultural developments. Thus, the transition from early to middle Hasaean corresponds to the beginning of the Hellenistic period, and late Hasaean begins with the middle Parthian, that is, roughly the beginning of the Christian era. Nevertheless, the scheme does provide an initial basis for consideration of dates.

Thaj and the other Arabian urban centers of the first millennium B.C. demonstrate close links with the ancient cities of Yaman. With these cities and their achievements in complex cultures and writing systems, demonstrated also at al-Faw (Ansary 1982), begins the civilization which existed at the rise of Islam to usher in the modern period.

Note

1. "Prehistory" is meant here to specifically denote the whole range of human settlements as well as hominid evolution in the Peninsula. Chronologically, the designation would include all developments prior to the 2nd millenium B.C. for which there is evidence attesting urban and literate development within that landmass.

References

Ansary, A.
 1982 *Qaryat al-Faw, A Portrait of Pre-Islamic Civilization in Arabia*. New York: St. Martin's Press.
Andrews, P., Hamilton, W.R. and Whybrow, P.J.
 1978 Dryopithecine from the Miocene of Saudi Arabia. *Nature* 224: 249–250.
Atlal, The Journal of Saudi Arabian Archaeology 1977.

Bibby, T. G.
    1968 *Preliminary Survey in East Arabia, 1968.* Copenhagen: Jutland
        Archaeological Society.
    1971 *Looking for Dilmun.* New York.
Braidwood, R. J., and B. Howe
    1960 *Prehistoric Investigations in Iraqi Kurdistan.* Chicago.
de Cardi, B., et al.
    1976 Ras al-Khaimah: Further Archaeological Discoveries. *Antiquity* 50:
        216–222.
Caton Thompson, G.
    1944 *Tombs and Moon Temple of Hureidha.* Hadramawt.
Cornwall, P. B.
    1946 Ancient Arabia: Explorations in Hasa 1940–41. *Geographical Journal*
        107:28–50.
Dayton, J. E.
    1975 The Problems of Climatic Change in the Arabian Peninsula. *PSAS*
        5:33–76.
    1979 A Discussion of the Hydrology of Marib, *PSAS* 9:124–129.
Fakhry, A.
    1948 Les Antiquités du Yaman. *Le Muséon* 61:215–226.
Fakhry, J., and G. Ryckmans,
    1952 An Archaeological Journey to the Yemen. *Service des Antiquités de
        L'Egypte.* Vols. 1–3. Cairo.
Fröhlich, B., and A. Mughannom
    1985 Excavations. of the Dharan Burial Mounds. *Atlal* 9:9–40.
Hamilton, W.R., Whybrow, P.J., and McClure, H.A.
    1978 Fauna of Fossil Mammals from the Miocene of Saudi Arabia. *Nature*
        274:248–249.
Inizan, M. L.
    1980 Premiers resultats des fouilles prehistoriques de la region de Khor. In
        Mission Archaeologique Français a Qatar. J. Tixier, ed. Vol. 2. Paris:
        CNRS.
Journal of Oman Studies 1980–89. Muscat, Sultanate of Oman.
Kapel, J.
    1967 *Atlas of the Stone Age Cultures of Qatar.* Arhus: Jutland Archaeological
        Society Publications.
    1973 *Stone Age Survey in T.G. Bibby, Preliminary Survey in East Arabia, 1968.*
        Arhus: Jutland Archaeological Society..
Kuml
    Journal of the Jutland Archaeological Society. 1962, 1965–70
Larsen, C. E.
    1983 *Life and Land Use on the Bahrain Islands.* Chicago.
Masry, A. H.
    1973 Factors of Growth in the Civilization of Southwestern Arabia: An

Ethno-Ecological Approach. *Bulletin of the Faculty of Arts*, Univ. of Riyadh, Vol. 3.

1974 *Prehistory in Northeastern Arabia: The Problem of Interregional Interaction.* Coconut Grove, Florida: Field Research Projects.

1976 Introduction. *Atlal* 1:1.

1983 Introduction. *Atlal* 7:1.

McClure, H. A.

1971 *The Arabian Peninsula and Prehistoric Populations.* Coconut Grove: Field Research Publications.

Oates, J.

1978 Ubaid Mesopotamia and its Relation to Gulf Countries, in *Qatar Archaeological Reports. Excavations 1973.* B. de Cardi, ed. OUP, Pp. 39–52.

Parr, P. J.

1970–1972

Preliminary Survey in Northeastern Arabia, 1968. *Bulletin of the Institute of Archaeology* 8–9:193–242; 10:23–61.

Parr, P. J., and M. Qazdar

1980 A Report on the Soundings at Zubaydah (Al-Amarah) in the Al-Qasim Region. *Atlal* 4:107–117.

Potts, D.

1983 Thaj in the Light of Recent Research. *Atlal* 7:86–101.

Pullar, J.

1974 Harvard Archaeological Society in Oman, 1973. PSAS 4:33–48.

Rice, M.

1985 *Search for the Paradise Land.* London: Longman.

Roaf, M.

1974 Excavation at Al Markh, Bahrain: A Fish Midden of the Fourth Millennium B.C. *Paleorient* 2:499–501.

1976 Excavations at Al-Markh, Bahrain. *PSAS* 6:144–160.

Smith, G. H.

1978 The Stone Industries of Qatar. In *Qatar Archaeological Report.* B. de Cardi, ed. Pp. 36–38.

Tixier, J.

1980 *Mission Archaeologique Française a Qatar.* Doha.

Van Beek, G. W.

1968 Hajar bin Humeid. Baltimore.

Whalen, N., et al.

1983 Excavation of Acheulean Sites Near Saffaqah in al-Dawadmi (1402/ 1982). *Atlal* 7:9–21.

Zarins, J. et al.

1981 Comprehensive Archaeological Survey Program on the Southwestern Province. *Atlal* 5:9–42.

PART II
FORGING IDENTITY IN THE NINETEENTH AND TWENTIETH CENTURIES

5 History and Patriotism in the National Museum of Mexico

Luis Gerardo Morales-Moreno

In this chapter, I consider the emergence of the National Museum of Mexico from the late 18th to the 20th centuries, a period in which the modern nation-state arose. This museum is the immediate predecessor of the present system of national and regional museums of history and anthropology. In the process of its formation, a highly technical and professional infrastructure was created that formed the basis of the National Institute of Anthropology and History (INAH), founded in 1939. The history of the National Museum reveals how cultural patriotism created a common past, which was supposedly shared by all Mexicans. While there are many definitions of museum (e.g., Leon 1986; Smith 1989), the contemporary definition of a museum does not refer to these historical and sociocultural processes. A museum is seen as

> an institute at the service of the public which acquires, conserves, communicates and presents, in order to increase the knowledge, the safe-keeping and the development of man's heritage, education and culture, possessions representative of man's nature. [Giraudy 1979:7]

Historical Beginnings

In Mexico, the collecting of historic, archaeological, and artistic objects began in colonial times with the encounter between ancient Mesoamerica and Spain. From 1521 onwards, in the eyes of the medieval Christian conquerors from Spain, the physical remains of the conquered civilizations—Aztec, Maya, Zapoteca, and others—were converted into exotic examples of idolatry (Weckman 1984). In 1523, the Emperor "D. Carlos in Valladolid" sent authorized representatives to "the Indies" with an order

> that the idols, and indian shrines should be torn down in all provinces, and sacrifices should be expressly prohibited with severe penalties to those idolatrous indians, and to those who eat human flesh. [*Recopilación de Leyes de las Indias . . . 1756*:2]

By the end of the 16th century, the Spanish Crown had legislated not only the prohibition of idolatry but also Spain's territorial jurisdiction with reference to the "discovery of treasures." Thus, in 1595, King Philip II commanded that

> anyone discovering treasure in the Indies should draw up an agreement first of all with us, or the Viceroys, Presidents or Governor, the part corresponding to what has been found and are obliged through his person and state, with sufficient guarantee to satisfy and pay damages incurred in the search of his house's property, or possessions of the owners where it is. [Law quoted in Valderrama Zaldívar and Velasco 1981, 1:]

In the 17th and 18th centuries, the Spanish and colonial governments made a complex and contradictory attempt to explain the Indian past through its material remains. In the process, objects of Indian idolatry were replaced with Roman Catholic objects representative of emergent New Spain, the colonial name of present-day Mexico. Nonetheless, the representation was varied and was made up of opposing elements: the collecting and plundering of art and the discovery and mutilation of Prehispanic relics.

In the early 18th century, Lorenzo Boturini visited New Spain to collect Indian manuscripts and religious documents, which he organized into the *Catalog of the Indian Museum*. Its purpose was to establish the divine origin of the Virgin of Guadalupe to promote her coronation. His project failed, but his catalog made a contribution by associating the word "museum" with the Indian past of colonial Mexico (Matute 1976; see also Bernal 1979; Brading 1980, 1991a; Fernandez 1987; Rivera Cambas 1880).

By the mid-18th century, some Europeans were already questioning the importance of Spanish colonization and New World cultures. In New Spain, Creole explanations of a patriotic historiography praised the

Aztec past—in stark contrast to the European Cornelius De Pauw's theory, for example (Brading 1980, 1991a; Duchet 1975, 1985; Gerbi 1982). A controversy between the New World and the Old World had begun. The Creoles, persons of Spanish descent born in Mexico, sought to create a national history capable of overcoming the "colonial stigma" and the "split nature" of a society that debated its remote indigenous past and its immediate "Creole-mestizo" present ("mestizos" are children of mixed Spanish and Indian parentage). Creole intellectuals tried to establish enlightened ideas of what was actually "Mexican."

The Jesuit Francisco Xavier Clavijero, from exile in Italy, wrote the *Ancient History of Mexico* (1780), which aimed to refute the European idea of "American inferiority" (Brading, 1980, 1991b; see also Gerbi 1982; Pacheco 1983). Clavijero proposed setting up a museum that would "not only be useful but interesting." He suggested that "the antiquities of our native land" should be preserved there. He also suggested that the disowned past be symbolically repossessed and linked to the present New Spain. Clavijero's idea was to have an enlightened memory of the past so that a common history and destiny could be built. Clavijero was not proposing the usual style of colonial collecting; he was thinking of a "Novohispanic" museum, which would gather together

> ancient statues which are preserved or which will be excavated, arms, mosaic structures and other similar objects, Mexican paintings scattered throughout the country and, above all, manuscripts, both those of the missionaries and other former Spaniards, and those of the Indians which are to be found in some of the monastery libraries, where copies should be made before the . . . woodworm gets to them or they are lost through some other disaster. [Clavijero 1982:xviii]

His vision may seem to have justified the plunder of indigenous cultural possessions by trying to insert them into a holistic Mexican history, but he also advised prudence in this reappropriation of the past:

> what a few years ago an erudite and interested stranger [Boturini] observed could be accomplished by our fellow countrymen, if diligence and clever wit were combined with the prudence necessary to extract these kind of documents from the Indians. [Clavijero 1982:xviii]

In 1787, King Charles III sent the Naturalist Commission to collect and study the plants, animals, and minerals of New Spain. The purpose was to complete and illustrate the manuscripts and drawings of Dr. Francisco Hernández, who had been in Mexico in 1570, during the reign of King Philip II (Fernandez 1987; Rivera Cambas 1880; see also Pino Díaz 1988).

To support this scientific mission, a botanical garden was also to be established (see the Royal Ordinance in Arrillaga 1831). The project was left in the hands of the viceroy at the death of King Charles III. To commemorate the ascent of King Charles IV to the Spanish throne, the first Natural History Museum was opened in August 1790. The founding of the museum was based in part on the Creoles' interest in giving an American cast to the lush vegetation in Mexico and in displaying the scientific knowledge of the time. The splendid new Natural History Museum exhibited elephant skeletons, as well as scientific instruments and equipment of the period, such as microscopes, barometers, and *cameras obscuras*. The Novohispanic society greeted "with enthusiasm the existence of the first museum, and donations to enrich the collection began to come in by the dozen" (Lozoya 1984:105; see also Fernandez 1987; Rivera Cambas 1880).

The museum of antiquities proposed by Clavijero happened by chance. In 1790, some important monoliths were accidentally discovered during repair of the Zocalo (main square) in Mexico City. The archaeologist, Ignacio Bernal, commented:

> Even if it was a chance find, the change of attitude in the Viceregal government was no accident. The Viceroy, Count of Revillagigedo, who would have ordered their destruction a few years earlier, now ordered the sculptures to be preserved. This change of attitude mirrored the alteration in attitude of Charles III and some of his advisors. [Bernal 1979:75; see also Gonzalez 1987]

A palace official of New Spain, José Gómez, recorded the monoliths' discovery and wrote in his diary on September 4, 1790:

> Opening up some foundations, they dug out a local idol which was a highly carved stone figure with a skull on the back, and on the front was another skull with four hands [and] *carvings* on the rest of the body but with no feet or head, and the Viceroy was Count of Revillagigedo. [Gómez 1986:25]

The pieces preserved by Revillagigedo were made available to the learned men of the time for study. The visits by Baron Humboldt in 1803 and 1804 flattered the enlightened monarch's enthusiasm for the natural sciences (Humboldt 1984:80). It is said that some of the documents collected by Lorenzo Boturini and deposited in the Viceregal Secretariat were acquired by Humboldt, the traveling Prussian philosopher (Bernal 1979:121, 125). King Charles IV continued the enlightened ideas of the former king. He allowed Guillermo Dupaix, a Franco-Austrian, to seek out ancient ruins. Between 1808 and 1813 there was an attempt to start an antiquities council, but work was interrupted by the insurrections and calls for national independence that began in these years.

The Transition to Independence in the 19th Century

The political crises related to the struggle for independence, from 1810 to 1821, revised the Creole and imperial Spanish approach to the recovery of Mexican "antiquities." The writings of Friar Servando Teresa de Mier and Carlos Ma. de Bustamante were to become the point of departure for the rediscovery of ancient Mexico.

> The spokesmen for the revolution tried to establish, through every possible means, the continuity of Mexican history and nationality from Aztec times until the present day. They unearthed a Nahuatl geographic term of uncertain meaning, *Anahuac*, and applied it to the immense territory of New Spain. [Keen 1984:327; see also Brading 1980; Duverger 1987; Ocampo 1969]

The Creoles' sanctification of the new fatherland, or nation, through an antiquities museum became a reality from 1821 onward. It was the result of a process of appropriation and expropriation of history, taken from the Indians and their culture to represent the Mexicans. Patriotism-motivated collecting provided the principal cornerstone of the modern National Museum at the end of the 19th century.

There was, however, much ambivalence about the Indian antiquities. One of the pieces discovered in 1790, the *Coatlicue*, a stone sculpture of the Aztec mother goddess, was sent to the university for study (Figure 5.1). It was kept out of sight because it was not considered worthy of

Figure 5.1   The Goddess *Coatlicue*, National Museum, Mexico City. Photograph courtesy of the Archivo General de la Nación, Mexico City.

exhibition next to the Greek and Roman replicas already on display (Gonzalez 1987:247–248; see also Bernal 1979:78). It was then reburied, like some evil spirit, until Alexander Humboldt requested its temporary disinterment so that he might observe it more closely. It was returned afterwards to storage, the *museum of oblivion.* The Creoles' refusal to exhibit the *Coatlicue* monolith is illustrative of the colonial elite's divided feelings about the indigenous past. Many early remains were saved but remained hidden, deep below ground, for years; and many were stored in warehouses and inaccessible to the public (for a "classic" essay about indigenous thought, see Villoro 1950; for Mexican art and the aesthetics of *Coatlicue*, see Fernandez 1967, 1972).

Founding a New Identity after Independence

After several attempts by the First Federal Republic of Mexico to found a museum, a decree was issued in 1825 by President Guadalupe Victoria through Minister of Internal and Foreign Affairs Lucas Alamán to the dean of the university:

> that the antiquities which have been brought from Sacrifice Island [Sacrificios in the Gulf of Mexico] and others existing in the capital should form a National Museum, and one of the university halls be set aside for this purpose and that the expenses incurred would be paid by the supreme government. [Castillo Ledón 1924:11]

This was the beginning of the Mexican government's control over and husbandry of cultural heritage. The museum would legitimize the practice of successive Mexican governments' gathering together all objects considered of "use and national glory." Finally and most importantly, the decree in 1825 initiated the museological process of converting idolatrous objects into museum pieces (Morales-Moreno et al. 1988; see also Morales-Moreno 1991a, 1991b). Forty years were to pass before the museum had an appropriate site, near the Presidential Palace, in the ancient building that had been the former mint. It remained there for the next 100 years (Figure 5.2).

The National Museum of the 19th century should be considered in terms of several historic periods. It was the republican triumph over the

Figure 5.2 Detail of building, National Museum, Mexico City, 1865–1964. Photograph courtesy of the Archivo General de la Nación, Mexico City.

French army and the failed attempt of Maximilian of Hapsburg to establish an empire (1862–1867) that had consolidated the power of a new ruling elite, which in turn had immediate repercussions for the museum. Up to that time, the museum had largely existed on paper and had depended on the good intentions of the national government and on the patriotic dreams of well-intentioned others. From 1867 onward, there was an established and growing budget for museums and archaeological explorations, particularly in the Porfirio Díaz regime (1877–1911).

The period from 1867–1887 was one in which the National Museum was influenced by the positivist, educational ideas of the republican regime of Benito Juárez (1858–1872) (De la Torre et al. 1982; Guerra 1988; Hale 1991; Monroy 1974; see also Sanchez 1877, 1887). This period ended with the establishment of a gallery of ancient monoliths, in 1887 (Figure 5.3). This gallery began Mexican archaeological museography and established the great Aztec monoliths, the Calendar Stone, and the *Coatlicue* sculpture, as representative of Mexican prehistoric culture (Galindo y Villa 1896a, 1913, 1923; see also Castillo Ledón 1924; Morales-Moreno 1991a).

From 1887, historic-museographic discourse adhered more and more to an official version of *Mexican* history as put forward in patriotic teachings (see Vazquez 1975). The initial presidential protection of the "Prehispanic titular gods" became the general policy in Mexican archaeology and was eventually centered in the State Department of Public Education and Fine Arts and in the newly created General Inspection of Archaeological Monuments.

The period between 1887 and 1910 was one in which the Mexican government gained considerable experience in mounting international exhibitions, and the National Museum played an important part in these exhibitions: the "Centenary of the French Revolution," in Paris in 1889; the "Fourth Centenary of the Discovery of America," in Madrid in 1892; the "World's Columbian Exposition," in Chicago in 1893; the "International," in Paris in 1900; the "Panamerican," in Buffalo, New York, 1901; and the "Archaeological," in Rome, 1910 (see the newspapers *El Imparcial* and *Monitor Republicano* for details; Valderrama Zaldívar et al. 1981. In addition, two international Congresses of Americanists were held in the National Museum, one in 1895, another in 1910. These activities conferred considerable prestige on the Porfirio

Figure 5.3 The Monolith Gallery, 1887, National Museum, Mexico City. Photograph courtesy of the Archivo General de la Nación, Mexico City.

Díaz period and used the display of archaeological pieces to open up international frontiers of trade and development outside Mexico.

Modern Times: The 20th Century

The symbiotic relationships among archaeology, the state, and the museum formed part of the myth of the Mexican origin.[1] In this sense, the museum contributed to an ideological process of sanctifying the history of the fatherland (Deloche 1989:31–69) and, above all, providing a new basis for national identity that included the Prehispanic past together with the War of Independence, 1810–1821. In this way, the National Museum and the Porfirio Díaz period added significantly to the late-18th-century Creole conception of the country. The National Museum paid homage not only to the mystified, fossilized native past, while ignoring the Indian present, but gave recognition to the national War of Independence (1810–1821) and to the heroes of the wars of the American and French interventions (1846–1848 and 1862–1867, respectively).[2] Modern museography combined political and historic museological discourse. Modern Mexico did, in fact, begin with the reinvention of its historic tradition in a nationalistic, anti-imperialistic, and pro-mestizo context (Hart 1990; Katz 1976, 1988; Powell 1974).

The collections of the National Museum were divided in 1909, when a presidential decree separated the history collection from the natural history collections and, consequently, from the natural sciences in general. The National Museum then acquired a longer and more precise name: the National Museum of Archaeology, History, and Ethnology. It included the three aforementioned departments and an industrial art department. Evidently, "el Señor Presidente" wanted to open the museum in time for the first centenary celebrations of the War of Independence. The new museum received its first visitor August 28, 1910, at 10 A.M., when President Porfirio Díaz and his general staff (Garcia 1911:268), accompanied by a small committee of research professors and public officials, arrived. It was noted that he lingered in the independence exhibition halls.

This relatively unimportant but peculiarly Mexican ceremony became standard practice in the Díaz regime. It shows that the relationships among the museum, archaeology, and power were part of a strategic plan by the state to control the past through the image exhibited in the National Museum. The president himself approved or disapproved the content of the exhibition halls, particularly those displaying the history of the fatherland. This control included the presentation of the Spanish Conquest; the heroes of the War of Independence; the 1847 war against the United States; Benito Juárez, the Indian president; the 1857 liberal Constitution; and the struggle against the French. All were scenes displayed by the museum as symbolic of the new nation and were emphasized by the state as an "incarnation of the state itself" (see the National Museum History Collection catalog for the contents of the museum; see also Galindo y Villa 1896a, 1896b, 1923; Mendoza and Sánchez 1882; for the concept of "Indian," see Herrera 1895). Independence Centenary festivities were congruent with these ideas and emphasized the mortal remains and portraits of heroes and personalities of the heritage museum, the *museopatria* (Morales-Moreno 1991a, 1991b). It was through these relics that the nation-state acquired historic splendor. It is evident that the Mexican identity was forged in the National Museum with an archaeological past, a "Creole indigenism," and a mestizo present.

In September 1910, Mexico City itself became a living patriotic museum. Cuauhtémoc; Cortés; Indian warriors; Spanish captains; "la Malinche," an Indian princess who became Cortés' mistress and interpreter; Miguel Hidalgo y Costilla; and the Trigarante Army were impressively represented in allegories. The month of patriotism for the populace began on September 2, with a solemn procession to the National Museum, taking the baptismal font in which "*the renowned instigator* of Mexico's emancipation was christened" (Garcia 1911:182). The captive public of this almost-religious procession were school-children, public employees, teachers, and headmasters of innumerable schools. The granddaughter of the "Liberator" Guadalupe Hidalgo played a conspicuous part in this civic homage in which "the first schools filed through Constitution Square forming a military parade from the entrance of the museum to the grand entrance of the Archaeological Hall" (Garcia 1911:186). Hidalgo's granddaughter entered the museum in a car decorated with tricolor ribbons and roses, and as she left there was a "long, rowdy ovation to greet her".

The mortal remains of the heroes of the War of Independence were popular. The ritual of their display reflects the collective pulse of 19th-century Mexican society—the colonial-religious and the civic-secular scientific. Past and present were reconciled, and two great traditional streams of patriotism in New Spain and Mexico were expressed both in civic-lay contexts and Catholic religious cults. This phenomenon is expressed in the symbolic representation of two pharaoh-like tombs: one contains "the relics of the Liberators in front of the altar of Pardons" in the cathedral; and the other is displayed in the central courtyard of the Presidential Palace, where a stone is inscribed "Fatherland 1810–1910." Thus, the mestizo notion of fatherland, or nationality, and its heroes promoted renewed acceptance of a common identity.

More than a museum hero, Porfirio Díaz had become a living re-incarnation of all heroes. Unfortunately for him and his administration, a few months later social unrest toppled the hero-soldier from his pedestal and lifted him, together with his medals and his official chroniclers, onto the pages of a new text of the past. His clothes, gifts, and way of life became museum pieces. The men of the Revolution of 1910 interpreted the display of the republican dictator for the study and the curious gaze of schoolchildren.

Discussion and Conclusion

The museographic content of the present National Museum of Anthropology reaffirms the 19th-century nationalist view of history and the fatherland. The museum expresses the liberal path of "enlightened coercion" that has dominated Mexico since 1867 (Aguilar Carín 1988:22). (By "enlightened coercion," he refers to a certain type of traditional political domination, paternalistic and authoritarian "at the service of a modern capitalistic state initiative.") The writings and politics of the period espoused their ideas under this essential supporting structure.

The National Museum between 1825 and 1925 was not merely a hollow concept or an abstract cultural symbol of the nation. It was, in fact, a collection of "events in movement"—wars, struggles, revolutions, military invasions, and political disorder—that were transformed into symbols and displayed as images. The exhibition halls served as kinds of "historiographic canvases" or "social scenery from the political imagin-ation." The various sources show that the physical objects of these events, the monoliths, the arms, and the scapulars, were always on permanent exhibition. It was their interpretation that changed according to the different values assigned them by society (Leon 1986; Smith 1989). The sources for these comments include various catalogs, a few photographs of the exhibition halls, and the many descriptions left by foreign visitors (Berger 1943; Bullock 1824, 1983:180–186; Calderon de la Barca 1987; Chabrand 1987; Charnay 1884:270–278; Gardiner 1952: 321–351; Lyon 1984).

The National Museum formed a crucial part of the patriotic culture from its beginnings. A public museum, it was used in a way similar to that of Napoleonic France: to discover "patriotic identity" and to resolve the "orphanage of the newborn nation."[3]

The development of the museum was marked by periods of activity and of stagnation. The Díaz regime actually invented Mexican history in the National Museum (Hobsbawm and Ranger 1984). It invented a new tradition and gave it an ideological function which inevitably became dogmatic within the context of a positivist doctrine (Guerra 1988; Hale 1991). This does not mean, however, that the museum's discourse was mere fiction. Rather, from this fiction of the ideas of the fatherland, the lost origins, the conquered King Cuauhtémoc, there developed archaeological, anthropological, and historical research, which, together with the legal custody of a unified memory and patriotic museography, tried to offer a "scientific" explanation of a historic past. The historic past, which the enlightened political elite tried to interpret as a guiding light, would, they thought, lead to a bright, bourgeois future and Mexico's integration into the world market.

From a museological point of view, one now asks, Where does the *concept* of nation lie? A close approximation of the answer can be found in part in recent writings by philosopher-historian Guillermo Zermeño, when he speaks of "administered history."

> Before talking about the living past, we have to refer to the past of the state which forged a "national identity." . . . If the nation is a creation or an invention, generally occurring through revolutionary violence whose idea is imposed upon an inarticulate ethnic, cultural, or social group, then it is obvious that the process is not homogeneous and that the creation of a national conscience is asymmetrical. Its acceptance will vary according to the region, the cultural group, historical precedents, etc. [Zermeño 1991:12]

The influence of the National Museum between 1867 and 1925 was limited to a city of approximately 1 million people, surrounded by a principally rural, illiterate society, ignorant of the concepts of liberal doctrine. It is precisely this audience that makes the existence of the museum interesting. It reflects the political beliefs of an intellectual elite hardly known in Mexican historiography (Camp 1988). It refers to an elite group of professionals and craftspeople: engineers, doctors, naturalists, taxidermists, draftsmen, printers, carpenters, photographers, professors, and scholars. The museum produced the first official historians, archaeologists, anthropologists, museographers, and museologists in modern Mexico. This political and intellectual elite was essential to the labors of creating patriotic self-awareness from the revolutionary civil war of 1911–1920. The National Museum, in leading the search for and discovery of patriotic identity, also converted a dead area into something full of meaning for the living. This dead area was filled with vitality through the magic of museography. The museum offered an alternative means of mass communication to those offered by the public schools, the press, and the cinema; in other words, it offered a more general knowledge and a worldview for a more homogeneous public.

Museography took into account individual, collective, scientific, and mythical beliefs that were seen to be "Mexican." The public exhibition of "found" identity, combined with the thought, conscience, aesthetics, philosophy, and ideology of what is "Mexican," transformed the National Museum into a living arena engaged in a social and educational discourse. Even though the state used the historic museum to pay homage to the fatherland, the museographic language presented a series of re-creations, reinventions, mutilations, and reconciliations from a collective memory. The museum's messages were transmitted through images, objects, symbols, and myths, many of which belonged to civic rituals that were traditions invented by those in power or belonged to popular culture and were customs that revived the past.

In the end, the national heritage museum may be seen as a depository, a funerary urn, symbolic of the hybrid cultures within. The recovered pieces are a mixture of goddesses and gods, *Coatlicues* and *Tlalocs*, sherds, crucifixes, swords, and statues of the Virgin, along with secular anti-imperialist heroes, who were neither Indian nor Creole, represented in portraits, wax figures, and plaster busts. The concept of the fatherland, or nation, underlies the present-day National Museum of Anthropology. It was used politically to legitimize a historical and mythic age, a Prehispanic and profoundly religious Indian past, and the colonial and secular state that was transformed into the independent Mexican nation.[4] The museum itself transformed Indian idolatrous objects from religious to aesthetic cult objects; and Creole objects became part of historical dramas of national patriotism.

Notes

1. The myth of the Mexican origin refers to the several ways of writing and thinking about the historical roots of Mexico's indigenous and colonial past. It was an ethnological and historical process (see Brading 1980, 1991b; Duverger 1987; Florescano 1987; Villoro 1950).
2. Throughout the 19th century, the native way of life began its own struggle against the mestizo way of life of modern Mexico. The liberal elite sanctified the Indian past in the National Museum; meanwhile, the landlords despoiled the real Indian's land or tried to "integrate" the Indians into their utilitarian meanings.
3. I have used the words "patriotism" and "patriotic" in terms of two traditions: the colonial Creole and the liberal modern. Both reflect ideological thoughts: Creole patriotism longed for "autonomous rights" related to the Spanish Empire; and liberal patriotism longed for total independence. Nonetheless, the liberal patriotism inherited from the Creole ideology is *indigenism*. In the National Museum, this kind of patriotism was triumphant.
4. The Mexican poet Octavio Paz (1969) wrote the first and best critique of the political function of the National Museum.

References

Aguilar Camín, Héctor
    1988 *Después del milagro.* México: Cal y Arena.
Arrillaga, Basilio José
    1831 Reglamento en calidad de ordenanza que por ahora manda S. M. Guardar en el real jardín botánico. In *Recopilación de leyes, decretos, bandos, reglamentos, circulares, y providencias de los supremos poderes y otras autoridades de la República Mexicana.* B. J. Arrillaga, ed. Pp. 499–535. México: Imp. de J. M. Fernández de Lara.

Berger, Max
1943 *The British Traveler in America: 1836–1860.* New York.
Bernal, Ignacio
1979 *Historia de la Arqueologia en México.* México: Porrúa.
Brading, David
1980 Patriotismo criollo. In *Los origenes del nacionalismo.* Pp. 15–42. Era, ed.
Mexico.
1991a El paraiso occidental. In *Orbe Indiano: De la monarquia católica a la
república criolla, 1492–1867.* Pp. 415–420. México: Fondo de Cultura
Económica.
1991b El triunfo de los jesuitas. In *Orbe Indiano: De la monarquia Católica a la
república criolla, 1492–1867.* Pp. 189–207. México: Fondo de Cultura
Económica.
Bullock, William
1824 *A Description of the Unique Exhibition, Called Ancient Mexico: Collected
on the Spot in 1823, by the Assistance of the Mexican Government and Now
Open for Public Inspection at the Egyptian Hall.* London: Printed for the
Proprietor.
1983 Capitulo XXV: Antigüedades. In *Seis meses de residencia y viajes en
México: Con observaciones sobre la situación presente de la Nueva España. Sus
producciones naturales, condiciones sociales, manufacturas, comercio, agricultura
y antigüedades, etc.* Pp. 180–186. México: Banco de México.
Calderon de la Barca, Madame
1987 *La vida en México durante una residencia de dos años en ese pais.* México:
Porrúa.
Camp, Roderic
1988 *Los intelectuales y el Estado en el México del siglo XX.* México: Fondo de
Cultura Económica.
Castillo Ledón, Luis
1924 *El Museo Nacional de Arqueologia, Historia, y Etnografia, 1825–1925.*
México: Imp. del Museo Nacional.
Chabrand, Emile
1987 *De Barceloneta a la República Mexicana.* México: Banco de México.
Charnay, Desiré
1884 El Museo de México. In *América pintoresca.* Montaner and Simons,
eds. Pp. 270–278. Barcelona.
Clavijero, Francisco Xavier
1982 *Historia antigua de Mexico.* México: Porrúa.
De la Torre, Guadalupe, and Dolores Enciso,
1982 *Historia de los museos de la Secretaria de Educación Pública.* México:
Instituto Nacional de Antropologia e Historia.
Deloche, Bernard
1989 L'Obsession du Sacré. In *Museologica: Contradictions et logique du Museé.*
Pp. 31–69. France: Collection Museologia.

Duchet, Michele
  1975 *Antropologia e historia en el siglo de las luces*. México: Siglo XXI.
  1985 Cornélius De Pauw ou l'histoire en défaut. *Le partage des savoirs: Discours historique, discours ethnologie* 1:82–104.
Duverger, Christian
  1987 *El origen de los aztecas*. México: Grijalbo.
Fernandez, Justino
  1967 *El arte del siglo XIX en México*, México: Universidad Nacional Autónoma de México/Instituto de Investigaciones Estéticas.
  1972 *Estética del arte mexicano: Coatlicue, El retablo de los reyes, El Hombre*. México: Universidad Nacional Autónoma de México/Instituto de Investigaciones Estéticas.
Fernandez, Miguel Angel
  1987 *Historia de los museos de México*. México: Banco Nacional de México.
Florescano, Enrique
  1987 *Memoria Mexicana*. México: Joaquín Mortíz.
Galindo y Villa, Jesús
  1896a *Breve noticia histórica-descriptiva del Museo Nacional*. México: Imp. del Museo Nacional.
  1896b *Guia para visitar los salones de Historia de México del Museo Nacional*. México: Imp. del Museo Nacional.
  1913 La nueva Galeria Arqueológica del Museo Nacional. In *Noticia de Diversos Escritos*. Pp. 33–39. México: Imp. del Museo Nacional.
  1923 *El Museo Nacional de Arqueologia, Historia, y Etnologia*. México: Imp. del Museo Nacional.
Garcia, Genaro
  1911 *Crónica oficial de los festejos del Primer Centenario*. México: Imp. del Museo Nacional.
Gardiner, C. Harvey
  1952 Foreign Travelers' Accounts of Mexico, 1810–1910. *The Americas Magazine* 8:321–351.
Gerbi, Antonello
  1982 *La Disputa del Nuevo Mundo*. México: Fondo de Cultura Económica.
Giraudy, Daniele
  1979 *Le musée et la vie*. France: S.p.i.
Gómez, José
  1986 *Diario curioso y cuaderno de las cosas memorables en México durante el gobierno de Revillagigedo: 1789–1794*. Intro. and notes by Ignacio González-Polo. México: Instituto de Investigaciones Bibliográficas de la Universidad Nacional Autónoma de México.
Gonzalez, Graciela
  1987 Antecedentes coloniales (siglos XVI a XVIII). In *La antropologia en México: Panorama histórico*. C. G. Mora, ed. Pp. 213–260, book 1. México: Instituto Nacional de Antropólogia e Historia.

Guerra, Francois Xavier
  1988 Las mutaciones culturales. *México: del Antiguo Régimen a la Revolución* 1:376–444. México: Fondo de Cultura Económica.
Hale, Charles
  1991 *La transformación del liberalismo en México a fines del siglo XIX.* México: Vuelta.
Hart, John Mason
  1990 *El México revolucionario: Gestación y proceso de la Revolución Mexicana.* México: Alianza Editorial Mexicana.
Herrera, Alfonso y Ricardo Cicero
  1895 *Catálogo de la Colección de Antropología.* México: Imp. del Museo Nacional.
Hobsbawm, Eric, and Terence Ranger
  1984 *The Invention of Tradition.* Cambridge, MA: Cambridge University Press.
Humboldt, Alexander
  1984 *Ensayo Politico sobre el Reino de la Nueva España.* México: Porrúa.
Keen, Benjamin
  1984 *La imagen azteca.* México: Fondo de Cultura Económica.
Katz, Friedrich, ed.
  1976 *La servidumbre agraria en México en la época porfiriana.* México: SepSetentas 303.
Katz, Friedrich, ed.
  1988 *Riot, Rebellion, and Revolution: Rural Social Conflict in Mexico.* Princeton, NJ: Princeton University Press.
Leon, Aurora
  1986 *El Museo. Teoría, Praxis y Utopía.* Madrid: Ediciones Cátedra.
Lozoya, Xavier
  1984 *Plantas y luces en México: La Real Expedición Científica a Nueva España, 1787–1803.* Barcelona: Ediciones de Serbal.
Lyon, George
  1984 *Residencia en México.* México: Fondo de Cultura Económica.
Matute, Alvaro
  1976 *Lorenzo Boturini y el pensamiento histórico de Vico.* México: Universidad Nacional Autónoma de México/Instituto de Investigaciones Históricas.
Mendoza, Gumesindo, and Jesús Sánchez
  1882 *Catálogo de las colecciones histórica y arqueológica del Museo Nacional de México.* México: Imp. de Ignacio Escalante.
Monroy, Guadalupe
  1974 Instrucción Pública. In *La República Restaurada: Vida Social.* Pp. 633–726. México-Buenos Aires: Hermes.
Morales-Moreno, Luis Gerardo
  1991a *Museopatria Mexicana.* México: Instituto Nacional de Antropologia e Historia.

1991b Museopatria revolucionaria. In *Memoria del Congresso Internacional sobre la Revolución Mexicana.* Pp. 398–411. México: Gob. del Estado de San Luis Potosi/Instituto Nacional de Estudios Históricos de la Revolución Mexicana.

Morales-Moreno, Luis Gerardo, Frida Gorbach, and Cristina Ma. Urrutia
1988 *Antropologia e Historia de los Museos de Antropologia.* México: Instituto Nacional de Antropologia e Historia.

Ocampo, Javier
1969 *Las ideas de un dia.* México: El Colegio de México.

Pacheco, José Emilio
1983 La Patria Perdida: Notas sobre Clavijero y la "cultura nacional." In *En Torno a la cultura nacional.* H. Aguilar Camín, ed. Pp. 11–50. México: Secretaria de Educación Pública/Fondo de Cultura Económica.

Paz, Octavio
1969 *Posdata.* México: Siglo XXI.

Pino Diaz, Fermin del
1988 América y el desarrollo de la ciencia española en el siglo XVIII; tradición, innovación, y representaciones a propósito de Francisco Hernández. In *La América Española en la Época de las Luces.* Fernando Murillo, ed. Pp. 121–43. Madrid: Ediciones de Cultura Hispánica.

Powell, T. G.
1974 *El liberalismo y el campesinado en el centro de Mexico (1850 a 1876).* México: SepSetentas 122.

Recopilacion de Leyes de las Indias . . . 1756.
2nd ed., vol. 1, book 1. J. de Paredes, ed.: Madrid.

Rivera Cambas, Manuel
1880 El Museo Nacional. In *México pintoresco, artistico, y monumental.* Pp. 175–81. México: Imp. de la Reforma.

Sanchez, Jesús
1877 Reseña Histórica Del Museo Nacional. *Anales del Museo Nacional* I:1–2.
1887 Informe al Secretario de Justicia e Instrucción Pública. *Anales del Museo Nacional* I:3–4.

Smith, Charles Saumarez
1989 Museums, Artifacts, and Meanings. In *The New Museology.* Peter Vergo, ed. Pp. 6–21. Great Britain: Reaction Books, Ltd.

Valderrama Zaldívar, Ma. del Carmen, and Ana Ma. Velasco
1981 *El arte prehispánico en el Porfiriato.* 2 vols. México: Universidad Iberoamericana.

Vazquez, Josefina
1975 *Nacionalismo y Educación en México.* 2nd ed. México: El Colegio de México.

Villoro, Luis
   1950 *Los grandes momentos del indigenismo en México*. México: El Colegio de
       México.
Weckman, Luis
   1984 *La herencia medieval do México*. 2 vols. México: El Colegio de México.
Zermeño, Guillermo
   1991 En Busca del lugar de la historia en la modernidad. Manuscript on
       file, Mexico: Universidad Iberoamerica.

6 The "Caribbeanization" of the West Indies: The Museum's Role in the Development of National Identity

Alissandra Cummins

The comprehensive slave codes of the Caribbean, fully established by the 17th century, formed the legal basis for planter-slave relations and were continually reinforced over the next 150 years. They sanctioned rigid segregation, legitimized the planters' absolute ownership of and control over their slaves, and sought to suppress all natural response. The 1688 Slave Code of Barbados, for example, made it illegal for slaves to "beat drums, blow horns, or use other loud instruments" (Beckles 1990:34). Gordon Lewis noted,

> One corollary of this situation was that both under slavery and emancipation, the world of the Caribbean masses remained a dark unknown void. Transplanted forcibly from his African tribal culture, the slave in the new milieu became a deculturated individual. Losing one world he was driven to create a new one. [1968:54]

Thus, a local culture was created that was derivative of European values (for generations the most dominant force) and bound to African sensibilities (Figure 6.1).

In 1834, more than 345,000 slaves in the British West Indies were freed by the Official Proclamation of Emancipation. The colonial government's only contribution to the process of the slaves' preparation for independent life was to declare a period of apprenticeship; in essence, this was an extension of a period of semiservitude that was equated, at least in the colonial mentality, with a period of training or preparation for the new life to come. The only *real* contribution to this process was

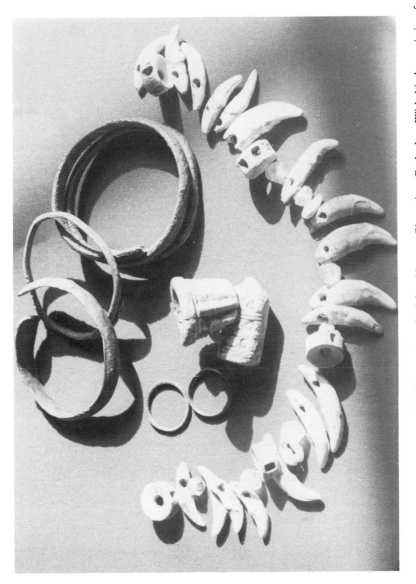

Figure 6.1 West African artifacts recovered from a slave burial at Newton Plantation, Barbados. With kind permission from the Barbados Museum and Historical Society. Photograph by Ronnie Carrington.

by Methodist and Moravian missionaries who established and expanded an educational system to accommodate black and colored persons.

Lieutenant Colonel William Reid (later Sir William Reid) as governor of Bermuda in 1839 gave a measure of official support to emancipation activities. On arrival in Bermuda, Reid, of his own volition, immediately set to work to ameliorate the conditions of the recently freed population. He said that "the best means of securing the loyal support of the people, must doubtless be through their own self-interest, by enabling them to prosper under British rule" (1839:nn). His unusually enlightened attitude earned him the title "the good governor" during his term in office (1839–1846). He established parochial schools and developed agricultural programs as a means of encouraging self sufficiency (Figure 6.2).

Reid, long a member of the Royal Society, was also instrumental in the creation of legislation to found the Bermuda Public Library in 1843. Part of its mandate was to house a public museum "containing a collection of natural history and works of art [which] would be beneficial to the community" (Bermuda Law 1843:nn). He was a major exponent of enlightened ideals, recognizing the link between education and emancipation on many levels, but in reality these were limited, at best: the dispossessed were to realize they were all beneficiaries of the British Empire and were to be educated to accept and appreciate that reality.

Reid's influence was extended to other islands when he left Bermuda in 1846 to become governor-in-chief of the Windward Islands, based in Barbados. Between 1847 and 1848, under his leadership, legislation virtually identical to that of Bermuda was enacted to establish public libraries and museums in St. Lucia, Bahamas, Barbados, and Grenada. The trustees of these institutions were charged with the task of collecting "natural and scientific subjects and productions of Art" and were empowered "to purchase . . . books, maps, prints, philosophical and other instruments and apparatus, and such curiosities as they deem proper from time to time place therein" (Bermuda Law 1843:nn).

All of these institutions were to be opened free of charge to all residents, in keeping with Reid's philanthropic ideals of ensuring intellectual stimulation for the masses. In reality though, this privilege was only exercised within a limited framework. The restrictions for a population struggling to survive were obvious; lack of available time for leisure activities and lack of available transport were real deterrents to

Figure 6.2 Engraving of Governor Sir William Reid (1839–1846). With kind permission from the Barbados Museum and Historical Society. Photograph by Alissandra Cummins.

those who might have had an interest, as was the rarified atmosphere engendered by the presence of scholarly society. However, it was the inaccessibility of the European concept of "museum" to the African cultural sensibility that proved to be the greatest barrier of all. Despite the liberal intentions of the governor, these early island museums were, for the most part, incomprehensible to the majority of the population and were soon generally subsumed by the interests of the libraries.

There is little other evidence to suggest that the colonial government was an active participant in the initial development of museums in the Caribbean; rather, its contribution was incidental where it coincided with plans for territorial consolidation through the "civilization" of foreign lands and foreign peoples. In keeping with the prevailing enthusiasm for scientific investigation and acquisition, they encouraged the collection and exhibition of scientific specimens and ethnographical artifacts, usually under the auspices of local agricultural and commercial societies. These two types of collections were clearly representative of the wealth of natural resources characteristic of the colony that were available for industrial exploitation.

During the first decades of the 19th century, the symbiotic relationship between scientific development and imperial expansion encouraged the diffusion of knowledge from one part of the world to the next. Local societies, formed by businessmen to focus on special interests, existed in Jamaica from 1807 and in British Guiana from 1814, and were as much a part of this network as recipients of emerging concepts and attitudes generated by the race for industrialization. By the middle of the 19th century, similar societies existed in most Caribbean islands, many of them forming the core of organizing committees to develop the exhibits needed to contribute to the "Exhibition of Industry of All Nations in London," the Great Exhibition of 1851.

This activity inspired other similar large-scale national exhibitions (British Guiana, 1855; Trinidad, 1858; Jamaica, 1891) throughout the second half of the 19th century and the first decades of the 20th. The popularity of these exhibitions influenced the development of the earliest West Indian museums and was, in many cases, the catalyst for the formation of the first national collections—since duplicate collections were often retained by the colonies. Other factors that contributed to early regional museum development included the West Indian Geological Survey, started in 1860, and the general increase in archaeological and anthropological activity in the Caribbean.

The Royal Agricultural and Commercial Society of British Guiana (1844) had as one of its primary goals the establishment of a museum and model room in which would be kept "both indigenous and introduced minerals, soils, timbers, fruit, seeds, gums, resins, dyes and drugs, specimens of zoology. . . . Also models of such implements and machinery connected with agriculture and manufactures." Robert Schomburg (later Sir Robert), following the completion of his boundaries survey of British Guiana, became one of its first members and donated a comprehensive collection of the colony's native woods.

Mineralogical, biological, and geological specimens offered by private donors soon augmented the collection, and by 1853 the society's museum became a legally incorporated entity. The Natural History Society of British Guiana (1861) also became an influential donor interested in forming "a local exhibition to bring to light these hidden sources of wealth and stimulants to industry [as well as] a general view of what [the] country offers to the research of scientific and intelligent curiosity" (Natural History Society of British Guiana 1863). The result was a distinct bias toward natural history as the core of the museum.

A fire in 1864 led to a renewal of volunteer efforts to provide the country with a museum as "a means of instructive recreation to all" (Roth 1953:2). In reality, however, the issuance of a prospectus for the "British Guiana Museum Co., Ltd.," in 1867, with shares at £10 each, sealed the fate of the institution as a private commercial enterprise. Its Eurocentric bias ensured that other cultural remains would be curiosities at best, and their material culture, trophies of Western civilization.

In Jamaica, the Royal Society of Arts and Agriculture was formed in 1864 with the amalgamation of two earlier organizations—The General Agricultural Society of Jamaica and The Royal Society of Arts (Jamaica). The intention was "augmentation of the sources of public industry and the extension of the arts and manufactures of the colony." The society's collections and those of the Sawkins and Brown Geological Survey in 1879 formed the nucleus of the Institute of Jamaica. The institute aimed to develop representative natural history and anthropological collections, to host lectures and exhibitions, and to hold examinations in science, literature, and the arts.

Even though the institute contributed significantly to the growth of science and industry within the island, the membership fees, along with the social mores of the period, ensured that its management (and by extension its collection and exhibition criteria) was dominated by an exclusive clique of middle-class white men. The focus on natural history (and later art) found little response among the populace, even though entrance to the museum cost nothing.

Like its sister nations, Trinidad saw the need for an institution that would embody the cultural heritage of the country but that, at the same time, would act as a kind of vocational training center, with regular classes in arts and crafts. In 1870, the Trinidad Society of Arts and Sciences was formed and spearheaded the movement to build the Victoria Institute (later, the Royal Victoria Institute), using the Victoria and Albert Museum as its model.

The institute, with the help of the Trinidad Field Naturalists Club, immediately began to develop a collection of local fauna. By the time the new building was opened to the public in 1892, archaeological and geological specimens had been added to the collections. Initially the institute seemed to have had more success in garnering the support of the working-class population with its training courses and annual exhibitions, than as a museum. The managing committee was comprised of scholars, scientists, and businessmen, and the collections acquired were agricultural samples, zoological specimens, botanical specimens, and so on, once again giving a natural-history focus to an early museum.

These early Caribbean museums had several things in common: they were all private organizations, they were developed to meet the needs of the colonies' commercial and agricultural interests, and they operated with little more than token patronage from their governments. While their formation occasioned the expression of lofty ideals of education for the masses and of development of science, the primary catalyst for these activities was enlightened self-interest. Museums were principally regarded as an invaluable means of informing visitors about the resources of the colony and the potential benefits of investment in local industry.

Because industrial and commercial enterprises were so important to the economy of the colonies, museums were justified in helping to identify and enhance national resources, which included anthropological collections. African and Amerindian cultural heritages were part of the exotic baggage acquired with territorial prizes. In fact, a process of separation and disinheritance eventually plagued the majority of the West Indies' population for decades to come. As Gordon Lewis points out, "The fact is that, all in all, the West Indian person has been deprived of a meaningful kinship with his origins and has sought relief in sheer movement—dance, cricket, and activist religion, migration itself" (1968:30). For officialdom, such expressions of folk culture had no legitimate place in the museum context.

The World's Columbian Exposition in 1893, held in Chicago to commemorate the 400th anniversary of Columbus' discovery of the New World, generated enormous interest in every aspect of West Indian life and culture. A special trip by Frederick Ober was made to Dominica and St. Vincent to persuade a group of Carib Indians to go to the exhibition. Jumping on the bandwagon, P. T. Barnum and James Bailey also imported some Indians to join the "Great Show in New York." However, it was the United States of America's acquisition of Puerto Rico, at the close of war with Spain in 1898, that led to a fascination with the Caribbean.

Archaeological fieldwork in the West Indies began in earnest in 1900, under the auspices of the Bureau of American Ethnology and the Smithsonian Institution. This was an important step, Fewkes suggested, because "Archaeology is thus able to illuminate obscure chapters overlooked or unrecorded by the historian and ethnologist. It offers the only exact data by which the manners and customs of the aborigines before the advent of Columbus can be interpreted" (1907:17). As scientific knowledge increased in the United States, so did the interest of private collectors. George Gustav Heye, for example, amassed a huge Caribbean collection for his private museum, the Heye Foundation, which only recently—1991—became the National Museum of the American Indian, Smithsonian Institution.

Local collecting during the first half of the 20th century was mostly confined to enthusiastic amateurs, and many collections soon found homes in the island libraries, which eventually became the nuclei of the small museums that exist today. The problem was that, while museums and institutes were viewed as being educational for the local populace and as giving pleasure to the visitors, the focus of attention on Amerindian culture produced little emotional response within the larger community. For the majority of Caribbean people, the early eradication of the Amerindian population from most of the territory, effected by the end of the 17th century, meant that there were no bonds of blood, language, or culture, with the exception of Guyana and to a lesser extent Dominica and St. Vincent. There was no experience of living culture coexisting side by side with relics of the past. The indigenous clay pots, shell tools, and stone axes held little meaning to the majority of the Caribbean community.

Alongside an increase in regional archaeological investigation, a concern with the status and preservation of historic buildings was developed in the West Indies. The Colonial Office carried out a comprehensive survey of all public and military structures of historic interest in the region during the early years of the 20th century. Later, in the 1940s, the Georgian Society of Great Britain paid equal attention to the wealth of historic houses that still remained in the region. Both groups emphasized the potential for development of these sites and museums as tourist attractions. But once again the Eurocentric focus of local preservation efforts failed to involve the majority of the populace by ignoring the relevance of the African and non-European Caribbean experience.

Bather and Sheppard's report on museums of the West Indies for the Museum Association in 1933 provides no insight into the future of cultural identity. Even their advocacy of "an adequate museum service" for every town with at least 20,000 people was qualified by their introduction of the word "literate." The commissioners' statement, that "It might seem slightly fantastic to imagine education museums being provided for an illiterate population, although in years to come educationalists may be sufficiently advanced to utilize a museum or museum methods in the education of illiterates," may have been in keeping with the professional views of the period (1933:33).

Despite the disclaimer that "there is, so far as museum visitors or officers are concerned, no reason to make any distinction of race," they seem to have been complacent and satisfied that "in several of these island territories the literate population was sometimes less than 5% or 6% of the whole." In all likelihood, these notions contributed to the locals' view of museums as institutions of the elite, although some Negroes and Chinese were included by reason of "intelligence" and as "cultured" members of society. They seem also to have been largely unaware of the determination of the working-class leaders to give priority to formal education for all children, and indeed they criticized those leaders for what seemed an overemphasis on education. They were surprised that, despite their inability to read the labels, most visitors to the museum were "natives" who took a special interest in exhibits connected with their own customs and in specimens familiar to them.

Bather and Sheppard recognized that it was not government but semiprivate enterprises which had been "the chief agents in providing the only effective museums." They acknowledged that further development in the smaller islands would only be likely if voluntary effort were supported by professional staff. Their solution, a "federation of islands for museum purposes" sharing resources and one or more curators, was far ahead of its time. Although this concept was received with some interest, it was never supported by the Home Office and never came to fruition.

The long-term Caribbean economic depression that was suffered from the end of the 19th century had become chronic during the 1930s and produced an impoverished working class. Although patterns of landownership had begun to change, primarily due to the influx of "Panama money," an artificial prosperity experienced as a result of the wartime boom in sugar production collapsed during the 1920s. The austerity of the Caribbean economy heightened the differences in life-style between the planter-merchant class and the working class. In the late 1930s, extensive rioting erupted throughout the region. At the same time, independent black organizations emerged with the development of mutual support groups, such as friendly societies, cohesive church congregations, and other community groups.

Black socioeconomic consolidation fostered an awareness of the need for political mobilization among the working classes. Marcus Garvey's Pan-Caribbean movement was the major stimulus to the development of West Indian political consciousness and trade unionism. By extension, Caribbean blacks sought to redress the disenfranchisement they had suffered by demanding social and economic reforms. For the first time, they also addressed the issue of deliberate European suppression of black culture and attempted to establish a policy of black cultural nationalism as a counterpoint to the Eurocultural model that dominated West Indian society. In Jamaica, Edna Swithenbank (later, Edna Manley, wife of Jamaica's first prime minister, Norman Manley) exhibited in 1937 her sculpture *Negro Aroused* in her first solo exhibition on the island. It soon became the icon of this movement. This powerful torso came to symbolize the Jamaican people and presaged the break with British colonial rule. Nationalist pressure led to the acquisition of *Negro Aroused* by the Institute of Jamaica, where it became the centerpiece of the national art collection (Figure 6.3).

The Moyne Commission, appointed by the British Government, thoroughly investigated the social and economic conditions of the laboring classes in the West Indies in 1938–1939, and its report (1945)

Figure 6.3   *Negro Aroused*, sculpture in wood, by Edna Manley (1935). With kind permission from the National Gallery of Jamaica. Photograph by Maria La Yacona.

both raised many questions and offered a number of recommendations to ameliorate the West Indian way of life. Local reformers pressed for a more equitable distribution of economic resources and a liberalization of social institutions.

While the commission's report in particular commended the Carnegie Corporation's role in improving educational standards (by assisting in establishing a central Caribbean library system), their report also drew attention to the paucity of aesthetic stimuli for the people. They noted that

> One of the strongest and most discouraging impressions carried away by the investigators is that of prevailing absence of independence and self help, the lack of tradition of craftsmanship and pride in good work . . . without some such tradition, no amount of external and governmental help will create a sound and self-perpetuating social tradition. [Moyne 1945:35]

For the commissioners, the solution was to encourage government in recognizing the importance of developing a handicraft industry to service the growing tourism in the region. Their vision encompassed economic security without appreciating the dynamic of cultural identification and cohesion it generated.

The onset of World War II brought with it a determination by the Home Office to gather as much support as possible for Great Britain in its time of crisis—despite moves to dispense with the historical bonds of the empire. The British Council was to serve as an organ of British cultural and visual propaganda. In the West Indies, the assessment of the desirability of and other needs for ensuring the development of arts and crafts led to the decision to establish by 1943 colonial offices of the council in Trinidad, British Guiana, and Barbados (to serve the eastern Caribbean and Jamaica).

Apart from its stated function, to support the development of the arts, though naturally with an Anglophile bias, the British Council's presence in the West Indies probably contributed to the development of national arts societies and, indirectly, national collections throughout the 1940s and 1950s. The inauguration of such bodies as the Barbados Arts Council and the Grenada Society of the Arts, both launched in 1944, was encouraged; while in British Guiana, the National Collection of Fine Art was formed six years later in 1950. Similarly, the founding of the

Jamaican School of Art in 1950 gave significant impetus to the development of Jamaican aesthetics.

The council also became the conduit for museum development proposals to the Colonial Office. The establishment of the Children's Gallery at the Barbados Museum in 1947 grew out of a reluctant acceptance that the development of a visual arts department within such an institution could contribute significantly to the educational system in Barbados. The Institute of Jamaica was already playing a similar role from 1938 onward. It was via these small outlets that museums were assigned a significant role in the development of national identity through the nurturing of a still-youthful Caribbean aesthetic consciousness. Nevertheless, the 1940s and 1950s saw scant development of the smaller museums in the Caribbean, and many museums continued a precarious existence as mere appendages of the local public libraries.

The rise of the regional tourism industry crystallized in 1951 with the formation of the Caribbean Tourism Association. In the years immediately following World War II, the islands of the British West Indies were promoted as an ideal holiday destination, and a much more aggressive marketing strategy was put in place. Commercial aircraft travel made the West Indies more accessible by the end of the decade and created an immediate market for the smaller islands in the region. At the same time, the Cuban Revolution closed that country off to the burgeoning United States tourism industry, thereby increasing interest in other Caribbean destinations.

As tourism expanded, sympathetic support for the restoration of historic sites grew. Acworth's survey in 1951 suggested that official support of hitherto neglected sites could yield even greater economic returns by opening them to the tourism market. It was the right time for the development of a heritage industry. Private initiative in the form of national trusts met few official barriers, although no funds were made available to help develop viable cultural resources.

Acworth's recommendations created local interest in historic buildings. Subsequently, open-air museums were developed as well (e.g., English Harbour [Antigua] and Brimstone Hill [St.Kitts]). As stated, another direct response to this new interest was the formation of the first national trusts in the region, including Jamaica (1958) and Barbados (1960) (Figure 6.4). In his report, Acworth noted with concern that "popular indifference to architecture of all sorts has been matched

Figure 6.4   Barbados Museum and Historical Society, Jubilee Gallery, early 1960s. With kind permission from the Barbados Museum and Historical Society.

by official neglect of the need for protecting the Islands' architectural heritage from damage or destruction." The major focus of Acworth's report was the European-style great houses and official buildings, and attention to any vernacular architecture that coexisted was lacking. The result was a distinct Eurocentric bias in both public and private priorities, one that gave little recognition to the more humble structures. The lack of popular support for these projects can clearly be tied to the lack of identification with its focus.

During the 1950s, the British West Indies gave consideration to the question of a "Federation of West Indian Nations." Negotiations had started in earnest almost a decade earlier, and by 1956 a federation seemed inevitable. At a time when the island governments were contemplating a political and economic union, which might strengthen the vulnerable positions of so many tiny nation-states, the concept of cultural unity was also mooted. In August 1956, Lynndon Clough, representative for the British Arts Council in Barbados, wrote,

> After Federation one hopes and presumes that the nation will develop a cultural unity to cement the political and economic joints, though perhaps each island will preserve its individuality in much the same ways as English counties, American states and Canadian provinces cling to personal characteristics. [1956:22]

He also emphasized that a federal museum should be a major consideration in the process of regional unification.

The first federal government was elected in 1958 and by May 1959 had approved plans for a national (Caribbean) art collection. Plans for the future were hopeful. This was the first time that a cultural policy for the region as a whole was promulgated. Political events, however, militated against the achievement of this ideal. In May 1962 after only four uncertain years of political unity, the Federation of the British West Indies was disrupted by calls for independent status. Jamaica was the first to go, achieving independence in 1962, followed closely by Trinidad and Tobago and later by Guyana and Barbados in 1966. With the departure of these nation-states, the vulnerable federation disintegrated, leaving cultural unity in the Caribbean unfulfilled.

The activities of the artistic community, through an exchange of cultural programs and exhibits among regional counterparts, were of little benefit to the local museums, whose existence was overshadowed, especially in the smaller territories. The Caribbean continued to suffer from a colonial viewpoint in which preservationists were seen primarily as an expatriate element seeking to cling to the last vestiges of an exploitative past. Thus, preservation-oriented groups, including historical societies and national trusts, tended to remain marginal organizations whose administrative structures and memberships were "exclusive." The National Trust of Jamaica and that of Guyana, being governmental bodies, largely escaped this stigma, but other private groups did not.

One exception was the Institute of Jamaica. In 1961, the Jamaica Peoples Museum of Craft and Technology was established in the stables of the Old King's House at Spanish Town. The Jamaican government sought to move beyond the confines of Kingston and to create an appreciation of traditional Creole culture and crafts within the rural community. The exhibits of this new museum presented traditional techniques in the arts, in architecture, and in crafts within a relevant cultural context. Later, in 1965, the institute established the Arawak Museum at White Marl in St. Catherine, at the largest Amerindian site yet discovered on the island. It was constructed in the octagonal shape of an Arawak house and was designed to interpret the prehistory of Jamaica, including aspects of the social, spiritual, and economic life of the Indian population. The museum was intended to be a prototype of similar interpretive centers to be established around the island. Both the Jamaica Peoples Museum and the Arawak Museum attempted to create a sense of identity among the local populace and to encourage a sense of national pride throughout a disparate community.

During the late 1960s, with the founding of various regional organizations, the concept of Caribbean unity again began to gain currency. Concern for conservation issues led to the formation of the Caribbean Conservation Association (CCA) in 1967. Conceived as a regional, nongovernmental organization to preserve and protect the islands' natural and man-made environments, the CCA was to act as a coordinator for technical assistance and as a persuasive lobbyist for action by various governments. In addition, the CCA wanted to serve as a link between governments, nongovernmental associations, and funding agencies. Part of the CCA's mandate was to help coordinate and assist the activities of trusts, governments, and private agencies on a regional basis. The influence of such a body was almost immediate, and by the end of the decade several new conservation bodies had been set up in the West Indies. The Grenada Trust was incorporated in 1967 by an act of legislation, followed closely in 1969 by the formation of a National Trust in Montserrat, in St. Vincent, and in the Grenadines.

However, despite this early success, there was little official support for the CCA during the first seven years of its existence until September 1974, when the government of Barbados became the first full member of the association. During the opening ceremony of the CCA Annual General Meeting in September 1976, Prime Minister Forbes Burnham of Guyana delivered an address calling, perhaps for the first time, for the safeguarding of the natural and cultural heritage of the Caribbean. Evidently influenced by the concerns expressed with increasing fervor by both African and Asian countries, he also called for the repatriation of materials of cultural and historical significance held outside the region and also expressed his belief that the CCA was the obvious body to coordinate these activities.

The CCA was also the facilitator for a major analysis of Caribbean museum development. In their report to the CCA, Canadian consultants found that most of the institutions visited were small, general in the scope of their exhibits, badly organized, understaffed, and inadequately financed. None of the institutions, with the exception of Barbados, had professionally qualified staff. They noted, however, that

> within recent years there had been a cultural reawakening and many of the island states in their development plans provided for the rehabilitation of existing museums, or the establishment of historical and natural history museums to complement the preservation and restoration of military monuments and forts, linked closely with the tourism strategy of the developing territories. [Lemieux and Schultz 1973:1]

In addition, this plan emphasized the need to encourage West Indian unity and to develop a closer working relationship between museums to maximize the use of available professional staff.

It was hoped that ultimately "a Caribbean Museums Association would be established to coordinate and develop regional programs at all levels and establish links with international museums associates" (Lemieux and Schultz 1973:2). One such effort to forge a regional museums association was developed by Dr. O. Marcus Buchanan, who sought the "reawakening of internal interest in the definition of our cultural and social interest [which] had demanded the establishment of institutions preservative of those elements which are indicative of that heritage" and felt that "the modern museum . . . must be considered a complementary adjunct to the educational and cultural resources of the community, not an organization competing against them" (Buchanan 1972:2). Throughout his career in the Caribbean, Dr. Buchanan encouraged the development of professional standards in West Indian museums. He struggled single-handedly to establish a network of museums, attempting to improve lines of communication between museums in the Caribbean and external organizations that might benefit the regional institutions. But with his death in 1976, this effort seemed largely unsuccessful.

Meanwhile, Jamaica maintained its lead in museum development. In 1972, the Institute of Jamaica assumed responsibility for all state cultural activities. It was the first Caribbean national institution to gain such prominence and responsibility, a fact reflected in a program of research designed to analyze museums and enable them to develop their potential in terms of the needs of the total Jamaican community. The National Gallery of Jamaica was established at Devon House in 1974 to house the institute's extensive Jamaican art collection and to highlight it as an important component of the national heritage. This was the first such institution to legitimize art in a Caribbean culture; it immediately became the major catalyst for the development of a distinctly *Jamaican* artistic language.

Caribbeanization

During the 1970s, the English-speaking Caribbean nations renewed their pursuit of a regional identity, primarily through economic cooperation in 1973 with the Caribbean Common Market (CARICOM). The earlier Caribbean Free Trade Association was replaced to coordinate trade among the member nations. A culture desk was established within CARICOM in 1976 and was given responsibility for planning and coordinating regional cultural festivals and advising client nations on cultural matters. During the period immediately following the formation of CARICOM, museum development consciously began to move in a different direction—though to what extent CARICOM was necessarily the vehicle for that change is still in question.

Another regional museum report was initiated by CARICOM in 1978. Dr. Raymond Singleton, a consultant for the United Nations Educational, Scientific, and Cultural Organization (UNESCO) saw the need for one or more regional centers attached to certain larger museums to provide technical aid and conservation work when required. Because of the unique situation in the Caribbean, Singleton felt that CARICOM as a "suitable, independent, central agency . . . should act as a clearinghouse for museum aid of all kinds" and "that the basic principle for the distribution of such aid should be the 'community value' of the institution concerned" (Singleton 1978:8). He was particularly sensitive to "the diversity of character between the various communities [as] one of the principle features of the Caribbean" and felt strongly that "any tendency to develop standardized, stereotyped museums should be resisted" (Singleton 1978:9). Rather, he recommended that each institution develop its own character in close relation to that of the community; and, while developing a number of activities and services to confirm its identity as a museum, "the form these should take should be allowed to depend very largely on local traditions, local needs, and local initiatives" (Singleton 1978:9).

Singleton also recognized the great importance attached to tourism in the region. He noted that tourists visiting the region would benefit considerably from viewing exhibits that focused on the diversity of cultures. Nevertheless, he was careful to stress that these institutions should be developed primarily to meet the needs of the local community, without catering exclusively to the interests of any of the specialist groups. Finally, he concluded:

> A virtue should therefore be made of diversity, encouraging each museum to develop its own highly individual character . . . each museum . . . should be strongly community-oriented, reflecting not only the complete history, but the character of the community it serves. In this way, the unique form of cultural contribution which only a museum can make is likely to be most effective and most readily understood, accepted, and valued locally. [Singleton 1978:10]

Following the Singleton report, CARICOM took the initiative in organizing the first Caribbean workshop on museums, monuments, and sites. Modern museum development took a major step forward when CARICOM made it a priority in the region's program of cultural cooperation. The program was devised to increase cultural awareness throughout the region and to promote the development of museums and the preservation of monuments and historic sites as important instruments of historical awareness and cultural identity. The significance of the workshop was that it marked the first "regional" consciousness of museums as catalysts and generators of culture and established, in some ways, the professional status of museum work.

The regional views of cultural development were presented by Mr. A. A. Moore, chief of the Education and Culture section of CARICOM. He noted that it was one of the essential components of national development. . . . [CARICOM] is convinced too that the region with its rich cultural heritage, reflecting strains and influences from almost every part of the world, has a great deal to gain from the promotion of education and information about and an appreciation and understanding of this heritage. [Moore 1978:1]

He noted the important role of museums, monuments, and sites in fostering national and regional identity. The need to establish a Caribbean museum association was emphasized. With the exception of Belize, no country had functioning legislation for the protection of cultural heritage. This heralded a significant change in the official attitude toward museums and gave them new credibility in the political community that had not previously existed.

During the 1970s, the trend toward self-government accelerated, and eventually smaller islands followed the example given by larger states. In 1974, Grenada led the way, gaining full independence. The other islands followed quickly: Dominica in 1978; St. Lucia, St. Vincent, and the Grenadines in 1979; Antigua in 1981; and St. Christopher (St. Kitts) and Nevis in 1983. The political creation of these micronations—combined with the impact of CARICOM—had considerable influence on contemporary museum development in the region and on the national pride they inspired in these newly independent island communities. In turn, this development was nurtured, and other nonindependent islands were influenced, including the St. Eustatius Museum (1974), the Museum of the Montserrat National Trust (1976), and the Eco Musée de Marie Galante, Guadeloupe (1980) (Figure 6.5).

By the 1980s, the leaders of the self-governing states were drawn primarily from the black working-class and middle-class majority. Independence brought a search for a positive national image and an independent society, in place of the British cultural image and the habit of colonial dependency. On the eve of St. Vincent's independence in 1978–1979, for example, Premier Milton Cato opened the first island museum devoted to its earliest inhabitants. Stressing the significance of cultural patrimony, he emphasized history as essential to the growth of a nation. A group of 40 Carib children from the Sandy Bay area joined in the ceremony; many of them had donated artifacts and considered it to be their museum. In St. Kitts, Premier Kennedy Simmonds paid similar attention to the role of a new museum at Fort George, Brimstone Hill.

Figure 6.5   Front facade of the Museum of the Montserrat National Trust. With kind permission from the Barbados Museum and Historical Society. Photograph by Alissandra Cummins.

The Institute of Jamaica underwent an extensive reorganization from 1976 to 1981. The Museum Division formulated a new national museum plan, which aimed at decentralizing the collections related to specific periods and events around the island. The plan was to be funded entirely by the government through its Ministry of Mobilization, Culture, and Information.

In 1982, the Jamaica National Gallery of Art was relocated from historic Devon House to a spacious, modern building in an urban development, New Kingston. The building, which was originally designed as a supermarket and business center, was acquired by the Institute of Jamaica to house its contemporary art and African collections and to provide space for new conservation and technical workshops.

In Barbados, Michael Chandler (1977), previously chief archivist, provided a critical analysis of the Barbados Museum that revealed many deficiencies in the staffing, exhibits, collections, and space. Overall, the museum was not fully representative of national history and culture. For the first time, both government and board gave full consideration to the role the Barbados Museum should play within the local community and beyond. In 1980, the minister of information and culture expressed concern that the Barbados Museum was "not really representative of the various aspects of Barbadian life" and that "while the collection tells the visitor a great deal about Barbadian merchants and planters, their life-style and their adoption of European material culture, it says little or nothing about slaves, plantation labourers or peasant farmers" (Barbados Museum and Historical Society 1982:2).

The collections focused attention "mainly on one segment of society and culture and therefore [did] not present a coherent or complete story of Barbados in history." A select committee was set up to examine these deficiencies and developed plans for the modification and improvement of the museum in all these areas. The government, in exchange, would supply the necessary funding for the museum to become "an instrument of national identity" and an institution "in the service of national development." This partnership spurred future cultural development and the museum by making it part of the national agenda.

In Trinidad, an initiative by Mrs. Sheila Solomon (the secretary-general of the Trinidad and Tobago National Commission for UNESCO) produced a UNESCO consultancy on museum development.

Between November 1976 and January 1977, Dr. Fernanda de Carmago de Almeida-Moro visited the country and prepared a report on its museums (de Carmago de Almeida-Moro 1977). She proposed plans for national museum development and advised on community outreach programs to reflect social awareness and change among the local people; she also gave advice on exhibit design and installation and recommended that legislation to protect cultural property be drafted. The government and the individuals involved in these activities expressed the developing role of the museum as a "centre for cultural dynamism [within] the community" (1977:2). She also proposed the establishment of a number of new facilities: (1) a living museum of festivals, music, and dance to highlight the importance of these activities among the local majority population; (2) a museum of agriculture in the Caroni area to give a basic understanding of the country's environment, ethnography, and natural history, as well as the development of agriculture in Trinidad; (3) a petroleum museum, illustrating the development of the refinery process from the early 20th century, as well as the transformation of society brought through petroleum development; and (4) the creation of a series of minimuseums at civic centers throughout the country to house temporary exhibits for the benefit of local communities.

One year later, in May 1978, the government of Trinidad took up one of Dr. de Carmago de Almeida-Moro's recommendations and requested that UNESCO provide a seminar: "Concepts of Cultural Heritage and Preservation." During the seminar, Minister of Education and Culture Cuthbert Joseph placed emphasis on the role of modern museums as "dynamic instruments of education, cultural activities, and interaction within communities" (UNESCO 1978:4). These discussions revealed the island's vulnerability, with regard to cultural destruction, because it lacked protective legislation for architectural and archaeological remains. Thus, for a short time, the stage was set for truly innovative museum development in Trinidad. Within five years, however, the bottom dropped out of the country's oil market, and its collapse heralded the disintegration of a dream (Figure 6.6).

In Guyana, similar attempts were made over the years to establish a national museum system. The Vincent Roth Museum of Archaeology was established; and under the able direction of Dr. Denis Williams, it housed the extensive archaeological and ethnographic collections of the Guyana National Museum. The Guyana National Museum itself now

Figure 6.6 Front facade of the Trinidad National Museum and Art Gallery (Originally, the Royal Victoria Institute). With kind permission from the Barbados Museum and Historical Society. Photograph by Alissandra Cummins.

concentrates almost exclusively on the natural history of the territory, although there are also small history exhibits.

In the decade following, three further museum reports were compiled, including Towle and Tyson (1979), Rivera and Soto Soria (1982), and Whiting (1983). In each case, the authors emphasized that the role of cultural-resource utilization in the overall insular development process had not yet been fully recognized or defined by Caribbean nations. Cultural development could also promote " a sense of pride, self-esteem and national identity that will help the people of developing nations overcome the debilitating sense of cultural inferiority and dependency induced by colonialism and slavery" (Towle and Tyson 1979:9).

The lack of professional curatorial and technical staff was identified as a major deficiency, as was the need for professional training at all levels. Creating a viable information network was regarded as a priority, so was ongoing professional contact with other museum colleagues; and the exchange of curatorial advice and technical assistance, it was emphasized, could be done most effectively if a regional association of museums were established. This idea finally became reality with the formation of the Museums Association of the Caribbean (MAC) in 1989. The establishment of regional conservation and training centers was regarded as essential for resources to be shared most efficiently. In the final analysis, all consultants identified that the key to further improvement and strengthening was greater governmental participation in museum activities—incorporating museums into the educational and cultural machinery as part of the national-development plans of each country.

Every report has recognized that museums, as contributors to the foundation of national development, should form linkages with education and tourism, with a carefully balanced orientation. That they have something of great value to offer in both areas is a concept yet to be fully accepted by various island governments, although the words are mouthed on appropriate public occasions. The refrain of informal educational and cultural tourism resounds whenever museums are mentioned. Yet, while it may be accepted in principle, there has clearly been very little done to put it into practice. Even though, for most of these governments, departments of education and tourism remain the greatest priorities, with the largest designated budgets within the development process, museums and historic sites are consistently relegated solely to culture and are generally given the smallest budgets in the various governments. Nevertheless, the linkage of cultural activity with national identity and independence, and with tourism and development, continues to have important ramifications for the Caribbean today. Each country in the region has sought to incorporate a cultural-development policy in its overall national-development strategy; but all too often, the policy option chosen has been one of "cultural tourism," in an attempt to justify future investment with an economically viable solution, while at the same time facilitating integration within the region. Nettleford (1988) suggests that, "at best this speaks to our cultural pluralist texture of which we are, indeed, proud. At worst it reinforces the lack of confidence in what we ourselves have created for ourselves and panders to the perception of a glamorous paradise" (1988).

The authors of museum reports have recognized that museum establishment and development have been the realm primarily of private, nonprofit organizations, resulting in benign indifference on the part of the governments. While some of the oldest and largest institutions in Guyana, Trinidad, and Jamaica have become government institutions, this does not necessarily guarantee any greater share of national resources. Jamaica, however, seems to have benefitted from the sympathetic interest of Prime Minister Michael Manley at important periods in its development: that is, 1976–1981 and to the present. Nevertheless, this interest has unwittingly served to politicize the cultural-development process; and ambitious plans for a new home for the National Gallery of Jamaica have become the target of bitter attack by the opposition.

In her article, "How Sweet It Is: Cultural Politics in Barbados," Jeanne Cannizzo examined the role of museums as "symbolic structures which make visible our public myths" (1987:22). Her analysis of the process is that museums as "visual ideologies, are expressive of a relatively coherent [cultural] system of ideas, values, beliefs etc." (1987:22). Her exploration of the Barbados Museum's redefinition of local culture may be used, to a greater or lesser extent, to see a pattern of museum development in the other English-speaking islands. While Caribbean museums were often active agents in shaping identity, they have, until recently, expropriated culture, using it on behalf of the ruling classes to achieve "self-definition by majority exclusion" (Cannizzo

1987:23). She reflects that, "by not displaying the cultural heritage of the majority of the population, the museum has taken from them, by implication, their role as history makers, as active participants of their own past" (1987:24).

How is this bias and imbalance to be corrected? Cannizzo suggests that, while we may disagree with the government's interventionist policy, in which popular sentiment is manipulated, the Barbados government's initiative might be viewed as a kind of cultural affirmative action, by which people assert their cultural independence or restore a collective heritage. Changes in exhibit interpretation present Barbados as a pluralistic society, "a present growing out of its past and history is not based solely on dates and objects but on meanings." Throughout the museum, black culture is shown as worthy of serious museological investigation and display (Cannizzo 1987:25, 26). In this way, the museum acknowledges and legitimizes Caribbean culture, making visible what was once a hidden past. The museum serves a number of functions in the Caribbean, where popular culture was for centuries alienated from officialdom. At this time—when a Pan-Caribbean political ideology remains in its infancy—regional museums, through the process described above, may do much to help the Caribbean community to adjust to far-reaching social, economic, political, and cultural trans-formations.

References

Acworth, A.
  1951 *Buildings of Architectural or Historic Interest in the West Indies: A Report.* Colonial Research Studies, 2. London: HMSO.
Barbados Museum and Historical Society
  1982 *Final Report of the Museum of Development Plan Committee.* Unpublished Report, Barbados.
Bather, F. A., and T. Sheppard
  1933 *The Museums of the British West Indies: Report on the Museums of Ceylon, British Malaya, The West Indies etc. to the Carnegie Corporation of New York.* S. F. Mark, ed. Pp. 27–58. London: The Museums Association.
Beckles, H.
  1990 *A History of Barbados: From Amerindian Settlement to a Nation-State.* Cambridge: Cambridge University Press.

Bermuda Law
1843 An Act To Establish a Public Library in This Island. 1843. *Laws of Bermuda.*

Buchanan, O. Marcus
1972 Personal Correspondence to M. Harif, Caribbean Conservation Association. May 1972.

Cannizzo, J.
1987 How Sweet It Is: Cultural Politics in Barbados. *Muse* 4(4):22–26.

de Carmago de Almeida-Moro, Fernanda
1977 *Development of Museums in Trinidad and Tobago.* Paris: UNESCO (FMR/CC/CH/77/192).

Chandler, M.
1977 *Status Report on the Barbados Museum.* Unpublished Report, Barbados Museum.

Clough, L. W.
1956 Culture and Federation. *Bajan Magazine* 3(12):22–31.

Fewkes, J. W.
1907 *The Aborigines of Puerto Rico and Neighbouring Islands.* Annual Report 25. Washington, D.C.: Bureau of American Ethnology.

Jamaica Law
1864 Act for the Establishment of the Royal Society of Arts and Agriculture. *Laws of Jamaica* ACT 27 Victoria, Cap 22.

Lemieux, L., and H. Schultz
1973 *Report on Caribbean Museums.* Bridgetown, Barbados: Caribbean Conservation Association.

Lewis, G. K.
1968 *The Growth of the Modern West Indies.* New York: Monthly Review Press.

Moore, A. A.
1978 *Introduction to the Report on the CARICOM Workshop on Museums, Monuments and Sites.* Guyana: CARICOM.

Moyne, Lord
1945 *Report of the West India Royal Commission.* London: H.M.S.O., Cmd. 6607.

Natural History Society of British Guiana
1863 *Proceedings of the Natural History Society of British Guiana.* Georgetown, British Guiana.

Nettleford, R.
1988 Cultural Identity. 4th Conference of Commonwealth Arts Administrators. April 25, 1988. Barbados.

Reid, W.
1839 Private Communication to Normanby. July 12, 1839. *Public Records Office* (C.O. 37/101). London.

Rivera, R., and A. Soto Soria
   1982 *Museum Development in English-Speaking Caribbean Countries. Report of the Mission.* Washington, D.C.: OAS.
Roth, V.
   1953 *The British Guiana Museum of the Royal Agricultural and Commercial Society: Centenary History and Guide.* Georgetown, British Guiana: The British Guiana Museum.
Singleton, R.
   1978 *Museums in the Caribbean: Their Immediate Needs and Their Suggested Objectives.* Guyana: CARICOM.
Smith, T.
   1976 Without Revolutionary Theory. *Studio International* 191:134–137.
Towle, E. L., and G. F. Tyson
   1979 *Towards a Planning Strategy for the Management of Historical/Cultural Resources Critical to Development in the Lesser Antilles. A Concept Paper.* U.S. Virgin Islands.: Island Resources Foundation.
UNESCO
   1978 *Concepts of Cultural Heritage and Preservation—A Report on the Trinidad and Tobago Government Seminar, May 8–12, 1978.* St. Augustine, Trinidad: University of the West Indies.
Whiting, J.
   1983 Museum-Focused Heritage in the English-Speaking Caribbean. *UNESCO Technical Report 1981–1983/4/7/.* June 4, 1983. Paris.

7 Nostalgia for a Gilded Past? Museums in Minas Gerais, Brazil

J.P. Dickenson

The increasing importance of preserving the past is becoming commonplace, at least in the developed world. In the case of the United Kingdom, Robert Hewison could envisage the whole country becoming one vast museum, in which the "heritage industry," producing heritage as a commodity, had begun to supersede the manufacture of industrial goods (Hewison 1987). While that might be a deliberately exaggerated view, the preservation of the past, in which museums are an integral element, is undoubtedly a growing activity. The geographer David Lowenthal has suggested that awareness of the past is essential to the maintenance of life, offering a sense of continuity and knowledge of causality and of our own identity (Lowenthal 1979:103). Similarly, at a United Nations Educational, Scientific, and Cultural Organization (UNESCO) conference on conservation, the architect Graeme Shankland talked of the "almost magical power of the past," not merely in terms of beauty but of the identity that preserved items confer; he asserted that "a country without a past has the emptiness of a barren continent" (Shankland 1975:25–27). Such views have clear Eurocentric perspectives and are part of well-established European, and latterly North American, concerns with the past and its retention.

Lowenthal notes a universal in the impulse to preserve that includes communist and capitalist countries, former imperialist powers, and newly independent states. One may ask if such impulses are consistent around the world, particularly outside Europe and North America, in their strength and objectives. In Lowenthal's view, the aims and force of preservation may be specific to national and local circumstances. Increasing numbers of people share a concern with their various national

heritages, but differing impulses may animate the preservation movement in different places (Lowenthal 1981:12).

In the present chapter, I seek to explore the relevance of these views
of the role of the past to a developing country: Brazil. I appraise the
contribution of museums to the creation and sustenance of identity at
the subnational level, in the state of Minas Gerais.

Early Museums

Brazil's first museum, the Museu Nacional, was established in Rio de
Janeiro in 1818. It holds claim to being the oldest museum in Latin
America and is derived from collections of natural history intended to be
sent to Lisbon by the Portuguese viceroy (Lopes 1992:193). It developed
a heterogeneous collection in botany, zoology, mineralogy, and geology,
and in anthropology and ethnology. The second, the Museu do Instituto
Arqueológico, Histórico e Geografico de Pernambuco, in Recife, was
not founded until 1862, followed by others in Pará and Bahia in 1883
and 1894, respectively (Carrazzoni 1972). Many of these early museums
originated as private collections made by intellectuals, clerics, and rich
businessmen and were given to or acquired by public authorities. They
contained material from the natural environment, from Brazilian culture,
and from the country's European heritage. The Instituto do Patrimônio
Histórico e Artistico Nacional (IPHAN) was created in 1937 to protect
those elements of the national historic and artistic heritage whose
conservation was deemed to be in the public interest, elements that
included material relevant to Brazil's history or of exceptional archaeological, ethnographic, bibliographic, or artistic merit (Carrazzoni
1987:11). The preservation of historic buildings saw the establishment of
several regional museums, which combined listed buildings with
collections of historic and artistic material. These included the Museu da
Inconfidência (1938) and the Museu do Ouro (1945) in Minas Gerais,
and Museu das Missões (1940) in Rio Grande do Sul. Art museums were
founded in São Paulo in 1947 and in Rio de Janeiro in 1950. In
recognition of the role of European immigration in Brazil, museums of
colonization were established in Santa Catarina in 1957 and 1970 and in
Espírito Santo in 1968. There were in total, by 1985, a recorded 895
museums in the country: 129 administrated by the federal government,

282 by states, 264 by municipalities, and 220 privately owned (IBGE 1991). The principal concentrations are to be found in the states of São Paulo and Rio de Janeiro, followed by Bahia and Minas Gerais.

Museums in Minas Gerais

Minas Gerais is the fourth-largest and second-most-populous state in Brazil. It was settled relatively late in the period of Portuguese colonial rule, following the discovery of gold in the final decade of the 17th century. These riches, together with the later discovery of diamonds, sustained what Charles R. Boxer called "the golden age" of Brazil, from 1695 to 1750 (Boxer 1962). The gold and gems generated great wealth for the Portuguese Crown and for Minas Gerais. A contemporary commentator described the province as "the head of the whole of America" and "the precious pearl of Brazil" (quoted in Boxer 1962:163).

The prospect of sudden affluence drew migrants from other parts of Brazil and from Portugal, creating the first substantial area of settlement in the interior. The population became a mixture of Paulistas (migrants from São Paulo who had first discovered the gold), Portuguese immigrants, Indians, and African slaves brought in as mine laborers. By the end of the 18th century, there were possibly 500,000 inhabitants and, in contrast to many other gold-rush areas, a firm urban base developed: 14 settlements had been given town (*vila*) status, and Mariana was created a city in 1745, providing one of the earliest urban societies in Brazil, with an elite of government officials, successful miners, clergy, and prosperous merchants.

The wealth from gold and diamonds fostered striking civic and religious architecture in such towns as Mariana, Ouro Prêto, Sabará, and Diamantina. This gave 18th-century Minas Gerais a unique cultural standing in Brazil, based on its architecture, sculpture, art, literature, and music (Barata 1968:6). The Roman Catholic church made a significant contribution to this status, deriving from religious fervor and from endowments made by successful miners for building and embellishing churches. Rivalry between towns and their religious brotherhoods prompted the building of numerous elegant churches, particularly in the baroque and rococo styles distinctive to Minas Gerais.

The province was the scene of the first significant protest against

Portuguese colonialism, the Inconfidência Mineira of 1789, a protest that was inspired by the ideas of the French and American Enlightenment and prompted by threats of higher taxation at a time of falling gold production and revenue. Though it aimed to declare a republic, it was essentially a localized Mineiro conspiracy involving Brazilian-born bureaucrats, clerics, intellectuals, landowners, and soldiers. The plot was discovered and its ringleaders executed, serving to create Brazilian martyrs and a sense of regional identity.

Minas Gerais was also involved in Brazil's achievement of independence in 1822, which drew inspiration from the Enlightenment and from the achievement of independence in most of Spanish America about this time. Along with São Paulo and Rio de Janeiro, Minas Gerais gave support to the prince regent. The Portuguese court had been resident in Brazil from 1808 to 1821, in exile from the Napoleonic invasion of Portugal, with Rio de Janeiro as the capital of the empire. Following the return of the king to Lisbon, it was his son, left behind as regent, who declared independence against economic and political pressures from Lisbon.

However, by the early 19th century, the state's precious mineral resources were exhausted, and its economy stagnated, depending mainly on cattle and coffee. In the 20th century, more prosaic minerals, particularly iron ore, have stimulated industrialization, to make Minas Gerais again one of Brazil's most prosperous states.

Museums in Minas Gerais

The state of Minas Gerais currently has some 50 museums (Quatro Rodas 1991), including historical, economic, and archaeological museums, fine- and sacred-art museums, as well as institutions linked to significant figures in the history, politics, and culture of the state (Figure 7.1). They are variously administrated. Some "regional" museums, mainly those housed in listed buildings, are administrated by the IPHAN; others by the state Secretaria do Estado da Cultura; still others belong to federal agencies, local government, universities, the Catholic church, trusts, and private groups.

Most Mineiro museums appear to be impoverished. Their buildings are often in a poor state of repair and their displays "old-fashioned,"

Figure 7.1 Map of Minas Gerais, showing location and nature of each of its museums. Map by Sandra Mather and John Dickenson.

offering limited contextual information. Few museums provide details about the nature, purpose, and origin of their collections. Labeling is often minimal, limited to an adjacent typewritten notice giving the title and sometimes the date and provenance. Staffing is modest, frequently comprised of only a doorperson or ticket seller and a security guard; there is rarely evidence of a curatorial presence. Most museums levy a small entrance charge. They usually ban photography, but the reason for doing so is unclear since few museums have postcards or slide sales to protect, and guidebooks and informative brochures are uncommon.

The museums of Minas Gerais fall into four specific categories, leaving a fifth more heterogeneous residual group. The most distinctive category is that of the museums of religious art, or *arte sacra*. The gold boom stimulated the florescence of what Boxer described as "a peculiar

Mineiro civilization" (Boxer 1962:162), expressed and preserved in the rich baroque churches and public and private buildings in the towns of Ouro Prêto, Mariana, São João del Rei, Congonhas do Campo, Serro, Diamantina, and others. The townscapes themselves are, perhaps, the most important "museums" in the state, dominated by the plethora of churches. Besides distinctive architecture, the religious exuberance generated by gold also sustained a great output of decorative art and ecclesiastical artifacts. These works are the basis of the collections of the museums of *arte sacra*—statues in wood, clay, and soapstone of Christ, the Virgin Mary, and a host of saints; together with oratories, ex-votos, altar plates, processional crosses and banners, reliquaries, vestments, and occasionally pulpits and other items of church furniture. These specialized museums in Ouro Prêto, Mariana, Sabará, São João del Rei, and Santo Antônio do Monte provide rich, even lavish, collections of the flowering of colonial Catholic art.

The prosperity of the 18th century sustained not only rich religious architecture and artifacts but also distinguished artists, of whom the best known is Antônio Francisco Lisboa (1738–1814), usually referred to as "Aleijadinho" or "Little Cripple" because his hands were deformed by disease, thought to have been leprosy. Work by or attributed to him is found in several Mineiro museums, especially in the Aleijadinho and Inconfidência Museums in Ouro Prêto (Figure 7.2). The finest examples of his work, however, are in the extraordinary life-size *Stations of the Cross* and the terrace of Old Testament prophets at Congonhas do Campo (Figure 7.3). Religious art also makes significant contributions to most of the historical museums and to the three IPHAN regional museums at Caeté, São João del Rei, and the Inconfidência. Such material, along with austere domestic furniture of the colonial period and the 19th century, forms the bulk of the displays. The state's "historical" collections tend to be limited in both artifacts and time to the 18th and 19th centuries, to religious art, and to domestic furnishings.

"Economic" museums are a distinctive type of Mineiro museum. There are more than a dozen such museums, and the most important are those linked to the state's mineral resources. These are essentially geological collections, containing a diversity of rocks, crystals, gems, and mineral ores. However, few make any real attempt to link their displays to the state's economic history or current development, and they commonly include an admixture of specimens from other parts of

Figure 7.2 The Inconfidência Museum, Ouro Prêto, Brazil. Photograph by J. P. Dickenson.

Figure 7.3   Statue of a prophet by Aleijadinho, Congonhas do Campo. Photograph by J. P. Dickenson.

Figure 7.4   The Gold Museum, Sabará. Photograph by J. P. Dickenson.

Brazil and abroad. Only the Museu do Ouro (the Gold Museum) at Sabará relates specifically to the gold-mining era (Figure 7.4); and it includes displays of geology, gold products, and equipment. Other museums are devoted to iron- and tin-working.

Of particular interest with regard to the state's economic development are three railway museums that, administered by Brazil's railway corporation, the Rede Ferroviária Federal S.A., form part of a nationwide net of a dozen transportation museums. Those at São João del Rei and Belo Horizonte have displays of high quality, being well maintained and providing a good context of railway history—internationally, in Brazil, and in Minas Gerais—for a range of artifacts (Figure 7.5). A great deal of historical railway material was destroyed when steam traction was abandoned in Brazil as elsewhere, so that most of these collections consist of station and permanent way materials. The São João del Rei Museu do Trem includes a roundhouse with a dozen steam locomotives from the period 1889–1923 and other rolling stock;

Figure 7.5   The Historical Museum, Belo Horizonte. Photograph by J. P. Dickenson.

and it maintains an active steam link to the town of Tiradentes, 12 km away (Figure 7.6).

Tiradentes takes its name from Joaquim José da Silva Xavier (known as Tiradentes or 'toothpuller'), the leader of the Inconfidência rebellion against Portuguese rule in 1789 (Figure 7.7). The remains of Tiradentes' house is a historic, listed building, and that of Padre Toledo, another rebel, is a museum to the revolt. Similarly, the house of Padre Rolim, a third conspirator, forms the Museu do Diamante at Diamantina, which, despite its associations and name, is a heterogeneous collection of minerals, furniture, porcelain, and religious art. The most important link with the rebellion is the Museu da Inconfidência at Ouro Prêto, which contains an austere pantheon of the rebels. This museum was established in 1938 to house items connected with the revolt, together with works of art or of historical value relevant to the formation of the state of Minas Gerais. Besides the remains of the rebels executed in 1792, the museum contains documents relating to the rebellion, religious artwork

Figure 7.6 Steam locomotives in the roundhouse, Museu do Trem, São João del Rei. Photograph by J. P. Dickenson

Figure 7.7   Likeness of "Tiradentes" (Joaquim José da Silva Xavier). Reproduced from *Historia Geral do Brazil* (5th edition), F. A. de Varnhagen, 1956.

Figure 7.8 Drawing of the passing of sentence on the Inconfidência rebels, April 19, 1792, by Leopoldino de Faria. Reproduced from *Historia Geral do Brazil* (5th edition), F. A. de Varnhagen, 1956.

collected by the local archbishop, and furniture from the late 18th and early 19th centuries. (Figure 7.8).

Such collections, devoted to important figures in the history and culture of the state, constituted a third major group of museums, located mainly in the birthplaces of "favorite sons." They include the novelist Guimaraes Rosa (1908–1967) at Cordisburgo; the pioneer aviator Santos Dumont (1873–1932), whose birthplace also now bears his name; and Carlos Chagas (1879–1934), a medical pioneer, at Oliveira. Three Mineiros who have become presidents of the nation also merit personal museums—Wenceslau Bras (president from 1914 to 1918) at Itajubá;

Juscelino Kubitschek (1956–1961) at Diamantina; and Tancredo Neves (1985) at São João del Rei. Neves was Brazil's first democratically elected president after 20 years of military rule, and the museum devoted to him is the newest and most impressive in the state. Neves' long involvement in Brazilian politics, his symbolic role in the return to democracy, and his premature death make him a particularly significant figure in the country's recent political history. The museum, in his birthplace, stands in marked contrast to most others in the state. It is jointly funded by the government, a multinational company, and a trust; it is well staffed and offers a wide range of literature and facilities. It uses contemporary display techniques to portray Neves' life in memorabilia, photographs, press cuttings, posters, and recordings.

These four basic categories, sacred art, historical and regional, economic, and personal museums, account for four-fifths of the collections conserved in Minas Gerais. The remaining dozen museums are heterogeneous. They include art and natural-history museums in Belo Horizonte; an archaeological museum at Lagoa Santa; a colonial mint at Ouro Prêto; two municipal museums at Sete Lagoas and São Sebastião do Paraíso, respectively; and a commemorative museum to Brazil's involvement in World War II, at São João del Rei.

The strengths of the Mineiro museums, as repositories of past and of regional identity, lie in their collections of historical and religious artifacts from the heyday of the gold-mining period under the Portuguese. They provide evidence of the state's rich natural-resource base and of the adulation of its favorite sons. Conversely, one may ask, What are the weaknesses of the state's museums? What is missing? Aside, that is, from the gender bias of the museums of personality, with women conspicuous by their absence; this phenomenon may be noted in the patriarchal museums of Europe as well (Horne 1984:4). It is only in the museums of *arte sacra*, in statuary of the Virgin Mary and the saints, that women are much in evidence in Mineiro museums.

There is little reference to the precolonial past in the existing museums. Although Brazil sustained no advanced civilizations, such as those in Mesoamerica and the Andes, Minas Gerais was the site of some of the earliest identified settlements in Latin America, dating from at least 10,000 years B.P. The largest public display of the latter materials is essentially in the private collection of an individual archaeologist at Lagoa Santa. It is adjacent to the limestone caves from which the artifacts and human remains were collected. The display gives some explanation of the region's prehistory and of the pioneering excavations carried out by the 19th-century Danish archaeologist Peter Lund. However, a symptom of the disregard for the precolonial past is that many of the limestone knolls in this area are being excavated to feed the local cement industry. As the Mineiro poet Carlos Drummond de Andrade observed in a centenary tribute to Peter Lund, "Minas Gerais sold its soul to development and cast aside its prehistory" (Drummond de Andrade 1974). In Belo Horizonte, the Natural History Museum has some archaeological material, but its relationship to the human development in the region is scarcely explored. Although a few Indian groups survive in Minas Gerais, there is little reference to the contemporary Indian population; and the museum devotes only a single small room to the Maxacali tribe, whose territory, on the Minas Gerais-Bahia border is now threatened by outsiders invading their land.

Contemporary Issues in Minas Gerais Museums

In recent years, ethnocultural displays in museums in Britain and North America have provoked considerable controversy (Fulford 1991; Ramamurthy 1990). In Minas Gerais, black slaves were a major labor source in gold and diamond mining; and in 1980, "blacks" and "browns" (as defined by the Census) constituted 40% of the state's population (IBGE 1981:350). However, neither the past not the present of this segment of the population is made apparent in the state's museums. There is little reference to slavery (and there are very few artifacts, such as shackles from the period). It might be argued that, by its very nature, slavery generates few heirlooms among its victims. It is also perhaps significant that few of the displays relating to the colonial artist Aleijadinho reveal that he was the mulatto son of a black slave woman. An exception to this silence is the Museu de Arte Sacra do Carmo in Ouro Prêto. This museum suggests that the emergence by miscegenation of a free mulatto middle class sustained the province's intense architectural and artistic ferment of the 18th century and had neither the preconceptions of the whites nor the constraints imposed upon black slaves (Museu de Arte Sacra do Carmo 1987:5). There is, however, little evidence of the nonwhite population in post-emancipation Minas Gerais. The Mineiro museums offer little relating to Indians, Africans, or women. There are few "prehistoric" materials from before 1700, and few exhibits from the periods of the Empire (1822–1889) and the Republic (1889 to the present). Mineiro museum collections are "urban" in derivation, and there is little evidence of the important rural dimensions of the state's history and economy.

The museums and collections of Minas Gerais define the identity of the state narrowly—beginning circa 1700, terminating largely before 1920. The emphasis is strongly on the colonial period and upon the religious past.

In addition to the nature of what items are contained within museums and what they say about the past and identity, a further crucial issue, in a country such as Brazil, is the geographical distribution of museums. Boylan (1990) emphasizes the role of "national" museums in cultural identity. But can such museums wield the same influence in a subcontinent the size of Brazil or China as that in a small nation like Costa Rica or Qatar? The query is compounded in the Brazilian case by the fact that most national cultural institutions—the National Library, the National Archives, and the National Museums of History, Natural History, and Fine Arts—are in Rio de Janeiro, more than three decades after the national capital was shifted to Brasília. What is the impact of such institutions when they are located in a single city but are in a country with 8.5 million sq km and 150 million inhabitants. Accessibility is clearly a fundamental constraint, as is cost of travel and entrance fee, relevant in a country with a low per capita income. The last available national figures for museums, for 1985, record 20 million museum visitors, of which one-quarter were schoolchildren (IBGE 1991:218). The role of designated national museums in cultural identity may be limited in a country the size of Brazil, and those of regional status may be of greater significance. In the case of Brazil, with five macroregions and 27 states, the locus of identity-creating functions may well be at the state level. Yet as the present case study indicates, provisions may be modest and spatially constrained, even at this level.

Minas Gerais has a territory of 586,000 sq km, but 70% of its museums are within 150 km of the state capital, Belo Horizonte. The remainder are scattered across the southern part of the state, with only one, at Januária, in the poorer and much less developed northern half

(230,000 sq km). Only 30 of the state's 720 *municipios* (the basic administrative unit, akin to U.S. counties) have museums; and in most cases these are lone institutions. Only three centers, Belo Horizonte, founded in 1897, and the gold-mining towns of Ouro Prêto and São João del Rei have significant "museum industries."

Belo Horizonte has seven museums, including several ostensibly of statewide importance, but their contents are modest, their presentations limited, and their state of repair poor. The Museu Histórico is housed in the only surviving (and heavily restored) building that predates the founding of the city, has a small collection of furniture, and contains maps and aerial photographs of the city at various dates. It is surrounded by a yard holding a miscellany of objects: an old locomotive, religious statuary, an early elevator, and a model of the village that preceded the planned city. The Museu Mineiro (Minas Museum) is limited to sacred art and temporary exhibitions. The Museu de História Natural is similarly poorly housed and contains a geological collection, pickled fauna, and limited archaeological materials. The significance of these faunal specimens is unexplained; neither their provenance in nor their relevance to Minas Gerais are given. The Museu de Arte has similarly modest collections, but it is at least housed in one of Brazil's few 20th-century listed buildings. It was designed by the distinguished architect Oscar Niemeyer and was set in elegant gardens created by Roberto Burle Marx. Other museums in the city are dedicated to minerals, to railways, and to the telephone.

Two former mining towns have good collections of museums. Both towns are closely tied to the prosperity of colonial gold mining and to their religious past. In Ouro Prêto the Museu da Inconfidência provides a sense of the province's colonial history. It played a role, albeit abortive, in the independence movement. It also plays the most overt role in trying to articulate Mineiro identity. Other museums are dedicated to silver, the artist Aleijadinho, numismatics, and sacred art; they are associated in various ways with the colonial period, particularly with the religious art fostered by the gold boom. The Museu de Arte Sacra do Carmo is probably the most impressive of its type, with extensive displays and a serious attempt to explain the general evolution of the Mineiro baroque style and the details of its various displays of altar ware, religious paintings and statuary, processional crosses, and vestments.

São João del Rei is less exploited by tourism than Ouro Prêto but retains a number of colonial streets, churches, and secular buildings. With its museums, it offers a microcosm of the state's history. The Museu de Arte Sacra is smaller than that at Ouro Prêto, but it is similarly presented. The Museu Regional also contains religious art, but its collections of domestic furniture, agricultural implements, and early-20th-century equipment from the town's industries give a broader and more in-depth perspective of local history. In addition, the Railway and Tancredo Neves Museums also provide more extended contexts for railway history on an international, national, and regional scale, in the former case, and of state and national politics, in the latter. The Museu dos Ex-Combatentes (temporarily closed in 1991) records Brazil's participation in the Italian campaign of World War II. It memorializes the losses sustained by a regiment raised in the town.

Outside these three centers, museums are relatively few in number, limited in range, and constrained in subject. In the case of towns with a single institution, museums of *arte sacra* focus essentially on the colonial era, while the economic museums are linked to local economic activities. The museums associated with famous personalities are also essentially locally oriented. Even museums categorized as "miscellaneous" frequently have particular local roots; and only two towns boast small municipal museums that seek to portray the local community. It is only in the half dozen settlements that have historical museums that there are at least modest efforts at offering a broader sense of regional history and society. Thus, despite being a major state in terms of size, population, and prosperity, Minas Gerais must be viewed as deficient in the number, location, content, and quality of its museums. In such circumstances, the efficacy of museums in fostering cultural identity at the subnational or regional level must be questioned.

While Boylan suggests that a national museum ranks with a national defense force, a broadcasting system, and a university as a vital instrument for the creation of national identity, this ranking presupposes judgment and policy about what a museum should contain and what images it should present (Boylan 1990). In the case of Brazil, 170 years of independence seem to have made this less relevant. In addition, sheer territorial size diminishes the impact of any such national institution. The possible contribution of museums to national identity via some hierarchical or spatially diffuse structure of "official" museums requires a degree of planning and manipulation not evident in Brazilian public policy. For example, the Museu Histórico Nacional in Rio de Janeiro, administrated by IPHAN and the Ministry of Education and Culture, has declared as its role the collection, preservation, conservation, study, and display of historic and artistic objects linked to national history—a fairly bland and universal statement of the role of any museum (Carrazzoni 1972:51).

In the absence of a strategy at a subnational level, the Minas Gerais experience suggests a similarly amorphous and uncoordinated structure. Museums have various specialties, often with local roots and a diversity of administration. There is certainly a lack of any coordinated structure to make museums part of public education and accessible to the whole population.

Within the context of the developed world's views about the significance of the past and the role of the museum, the Mineiro museums' endowment raises a series of broad questions. Various authors cited above emphasize the importance of the preserved past in defining identity. Horne, for example, suggests that museums help people define who they are and what matters in the world (Horne 1984:2). If so, contemporary influence on Mineiro museums is piecemeal and partial.

In the case of Third World countries, the nature of the past has particular qualities, since it encompasses a colonial experience, which is often viewed negatively by an independent nation. Lowenthal suggests that countries freeing themselves from colonial rule, whether in the distant past, in the case of the United States, or more recently, in the case of African and some Asian countries, seek to erase the colonial experience and try to find an autonomous national identity in the precolonial past (Lowenthal 1976:89). Moreover, former colonial powers have in recent years come under pressure to reappraise their representations of the past, especially those related to imperialism (Cannizzo 1991; Ramamurthy 1990). However, this is not the case with the museums in Minas Gerais, since their predominant strength and focus is the colonial period.

Minas Gerais' colonial inheritance, in which gold provided the wealth and the Catholic faith the inspiration, sustained a period of great cultural and artistic activity in the 18th century. This linkage between affluence, the church, and fine art is of particular significance, in that artifacts designed to embellish religious buildings or to be used in church services subsequently also became the country's artistic treasures, to be preserved. Several museums of sacred art have as their nuclei collections from diocesan or archdiocesan sources. The churches were an integral part of the colonial townscape; and as a consequence of the economic stagnation of the 19th century, these towns survived with few modifications. Their aesthetic merits were eventually recognized and preserved. IPHAN was responsible for designating large tracts of Ouro Prêto, Mariana, Diamantina, and other old mining towns for conservation from modernization and economic "progress."

Moreover, Minas Gerais was a pioneer in Brazil's preservationist movement. There were efforts to record the state's architectural and cultural treasures as early as the 1790s. In the 20th century, the loss of pieces of sacred art and colonial furniture to other states and overseas prompted the state government to establish in 1925 a commission, which included clergymen, politicians, historians, and others, to seek ways of protecting the Mineiro heritage (Andrade 1969:24–25). The Mineiro initiative contributed to the creation of IPHAN, and this agency was then responsible for protecting the colonial townscapes and historic buildings and for converting them into museums. The act of designation serves to define identity, because what is designated both is protected and acquires status. In 1938, legislation creating the Museu da Inconfidência specified that it should collect materials from the time of the conspiracy and of later events that contributed "to the formation of Minas Gerais." Seven years later, the Museu do Ouro in Sabará was designated to collect material related to gold mining, referring not only to its evolution and technology but to the influence of gold "on the economic development and social formation of Minas Gerais and all Brazil" (Ministerio da Educação e Cultura-DPHAN 1967:59, 63).

The preponderance of an essentially colonial heritage in Brazil may truly reflect the fundamental richness of that inheritance and its preservation. But there may be additional factors. After the gold was exhausted, the Mineiro economy stagnated, and there was no cultural legacy in the 19th century to match that of the colonial period. One commentator saw the period from 1850–1940 in Minas Gerais as one of cultural inertia. In architecture there was no significant progress: "They were a hundred years of paralysis" (Vasconcelos 1970:208–209). Not only did the early years of independence seemingly fail to stimulate cultural progress in Minas Gerais, but the way in which independence was achieved in Brazil may have mitigated the anticolonial sentiments identified by Lowenthal in the United States and, more recently, in independent states in Africa and Asia. In contrast to events in most of Spanish America, Brazil's independence was achieved without violence. After the Portuguese court returned to Lisbon in 1821, it was the prince regent who declared independence—against attempts by Portugal's Parliament to reimpose colonial status upon Brazil. There was little opposition to this declaration in Brazil, and the regent and his son ruled as emperors of independent Brazil until 1889, when it became a republic. The continuity and the absence of a violent overthrow of Portuguese rule and influence served to dilute any rejection of the colonial cultural legacy.

For Minas Gerais, with its three centuries of history, the gold boom represented the heyday of economic prosperity and the creation of a rich and distinctive culture. The Inconfidência was, in a modest way, a gesture toward regional independence and identity; it remains a source of Mineiro pride. A significant legacy of those times is preserved in the conservation areas, the listed buildings, and the state's museums. Hints of the nostalgia for this period are to be seen in the incorporation of features of colonial architecture in the modern residences of the affluent. The neocolonial style is as evident in the modern urban scene in Minas Gerais as the neo-Georgian is in England or the Spanish-colonial revival is in the southwestern United States.

This Mineiro colonial legacy may also have a wider significance. It has been argued that its emergence in the interior, funded by the wealth from gold and created by a mixture of immigrant peoples—from Portugal, from other parts of Brazil, and from Africa—represented the first flowering of a distinctive and autonomous Brazilian culture (Melo Franco 1977:17). In this way, it has contributed to the creation of a national identity. The Mineiro baroque has been described as "one of the most significant . . . and most beautiful phenomena of all the cultural history of Brazil" (Gomes Machado 1973:25). Yet, if such a rich legacy survives, not "as simple nostalgia, but as an oasis which serves an indispensable and actual function in the modern world," there are also countervailing pressures (Barata 1968:5).

Conclusion

The importance of a museumified past draws mainly upon the perspectives of Britain, Europe, and the United States. But does the concept of the past have the same resonance in the Third World? Lowenthal, for example, suggests that the past is a refuge against the uneasy present and the uncertain future (Lowenthal 1979:104). In the Third World, if the past was colonial, if the present is an era of deprivation, and if it is only the future that holds the prospect of amelioration, then the past may have little value and may even be expendable in the search for a better future. The evidence from Minas Gerais is ambivalent because the past preserved in the museums is temporally confined, mostly to the colonial period. However, there is evidence that some elements from the past, such as old buildings, are also seen as obstacles to economic progress, hence expendable.

In a developing country of limited resources, preserving the past by conserving old buildings or maintaining museums is often given low priority. If the past has an intrinsic value, it also has a real price. The cost of collecting, classifying, and displaying objects, within a Third World country of poverty, debt, and economic adversity, may be viewed as a luxury in comparison with other needs, both perceived and real: schools, medical clinics, and factories. This seems to be the case in Brazil. As part of the austerities in federal expenditure of the government of President Fernando Collor de Mello, few funds were made available for IPHAN; and economizing measures in the federal railway system have forced the closure of three railway museums and a reduction in the activities of others (ABPF 1990:4). Minas Gerais gives low priority to museum funding. A Mineiro museum was included in the original plan for the city of Belo Horizonte, but it was not formally approved until 1977 and not inaugurated—and then only on a modest scale—until 1982. The state agency responsible for museums more recently declared, "Minas Gerais is tradition: Minas is culture. Our past is alive and it is necessary to preserve it" (Secretaria do Estado da Cultura n.d.). However, in 1990, the agency received only 20% of the funding it asked for, 0.1% of the state budget (Hoje 1991).

A recent proposal for a new museum elsewhere in the country

prompted the observation that, because of its limited past, Brazil lacks cultural material. The opening of new museums, it was suggested, would only diffuse this limited heritage further and spread the number of visitors too thinly (Jornal do Brasil 1991:10).

Preservation of the past in Brazil is narrowly defined in colonial terms and is given low priority in governmental-resource allocation. The absence of precontact indigenous high cultures means that there are fewer surviving artifacts. Other items, especially those of natural history and of the colonial period, were probably removed to Portugal or were taken away by 19th-century European travelers and members of expeditions. In the case of Minas Gerais, the late-colonial period was one of great cultural richness, fostered by gold. It has left a substantial legacy in the urban scene, and its artifacts are a major component of the state's museum collections. The period was a crucial one in the formation of the state, and its tangible remnants are notable elements in the external image and internal identity of Minas Gerais. There is, nonetheless, a discrepancy between the significance ascribed to this heritage and the resources available for its preservation.

Generalizations from any single case study carry with them many risks, but so do presumptions of universality. Brazil's circumstances were distinct. The "European" period was short: five centuries in the case of the country, three in the case of Minas Gerais. In the latter, evidence of the past is limited in its themes and in those artifacts available; its contribution to national and regional identity is inhibited by size and distance.

Brazil's government and patrons have made economic judgments about the relative utility of museums and art galleries when compared with schools and hospitals. It also seems evident that "national" museums cannot be expected to function on a national scale—at least in a geographical sense. As is clear in Minas Gerais, regional or local identity is also both incomplete and imperfectly realized.

Clearly, several crucial issues remain if the developed world's perspective of preservation and museums is correct. Is preservation an essential component in the sustenance of national identity? How is such a heritage to be created and sustained in the Third World? How should scarce resources be allocated among competing priorities? How is national identity expressed at regional and local levels in museums?

Acknowledgments

The fieldwork on which this essay is based was carried out whilst I was a visiting professor at the Instituto de Geociencias, Universidade Federal de Minas Gerais (UFMG), Brazil. I wish to acknowledge the support of the UFMG, the Conselho Nacional de Pesquisas, the British Council, and the Institute of Latin American Studies at the University of Liverpool.

References

ABPF (Associação Brasileira de Preservação Ferroviaria)
    1990 Museus ferroviarios em crise. *Trem de Ferro* 1(4):4.
Andrade, R. M. F. de
    1969 Palestra. *Revista do Patrimônio Histórico e Artístico Nacional* 17:11–27.
Barata, M.
    1968 Minas setecentista. In *Imagens do passado de Minas Gerais*. P. Scheier, ed. Pp. 5–10. Rio de Janeiro: Livraria Kosmos.
Boxer, C. R.
    1962 *The Golden Age of Brazil*. Berkeley: University of California.
Boylan, P.
    1990 Museums and Cultural Identity. *Museums Journal* 90:29–33.
Cannizzo, J.
    1991 Exhibiting Cultures: Into the Heart of Africa. *Visual Anthropology Review* 7:150–160.
Carrazzoni, M. E.
    1972 *Guia dos Museus do Brasil*. (2nd edition). Rio de Janeiro: Expressão e Cultura.
    1987 *Guia dos Bens Tombados Brasil*. (2nd edition). Rio de Janeiro: Expressão e Cultura.
Drummond de Andrade, C.
    1974 Ao Dr. Lund, em seu reposa. *Estado de Minas*. March 13, 1974; 2° caderno, 1.
Fulford, R.
    1991 Into the Heart of the Matter. *Rotunda* 24:19–28.
Gomes Machado, L.
    1973 *Barroco Mineiro*. (2nd edition). São Paulo: Editora Perspectiva.
Hewison, R.
    1987 *The Heritage Industry*. London: Methuen.
Hoje
    1991 O desafio de cumprir as novas velhas promessas. *Hoje*. March 13, 1991; 21.

Horne, D.
  1984 *The Great Museum.* London: Pluto.
IBGE
  1981 *Tabulacões Avancadas do Censo Demografico IX Recenseamento do Brasil, 1980.* Vol. 1, no. 2. Rio de Janeiro: Instituto Brasileiro de Geografia e Estatística.
  1991 *Anuário Estatístico do Brasil 1990.* Rio de Janeiro: IBGE.
Jornal do Brasil
  1991 Museus de tudo. *Jornal do Brasil.* March 14, 1991; 10.
Lopes, M. M.
  1992 Brazilian Museums of Natural History and International Exchanges in the Transition to the 20th Century. In *Science and Empires.* P. Petijean, ed. Pp. 193–200. Amsterdam: Kluwer.
Lowenthal, D.
  1976 The Place of the Past in the American Landscape. In *Geographies of the Mind.* D. Lowenthal and M. Bowden, eds. Pp. 89–118. Oxford: Oxford University Press.
  1979 Age and Artifact. In *The Interpretation of Ordinary Landscapes.* D. Meinig, ed. Pp. 103–128. Oxford: Oxford University Press.
  1981 Introduction. In *Our Past Before Us: Why Do We Save It?* D. Lowenthal and M. Binney, eds. Pp. 9–16. London: Temple Smith.
Melo Franco, A. A. de
  1977 Continuidade e atualidade politíca de Minas. *IV Seminario de Estudos Mineiros.* Pp. 13–40. Belo Horizonte: Universidade Federal de Minas Gerais.
Ministerio da Educação e Cultura-DPHAN
  1967 *Legislação Brasileira de proteção aos bens culturais.* Rio de Janeiro: M.E.C.-DPHAN.
Museu de Arte Sacra do Carmo
  1987 *Catalogo.* Ouro Prêto: Museu de Arte Sacra.
Quatro Rodas
  1991 *Guia Quatro Rodas do Brasil 1991.* Rio de Janeiro: Quatro Rodas.
Ramamurthy, A.
  1990 Museums and the Representation of Black History. *Museums Journal* 90(9):23–35.
Secretaria do Estado da Cultura
  n.d. *Minas investir na cultura e projetar o futuro.* Poster. Belo Horizonte.
Shankland, G.
  1975 Why Trouble with Historic Towns? In *The Conservation of Cities.* UNESCO. Pp. 24–42. London: Croom Helm.
Vasconcelos, S. de
  1970 Arquitetura e Artes Plásticas. In *Minas Gerais: Terra e Povo.* G. Cesar, ed. Pp. 201–222. Pôrto Alegre: Editôra Globo.

8 The First Greek Museums and National Identity

Maria Avgouli

The immense contribution of ancient Greece to Western civilization is both a source of pride and a burden for the people living in Greece today. Excavations carried out since the 19th century in what is now modern Greece disclose the remains of ancient civilizations, which in some cases have their roots in the fourth millennium B.C. The country's ancient past, the emphasis of the neoclassical movement on the classical era, and the emergence of a national identity that harks back to the ancient Greeks were reflected in the first museums, which were archaeological in content. These public museums were founded soon after the formation of the new Greek state in the 19th century and had displays that stretched from the Neolithic to Late Roman times.

Of the more than 400 museums that exist in contemporary Greece, half are archaeological and are under the supervision of the Ministry of Culture.[1] Museums were not, at first, housed in specially designed buildings. The first museum used the orphanage along with other newly established institutions like the central school, the public library, and the National Printing Press (Kokkou 1977:61–68). In 1834, when Athens became the capital of Greece, the National Archaeological Museum was founded, and the collection of its predecessor on the island of Aigina was moved to Athens.

Following the proclamation of independence from Turkey, scholars in Athens worked tirelessly to widen, explore, and reaffirm the history of Greece. A collective undertaking, the government launched a program of consolidation, restoration, and protection; and established historical zones, expropriated sites, and implemented both long-range excavation projects and emergency rescue operations. The maintenance of extraordinarily rich museum collections involved cataloging, cleaning, and conserving bronzes and pottery, statues and inscriptions, and so forth.

In 1833, the Archaeological Service was founded as a department within the Ministry of Education.[2] One year later, the first law was enacted and set specific regulations for the establishment of new museums, excavations, preservation, and possession of antiquities (*Government Gazette* 1834). At this time, the state could not afford to erect new museum buildings, and some monuments themselves (churches, schools, and town halls), therefore, became the protective shells for finds. The first public archaeological collections became the nuclei of later, well-organized local museums at the beginning of the 20th century (see Kavadias 1890–92; Kokkou 1977:157).

Most of the antiquities gathered in Athens and housed in its monuments—the Acropolis, the Hephaisteion, the Stoa of Hadrian—constituted the museums of Greece for almost 40 years, until the Acropolis Museum and the National Archaeological Museum were built. After 1834, when it was no longer used as a fortress, the Acropolis became a subject of archaeological research. The Parthenon, the Propylaia, and the Pinakotheke housed freestanding sculptures, architectural components, inscriptions, and miniature artifacts (Figure 8.1). The Hephaisteion, designated the "Central Archaeological Museum" by royal decree in 1834, housed the collection of the first museum in Aigina (Figure 8.2). Its contents were continually enriched by abundant new finds discovered during the construction of public and private buildings in the new capital (Kokkou 1977:149–188).

Some of the most important other, nonarchaeological museums were founded later, during the early decades of the 20th century: the National Gallery, 1900; the Byzantine Museum, 1914; the Museum of Greek Folk Art, 1918; the National Historical Museum, 1926; and the Benaki Museum, 1930. The period following World War II marked an efflorescence of museums in Greece. I focus here on three types of museums (using specific examples), archaeological, Byzantine, historic and ethnographic, as expressions of the changing "meaning" of the country's national identity in the 19th and early 20th centuries.

Unlike the rest of Europe, whose concept of nationhood was born in the romantic movement and made the distinction between "we and the others," the Greeks were more idiosyncratic: the concept of nationhood

Figure 8.1 The northwest angle of the Parthenon in 1855. The Parthenon was used as a temporary museum, as were the Propylaia, the Pinakotheke, and the temple of Athena Nike on the rock of the Acropolis, from 1835 to 1877. Woodcut. By J. W. Whymper. Courtesy of the Gennadeios Library, Athens.

Figure 8.2 The Hephaisteion was designated the Central Archaeological Museum from 1835 to 1874. Gasparini, 1842. Courtesy of the Gennadeios Library, Athens.

came out of the Greek Enlightenment and distinguished between "we and the ancient Greeks" (Kyriakidou-Nestoros 1978:39).

Historical Background

The ancient Greeks emerged as a point of reference in national identity for the first time in A.D. 1204 among scholars.[3] However, it did not go beyond enclaves of intellectuals to the people (Vakalopoulos 1974:46). With the fall of Constantinople in 1453, Greece was occupied by the Turks for almost four centuries. During this long period, as the Orthodox church became the leading authority in education, the vision of a glorious and pagan past became increasingly dim.

By the end of the 18th century—while Greece was still under Turkish occupation—Greek intellectuals, influenced by the ideas of the French Revolution, took part in a movement called the Greek Enlightenment (1770–1820). This movement inspired the War of Independence of 1821 and led to the creation of the modern Greek state (Dimaras 1977). The Greek Enlightenment movement shared most of the characteristics of its European equivalent, as far as its perception of history was concerned, although its approach was romantic.[4] This romanticism was natively engendered and was not related to its more famous Western counterpart, which actually emerged somewhat later in the 19th century.[5]

Greek identity came to imply a collective consciousness of historical continuity. On the intellectual level, this was expressed by a growing independence from domination by the church, a development that left ample room for the ancient past to reassert itself. The new bourgeoisie that emerged at the end of the 18th century was in search of a unifying belief. Pride in their ancestors and awareness of historical continuity were inherent in their belief. The choice was not difficult: western European neoclassicism was already full-blown, and Classical Greece was considered the finest period of human history. Neoclassicism not only pointed to an ideal, it provided instruction in how to achieve it— imitation. Returning to the past meant, for the Greeks, a liberal spirit and freedom from strict religious dictates; it also meant equal opportunity for all citizens and a democratic form of government (Dimaras 1975:160–161). These ideals served the emerging bourgeoisie.

In 1833, Otto I arrived in Greece, complete with a ready-made Bavarian court, and became king of the Hellenes. He established a monarchy based on the German model, contrary to the prevailing spirit of the postrevolutionary period in Greece and made evident in their first constitutions. The monarchy was the antithesis of traditional community-based Greek society. In this period of imported cultural and political models, alien to Greek social and intellectual mores, the Greeks once again found inspiration in their history. This time, however, their pride in a glorious past became a sterile form of ancestor worship (Dimaras 1975:263). Imitation was no longer a means of achieving a certain ideal or of fulfilling a vision: it became an obsession. The effort to prove all "unbroken continuity of the nation," the main ideological tenet of the time, was used in the service of 19th-century "historicism." History and evidence from the past were to solve practical, "national" problems (Gratziou 1986:55).

Protecting and Housing A Cultural Heritage

The 17th century marked the start of a growing interest in Greece and its monuments (Kokkou 1977:5–26). The first travelers had as their main motive not knowledge of the country itself but the hope of discovering *tresors* with which to enrich their private collections at home. The British formed significant, impressive collections in the first decades of the 17th century (see Michaelis 1882). Following their example, over the next two centuries, other European travelers, mainly French, focused on collecting Greek art (Simopoulos 1970–1975). These travelers affected Greece both positively and negatively—the former because they led to systematic research and the study of culture: the latter because those travelers, being fanatic collectors of antiquities, were responsible for damaging and removing some of the most important monuments in the history of art (Figure 8.3). (On the looting of antiquities in general see Bracken 1975.) The removal of the Elgin Marbles by Thomas Bruce to England in 1806 is one of the best-known and current cases, but it is far from unique (see Hitchens 1987; Simopoulos 1970–1975:557–582).

By the end of the 18th century, the Greek Enlightenment movement and growing nationalism focused on preserving cultural heritage and caused the first attempts at rescuing "ancestral remains." During the War of Independence in 1821 and afterwards, there was a collective awareness of the need to protect ancient monuments. Among the first constitutional acts of the new state, and among the roles and duties of the new governor of Greece, was the stipulation that "he shall not permit the selling or exporting of antiquities outside the country" (see Mamoukas 1971:537). In addition, almost all official decisions concerning the protection of antiquities were published in the press, an act that demonstrated the state's special interest in them.

In 1829, the first governor of Greece, Ioánnis Kapodístrias, founded the country's earliest archaeological museum on the island of Aigina, the capital of Greece at that time. It was called the National Museum, and its main goal was "to collect the antiquities that are under the classical earth of Greece (Protopsaltis 1967:142–5, no. 117). The first director, A. Moustoxidis, submitted a list of measures to the government to protect monuments and movable objects (1967:142–145). After these basic measures were enacted, interest in excavations grew rapidly. Provisional local governors all over the country began excavating in the areas under

Figure 8.3   The looting of the sculptures from the Temple of Apollo, Epicurius at Phigaleia in Arcadia, 1812. Painting by C. R. Cockerell from the Temples of Jupiter Panhellenius at Aigina and Apollo Epicurius at Bassae near Phigaleia in Arcadia.

their charge, sending the findings to the National Museum, and reporting on their discoveries (Kokkou 1977:53). The provisional governor of Elis (Peloponnese) in 1829, made an effort to educate the people of the area. He wrote that "Museum is the word for the place where antiquities are kept and guarded. Antiquities is the word for old works of art which were made by our Greek ancestors and which were kept safe above or under the ground" (Protopsaltis 1967:107–109 no. 82).

Building New Museums

The Acropolis Museum and the National Archaeological Museum in Athens were the first Greek museums ever built. Both were erected in the late 19th century. The former contains finds from the Sacred Rock of the Acropolis; the latter is the repository of the most important ancient artworks from all over Greece.

The Acropolis Museum

The need for an organized museum of the Acropolis itself was apparent from the earliest years of the Greek state. The thought was that the museum would be dedicated to housing the remains of the shrine, unparalleled masterpieces that expressed the majesty of the conception and the superb workmanship found on the rock: large, freestanding and group sculptures and architectural elements dating from the sixth to fourth centuries B.C. (Andronikos 1974:112–148; Brouskari 1974; Dickins and Casson 1912–1921; Miliadis 1965). In 1862, the Ministry of Education officially announced the decision to found such a museum. Preliminary work, begun two years later, ceased almost immediately, however, when excavations for museum foundations revealed still more ancient ruins (Kavadias and Kawerau 1906:15). It thus became evident that this site constituted a major problem. Archaeological research on the Sacred Rock of the Acropolis was still incomplete, and the topography of the site was unknown. The project was reassigned to another location, southeast of the Parthenon, and was concluded in 1874. It was intended to house the remaining marbles scattered about the Acropolis, but the museum was also later enriched with unique works of art found during the extensive excavations carried out on the rock between 1885 and 1890 (Dickins and Casson 1912–1921:1–9; Kavadias and Kawerau 1906). Exceptional archaic statues, together with the Parthenon marbles, offer the visitor the clearest picture of Attic plastic arts at the peak of the historic age (sixth to fifth centuries B.C.).

Before long, space in the new museum was too limited for the wealth of material. In 1888, a second, smaller museum was erected near the original building. After the Second World War, the first structural works were carried out for the preservation and expansion of the museum. From that time until 1964, the museum underwent numerous transformations. In 1991 it was decided to move its collections to another building and in the same year an international architectural competition was held in Athens for the new museum, yet to be constructed, in the vicinity of the Acropolis, not on the rock itself.

The National Archaeological Museum

The founding of the National Archaeological Museum coincided with the legal establishment of the Greek state in 1834. The first archaeological law of 1834, article 1, provided that a "Central Public Museum for Antiquity" be built in Athens. To this end, a succession of architectural competitions was declared for the design of the building, which—and this was stressed—must be worthy of the masterpieces of antiquity it was to house (*Government Gazette* 1858).

In 1860, German architect Ludwig Lagge (1808–1868), a professor at the Munich Academy and designer of the Leipzig Museum, was commissioned to prepare the plans for the museum, and in 1866 the official ground-breaking ceremony was held. Ernst Ziller (1837–1923), another German architect, was placed in charge of completing the building (1889) (Figure 8.4). It was he who introduced many changes and left his stamp on what is both one of the most important neoclassical monuments in Athens and a typical example of museum architecture from the late 19th century.[6]

The transfer of antiquities to the new building was begun in 1874. The public collections that had been housed in various Athenian monuments, public buildings, educational institutions, and societies were transferred to the new National Archaeological Museum. Antiquities from archaeological sites in and around Athens and some occasional finds were also taken there.

In 1893, the aims of the institution were set down: "The National Archaeological Museum is dedicated to furthering the study and teaching of the science of archaeology, to promulgating archaeological knowledge and to developing a love for great art." At the same time, the departments of the museum were also defined: sculpture; pottery; clay and bronze statuettes and various other ancient objects; inscriptions; works from early Greek periods (Mycenaean collection, etc.); and Egyptian works of art. Its collections covered finds from the Neolithic to the Late Roman period (*Government Gazette* 1893). Several new wings were added to the original museum building in the first decades of the 20th century, doubling the space available for exhibits. During World

Figure 8.4   The National Archaeological Museum, after its completion in 1889. From a postcard, private collection, Athens.

War II and until 1946, the museum was closed and its exhibits stored away for safekeeping.

The history of the National Archaeological Museum and the efforts by the state for almost half a century to establish an exceptional institution are indicative of the importance of its role in strengthening an already-entrenched national identity, rooted mainly in the ancient past. (For an analysis of the history of the National Archaeological Museum, see Kokkou 1977:201–258; for exhibits, see Andronikos 1974: 19–106; Karouzou 1979.)

By the late 19th and early 20th centuries, the emphasis shifted to later historical periods. The concept of a cultural and historical continuity was broadened to include the Byzantine, Post-Byzantine, and most recent times. Historians of this period saw ancient Greek civilization as passing through the Byzantine era to modern Greece and to western Europe. These shifting interests led to the founding of the Byzantine Museum (1914), the National Historical Museum (1926), and the Museum of Greek Folk Art (1918), all situated in Athens.

The Byzantine Museum

The history of the Byzantine Museum does not really begin with its founding in 1914 but considerably earlier, with the foundation of the Christian Archaeological Society in 1884. This society was established by private individuals for the purpose of preserving and collecting relics of Byzantine and Post-Byzantine Christian art from all over Greece. In 1897, the government entrusted the Christian Archaeological Society with the founding of a Christian Byzantine museum, but the first bill providing for this art did not become law until 1914 (Kokkou 1977:285). The society's collection was incorporated into the Byzantine Museum in 1923, but the problem of a permanent home for both was not solved until 1930. The museum was at that time transferred to the "Villa Ilissia," a mansion built in 1840, and was finally officially inaugurated (see Sotiriou 1929) (Figure 8.5). The museum collections include paintings (icons and frescoes), sculpture, and the minor arts and cover the whole Byzantine and Post-Byzantine periods in Greece, from the early days of Christianity to the last years of the Turkish occupation in 1821 (Sotiriou 1962); they came from archaeological excavations or were gathered from Byzantine monuments around the country.

The spirit and principles on which the museum's organization were and still are based reflect the ideological atmosphere of the period and the attitudes toward the historic past. In the late 19th century, the special significance of medieval Hellenism had begun to prevail. This notion of the importance of medieval Byzantine Hellenism was associated with the "diffusion" of ancient Greek civilization from antiquity to modern Hellenism (Noutsos 1981:115). According to the prevailing views of the time, objects displayed in museums were not to be appreciated solely as works of art but as relics of national history and as proof of the unbroken continuation of the nation from ancient times.

The widespread adoption of this notion went hand in hand with the restoration of Byzantium as a significant civilization, which the Enlightenment had dismissed or negated. It was also linked ideologically with the need to solve some practical national problems.[7]

In 1924, the text referring to the aims of the museum stressed that "the Byzantine Museum of Athens is and will be in time first and foremost the national museum of Greece," and

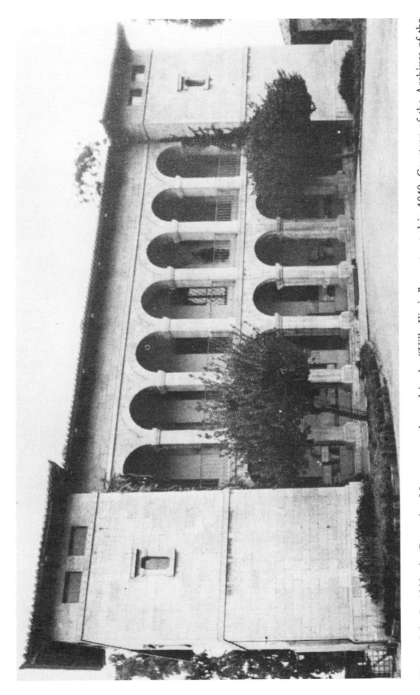

Figure 8.5 In 1930, the Byzantine Museum was housed in the "Villa Ilissia," constructed in 1840. Courtesy of the Archives of the Commercial Bank of Greece, Athens.

its contents, the Christian objects of Greek art of the Byzantine Museum, present the civilization of our forefathers, as the Archaeological Museum presents the civilization of our more distant ancestors. These ancestral works have an international character and they belong to other nations as much as to Greece, the Christian Greek work[s] on the other hand are closer to us . . . and have more obvious relevance to the whole cycle of ideas and customs within which we still live. [Sotiriou 1962:3]

This division of forebears into "ancestors" and "forefathers" makes it obvious that, "despite the indisputable value of the former, throughout the period between the wars the forging of the national identity was in the hands of the latter" (Gratziou 1986:72).

The National Historical Museum

A historical museum is defined in Greece in accordance with the legislative decree of 1926 establishing the National Historical Museum as one that "has as an aim the collection and conservation of relics dating from the Fall of Constantinople (1453) and subsequently, having reference to the history of the public and private life of the Greek nation" (Kokkinis 1979:266).

The National Historical Museum was founded through the efforts of private individuals. In 1882, a group of intellectuals interested in preserving memorabilia linked to modern Greek history formed the Historical and Ethnological Society in Athens (Kokkou 1977:280). The founding and aims of the Christian Archaeological Society towards the creation of the Byzantine Museum should be compared with the almost simultaneous founding of the Historical and Ethnological Society and the latter's campaign to establish a "truly national museum to bridge the gap [that exists] between antiquity and the years of the Revolution of 1821 and afterwards" (Gratziou 1986:63).

The society's museum was to have two departments, according to the Articles of Association: archives for written historical documents and the museum proper for "other artifacts of national life" (Kokkou 1977:280). The objects that were gathered from public and private collections included historical relics from the time of the Frankish and Turkish occupations, souvenirs of the War of Independence of 1821, original drawings from early travelers, historical mementos of the struggle for liberation, personal belongings of distinguished personages of modern Greek history, and a fine collection of ethnographic objects from throughout Greece.

In 1926 the National Historical Museum was officially founded. The objects in the society's collections formed the bulk of its exhibits, which were housed in various locations on a temporary basis until the problem of a permanent home could be solved. With the outbreak of World War II, the collections were placed in the storerooms of the National Archaeological Museum, as were the exhibits of other museums. After the war, the society obtained the first Greek Parliament Building for the museum. It is a historic architectural monument erected in 1858 (Figure 8.6). The museum was inaugurated in 1962, and the society's collections, document archives, library, and photographic archive were all transferred there (see Meletopoulos 1966).

The Museum of Greek Folk Art

The first Museum of Greek Folk Art to be founded in Greece was and is an ethnographic museum, whose purpose is to study and exhibit the regional traditions of the country. Within the context of 19th-century ideology and the attempts to demonstrate the historical continuity of the Greek nation, the study of beliefs and customs of traditional life was conducted solely with reference to antiquity. Research into folkloric phenomena was undertaken to establish their origins in ancient Greece (see Kyriakidou-Nestoros 1978:91–97). Comparisons between ancient and modern Greek customs became common in the early 19th century and constituted the principal tenet in the study of Greek folklore. The field was officially recognized among writers and scholars in 1909 with the establishment of ethnography as a scholarly discipline. The philosophy of the first folk-art museum was based on a general effort to trace the survival of ancient customs in the modern country.

The Museum of Greek Folk Art was founded in 1918 on the initiative of G. Drosinus, a poet, and K. Kourouniotis, an archaeologist, both of whom were civil servants in the Ministry of Education; its original name was the Museum of Greek Handicrafts. According to its first Articles of Association, its task was to collect

Figure 8.6 The National Historical Museum was housed in the first Parliament Building of the new Greek state, erected in 1858. Courtesy of the Archives of the National Historical Museum, Athens.

handicrafts found in Greece and in all countries where Greeks reside, dating from the Fall of Constantinople (1453 A.D.) up to the year of founding of the Greek state. . . . These handicrafts may be embroideries on fabric, costumes, household furnitures and utensils of any kind of material, tools used in all kinds of crafts and industries, and weapons.

In 1923, its name was changed to the National Museum for the Decorative Arts; and its purpose was the creation of a "national body of decorative art" and aimed "for the collection of decorative works from antiquity up to modern times, mainly of Greek origin" (for museum legislation, see Hatzinikolaou 1988:84; Kokkou 1977:296). It was decided in 1926 that the museum should become a part of the National Historical Museum, but this decision was never implemented. Nevertheless, it is indicative of the perceived common aims and goals held by historical and ethnographic museums in Greece. The museum in 1959 acquired the name it bears today, a name that is more in keeping with its collections: the Museum of Greek Folk Art. The collections, ranging from 1650 to the present, include Greek traditional embroideries, weavings, regional costumes, metalwork, silver, wood carvings, stone carvings, ceramics, shadow-theater puppets and props, masquerade costumes, and some paintings. The museum was first housed in an 18th-century mosque in the historic center of Athens (Figure 8.7). It remained there from 1918 until 1973, when it moved to its present quarters, which are still in the old part of the city.

Conclusion

The founding of the first museums in Greece—those of the 19th century— coincided with the founding and subsequent consolidation of the new Greek state. The purpose was not just to reinforce a sense of national identity; there was also a desire to protect a long cultural heritage, which was and still is obvious in every part of the country.

In establishing the various types of museums (archaeological, Byzantine, historical, ethnographic), a primary role was played each time by the prevailing view of the historical identity, which has never, though it may undergo some changes in points of reference, been questioned.

Figure 8.7   From the first exhibition of the Museum of Greek Folk Art's collections at the Mosque prior to 1960. Courtesy of the Archives of the Museum of Greek Folk Art, Athens.

Notes

1. These 400 museums do not include private collections or sacristies in monasteries. They are mainly state and public museums. (For more information, see Kokkinis 1979:278–281.) After archaeological museums, the second-largest category is ethnographic museums, of which there are 83 nationwide; these are followed by ecclesiastical art (38), historical (27), modern art (23), natural history (13), and Byzantine and Christian art (11) (see also Kokkinis 1979).

2. The Archaeological Service, which is under the jurisdiction of the Ministry of Culture today, is the main state body charged with the protection of monuments and archaeological sites and with the operation of the museums. The Archaeological Service has departments all over Greece.

3. In 1204, the military clash between two worlds–Byzantium and the West—was to terminate the dissolution of the Byzantine Empire. Up until the sixth century A.D., the conflict between Christian ideology and ancient Greek culture could be readily discerned; it continued up through the ninth century with numerous fluctuations. The more direct contact with ancient Greek arts and letters observed in the 10th and 11th centuries, subsequent to the first Renaissance in the ninth century, was a result of the intellectual turmoil provoked by iconoclastic controversy. The consciousness of the intelligentsia involved the cultural present and began to be linked to Greek antiquity. After 1204, Greek culture is presented by most writers as an ancestral heritage in which they took great pride. The name "Hellene" ceased to mean "pagan" and reacquired its dual cultural and ethnological content (see Svoronos 1983:145–161).

4. The Enlightenment was governed by reason, romanticism was ruled by emotion; both are generalizations. The differences between them can be examined on many levels. Here, the reference is to the perception of history. This perception, as formulated by the Enlightenment, does not include the nation as a concept, while romanticism, on the contrary, is inextricably linked with the "idea" of nationhood. Accordingly, the idea of the nation does not depend on sociocultural characteristics but is biological (see Kyriakidou-Nestoros 1978:30, 37).

5. The new notion of nationalism, which was the principal factor in molding both the public and the private lives of Europeans, developed within the context of 19th-century romanticism (see Kohn 1965:9).

6. Numerous public and private neoclassical buildings in Athens and in other Greek cities were designed by Ernst Ziller. For an extended consideration of his work, see Papastamos (1973).

7. The vision of recovering the old Byzantine Empire was the principal national issue in Greek politics during the first decades of the 20th century. It could be justified on the basis of the "diffusion" of ancient Greek civilization throughout the Levant (see Dimaras 1981:39).

References

Andronikos, M.
   1974 *The Greek Museums*. Athens: Ekdotike Athenon.
Bracken, C. P.
   1975 *Antiquities Acquired. The Spoliation of Greece*. London: David & Charles.
Brouskari, M.
   1974 *Acropolis Museum, Descriptive Catalogue*. Athens: Acropolis Museum.
Dickins, G. and S, Casson
   1912–1921 *Catalogue of the Acropolis Museum*. Vols 1 and 2. Cambridge:
      Cambridge University Press.
Dimaras, K. T.
   1975 *History of Modern Greek Literature*. Athens: Ikaros.
   1977 *The Modern Greek Enlightenment*. Athens: Hermes.
   1981 *Modern Greek Philosophy: The Ideological Dimensions of Its European
      Approaches*. Athens: Kedros.
Government Gazette
   1834 No. 22. June 16–28.
   1858 No. 30. July 31.
   1893 August 9. On the Organization of the National Archaeological
      Museum.
Gratziou, O.
   1986 From the History of the Byzantine Museum: The Early Years. *Mnimon*
      11:54–73.
Hatzinikolaou, T.
   1988 *Legal Protection of Ethnographic Museums*. Proceedings of the First
      Seminar on Ethnographic Museums. Athens: Ministry of Culture,
      Museum of Folk Art.
Hitchens, C.
   1987 *The Elgin Marbles*. London: Chatto and Windus.
Karouzou, S.
   1979 *The National Museum*. General Guide. Athens: Ekdotike Athenon.
Kavadias, P.
   1890–1892 *The Sculptures of the National Museum*. Athens: National Museum.
Kavadias, P., and G. Kawerau
   1906 *The Excavation of the Acropolis from 1885 Through 1890*. Athens:
      Archaeological Society.
Kohn, H.
   1965 *Nationalism: Its Meaning and History*. New York: Van Nostrand
      Reinhold Co.
Kokkinis, S.
   1979 *The Museums of Greece*. Athens: Estia.
Kokkou, A.
   1977 *The Care of Antiquities in Greece and the First Museums*. Athens: Hermes.

Kyriakidou-Nestoros, A.
　1978 *The Theory of Greek Folklore.* Athens: Society for the Study of Modern Greek Civilization and General Education.
Mamoukas, A.
　1971 *The National Assemblies.* Vol. 1. Athens.
Meletopoulos, I. A.
　1966 *The National Historical Museum.* Athens: National Historical Museum.
Michaelis, A.
　1882 *Ancient Marbles in Great Britain.* Cambridge: Cambridge University Press.
Miliadis, G.
　1965 *A Brief Guide to the Acropolis Museum.* Athens: Acropolis Museum.
Noutsos, P.
　1981 *Modern Greek Philosophy. The Ideological Dimensions of Its European Approaches.* Athens: Kedros.
Papastamos, D.
　1973 *Ernst Ziller.* Athens: Athenian Publishing Center.
Protopsaltis, E.
　1967 *Historical Writings on Antiquities and Other Monuments during the Revolution and Kapodistrias' Rule.* Athens: Library of Athens Archaeological Society.
Simopoulos, K.
　1970–1975 *Foreign Travellers in Greece.* Vols. 1–3. Athens: Ekdotike Athenon.
Sotiriou, G.
　1929 Le Musée Byzantin d'Athenes. *Mouseion* 8:146–8.
　1962 *A Guide to the Byzantine Museum in Athens.* Athens: Byzantine Museum.
Svoronos, N.
　1983 *Analects of Modern Greek History and Historiography.* Athens: Themelio.
Vakalopoulos, A.
　1974 *History of Modern Hellenism. Its Origin and Development.* Vol. 1. Thessaloniki: Aristoteleion University of Thessaloniki.

PART III
TRANSFORMING OBJECTS, COLLECTIONS AND "NATION"

9 Old Wine in New Bottles, and the Reverse

Douglas Newton

Old Wine

I have been lucky enough, as I would think, to work in museums for half my life, and I would happily have spent even more time in the same way. I am, and I think this must be true of all museum workers (and if not it should be), deeply committed to the material world, and above all to that area of the material world that is embodied and expressed by human beings in the objects that they make.

The museum, though itself an abstraction, is both flexible and capacious, changing and permanent. It is also a material reality, expressed in brick, metal and stone, vivified by the devotion of individuals, and powered by a number of curious impulses.

The history of the museum as an institution is familiar enough. It begins with a myth and takes its name from the characters of the myth, the Muses. The Muses of ancient Greece were originally only three, according to Robert Graves, who also claimed that they were a threefold aspect of a fierce, Great Goddess. Unlike other famous threes of classical mythology, the Fates for instance, they had aesthetic leanings and liked singing trios. They proliferated consequently into three threes: the nine Muses we know (Graves 1955: passim.). In this form, they are a manifestation of the ancient Greek impulse to the ordering by classification of a disorderly and turbulent world. In the Muses' honor, the Alexandrians built the Museion, with its great library, which lasted for about 700 years. Its later history is obscure (Canfora 1990). It recovered from semi-destruction at the hands of Julius Caesar, only to collapse under Christian religious absolutism at the end of the fourth century. The Museion's institutional descendant is the museum of today.

The Muses themselves were devoted to the arts of the word; their Museion was a scientific establishment for both theoretical and empirical research. The museum of today is involved with both the intellectual and, more prominently in the public eye, the material world.

As far as museums are concerned, we are the heirs not so much of the Greeks as of the Romans. They introduced to western Europe a certain cycle which has endured down to our own time. Conquest of an enemy, preferably rich, is followed by looting of his most prized possessions. These possessions, always objects of value, either as tokens of wealth or national icons, many works of art, are brought home in triumph. This practice led to a new fad among the wealthy Romans. The valued objects aroused admiration and the desire for possession of the same sorts of things, thus generating an art-market, complete with dealers, art-galleries and—to supply the unwary or the overconfident—the copyists and the makers of fakes. Initially looting is an expression of power. Later, something subtler takes its place: a somewhat wistful desire to assimilate the esteemed culture of the looted. Thus it came about that the Roman aristocrats made huge collections of Greek sculpture, some genuine, some counterfeit.

While works of art were the first targets of collecting, a new tendency began with the proto-museums of the Renaissance. The accumulation of sculpture and paintings by princely families continued; at the same time the period saw growth of cabinets of curiosities, semi-scientific collections that led, eventually, to the foundation of museums of science.

About 200 years ago, the age of the cabinet of curiosities and the palace gallery came to an end. The great private collections of the aristocracy and royalty, previously sometimes available to select visitors, began to become public institutions. This change did not take place overnight, and the formation of many great museums took place in a decidedly haphazard manner. However, museums gradually became manifestations—and—sources of national pride rather of than personal prestige. The collections began to be fed by legitimate acquisitions rather than by loot, though some flurried, and belated, steps backwards were still taken. Napoleon's imperial depredations in Italy and Germany in the name of France's glory were a notorious example.[1] One must also mention Hitler's astonishing thefts, often disguised as legitimate acquisitions, of works of art intended for a visionary, total museum in Linz. More recently still there were the plundering of German museums at the end of World War II by Russian troops.[2] Latest of all are the thefts by Iraqi forces in Kuwait museums preceding the Persian Gulf War. These revert to Roman conceptions of legitimate, even appropriate, national actions.

About the middle of the 19th century, the museum world intensified a shift towards scholarship and away from vainglory and inquisitiveness. The face and purpose of the museum were changed by the didacticism typical of the period, by increasing competition in the field of manufactures, which had to be powered fed by increasingly knowledgeable and better trained workers, and by the imperialism which provided markets for manufactured products. For example, the Victoria and Albert Museum in London owed its inception not to any ambition to create yet another art museum but to providing a showcase for prizewinning objects from the Great Exhibition of 1851. They were intended to be a permanent stimulus to the British artisan and his employers to raise their standards of skill and design. Museums were no longer to be (or not quite so much to be) tokens of national or private grandeur, but to play socially useful moral and educational roles.

National Museums: New Bottles

The rise of ethnographic collections in museums took place at about the same time for two reasons, the theme of national glory aside. Anthropologists themselves hopefully postulated that such collections would be of value to future proconsuls in western Europe's empires (though there is little evidence that governments took this too seriously). The second motive was somewhat more honorable. It was a commonplace that the "primitives" now coming into increasing contact with Western culture were probably doomed—perhaps physically, certainly as far as their cultures were concerned. It was an historic duty to preserve as far as possible the traces of an "earlier stage" of human history, as they could throw light on the "ascent" of modern man from savagery. The political naivete of the first reason and the misconstrued Darwinism of the second are, nevertheless, still didactic in intent.

The museum today functions more than ever as an educational establishment, owing an increasing social consciousness on the part of those who are often the source of museum financing—that is, federal and local governments, who want to know that the money they disburse is serving some good social purpose. The same consciousness informs, if sometimes less immediately, the enormous and indispensable body of private patrons. There is now not only a strong emphasis on the educative function of the museum, but indeed a running debate on how that function is to be fulfilled. The intellectual level to be attained by the museum's exhibition function has been widely debated, and in fact certain programs that have been undertaken are highly debatable. As far as ethnographic collections are concerned, the general point of agreement is that the museum can teach us about the lives of others, and about our own.

"Our own"—but who are we? "We", as in "Westerners", are rather different from those we used to be; we are no longer members of the nations that absorbed and drew on the others of the world. In recent years, most of the countries formerly colonized by Westerners have become independent, sometimes rich, often ambitious and nearly always self-conscious. These things almost inevitably lead to the desire for modernization. This in turn leads to the frustration of seeing precisely what makes a country distinctive, what gives it meaning to the outside world and itself, eroding rapidly away. This is a terrible dilemma which countries often attempt to solve by founding national museums to preserve traditional national cultures. This conception of the national museum actually arose quite early. Bernal shows, for instance, that the rise of Mexican nationalism in the late 18th century was closely associated with archaeology and the preservation of antiquities, though nothing much came of the idea of a national museum for another century (Bernal 1980: 72–77).

The idea of a single national museum is not familiar in the United States. This country, according to a recent listing, rejoices in over 6,700 museums of all shapes, sizes, and subjects from Art to Zoology, not to mention specialized establishments for fly-fishing, tennis, Elvis Presley (two of these), barbed wire, and the National Cowgirl Hall of Fame. If the United States has no single national museum—those of the Smithsonian Institution are really National by courtesy title only—but only an enormous number of museums, perhaps one can think of the aggregate of them all being our national museum, and expressing our perceptions of our culture in all its fantastic variety. For purely practical reasons, most countries must subsume the major part of its museum resources into one establishment.

New Wine

The new type of national museum's role as preserver of culture has not been expressed with higher hopes than by Sir Michael Somare, the first prime minister of Papua New Guinea, and the leader in founding Papua New Guinea's National Museum and Art Gallery. In his own words,

> Many people have thought of museums as places for visitors and tourists to spend an afternoon marvelling at the past and absorbing a little culture. But in Papua New Guinea the Museum [has] a far greater responsibility to the nation that [it] serves. Papua New Guinea, during the past 100 years, has been subjected to a cultural revolution. The arrival of the Germans, British, Australians and Japanese had a great impact on the culture of our people. Many of our ways, our arts and our beliefs have already been forgotten. In the struggle to hold our own in a modern technological world it will be all too easy for our own culture to be lost forever.
>
> I believe that the Museum has a vital role to play in preserving that culture. The museum must not be a place where our past is stored and displayed, but must act as an inspiration to our people in the effort to keep our culture alive. (Somare 1974: iv)

Sir Michael's statement challenges us to consider in which directions the museum concerned with the preservation of a cultural heritage is to go. It defines the new national museum as a place which will set out to preserve and exhibit the local culture above all, perhaps exclusively, rather than attempting the worldwide coverage of the traditional national museum. It calls for an activist approach: such new museums, by nature of their charter and possibilities, must play their part in defining national identity by a process of exclusion.

The new national museum, we begin to see, is a child of this century, but not a single child: it is a twin. On the one hand, it is not intended as an exposition of the works of other cultures as a testimony to national power's ability to take them over; on the other hand it demonstrates a nation's power to be itself. It is a statement about the nation itself and its heritage. The potential of the national museum to provide a focus for its nation's culture may well be its clear charter.

This agenda suggests three things: that there is such a thing as culture, that it needs help in maintaining itself, and that museums can provide that help.

What is culture? A simple answer to this complex question—if there can be such a thing, and many respectable authorities would say one cannot—is that culture is the basic suppositions and convictions of a group of people, how they act as a result, and the material evidence of their thoughts and acts in what they make (using "make" in its broadest possible sense). The convictions and suppositions are fundamental. As a friend of mine said to me recently, "Culture is what we are committed to; each of us can only have one culture, but we can be tourists in others." He might well have added that in the complex world of today we must be all be tourists in other cultures if our own is to survive, and if we are to understand it ourselves.

Old Bottles

To have had the experience of working in a museum that houses the products of numerous cultures makes one acutely aware of this problem. English by birth, when I walk through the galleries of the Metropolitan Museum of Art in New York where works from England are on exhibition I admit to feeling a certain intimate kinship I do not experience in other parts of that vast building. I am not offended, by the way, that some American has removed the works from my native land and placed them here; my nationalistic pride, moderate as it is, makes me rather regretful that the Museum does not show more and better. In that way the huge, international public which fills the Museum could get an acuter, more elevated understanding of English culture. But I do become vividly aware of the different nature of that culture from others. I am not alone in this. I have had more than once the pleasure of conducting through the Museum a party of notables from Papua New Guinea. They view much of what they see with civility. But it is when they approach the cases with works from Papua New Guinea that their eyes light up with recognition, admiration, a sense that at last they are in the presence of something genuinely worthwhile.

This brings us to another question. Just what is the culture that we are talking about and that we wish to preserve? The culture of the past, which is generally what "preservation" is aimed at, contains a great deal that is not necessarily acceptable as behavior today. No present or future government of Papua New Guinea is likely to countenance the continuation or revival of, say, head-hunting, once an integral component of some New Guinea cultures. If head-hunting disappears in such cultures, as it has, inevitably there goes with it a large area of associated belief and behavior. The behavior patterns having become obsolete, the associated beliefs will become only fragmentary memories, and the culture radically changed.

For myself the fact is I can be sure that none of my ancestors ever owned the sorts of objects that have gone into museums; and more than that, however much I admire them, I doubt that as I am, I could survive in the periods and societies which created those objects. Culture changes, and one's knowledge of one's own culture is inevitably fragmentary. It has two components: one's experience of the present continuum, which is permanently in process of becoming the past; and a farrago of largely disconnected memories about historical events, religion, music, poetry, anecdotes, and so on. For all of us it is an entirely different compound, though there is a tacit assumption that some items are more or less essential if we are to be firmly embedded in our culture. The Englishman who has actually read the complete works of Shakespeare is firmly embedded in the general culture. So is the man who without having read them is aware Shakespeare is considered the culture's greatest writer; as is also the man who disputes this view. But what about the man who has never heard of Shakespeare but has, let us say, the history of cricket at his fingertips? He is an equal proprietor of the general culture. It is on the sum of all the millions of our little individual farragoes that our comprehension of our culture is based.

The attempt to define a cultural Garden of Eden, untouched, unsullied, and pure of diluting influences, is probably futile. Levi-Strauss addresses this point in writing about certain Amazonian tribes. When he saw them they were in a state of advanced cultural decay, and he wondered when was it that they were most themselves in a distinct culture, at their most pristine? He was unable to answer the question (Lévi-Strauss 1974: 43). When we cannot answer it precisely about our own, as I suggest none of us can, the best we can do is to say that we will choose arbitrary points and nominate them as defining what we will call our culture. This means some falsification and some idealization, but is usually thought better than nothing and is at least workable.

Old Wine in New Bottles

René d'Harnoncourt (a former director of the Museum of Modern Art in New York) once told me an exemplary story. In the 1940s, he and the anthropologist Frederick H. Douglas were invited by a California Indian tribe to attend an important ceremony. This came as a surprise to them, as they were under the impression that these Indians had abandoned their culture, and had held no ceremonies in living memory. They were even more astonished to find that the ceremony appeared to be carried out in authentic traditional detail. The building, the paraphernalia and songs corresponded exactly to records and specimens they had seen.

When it was all over, d'Harnoncourt congratulated one of the leading men, and asked tactfully how they had managed to perform this ancient ceremony so precisely. "We had this," was the reply. "This" was a Bulletin published decades before about the tribe by the Bureau of Indian Ethnology of the Smithsonian Institution.

The printed word, as we all know, is a technique of recording which is historically dear to Westerners, but has great limitations. Electronic and photographic recording is relatively cheap and relatively speedy. It is also easily disseminated. An example of this took place in the Sepik District of Papua New Guinea in the 1960's. In 1965 I and others doing research there found ritual life in abeyance. Two years later it was reviving, and by 1970 was in full swing. It appears that in 1966 the local radio station had sent teams around the area to record traditional music and had then broadcast it for all to hear. The interest, pride and admiration generated by this had inspired the people to reevaluate their culture and to revive an important part of it.[3]

As time goes on modern recording devices are passing increasingly into the hands of participants in other cultures, not those of their observers. I know of at least two occasions when important ceremonies in New Guinea have been tape-recorded by men taking part in them, and undoubtedly there have been many more. At least one forest tribe in Malaysia, the Senoi, have made a film about themselves. One of the Amazonian tribes (the Yąnomamő) has acquired videocameras and uses them to record local events, but also to make records of encounters and conflicts with bureaucracy that can be put to political use. An interesting aspect of all this is that given fairly advanced technological devices, the people do not use them to make records of outside events and visitors as such; they do not record the sayings and doings of their visitors, their songs and myths. They concentrate on the things they value most—themselves. They are self-regarding; they are concentrating on the preservation of their own cultures.

It is generally assumed that the first task of the museum has always been to gather together the material expressions of a culture, to see that they are well housed, looked after, and made accessible to an interested public. This is an excellent first step, but if it is the only one it may lead us towards the storehouse museum, the closet whose door no one bothers to open. Preservation is only the groundwork for communication achieved through exhibits.

Ideally an exhibit that is well done can evoke a culture for someone grounded in that culture; each object is intended to start a train of associations, conscious or not, as it does in real life. Suppose that, as time goes on and culture changes, and those associations fade, as they probably will, we can only resort to the museum techniques of explanation: labels, photographs, and so on, which inform us of what we have forgotten or never knew. This can take us as far as the diorama, or reconstruction of a scene (a technique I personally dislike because it fossilizes life rather than conveys it—I admit that millions of visitors to the Disney establishments would say I am wrong). Suppose, though, we want to go further than preserving objects and telling about them; suppose we want to take a step beyond and actively to preserve the ideologies of the cultures we care about?

So far the tendency of the new national museum has been to follow closely the long-established Western models. But new situations may call for different solutions, for quite different kinds of institutions from our conventional museums; in fact there may be some countries which do not want or need the conventional museum at all; they may need something closer to what is often called a "cultural center", where direct interaction between people can take place. In the city of Auckland in New Zealand, for example, there is a Maori-run center where children and adults who normally lead Western-style lives can learn the language, traditional skills including woodcarving, the use of traditional weapons and so on, and can have illnesses treated with traditional remedies. The center is devoted to creating in Maori a sense of their culture's worth, and instilling elements to be carried into the future. Though not formally a museum, the center performs some of the functions that new nations evidently want from their museums. There have also been suggestions that Pacific countries need both kinds of institutions in tandem (Dark 1987).

Dirk Smidt, the former director of Papua New Guinea's National Museum, has analyzed (Crowe 1991: 3–4) differences between Westerners' and Pacific islanders' approaches to museums. He cites no less than 16 points; in summary, only a few are held in common; several are complementary. For the rest, the perceived difference between the ideal Pacific Islands museum and the Western museum with Pacific collections is striking. The Pacific Island museum stresses, admires and represents its own culture, restricts sacred objects from view, considers objects as living beings, displays them in their cultural context and for their spiritual strength, and values living traditions. The Western museum, on the other hand, relativizes its own culture and values others, desacralizes objects, displays with "aesthetic" aims, and values the old above the contemporary.

The impact of some non-western attitudes is already making itself powerfully felt outside purely local environments. Leaving aside the vexed question of repatriation of collections made in many cases long before even contemporary times, a powerful impact upon museums has recently been made by the attitudes and claims of at least two non-western groups of people. These are the Australian Aborigines and the Native Americans. Each represents the indigenous inhabitants of a country swamped by foreign newcomers, and each descends from ancestors maltreated by the incursion. They therefore are the holders of powerful moral debts, and have used these, among other ways, to control the holdings of a number of museums in Australia and the United States. Among other actions, sacred Aboriginal objects have been withdrawn from display in Australian museums. In the United States objects have been returned from museums to tribal authorities who intend to place them in outdoor shrines where they will assuredly, as in the past, eventually rot and disappear. The museum curator who may feel the justice of tribal demands, but equally thinks his responsibility is to preserve the heritage of the past for the future is in a dilemma. Is it now his duty to preserve the tokens of tradition or the tradition itself? And what may future generations say to his having allowed the material heritage to be destroyed?

The fact is that cultures are fragile, and yet aspects of them are impressively durable. Like some natural species, they may be suppressed, they may be endangered, but given half a chance at survival they will recover to a remarkable degree. Cultures are phenomena existing in history: they continually fluctuate and change, but it takes almost the annihilation of all those committed to a culture to eliminate it altogether. Whatever its limitations, the traditional museum also can play a role in cultural preservation. I can illustrate this, in part from personal experience, by way of an exhibition called "Te Maori", on which I collaborated and which opened at the Metropolitan Museum of Art in 1984.

It was a show of the art of the New Zealand Maori: the indigenous people of the country, as the Native Americans are of the United States. Sometimes when one says this to the unwary, they become eager, and ask where one can see Maoris. The answer, on the streets of Auckland, Wellington and other cities, is not taken well by the romantic. It leads to the question, but are there no real Maoris to be found in the remote interior? What one finds in the remote interior of New Zealand is of course what one finds in the remote interior of America: towns, motels, tourist resorts, and so on. The "real Maori" of today are farmers, doctors, clergy, lawyers, writers, professors, civil servants, and others in the general spectrum of modern employment and, unfortunately of unemployment. Since the arrival of Westerners (mainly British) first in 1769, then as colonists in significant numbers after 1840, Maori culture has undergone many vicissitudes. The original population may have been as many as 100,000 people; it fell to 60,000 by 1860, and to about 40,000 by 1900. Much of this loss was due to introduced diseases; some at least because the Maori, always extremely warlike and violent, seized upon the European firearm with an avid appreciation for its power of slaughter. It suited the colonial power to think of the Maori as a dying race. The forecast proved premature; in the last 100 years, with an improved birthrate, the Maori population has risen to nearly 400,000. Among New Zealanders of Western descent there was, perhaps still is, a sentimental respect for "our Maoris" with their prowess in war and sports. Even so, the Maori remain to a certain extent second-class citizens in New Zealand, a minority in the land they once owned in its splendid entirety. Not only numerically but culturally the Maori were at a low ebb in the late 19th century. Their ancient customs—warfare, cannibalism, religion, dress, tatooing, and much else—were long gone.

Even the mellifluous language was discredited in the government's schools and seemed to be disappearing.

How this situation change is at least partly the story of great Maori intellectuals like Sir Apirana Ngata and Te Rangi Hiroa (Sir Peter Buck) and others with their insistence on the importance of *maoritanga*, Maoriness or Maorihood, coupled with their recognition of the need for modern education and participation in politics (Ngata and Buck 1986). They had much to build upon. No matter what were the colonial governors' expectations, the Maori themselves had no intention whatever of becoming totally assimilated into Western culture. Maorihood, because much of Maori culture had survived, still exercised great power among the people. The sense of the individuality, the personality, of Maori culture, was intact. It is significant that the very word *"maori"* simply means normal or natural; the rest of the world is *"pakeha"*, foreign, different but no better. In Maori perceptions, the line was, and is, very clearly drawn.

One of the bases of Maori culture is consciousness of the past, of the ancestors whose *mana*, or power[4] increases with time and is bestowed upon their descendants. The communal meetinghouse, no matter how humble it may often be today in contrast to the great carved buildings of the past, is still the place where the ancestor symbolically gathers his children within his own body. The relics of the ancestor, of all ancestors are sacred. They are the *taonga*, the treasures inherited from the past.

New Wine in New Bottles

This is a hint of the complex situation I stepped into one day in 1973, all innocent enthusiasm. I was the curator of the Museum of Primitive Art in New York when I had a visit from Paul Cotton, then the consul-general of New Zealand. He wanted to find out whether we would be interested in a show of Maori art from New Zealand museums. At that time I frankly knew very little about Maori art. I did know that the large scale of many important objects would make it impossible to hold such a show in our tiny museum. I knew that such an exhibition had not been done before, and the subject certainly merited attention. I introduced Cotton to my friend Wilder Green, who had just gone to head the American Federation of Arts, an organization that circulates loan shows to museums around the United States. Wilder Green agreed to take the show on.

Easier said than done, though a great deal was done over the next few years. The New Zealand government wanted the show to take place and promised a great deal of support; but the country fell on hard economic times, and the government had to withdraw some financial support, though never its assistance and goodwill. Forward steps were taken, even if with reservations: a stack of 700 photographs of the most important objects in the museums arrived, even though accompanied by a note that these were not all to be assumed as available for loan. As we studied them, we became increasingly aware of the beauty and importance of the works, and of how splendid an exhibition of Maori art could be.

In 1979 representatives of the Art Galleries and Museums Associations of New Zealand and the Queen Elizabeth II Arts Council came to meet the New York group and to discuss progress. They made clear to us was just what the Maori part in the project had to be. The museums might nominally own the objects, but the Maori had never relinquished their spiritual ownership of them and their right of control, a position with which many of the museum's curators were in agreement. There would have to be full Maori participation in, and agreement to, anything that was to take place, and the New Zealand themselves had already fully accepted this principle. Naturally, we also did so, not only because we had no alternative but because we believed the principle was just.

We then agreed on several technical points: we would show the rich tradition of sculpture in wood, stone, bone and ivory. We would not show preserved tattooed human heads: as actual, physical parts of ancestors, they encroached too far into the realm of sanctity, and the Maori bitterly resented their being displayed. Tattooing was art: human remains were not. We would not ask for weavings and featherwork because they had had too much bodily contact with the ancestors, for one thing, and, for another were extremely fragile. As it happened we were later reproved by some Maori for not showing this, the major art of women.

There was in any case considerable scepticism, we knew, on the part of both Maori and Pakeha about whether the exhibition should or could take place at all; some of my Pakeha New Zealand museum colleagues, in fact, were quite confident that it never would. Some older and many younger Maori were bitterly opposed to the project from the start. Others were already in full support, including the Minister of Maori Affairs Ben Couch; Secretary for Maori Affairs Kara Puketapu and his successor Dr. Tamati Reedy; and other important Maori such as Maui Pomare, a trustee of the National Museum in Wellington. To my personal pleasure old friends, the distinguished Maori scholars David R. Simmons and Hirini (Sidney) Moko Mead, agreed to be my cocurators. Mead was also to become our most active advocate. With government agreement, a special Maori subcommittee was formed to monitor the Maori interests in the exhibition, which eventually, and after much to-and-fro was given the rather bland name "Te Maori".[5]

We worked out a wish list of works, the Metropolitan Museum of Art accepted the exhibition, and allotted space and time for it. It was the moment, this was now 1981, for someone of "our" side to go to New Zealand to put our case to the Maori and the museums. That someone was me, and willy-nilly I was launched into one of the most extraordinary experiences of my life. I knew that a good deal of negotiation would be involved; I had no idea how much. In 29 days I visited 14 museums throughout the country, from Auckland in the north to Invercargill in the south, to have meetings with museum trustees, directors and curators, and above all with leading Maori elders.

These meetings took on various tones. While the majority of the museum officials were sympathetic, many were apprehensive because they were unaccustomed to the idea of objects being shifted out of their home collections to anywhere else. Large-scale loan exhibitions, routine in the United States and Europe, were outside their frames of reference. In the end, though, even those who at first were opposed became caught up in the show's possibilities.

In the case of the Maori, meetings over a matter of large importance should ideally be held on the *marae*, a community's sacred open air space. Most of ours were not; they took place in conference rooms, offices, restaurants, and even in hotels (Figure 9.1). Mead later explained that this was partly a way of finding "a neutral place, and of emphasizing the role of the Maori in a modern society" (Mead 1986: 99), but it caused dissatisfaction on a number of occasions. Maori protocol is rigid, and also varies from tribe to tribe. Whether I was meeting one elder or 50 at a time, there was a set pattern of speeches, often in Maori. Kindly I was

Figure 9.1 Prayers are said at the beginning of a meeting of Maori elders at a hotel in Wellington, New Zealand. The meeting was typical of many held to discuss plans for the exhibition "Tc Maori" shown in the United States. Kara Puketapu is second from right. Photograph by Kathleen Haven Newton.

always provided with someone to help, translate and advise me, and of course most often it was he in actuality who did much of the work. This did not protect me from a constant disquieting conviction that the ice under my feet was very thin indeed.

My job was to explain what an American museum was, and what it did, and why the exhibition was worth doing. Many Maori had never laid eyes on the inside of a museum; they felt museums were merely instruments of the Pakeha who, not content with stealing their land, had usurped their taonga and that their life, their power, their mana had been betrayed. Many were afraid that the taonga would be stolen from them finally if they went overseas—quite literally stolen like so much else, by still another brand of Pakeha, and sold away forever. That sort of fear came as quite a shock to a museum curator. And then of course there was the crucial question, what good would such an exhibition do for the Maori anyway?

By this time I had learned enough about the Maori and their situation, or thought I had, to be able to answer such questions, and at least could do so with perfect sincerity. They felt that much of their power resided in their taonga; and they also felt, correctly, that as a people and as a culture they had been slighted. In the modern world, if one hid one's light under a bushel no one was going to come looking for it. The Metropolitan had 3 million visitors a year, equivalent to the population of New Zealand[6] ("I can't begin to think in those numbers," one lady exclaimed). Large numbers of people would see "Te Maori." One way to have the value of maoritanga understood was to exhibit its greatest material works to the world, through which the Maori ethos could be manifested to the Pakeha. This was an accepted path among Pakeha, and one they understood. The exhibition would be displayed in a space, already approved for scale and location by Kara Puketapu. It had earlier housed the ancient treasures of China, Egypt, Turkey, and Russia, and the Maori's art would take its place in that company as representing a great culture.

Not altogether unexpectedly, it was the militant members of the younger generation of Maori who were most bitter about the exhibition. They were allowed their say, but in Maori society their voices counted for very little. It was the elders who debated the question, and made the final decision for the taonga to travel. In at least one case, Maori overruled Pakeha curators who had wished not to send works, in particular the great carving of the rainbow war god Uenuku. His tribal custodian Ariki Nui Dame te Ata i Rangi Kaahu said grandly that Uenuku had led the ancestors to New Zealand, and that he should lead them to New York. In other cases, the elders had second thoughts about sending certain works, and we accepted their wishes. It was a given that whatever they chose was to be their decision and binding upon the rest of us; no one would force anything on them or go over their heads. There was intensive discussion almost up to the last minute, and it was disappointing that in the end a few major works were disallowed. Only one elder took it upon himself, without consultation with anyone, to refuse contributions totally; and I heard later that he was later much berated when his fellow elders realized that, by cutting their tribe out of a highly successful enterprise, he had diminished its mana.[7]

Finally, one September dawn in 1984, "Te Maori" opened at the Metropolitan Museum of Art, and it was an unforgettable occasion

(Figures 9.2 and 9.3). The actual ceremonial of the opening was carried out by a group of elders who had come to New York, with ritual, chanting, addresses and prayers to the ancestors. Nobody who was present was not deeply moved. It was not because of the exotic quality of the ceremonial, but because Maori had the power to transmit their belief, the mana of Maorihood, for all to see and, even if dimly, understand.

More than 200,000 people visited "Te Maori" in New York (not including thousands of schoolchildren). The exhibition moved on to St. Louis, Missouri; San Francisco, California; and Chicago, Illinois. Each time, it was accompanied by a different group of elders, and each time, it opened with ritual and great emotion. Cultural groups of performing artists augmented with song, dance and oratory the limited contents of the exhibition itself. Altogether over 621,000 people saw "Te Maori" in the United States; millions more heard of it through the media; and certainly among them were many who had never heard of the Maori before. After this there was no question that 'Te Maori" had to be shown in New Zealand itself, and it toured Wellington, Dunedin, Christchurch, and Auckland, with an ancillary exhibition in Honolulu, Hawaii. In the four New Zealand cities "Te Maori" was seen by more than 900,000 visitors, that is about 28% of the entire population. No other exhibition, so far as I know, had ever received so much attention in New Zealand. "Te Maori", to those who visited it, whether in the United States or in New Zealand, whether Maori or Pakeha, changed their perceptions of a culture. It will have a lasting effect on the young Maori; hundreds of them were recruited and trained as guides by Mead and Mrs. Mead at the several venues of the exhibition, and their evident pride in being placed in touch with their heritage was delightful to see.

Here then we have a case in which traditional museums performed effectively a job related to cultural preservation or, better still, inspiration. The very fact that great American museums had displayed Maori culture to great public acclaim brought it attention. There was also a considerable effect on New Zealand governmental policies for culture, both Maori and Pakeha. Very shortly after, and undoubtedly under the influence of the success of "Te Maori", plans were launched for the creation in Wellington, the capital, for a new national museum in three sections, devoted to a concept of reconciling the land itself, and

Figure 9.2   Dr. Peter Sharples, educator and expert in Maori culture, in traditional dress and stance at the opening of "Te Maori," September 10, 1984. He is in front of one of the works, a carved gateway from Rotorua. Photograph by Fred R. Conrad, *The New York Times.*

Figure 9.3 Maori *tohunga* Sonny Waru (center) chants *Karakia* (invocations) as he climbs the steps of The Metropolitan Museum of Art, New York, at dawn on September 10, 1984 for the opening of "Te Maori." He is accompanied by a party of *rangatira*, Maori elders. Dr. Sharples (near right) is one of the two *manutaki* (guardians). Photograph by Fred R. Conrad, *The New York Times.*

the two ethnic groups that inhabit it. No one would have dreamed of such a project two decades before. More important, let me quote some remarks of my colleague Hirini Moko Mead. His moving words say a great deal of what we hoped for the exhibition:

> We [the Maori] stand taller after "Te Maori," we speak with a greater assurance and dignity, we are more hopeful about our future, we are confident about being Maori, and we feel less threatened by others. We have a magnificent heritage and a beautiful future ahead of us. This is the message of "Te Maori." (Mead 1986: 118)

It would be misleading to convey that even after the success of "Te Maori" all Maori were enthusiastic about it. Opposition continued, more or less along the same lines as before, with certain elaborations and refinements of grievances.[8] This can only be to the good if opposition leads to positive action and reform rather than to introverted discontent.

The museum, on reflection, remains in whatever form it takes one of the few unquestionably beneficent achievements of modern civilization. It can educate, it can enlighten, bring respect for the stranger, and give the greatest pleasure in the accomplishments of others. The view of it taken here is narrow: nothing has been said to those museums which are in the fields of the science, only of the humanities—we can include in this range Elvis Presley, who is historically part of American culture, but not astronomy.

The museum can only work within the limitations imposed by history, and these are irrevocable. The museum can do many things; it can teach us about ourselves and "others," but cannot change anything except its visitors' minds. The Museum cannot bring the past back to life. It cannot make a contemporary Englishman into an Elizabethan Londoner, a Maori professor into a cloaked and tattooed chieftain. It can preserve the tokens of a culture and, by displaying, them cultivate and keep alive the memory of the times and people that created them. That memory enriches us all, and bestows upon us culture. Without it we have no past, and thus less sense of our own individuality and worth.

I often think of what I saw the first time I visited the great Museo Nacional de Antropología in Mexico. Its organization is brilliant: the first floor houses galleries of the Precolumbian monuments from the different areas of the country, the second floor has corresponding galleries of recent cultural materials from the same areas. On that first visit, I was struck by the many visiting families from rural districts. The men wore white cotton suits and wide straw hats, the women dark dresses and shawls, the children were similarly dressed, all were barefoot. At a glance, they could see, throughout the vast building, what their ancestors had created through the long history of Mexico. I often wonder what became of those people. Did they go back to their farms? Did they settle in the city? Did they become slumdwellers? Did those children become delinquents or good citizens? I'll never know. But I hope that day their visit to the museum gave them a sense of history, a sense of pride in their culture and in themselves. If the visit did, that pride justifies the long history of the museum as an institution.

Notes

1. Alsop (1982: 123) explains that many works were not returned to Italy after Waterloo because the Italian primitives were out of fashion, were thought "hardly worth the cost of packing and shipping"!
2. The situation is being remedied: for instance, repatriation of the ethnographic collection taken from the Museum fur Volkerkunde of Berlin began in 1991.
3. One must not overlook a number of other factors, the most important being that a great deal of ritual was still deeply embedded in memory as valid behavior. Social reasons—including dissatisfaction with the economic situation and introduced ideologies—must also have played a significant role.
4. The word "power" is a very summary equivalent of a complex concept which includes "prestige and authority" in dictionary definitions, and is linked to the supernatural.
5. On the possibility of future similar exhibitions, H.M. Mead remarked "When that time comes, we will not be so timid as to be afraid of calling an exhibition of our best examples of creative art "Mana Maori" as happened this time. After "Te Mana", "Mana Maori" is about as threatening as a teaspoon in the hand of a six-month-old baby." (Mead 1986: 118)
6. By now, both figures have increased considerable.
7. For some of the later adventures and problems of a Metropolitan Museum staff working on "Te Maori" see O'Biso (1987).

8. For details of one instance of this, see Adrienne L. Kaeppler's chapter in this book. Maori motives are often complex, and one should not underrate the possibility that the elder's actions may have been more than a simple bit of Pakeha-bashing. As appears from my text, he must have known his *rakau whakapapa* was to be shown in "Te Maori", and have had a chance to see it was properly described. It is not unthinkable that demonstrating the ignorance of the Pakeha also provided him an opportunity for subtly demonstrating the equal ignorance of his fellow-Maori, and thus increasing his own mana.

References

Alsop, Joseph
  1982 *The Rare Art Traditions. The History of Art Collecting and its Linked Phenomena Wherever these have Appeared.* Bollingen Series XXXV 27. Princeton University Press. New York: Harper & Row, Publishers.
Bernal, Ignacio
  1980 *A History of Mexican Archaeology. The Vanished Civilizations of Middle America.* New York: Thames & Hudson Inc.
Canfora, Luciano
  1990 *The Vanished Library. A Wonder of the Ancient World.* Translated by Martin Ryle. Berkeley, Los Angeles: University of California Press.
Crowe, Peter
  1991 *The Paris PAA: A Report.* Pacific arts no. 3, January 1991: 2–5.
Dark, Philip J.C.
  1987 *"The Living Museum": a Wenner-Gren Foundation Planning Meeting at Suva, Fiji, 9–14 November, 1986.* Pacific arts newsletter no. 24: 8–10.
Graves, Robert
  1957 *The Greek Myths.* 2 v. Baltimore: Penguin Books Inc.
Levi-Strauss, Claude
  1974 *Tristes Tropiques.* Translated by John and Doreen Weightman. New York: Atheneum.
Mead, Hirini [Sydney] Moko
  1986 *Magnificent Te Maori. Te Maori whakahirahira. He Korero Whakanui i Te Maori.* Auckland: Heinemann.
Ngata, Sir Apirana and Sir Peter Buck
  1986 *Na to hoa aroha. From your dear friend. The Correspondence between Sir Apirana Ngata and Sir Peter Buck 1925–50.* 3 v. Auckland: Auckland University Press.
O'Biso, Carol
  1987 *First Light.* Auckland: Heinemann.
Somare, Sir Michael
  1974 *Introduction. In Guide to the collection.* Papua New Guinea Public Museum and Art Gallery: Port Moresby.

10 Portuguese Art Treasures, Medieval Women and Early Museum Collections

Madalena Braz Teixeira

In the two parts of this chapter, I concentrate on the formation of Portuguese art museum collections. The first part covers the period of the nation's formation, A.D. 1123 and 1415, the dates established as the beginning of the "Discoveries," the period of Portuguese maritime expansion. In this period, treasures were not yet perceived as cultural patrimony. They were collected for specific qualities, as ornaments and as signs of wealth. Religious institutions were then the main places where treasures were gathered and kept, a situation that obtained until 1834 when all religious institutions were abolished. Consequently, the church treasures form the basis of today's collections in Portuguese museums.

The second part of this chapter covers the period between 1415 and the end of the 16th century, when the first collections that can be called "national" were formed. In it I also consider the roles of medieval women.

Historical Background

Iberia was first inhabited some 500,000 years ago in the Lower Paleolithic period. Later inhabitants of the Iberian Peninsula were the Iberos, who probably came from Africa about 1500 B.C., and the Celts, who came from northern Europe about 700 B.C. They are considered to be the ancestors of the present-day Portuguese people, the Lusitanos. Some important settlements were established by Phoenicians and Greeks in coastal areas, circa 1000 B.C. These areas were dominated by the Romans from the third century B.C. until the barbarian invasions of the fifth century A.D. In 711, the Moors landed on the peninsula and were to remain in present-day Spain and Portugal for eight centuries. They stayed in northern Portugal for only a few decades, but in the south they remained until they were finally expelled in the 13th century. The *Reconquista* of the peninsula from Arab domination was actually begun in the eighth century.

A dynasty of counts of Portucale was established in the ninth century. The name "Portucale" is formed from *porto* and *cale*, which means a small port. The first count to rule was Vimara Peres, in A.D. 868; he died in A.D. 873. His granddaughter, D. Mumadona, was responsible for enlarging Guimarães in the 10th century. She established the Monastery of Sta. Maria, and to it she donated much land and a valuable collection of manuscripts and religious ornaments. Her actions were accompanied by a great increase in the population of Guimarães, which later became the first capital of the kingdom. Another county in existence at the same time was under the count of Coimbra.

Both places, Portucale and Coimbra, were part of the Kingdom of León, but Portucale was the more important one and nearly autonomous. It was the region given as a wedding gift to D. Teresa, the bastard daughter of King Afonso VI of León and Castile, when she married D. Henrique of the House of Burgundy. Afonso VI also gave the county of Galicia to his eldest daughter, Urraca, on the occasion of her wedding to D. Raimundo, also of the House of Burgundy. Both cousins, D. Henrique and D. Raimundo, were among a number of European noblemen who came to the Iberian Peninsula to fight the Moors in a religious war known as the Western Crusades.

Afonso VI also had a bastard son, Sancho, by Zaira, the daughter of the Moorish Caliph of Seville, to whom he wished to leave his kingdom. Neither D. Raimundo nor D. Henrique approved of what they considered to be the dispossession of their wives. In 1106, they concluded a written agreement that would give Toledo and a third of all its considerable treasures to D. Henrique on the death of Afonso VI. If this should prove to be impossible, D. Raimundo would give his cousin the county of Galicia. Further, they pledged to give each other mutual support. However, D. Raimundo predeceased Afonso VI, and D. Urraca married again, this time to the king of Aragon, thus uniting the three kingdoms—León, Castile, and Aragon— and the county of Galicia. This unification, however, broke up after Afonso VI died, and a civil war ensued. D. Henrique refused to acknowledge his feudal duties to D. Urraca in 1112 or 1114, as did his wife, D. Teresa, after his death.

Their son, D. Afonso Henrique, fought with his mother over the freedom and power she allowed him and about her Galician lover. D. Henrique won the Battle of S. Mamede and banished D. Teresa from the country. She went to live in Galicia with her lover, Fernão Peres de Trava. Her son declared Portugal an independent kingdom in 1123; and it was recognized by Pope Alexander III in 1143.

Beginnings of the Kingdom, A.D. 1123–1415

First Treasures

The early treasures were to be found in the cathedrals, monasteries, convents, and churches, and in the castles. The religious institutions kept them mostly for liturgical reasons, whereas the treasures in castles were collected for wealth and prestige and as a ready source of funds in times of war. Church treasures consisted of sacred objects used for Mass and rituals, as well as other rare objects that were difficult either to make or to find in the country; these included textiles, rugs, leathers, ceramics, glass, wood, iron, and other metal objects made by skilled artisans, who were relatively few. Little remains from this period because everything that belonged to the infidels had to be destroyed or transformed. Nonetheless, an ivory Islamic cup, which belonged to the son of Almançor (A.D. 1160–1199), may be seen today and is part of the treasure of the Cathedral of Braga (Barreiros 1954:6). Almançor was an important Islamic ruler, well known for having built the Giralda Tower in Seville.

Medieval society as a whole was dominated by religion. In Portugal, there were four main religious centers: Braga, Coimbra, Guimarães, and Alcobaça. The primate and the church hierarchy were situated in Braga; Alcobaça led in social and economic development in the country; and Coimbra was to become its most important intellectual center. Coimbra University was established there in 1290. The religious centers were

influenced by the Cistercian order and up to the 13th century were
inclined to be austere. Mendicant orders were established and Romanesque architecture adopted. Twelfth-century cathedrals were fortified
and served as repositories for religious and other precious objects. The
military orders, Knights Templars, Knights Hospitalers, Knights of
Santiago, and Knights of Aviz, each had their castles, which contained
their arms and treasures. Monasteries constructed during this period
could be defended and served as places of refuge for the local
populations. Some of the treasures of castles, religious institutions, and
towns were acquired in the pillaging of lands conquered from the
Muslims (Teixeira 1983:39).

The conquest of Lisbon in A.D. 1147 is an example of a pillaged city.
Its conquest was greatly assisted by the English, German, and Flemish
Crusaders who stopped in Oporto on their way to the Holy Land during
the Second Crusade. The first bishop of Lisbon, Gilbert of Hastings, was
an Englishman who took an oath of obedience to João, Archbishop of
Braga (Livermore 1989:10). The mosque in Lisbon was transformed into
a cathedral, and the new bishop's deans were appointed from among his
compatriots.

Royal Treasures

During the medieval period, royal treasures were personal and associated
with individual kings; they did not belong to the state. Works of art
were kept and commissioned to add prestige and wealth to royalty, the
leaders of society.

The king, carrying his royal treasure with him, and his court traveled
around the country for military, political, and administrative reasons: to
exert local and regional control and to collect taxes. They often lived in
tents because so few places had buildings large enough to receive them.
We know something of these treasures from written testaments; they
included precious personal and religious objects, items of dress, and
gold and silver coins. Up to the 13th century A.D., testaments were
written in Latin and recorded how the various belongings were to be
divided and to whom they should be given (Teixeira 1983:51). Princess
D. Mafalda (1200–1256), for example, included some artworks in her
last will and testament, written in 1256. She willed the *duae sortillias*
(archaeological pieces considered to be *porte bonheur* or good luck) and

tre lapides saphieos et reservatur in thesauro to the Convent of Arouca, and to her brother Pedro she willed *monum* (coin not in use) *et lapidem sapi et alliam sortelliam magnum*. These objects were antique pieces, jewels and coins from Roman times or earlier. Medieval society believed that these items would bring good luck, which meant health and peace. Queen D. Beatriz (1373-ca. 1409), in her will written in 1354, left to her grandson *a camafeo*, representing a lion, which was found in an old monument (Vasconcelos 1923:9). D. Dinis (1261–1325) in his will left to his eldest son (the future King D. Afonso IV) a variety of objects, including jewels and all of his table sets made of gold and silver (Sousa 1946:239). The inventory of the possessions of D. Dinis, dated 1278–1282 and richly detailed, yields an idea of his treasure: tapestries, furnishings, tableware, goblets, items of dress, jewels, and other personal belongings. Among them, two objects are of particular interest: one, a copper barrel, was used to decant water for the relief of pain; the other, glass stones with Arab symbols, was decorated with silver (Anselmo 1916:41). The first is for medical purposes, and the second testifies to the importance of that particular Islamic object. By the 13th century, the *Reconquista* was already far away and was remote from prejudices against Muslims. The second object is rare, reason enough for it to carry prestige and for it to be described as part of the royal treasure. Nothing remains of D. Dinis' inventory today, war being just one of several reasons.

The above-mentioned testaments and inventories are intended to show what sorts of things were considered precious in medieval times. Other objects mentioned include religious ornaments, jewels, precious and semiprecious stones, clothing, articles of personal adornment, chests, tapestries, linen, and leather, as well as vases, tableware, and occasionally some medicomagic equipment and medicines (Marques 1973:75).

In 1345, a law decreed that all found treasures were to be divided, with half to go to the king, half to be retained by the discoverer. If a discovery were to take place by magic or witchcraft, everything would go to the king. Another such law was enacted in 1433. These archaeological treasures were mainly Roman coins (Teixeira 1983:36).

The political system at this time was not feudal in the same way that northern Europe was feudal. Power was centralized in the hands of a king, not delegated to noblemen, and local administration was carried out by *"alcaides"* appointed by the king, who were also responsible for local defense. Neither the noblemen, unless they belonged to the royal family, nor the *alcaides* were sufficiently powerful to accumulate treasure of any importance.

Church Collections

The church may be considered the most important repository of artistic treasures in the medieval period. Religion dominated the life and the emotions of the whole society. Kings, nobles, and individuals made many donations to the church and to its parishes, cathedrals, convents, and monasteries for a number of reasons: for fear of death, disease, hunger, and war; for personal beliefs and attachments; and for other political, military, or social problems that could be solved through the influence of priests, monks, or nuns. Thanks to medical and pharmacological help, results were frequently attributed to miracles, and many people throughout society became dependent on the church for solutions to problems. Thus, donations poured into various church institutions and into its coffers.

Religious institutions dominating society through God, acquired objects for liturgical purposes, for the decoration of their buildings, for investment, and for signaling the wealth attached to the faithful. The strength of the church's power was well illustrated in the documents of this period and throughout European history: the power of wealth, of treasure, of land, and of souls.

There was an important difference between church treasures and treasures belonging to royalty and noblemen. The former remained in the possession of the church, while the latter changed hands with each generation. The church constantly added things, which greatly increased its wealth. One significant aspect of church treasures for this study is their utility in illustrating changing styles and tastes. The priests, who were the teachers and scholars, played a decisive role in cultural development (Almeida 1930:243). They were able to identify precious objects; and they were normally immune from robbery. Church treasures remained essentially intact until 1834, when members of religious orders were expelled from the country, and religious property was nationalized.

Women and Treasures

It had been quite common for Portuguese women to take the veil. The reasons for their doing so were many: poverty, to escape from arranged marriages and frustrated love, and to escape from family pressures. Many women also withdrew to convents after being widowed; others were simply following their vocations.

Establishing convents was important in populating the country, in developing agricultural activities, in trading, and in promoting the social status of the local population. Around the convents and under their patronage, new agricultural products and techniques were introduced and encouraged, which consequently led to flourishing trade among the communities. New buildings and new villages appeared. Artisans, attracted by the prestige of the convents, came and were able to improve their skills.

Two princesses of this early period were D. Sancha (1160–1229), who lived in the Convent of Lorvão, and D. Mafalda (ca. 1200–1256), who lived in the Convent of Arouca. The two daughters of D. Sancho I established two new convents: the Convent of Sancha in Celas, and the Convent of Mafalda in Bouças. These four convents are important for their treasures and for farming and fishing developments in their locales.

Princess D. Sancha with her sister, D. Teresa, retired to the Convent of Lorvão due to a quarrel with her brother, King D. Afonso II, about her wealth and power. D. Sancha and D. Teresa both decided to take the veil in Lorvão, away from court problems and intrigues. They established the Convent of Sancha in Celas, circa 1213. D. Sancha purchased a great number of properties, which she donated to the convent, and commissioned a magnificent building in the Romanesque style, a building that can still be seen. She acquired for its church numerous works of art, some of which are today kept at the Museu Nacional Machado de Castro, in Coimbra.

D. Mafalda, though she was fiancée to Henrique, the eldest son of the king of Castile, never married, as Henrique died at the age of 14. She returned to Portugal and devoted her life to promoting social work and to helping to establish convents. Like her sister D. Sancha, she had problems with her brother the king about her wealth and power. Among the newly established convents, there was Bouças for which she especially cared, donating to this convent several properties and artistic treasures. When she died, she left all of her personal belongings and property to various religious institutions.

The will of Mafalda informs us that she left two amulets and three sapphires to the Convent of Arouca. The amulets were of Roman origin and were thought to bring luck. Arouca, in the center of Portugal, became very important in cultural terms for its treasures (Teixeira 1983:113). Some of the artworks gathered by the nuns through the centuries are today housed in the Grão Vasco Museum in Viseu.

Lorvão was at first a monastery, and we presume that its foundation dates from the end of the 11th century. However, Lorvão became a convent from the 13th century onward and an important cultural center (Borges 1977:50). Although the building has some remains of "moçarabe" and Romanesque styles, its appearance dates from the end of the 17th century and from the 18th century. Most of its treasures are still kept at the Museu Nacional Machado de Castro, in Coimbra, where one can observe the evidence of the highly sensitive tastes of its abbess. In the convent, there are still a great number of paintings and sculptures, dating from the Renaissance and baroque periods. Its famous manuscripts are kept at the University of Coimbra Library. A while later, in 1336, Queen Santa Isabel left part of her treasure to the Convent of Santa Clara in Coimbra, where what remains of her treasure is on view today in the Muesu Nacional Machado de Castro (Teixeira 1983:50).

Queen D. Isabel (1274–1336) (Saint Elizabeth), wife of King D. Dinis, is known as "Rainha Santa" ("The Saint Queen"). She is today the patron saint of the city of Coimbra, its university, and its students. She lived at the Convent of Santa Clara in Coimbra after being widowed. She enlarged this Gothic building and sponsored the construction of its new church (today in ruins). She also erected a hospital for the poor of Coimbra and built two others in the castles at Leiria and Santarém. Many churches and chapels and their ceremonial treasures were established by Queen Santa Isabel, as was the Convent of Almoster. Her charitable personality and the legend of her immense generosity make her one of the favourite individuals in the history of Portugal. Her sacred image—always representing one of her miracles, the miracle of the roses—appears in a great number of Portuguese altars.

Santa Joana (1452–1490) was a princess, a daughter of King Afonso V: her convent is now the Museu de Aveiro. Princess Joana refused to get married. A number of ambassadors from various countries asked her father, the king, and later asked her powerful brother, King D. João II, for her hand. Her answer was always no. She returned to the Convent of Jesus in the city of Aveiro. All of her belongings were then engraved with Jesus' thorn crown, which became her insignia. A portrait of her dressed in court costume gives us an idea of her personality: sad, strong, and obstinate. She devoted her life to the Convent of Jesus and greatly increased its art treasures.

The Convent of Jesus was considered one of the richest and most important in the country, but many convents commissioned works of art or received them as gifts from royalty and the aristocracy. Nuns from well-to-do families would often take their favorite possessions with them into the convents to make their lives more comfortable. Thus, the convents built considerable collections, most of which represented sacred art. Sacred images, also adorned with costumes and jewels, were brought into the convents and left to them by all sorts of followers (Teixeira 1983:38).

Queen D. Leonor (1458–1525) was of great importance as a collector (Figure 10.1). She was the wife of King D. João II and lived during the golden age of Portuguese history, the age of the discoveries and the navigators. She devoted herself as much to social welfare as to cultural patronage. In 1498 she founded the *Misericórdia*, a charitable and religious organization, which devoted itself to caring for the health of the poor and to providing them with food. In the Convent of Madre de Deus, where she went to live after being widowed, she surrounded herself with precious objects. The convent, which incidentally is one of the finest examples of Portuguese baroque interiors, today also contains part of her collection; the other part of her collection can be found in the National Art Museum, along with objects commissioned by her. These items include a reliquary, paintings by Portuguese and foreign artists, and the so-called *Custódia de Belém*, a masterpiece of jewelry designed by Gil Vicente (ca. 1465–ca. 1536), who was also a writer (Figure 10.2), His plays were often commissioned by Queen D. Leonor, as she was also a patron of scholars, musicians, and writers (Couto 1958:15).

Further examples of fine collections exist among other monasteries,

Figure 10.1 *Queen D. Leonor* in *Jerusalem View*, by Flemish author, second half of the 15th century, Museu Nacional do Azulejo. Donation of the Emperor Maximilian from Austria. The portrait of the Queen was commissioned by her from a Portuguese painter after the arrival of the picture in Portugal. Belonged to the Convent of Madre de Deus.

most of which are now national monuments with their own museums. The same is true of the cathedrals that keep their remaining treasures in museums. Only a few of the religious institutions that were established during medieval times are mentioned here for their great art treasures: the Cathedrals of Braga, Lisbon, Oporto, Coimbra, and Évora; the Monasteries of Alcobaça, Guimarães, Santa Cruz de Coimbra, Cristo in

Figure 10.2 *Custódia de Belém*, gold and enamel, by Gil Vicente, 1506, Museu Nacional de Arte Antiga. Commissioned by Queen D. Leonor; belonged to the Monastery of Jerónimos.

Tomar, Batalha, and St. Vincente de Fora in Lisbon and Varatojo; the Convents of Santa Clara and Santa Maria of Reforios, and the Convent of Odivelas (Teixeira 1983).

A New Approach to the Formation of Collections, 1415–1580

After 1415, with the conquest in that year of Ceuta by D. João I, a new period of collecting objects of aesthetic and historical value commenced. Ceuta, located in North Africa, became the first Portuguese fortress on that continent. While pillaging was going on in Ceuta, D. Afonso (1380–1461), the bastard son of King D. João I (the first duke of Bragança), acquired the Islamic marble columns for the chapel for the Gothic palace he built for the dukes of Bragança in Guimarães. He also brought back a wood-carved ceiling in the Islamic style, some jasper columns, an entire window, and a marble table where Governor Sala-ben-Sala of Ceuta used to have his meals (Silva 1973). In his later years, D. Afonso retired to Chaves, formerly a Roman town called Aquae Flaviae, where he collected archaeological specimens, manuscripts, and antiques. He also had an important collection of tapestries (Machado 1963:15).

Another collector of this period was D. Pedro (1429–1466), grandson of D. João I. Pedro became the king of Catalonia. He acquired a considerable numismatic collection. An inventory of his collection gives a description of each piece and its weight (Vasconcelos 1923:51). Both men, Afonso and Pedro, are early examples of humanistic collectors.

D. Jaime (1479–1532), grandson of D. Afonso de Bragança, built a palace at Vila Viçosa in the Luso-Islamic style using local marble. This palace became the principal residence of the Bragança family, even after they became the royal family in 1640, and was filled with rare and beautiful objects. The collections grew through the centuries and remained virtually intact until the establishment of the republic in 1910 (Dionísio 1942:20). Apart from its eclectic possessions, the Bragança family also had one of the most important collections of armor, which can still be seen at Vila Viçosa, along with works covering all periods of Portuguese history.

Collections of the 15th and 16th centuries contained numismatic, epigraphic, archaeological, and ethnographic specimens, as well as works of art and botanical and zoological specimens. Some examples are described below and reveal the deep interest in culture and environment among the populations met by the Portuguese during the Discoveries.

Two examples illustrate ethnographic acquisitions. Afonso Gonçalves Baldaia arrived at Ponta da Galé (near Guinea) in 1436. He brought back nets and other fishing equipment made out of a material similar to linen in order to show Prince Henri "The Navigator" the artifacts used by the local population (Baião 1940:140). Another description was reported by Valentim Fernandes, whose manuscripts cover the years 1506–1516. Speaking about Sierra Leone, he described the beauty of several objects manufactured from ivory in whatever design was submitted to them (Monod et al. 1951:104).

Nearly all scholars at this time were either priests or monks. André de Resende (1500–1573), a scholar who lived primarily in Évora, organized an open-air collection of epigraphic specimens, mostly Roman, in his garden. This collection was pedagogical and was used in the education of students from the local University of Évora, where Resende was a master. Most of the specimens had been discovered in and around Évora, an important town in Alentejo, where a royal palace had been built by King D. Manuel I (1469–1521). Resende was one of the scholars of this period who were also collectors (Vasconcelos 1785:26).

Another important ecclesiastic who started a numismatic and archaeological collection was Archbishop D. Diogo de Sousa (1461–1532) of Braga. He also had a garden of epigraphic specimens from Braga. Braga had been a bishopric since A.D. 216, so it was not difficult to find specimens from Roman times when this town was called Bracara Augusta. His collection too was pedagogical and was used in the education of student priests (Teixeira 1983:50). The bishop's palace, like other bishop's palaces in the country, contained collections of tapestries and fine art. D. Diogo de Sousa published a book in 1497 entitled *The Synodic Constitution*, which was one of the first books to be published in Portugal. Among a number of church laws in this book was one that forbade the sale or pawning of books, chalices, crosses, and other religious objects under penalty of excommunication, fine, or annulment of contracts. This document was the first published definition of canon law in Portugal and protected the patrimony of the church. Similar sets of laws were subsequently published in other dioceses (Anselmo, 1981:279).

The Portuguese exported exotic animals, feathers, jewels, pearls, gold,

Figure 10.3 *St. Jerónimo*, by Albrecht Dürer, 16th century, Museu Nacional de Arte Antiga. Belonged to Rodrigo Fernandes de Almada.

medicines, leather, ivory, cotton, sugar, salt, wine, olive oil, and fruit to Flanders and imported works of art, including paintings, sculptures, and tapestries, among other goods. Albrecht Dürer wrote in his diary that, on October 28, 1520, he bought a skull for the study of St. Jerónimo; he later offered it to the Portuguese *"feitor"* Rodrigo Fernandes de Almada (Vaisse 1964:134, 142). This painting can be seen today at the Museu Nacional de Arte Antiga (National Art Museum Figure 10.3).

Damião de Góes (1502–1574), an intellectual from Lisbon who became the head of the Portuguese Factory in Flanders, organized the most interesting art collection of the time, a collection that he moved from Antwerp to Portugal. He was well connected both in Flanders and in Portugal, and part of his collection can still be seen in the National Art Museum in Lisbon, along with *Tentações de Santo Antão de Jerónimos' Bosh* and the *Crucifixion* by Quentin Metsys (Massys) (Segurado 1978:149). Damião de Góes, one of the victims of the Inquisition (established in 1536), claimed during his trial that he possessed paintings only of religious themes. Although he was imprisoned by the Inquisition, he later lived for some time in the Monastery of Batalha before he died.

The Inquisition in Portugal was all-powerful up to the 18th century; therefore, few artworks had mythological or classical themes. Almost all of them were portraits, still lifes, or social scenes, and had religious themes. The noble palaces of Portugal held few works of art that were not religious or that could be construed as antireligious.

Many paintings, even those of religious significance, however, were often a pretext for portraits of patrons. A poliptic attributed to Nuno Gonçalves (fl. 1450–1472), known as the *Painéis de S. Vincente*, is composed of six woods, in which the patron saint of Lisbon is surrounded by the royal family, nobles, bishops, clergymen, scholars, merchants, fishermen, and a Jew, who was one of the financial patrons of the Discoveries. This painting is supposed to have belonged to the Cathedral of Lisbon and can be seen today at the National Art Museum (Figure 10.4). It is considered the masterpiece of all periods. It expresses the national aims and goals of maritime expansion, which were held by virtually all members of Portuguese society. Another is the house that belonged to Vasco da Gama, which still exists in Évora. Its apocalyptic frescoes, which subtly depicted exotic elements to be found in Paradise, were based on the then-recently discovered flora and fauna of South America, Africa, and India.

Animals and plants from distant lands were often depicted in paintings of the period. So, too, were Brazilian Indians with their feathers and dark skins. There are two famous paintings: one represents Hell, where the Devil is shown as a Brazilian Indian (Figure 10.5); and the other, signed by Grão Vasco and belonging to the Cathedral of Viseu, depicts one of the Three Kings as a Brazilian Indian.

Viceroy D. João de Castro (1500–1548) returned with trophies of his victories in India and some stones inscribed in Sanskrit, all of which can

(a) Monk's pane   (b) Fishermen's pane   (c) Infante's pane

(d) Archbishop's pane   (e) Knight's pane   (f) Relic's pane

Figure 10.4 *Painéis de S. Vincente*, attributed to Nuno Gonçalves, second half of the 15th century, Museu Nacional de Arte Antiga. May have belonged to the Cathedral of Lisbon.

Figure 10.5 *Hell*, by an unknown Portuguese master, first half of the 16th century, Museu Nacional de Arte Antiga.

be seen today in Quinta da Penha Verde, in Sintra. He also had a remarkable collection of tapestries manufactured at Tournai (Belgium) at the beginning of the 16th century (Keil 1928:6).

Garcia da Horta (1501–1568), a doctor from a Jewish family, went to Goa in India. He dedicated himself to cultivating medicinal plants, thereby creating a botanical garden and herbarium. He also collected natural-history specimens. Garcia da Horta wrote a great deal about pharmacology and the medicinal uses of plants and herbs. For a long time, his book—*Colloquios dos Simples*—remained the only scientific volume about this subject in India; and it became very well known elsewhere (Carvalho 1934:31).

Important ethnographic collections from the Discoveries were housed in the Royal Palace in Lisbon and on its grounds. Specimens came from Brazil, Sierra Leone, the Congo, Zimbabwe, Mombasa, Hormuz, Goa, Malacca, Ceylon, China, and Japan. King D. Manuel I established a zoological collection, becoming one of the first-known zoos in Europe.

An important 20th-century writer and anthropologist, Leite de Vasconcelos, used to say that the first ethnographic museum of Portugal was the Royal Palace of King D. Manuel I in Lisbon. The king's store, called *"Casa da India,"* organized and displayed everything in an artistic way, wrote a chronicler at the time (Góes 1554:51). Destroyed by the disastrous earthquake of 1755, nothing remains of these buildings.

During the late 15th and the 16th centuries, it is apparent that scientific interest was awakened by the objects brought back from newly discovered lands. This interest can also be seen in the architecture of this period, called *manvelino* and sometimes "Portuguese". Cathedrals, convents, and monasteries, as well as private palaces, were built in this style. Thus, the collections established in Portugal reflect a broad spectrum of interests—archaeology, history, art, natural history, and ethnography—interests that were extended by the widened horizons of the period of the Discoveries.

Most Portuguese museums today are a result of the treasures first gathered in religious institutions (Figure 10.6) and in royal palaces (Figure 10.7) and acquired by individuals, many of them distinguished women, during the humanistic period, giving Portugal its unique cultural identity.

Figure 10.6   *Chalice*, gilded silver 12th century, Museu Nacional de Arte Antiga. Belonged to the Monastery of Alcobaça.

Figure 10.7 *D. Afonso's Chair*, Gothic oak chair, second half of the 15th century, Museu Nacional de Arte Antiga. Belonged to the Monastery of Varatojo.

References

Almeida, Fortunato de
   1930 *História da Igreja em Portugal*. Porto: Portucalense Editora.
Anselmo, Artur
   1981 *Origems da Imprensa em Portugal*. Lisboa: Imprensa Nacional-Casa da Moeda.
   1916 *Arquivo Histórico Português, 1916*. Vol. 10. Lisboa.
Baião, António
   1940 *O Manuscrita de Valentim Ferandes*. Lisboa: Academia Portuguesa de História.
Barbosa, I. de Vilhena
   1885 *Apontamentos para a História des coleções e dos estudos de zoologia em Portugal*. Lisboa: Edição la Sociedade do Jardim Zoológico e de Aclimatização em Portugal.
   1907 Museum creados em Portugal até ao fim do século XVIII, *Boletim da Real Associação dos Arquitetos e Arqueologos*, 10, 4, Lisboa.
Barreiros, Conego Manuel de Aguiar
   1954 *Catálogo e Guia da Tesoiro da Sé Primaz de Braga*. Porto: Marques de Abreu.
Borges, Correia
   1977 *O Mosteiro do Lorvão*. Coimbra: Epartur.
Carvalho, Augusto da Silva
   1934 *Garcia d'Orta*. Coimbra: Imprensa da Universidade.
Chaves, Luis
   1946 Bronzes de Benin, *Congresso comemorativo do quinto centenário do descobrimento da Guiné*. Lisboa: Sociedade de Geografia de Lisboa.
Cortesão, Jaime
   1943 *Carta de Pero Vaz de Cominha*. Rio de Janeiro: Livros de Portugal.
Couto, João
   1958 A Rainha e os artistas. In *A Rainha D. Leanor*. Lisboa: Fundação Calouste Gulbenkian.
Dionísio, Sant'Ana
   1942 *Museu-Biblioteca de Vila Viçosa*. Lisboa: Fundação da Casa de Bragança.
Góes, Damião de
   1554 *Lisboa Quinhentista*, 1911 ed. Lisboa: Transcrição de Raul Machado.
Keil, Luis
   1928 *As tapeçarias de D. João de Castro*. Lisboa.
Livermore, H. V.
   1989 The Conquest of Lisbon. *British Historical Society of Portugal Review*, Lisbon.
Machado, J. T. Montalvão
   1963 D. Afonso 8° Conde de Barcelos fundador da Casa de Bragança, *Revista de Guimarães*. Vol. 73. Guimarães.

Marques, A. H. Oliveira
   1973 *A Sociedade Medieval Portuguêsa.* Lisboa: Sá da Costa.
Monod, T., Mota, A. Teixeira da, Mauny, R.
   1951 *Description de la Côte Occidental d'Afrique (Senegal au Cap de Monte, Archipels par Valentim Fernandes (1506–1510)).* Bissau: Centro de Estudos da Guiné Portuguêsa.
Porfirio, José Luis
   1977 *Museu de Arte Antiga.* Lisboa: Verbo.
Sousa, D. António Caetano de
   1946 *Proves da História Genealógica da Casa Real Portuguêsa.* Vol. 1. Coimbra.
   1948 *História Genealógica da Casa Real Portuguêsa.* Vols. 2 and 3. Lisboa.
Teixeira, Madalena Braz
   1983 *Do objecto ao museu.* Lisboa: Universidade Nova de Lisboa.
   1984 Os primeiros museus criados em Portugal. *Bibliotecas, Arquivos e Museus.* Lisboa: Instituto Português do Património Cultural.
Serrão, Joaquim Verissimo
   1980 André de Resende, o Humanista Eborense, *A cidade de Évora*, 32, 58, Évora.
Silva, Jorge H. Pais da
   1973 Paço dos Duques em Guimarães. *Palácios Portuguêses.* Vol. 1. Lisboa: Secretaria de Estado de Informação e Turismo.
Vaisse, Pierre
   1964 *Dürer, lettres, ècrits théoriques et traité des proportions.* Paris: Hermann.
Vasconcelos, Diogo Mendes de
   1785 Vida do licenciado André de Rezende. *Coleção de Antiguidades de Évora.* Évora: Na oficina de Filipe da Silva e Azevedo.
Vasconcelos, J. Leite
   1923 *Da Numismática em Portugal.* Lisboa: Arquivo da Universidade de Lisboa.
Viterbo, Sousa
   1904 *O Tesouro da Rei de Ceylao.* Lisboa: Tipografia da Academia.

11 Archaeological Museums in Israel: Reflections on Problems of National Identity

Magen Broshi

There is hardly a country where archaeology looms so large as in Israel. It is one of the most excavated and best surveyed countries in the world, an arena of intensive archaeological activities for the past one and one-half centuries. Israel, occupying some 20,000 sq km, is a little bigger than New Jersey in the United States and only 5% the area of France. Each year several hundred excavations are carried out, mostly by local archaeologists and by members of some foreign expeditions. A considerable part of the digging is done by the thousands of volunteers who come from the four corners of the earth.

This intense activity is all the more noteworthy considering the country's relative poverty in impressive finds compared with adjacent countries: Egypt with its fabulous art treasures and acres of inscribed walls; Mesopotamia (Iraq) with its colossal temples and palaces and hundreds of thousands of clay tablets. Not endowed by nature with giant rivers and fertile soils like Egypt or Mesopotamia or with natural resources like Cyprus (rich in copper), it was throughout history quite a poor country. The two main reasons, however, for the weight given to archaeology here in Israel are that this state is the land of the Bible and that the finds are an important component of the Israeli ethos. While I focus on the ethos here, I must first say a few words about the history of archaeological research in ancient Palestine, which today makes up the State of Israel, the Occupied Territories, and Jordan.

The first century or so of research, the period from 1838 to 1948, encompasses the pioneering work of an American, Edward Robinson

(1793–1863), to the founding of the State of Israel in 1948, in which archaeology was dominated by Christian scholars (Figure 11.1). Robinson, working in the country for a three-month period in 1838, founded Palestinian archaeology. His two main publications were *Biblical Researches in Palestine* (1841) and *Later Biblical Researches* (1856). These early scholars and their sponsors were motivated to study the land of the Bible: some 40% of the Christian archaeologists who worked in Palestine were either clergymen or devout laymen (Broshi 1987:17–26). The sites they chose for excavation were selected for their biblical interest: such were Jerusalem (the capital of ancient Israel), Jericho (the key site in the story of the conquest of the country by Joshua), Megiddo (an outstanding stronghold), and the like. In about 1918, 30 years before the State of Israel was founded, approximately one dozen local Jews were also active in archaeology. As might be expected, they showed a predilection for Jewish subjects and biblical sites, as exemplified by the work of Sukenik. The interests of Eleazar L. Sukenik (1889–1953), the founder of the Department of Archaeology, Hebrew University, Jerusalem, are typical of this early period (Figure 11.2). He concentrated on Roman-Byzantine synagogues, the Third Wall of Jerusalem, Jewish numismatics, and burial inscriptions. His expertise in Hebrew paleography made him the logical choice to become the first scholar to identify the Dead Sea Scrolls (November 29, 1947) (Figure 11.3).

The first generation of Israeli archaeologists continued to show a preference for Jewish themes after 1948, as the career of Yigael Yadin, the son of Sukenik, so well illustrates (Figure 11.4). The leading archaeologist of his time, Yadin chose to excavate large-scale sites, such as Hazor, excavated from 1955 to 1958, meant to elucidate the conquest of the land by Joshua (ca. 1200 B.C.); the Cave of Letters, excavated in 1960 and 1961, where papyri from the time of the Second Jewish Revolt (A.D. 132–135) were unearthed, including dispatches from Bar Kochba, the leader of the revolt; Masada, excavated from 1963 to 1965 by Yadin, was the last stronghold of the insurgents of the First Jewish Revolt (A.D. 66–73) (Figure 11.5); and Megiddo, the strata ascribed to Solomon and other Israelite kings (900–700 B.C.). The second generation of Israeli archaeologists, working as of the 1970s, showed more diversified interests, from early prehistory to the Middle Ages.

Figure 11.1 Edward Robinson (1793–1863), New England Congregationalist, was a spiritual descendant of the Puritans. His tour of the Holy Land in 1838 served to found Palestinian archaeology.

Figure 11.2 Eleazar L. Sukenik (1889–1953), founder of the Department of Archaeology, Hebrew University, Jerusalem. Almost all of his work dealt with Jewish subjects: ancient synagogues, burial caves, and numismatics.

Sukenik was appointed university archaeologist in 1927 and was promoted to the rank of lecturer only seven years later. His department, however, did not reach full maturity until the 1950s, when its staff was comprised of some of the best archaeologists ever to work in Israel: Nahman Avigad (1905–1992), Michael Avi-Yonah (1904–1974), Trude Dothan (1923–), Leo A. Mayer (1895–1959), Benjamin Mazar (1906–), Moshe Stekelis (1898–1967), and Yigael Yadin (1917–1984).

Figure 11.3   Qumran, one of the eleven caves where the Dead Sea Scrolls were discovered. Below the standing man is Cave 4, where the remains of some 600 scrolls were found.

As early as 1913, more than three decades before the State of Israel was founded, J.L. Magnes, a future chancellor of Hebrew University, established in 1925, suggested that the first department of such an institution ought to be archaeology. This department, he further believed, should ultimately be developed into a school of *Geisteswissenschaften* (i.e., the humanities and liberal arts, treated from a Jewish point of view) (Reinharz 1985:29, 379). The same year, the same idea was expressed, independently, by Baron Edmond de Rothschild (1985:19, 520).

Archaeology was later to assume an unparalleled role in the State of Israel (Elon 1971:365–378). Its uniqueness may be seen in the relative number of professional archaeologists, in the intensity of archaeological excavations, and in the public's response. More than 1,000 people took part in the conventions of the Israel Exploration Society in the early 1950s, approximately one per thousand of the total Jewish population at

Figure 11.4 Yigael Yadin (1917–1984), soldier, scholar, and statesman, was considered the leading Israeli archaeologist in the third quarter of the 20th century. Yadin (center) in a photograph taken in 1960, is shown planning a survey of the Judean Desert caves with a team of soldiers and archaeologists.

that time. This would be the equivalent of 50,000 participants if a similar conference were held in England, or of 250,000 in the United States. The number of participants at the Israel Exploration Society has remained constant over the years, but many new and comparable organizations have been formed in Israel since the 1950s: the Society for the Protection of Nature, the Ben Zvi Memorial Foundation for the History of Eretz (Land of) Israel (Figures 11.6 and 11.7), the Biblical Research Society, and many others. The importance attached to archaeology may also be seen in philatelic activity: 94 of the slightly more than 1,000 stamps issued by the State of Israel in its first 40 years have had archaeological themes (Tsachor 1989). Proportionately, this is about one-third of the stamps issued by Greece in the same period (Brinker 1990).

Figure 11.5 Masada, Herod's fortress-palace. Nearly 1,000 of its defenders against the Roman legions committed suicide on Passover, A.D. 73, rather than surrender. An outstanding archaeological site, it is an Israeli national symbol.

Figure 11.6 Eretz Israel Museum, Tel Aviv, where exhibits are arranged in galleries by category: for example, pottery, glass, numismatics. In its first three decades, the museum was called Haaretz Museum, but recently the name was changed to Eretz Israel Museum, a change with clear ideological motive. Shown here is the Glass Gallery with a 14th-century glass mosque lamp, probably made in Damascus.

Figure 11.7   The Ceramics Gallery of the Eretz Israel Museum, Tel Aviv. In the foreground are two clay jars, one from the Chalcolithic period and the other from the Early Bronze period.

Why Archaeology?

Among the reasons for the popularity of archaeology in Israel, one is simply intellectual curiosity—perhaps not surprising in a country holding the world record in per capita rate of scientific publications. All of the five Israeli universities—those in Haifa, Tel Aviv, Jerusalem, Bar Ilan, and Beersheba (Ben Gurion)—train archaeologists. Each, for example, has an area of specialization: surveys (in Tel Aviv), marine archaeology (in Haifa), (in Jerusalem) (in Bar Ilan), and desert archaeology (in Beersheba). All carry out regular site excavations and rely heavily on volunteers for labor.

For the Israeli Jew, archaeology plays an important role in forging national identity, but it does so only in the Israeli component of a person's personality, not in the Jewish. For the Jewish citizens of Israel, archaeology has very little to offer about their Jewishness. Judaism has, after all, survived for two and one-half millennia in foreign, frequently hostile lands, without a territory of its own. Moreover, *qua* Jews have not found much with which to identify among the archaeological discoveries. The past and its physical remains are supposed to produce an attachment to a territory. This phenomenon is aptly described by Nobel Laureate Siegfried Lenz in *Heimatsmuseum* (1978), where he gives in-depth consideration to the problems of "mother country," through reconstruction of ideology of the past and through museums. The past and its remains rarely work for the Israeli Jew. Most of the finds seem alien, often stemming from hostile cultures like the Canaanite, Hellenistic, pagan Roman, and Christian Byzantine. The Crusaders were notorious for their large-scale attacks on Jews; and the Arabs have been fighting the Israelis for decades. Canaanite fertility figurines and Byzantine mosaic floors studded with crosses excite interest and aesthetic appreciation but not a sense of identification.

Israel's fascination with archaeology instead seems to be based on two factors, which I have termed "roots" and "means of acquaintance." The roots factor is an aspect exemplified by the gift of an Old Testament to each new army conscript in Israel. The chief army rabbi states in his "Preface" that this Bible is Israel's title deed and registration document in the land of Israel. The archaeological finds are often regarded in the same way. These include the Wall of Jerusalem, the mighty fortress of Masada, and the mosaic floor of Beth Alpha, with its scene of the binding of Isaac. Hebrew and Aramaic inscriptions also bear eloquent testimony to the ancestors who are both far and near. It is of significance that the majority of the inscriptions and better-preserved Dead Sea Scrolls can still be read and understood by Israeli schoolchildren.

The second aspect to be considered is means of acquaintance. The phenomenon that is Israel, the return of a nation to its ancient land after some 2,000 years, is without parallel. The nation is in the process of renewing its acquaintance with itself and with its own ancient land. In this process, archaeology plays a major role. It is part of a larger process called *yediat haarets*; in Hebrew it means knowledge of the land and is probably derived from the German *Landeskunde*, in which "knowledge of the land" is made up of various disciplines, ranging from geography, history, and ethnography to bird watching (Katz 1985). Among them, archaeology holds a particular fascination, not unlike the charm of treasure hunting. For the European immigrants, however, they were returning to a land in which they felt, paradoxically, both a strong sense of kinship and a strangeness. Thus, in Israel, a *sui generis* state, archaeology becomes a means of dispelling the alienation felt by these new citizens. In both aspects, exploring old roots and putting down new roots, archaeology plays a predominant role.

It may be illuminating to compare two people living cheek by jowl in historical Palestine. One, the Israeli Jews, are trying to come to terms with their new territory. The other, the Palestinian Arabs, have a diametrically opposed problem—that of nationhood. They are in a process of nation building. The problem entails a concerted effort of "tradition invention" (Hobsbawn 1983), a tradition that is aimed at turning a territorial community into a 'community of memory," that is, a nation-state (Sivan 1988:141).

The Palestinian Arabs have little interest in and use for archaeology, and local Moslem remains offer them little with which to identify. These remains may belong to Ommayad, whose center was in Damascus; they may belong to Ayyubid, centered in Cairo and Damascus; Mameluk, which was in Cairo; or Ottoman, in Istanbul (Figure 11.8). Throughout Moslem times, for almost 13 centuries, starting in A.D. 636 and ending with the British occupation in 1917–1918, the country was under foreign, often oppressive colonial rule. Many monuments, like the Turkish military barracks in Safed, are not particularly attractive sites for the Palestinians.

Archaeological Museums in Israel

There are now between 120 and 180 museums in Israel, of which 34 are accredited museums that conform to the nation's Museum Law (1983) and its Museum Regulations (1984) (see also Rosovsky and Ungerleider-Mayerson 1989a, 1989b; Inbar and Schiller 1990). The majority of the museums in Israel are either fully or partly archaeological. They vary considerably in size and arrangement, period, subject matter, region, and site. Most of Israel's museums are public and belong either to the government or to the municipality, like those in Tel Aviv and Haifa; others are private, like the Israel Museum, which is the de facto national

Figure 11.8 Two Arab girls admiring Moslem jewelry displayed in the Mayer Memorial Institute for Islamic Art.

museum. Each private museum has different sources of funding, both local and foreign. The foreign sources amount to some 50% of the budget of the Israel Museum.

There were no archaeological museums in the new State of Israel. When the 1948 War broke out, the exhibits of the short-lived Mt. Scopus Museum were moved to Israeli Jerusalem, and they now form part of the study collection of the Department of Archaeology, at Hebrew University. There was a Palestine Archaeological Museum in Jerusalem before the war, also known, unofficially, as the Rockefeller Museum. It was housed in one of the most beautiful buildings ever built in Jerusalem, with excellent collections, but it was situated in eastern Jerusalem, which was under Jordanian rule until 1967; during that time, access was denied to the Israelis.

The basis for a central archaeological museum of the State of Israel was first established in Jerusalem in 1948 by the Antiquities Department. For use by the new department and nascent museum, Professor Samuel Yeivin, in keeping with the nationalistic spirit of the times, introduced an ethnocentric nomenclature for chronology. For example, Yeivin called the Iron Age the Israelite period, and the Late Hellenistic period, the Hasmonean. He divided the Roman period into the Herodian and the Mishnaic periods; and the Byzantine was called the Talmudic period. This system was discarded a few years later: the younger archaeologists found the nomenclature grossly inaccurate (e.g., Philistine pottery did not go well with Yeivin's Israelite period).

The Israel Museum was founded in 1965 in the Israeli sector of Jerusalem. Its archaeological wing, the Samuel Bronfman Biblical and Archaeological Museum, as stated, is the de facto national museum of archaeology. Based on the original collections of the Antiquities Department museum, it has the unofficial right of first refusal of every new find unearthed in the country. The spacious Bronfman wing is arranged chronologically from early prehistory and biblical times to the Middle Ages.

Another wing of the Israel Museum is the Shrine of the Book, the Samuel and Jeanne H. Gottesman Center for Biblical Manuscripts, which is the Dead Sea Scrolls Museum (Figure 11.9). This is an archaeological museum of a different kind; its exhibitions are far more eloquent than the mute objects unearthed regularly, and their emotional impact is clearly greater for the visitors. These manuscripts, written by Jews about 2,000 years ago, three-quarters of which are in Hebrew, one-quarter in Aramaic, are of utmost significance to those seeking their roots. Sukenik, drew attention to the symbolism of identifying the scrolls on the same day that the United Nations agreed upon the establishment of the State of Israel.

Conclusion

I have tried to show that the Israeli-unique penchant for archaeology is motivated by two factors referred to as roots and means of acquaintance. Archaeology (and history in general) are tinged by ideology everywhere (Lowenthal 1985); but in Israel, ideology plays a stronger role than in most other countries.

It seems to me, though, that ideological considerations are gradually exercising less influence on Israeli archaeology. After all, the ideology I described mostly served the needs of an immigrant society, and the

Figure 11.9 The Shrine of the Book, the wing of the Israel Museum that houses the Dead Sea Scrolls. In the center is the Isaiah Scroll, a complete Old Testament book, copied circa 100 B.C.

weight of immigrants in Israel is diminishing. While in 1951, 74.8% of the Israeli Jews were born abroad, in 1989 the figure dropped to 36% (Statistical Abstract of Israel 1954). Native Israelis appear to have a lesser need for the ideological reinforcements offered by archaeology. How will some half a million new Russian immigrants react to Israeli archaeology? It is still too early to say.

Acknowledgments

I wish to thank Professor Shaul Friedlander and Dr. Shaul Katz for their having discussed with me some of the topics included in this chapter. Special thanks are due to Dr. Edna Margalit for her insightful advice.

References

Brinker, M.
   1990 A Suggestion for a Research Project of the Official Culture of Israel from a Philatelic Viewpoint. *Igra* 3:9–14.
Broshi, M.
   1987 Religion, Ideology, and Politics and Their Impact on Palestinian Archaeology. *Israel Museum Journal* 6:17–32.
Elon, A.
   1971 *The Israelis*. New York: Bantam Books.
Hobsbawn, E. J.
   1983 *The Invention of Tradition*. Cambridge: Cambridge University Press.
Inbar, Y., and E. Schiller, eds.
   1990 *Museum in Israel*. Jerusalem: Ministry of Education and Culture and Ariel Publishing House. (Hebrew)
Katz, S.
   1985 The Israeli Teacher-Guide: The Emergence and Reputation of a Role. *Annals of Tourism Research* 12:49–72.
Lenz, S.
   1978 *Heimatsmuseum*. Hamburg: Hoffman und Campe Verlag. English: *The Heritage*. New York: Hill and Wang. 1981.
Lowenthal, D.
   1985 *The Past Is a Foreign Country*. Cambridge: Cambridge University Press.
Reinharz, J.
   1985 *Chaim Weizmann*. Oxford and New York: Oxford University Press.

Rosovsky, N., and J. Ungerleider-Mayerson
  1989 *The Museums of Israel*. New York: Harry N. Abrams.
Silberman, N. A.
  1989 *Between Past and Present: Archaeology, Ideology, and Nationalism in the Modern Middle East*. New York: Anchor Books.
Sivan, E.
  1988 *Arab Political Myths*. Tel Aviv: Am Oved. (Hebrew)
Statistical Abstract of Israel
  1954 *Onward Jerusalem*. 5:1989. Jerusalem: Central Bureau of Statistics, Government Printer.
Tsachor, Y.
  1989 *Israeli Postage Stamps 1948–1989*. Jerusalem: Israeli Philatelic Authority.

12 Repatriation of Cultural Heritage: The African Experience

Ekpo Eyo

The problem of the repatriation of cultural heritage to its country of origin is an old one, based on a 19th doctrine enshrined in the Treaty of Vienna that "scientific and artistic collections cannot be expatriated because they are destined to meet the permanent intellectual needs of the country" of origin (Rollet-Andriane 1979:6). Thus, the infamous exploits of Napoleon Bonaparte in Europe between 1804 and 1815 must constitute the starting point of this essay.

Napoleon looted a total of 2,065 paintings and 130 sculptures throughout devastated Europe, particularly from Italy and Belgium. Thereafter, in Paris, he staged a triumphal procession of soldiers, museum directors, and art professors to accompany carts and chariots loaded with renowned works, which included the *Apollo Belvedere*, the *Laocoön*, and the *Dying Gaul* (Alexander 1982:25). Most of these treasures were secured by one-sided treaties with the defeated countries. However, at the Congress of Vienna in 1815, France was forced by Napoleon's conquerors to restitute most of the looted artworks to their countries of origin. The rationale for that action was succinctly stated by none other than Viscount Castlereagh (Robert Stewart), the British delegate, who argued.

> It did not appear that any middle line could be adopted which did not go to recognize a variety of spoliations under cover of treaties, if possible more flagrant in their character than the acts were undisguised rapine by which these remains were, in general, brought together. The principle of property, regulated by the claims of territories from whence these works were taken is the surest and only guide to justice. [Hall 1982:37]

England had previously benefited in 1662 from the Treaty of Whitehall between Britain and the Netherlands, when the country received back works of art belonging to the Stuart collections (Rollet-Andriane 1979:6, n 7). It was in the same vein that the Treaty of Vienna in 1866 compelled the Duchy of Hessen to return a library taken from Cologne in 1794, and objects of art and science that had been plundered many years earlier also went back to Venice (1979:6).

Ancient Greece and Rome

If 19th-century Europeans considered cultural heritage as belonging to the permanent intellectual needs of its country of origin, the ancient Greeks and Romans regarded it as demeaning to plunder another country's heritage. For instance, the Greek historian Polybius is known to have frowned at the act of plunder by the Greeks when he said,

> The city should not owe its beauty to adornments brought in from elsewhere, but to the valour of its inhabitants . . . I trust that future conquerors will learn from these reflexions not to plunder the cities they bring into subjugation and not to take advantage of the distress of other peoples to adorn their homelands. [Rollet-Andriane 1979:9, n1]

Similarly, the Roman orator Cicero made Verres, the praetor of Sicily, pay retribution to the Sicilians for plundering their artworks for his personal use and praised the conduct of Scipio who, after taking Carthage in the Third Punic War, caused to be returned to Sicily the art pieces the Carthaginians had plundered from them (1979:1, n 4).

The 20th Century

In this century, numerous treaties based on the principle enunciated in Vienna in 1815 have been concluded. For example, Article 245 of the Treaty of Versailles required Germany to return to France those artworks that were removed not only during the First World War but also during the War of 1870. Similarly, the Treaty of Riga of March 18, 1921, provided for a total restitution of cultural property removed from Poland since January 1, 1772, that is, 150 years earlier (Rollet-Andriane 1979:6).

And, on January 5, 1943, at the height of the Second World War, a declaration was published simultaneously in London, Moscow, and Washington, D.C., in which the United Nations (UN)

> reserved the right to declare null and void any transfer of or traffic in property, rights and interests of whatever nature, which are or were situated in the territories occupied by or under the direct or indirect control of the governments with which they are at war . . . even if the said transfer and traffic are represented as having been effected without constraint. [*Department of State Bulletin* 8:21–22, in Rollet-Andriane 1979:7]

It is interesting to note that in all these examples the restitution process and the transfer or traffic in cultural property took place within Europe. These measures can, therefore, be seen as self-protective because most, if not all, of the countries of continental Europe had at one time or another been conquered territories. Plunder was thus seen as demeaning and unjust, and the right of each country to retain its cultural heritage to meet the "permanent intellectual needs" of its country of origin was emphasized and maintained.

The Post-Colonial Era in Africa

Before 1960, most African countries were still under colonial domination, but after that date, many of them became independent. With it has come the realization that, for political independence to be meaningful, it has to be buttressed by a program of cultural identity. Hence, such programs were worked out, aimed at creating cultural awareness and the assertion of national identity.

The usefulness of museums as mirrors of national ethos became obvious and imperative, yet in most cases few or no treasures were left to form the nuclei of such institutions. The newly independent African nations felt a deep sense of loss and alarm not only because of what they lost during the colonial period but because of the current rate of illicit traffic in cultural artifacts that severely affected them. They therefore welcomed the determination by the United Nations Educational, Scientific, and Cultural Organization (UNESCO), in 1964, to work toward a means of curbing this illicit trade, a move that was culminated in 1970 with the *Convention on the Means of Prohibiting and Preventing the Illicit Import, Export, and Transfer of Ownership of Cultural Property* (Monreal 1979).

I would like to point out that, although the developing nations were the immediate impetus for drawing up the convention, it was also meant to serve the purpose of the developed nations of the West because the problem of illicit ownership and transfer had also been and is still being experienced in Europe and other industrialized areas of the world. But my experience as a participant, from the early stages of the convention's inception to its final adoption, is that arguments were always polarized between the nonindustrialized and the industrialized nations, the latter always displaying hostility as if to say, "How dare You?"

The scene of the adoption of the convention at the General Assembly of UNESCO in 1970 was one of the most noisy in its history. That the industrialized nations had always been opposed to the convention was manifest. Ten years after its adoption, only 39 member states had ratified it: 34 were Third World countries, three were from the eastern European bloc, and two were from the industrialized West (Canada and West Germany) Monreal 1979:50, n3). Alas, the illicit trade has since continued, as if this convention had never existed—even today when the number of signatories has gone up to 64, including the United States.

Meanwhile, mainly due to the vacillation of the West on the 1970 convention, President Mobutu Seso Seko of Zaire added another dimension to the effort of building respectable collections of cultural-heritage materials in African countries for the purpose of establishing museums. At the UN General Assembly in New York City on October 4, 1973, Mobutu moved a resolution calling on those former colonial powers who held museum pieces from their former territories to return "a part of it so that we may teach our children their country's history." He added that these objects were not "raw materials," they were the "finished products of our ancestors." Finally, he emphasized the international implications of such action by adding that it would "constitute a means of strengthening international cooperation while making a just reparation of damage done" (Hall 1982:39). It is clear that President Mobutu was restating the points already made by the West, from ancient Greece to World War II, regarding a nation's cultural heritage and requesting that the same principle be applied to Africa.

In 1974, UNESCO, as an agent of the UN adopted the *Resolution on the Restitution of Cultural Property*. It took five years to work out its *modus operandi*, resulting in approval by the General Conference of the *Statutes of the Intergovernmental Committee for Promoting the Return of Cultural Property to Its Countries of Origin or Its Restitution in Case of Illicit Appropriation*. This long-winded title itself is a reflection of the argument by the West that, although they might return some items, the objects themselves were not removed illicitly and do not warrant use of the word "restitution." In other words, the Western nations maintained that it was *morally right* to have sequestered cultural objects from the countries that they had conquered. This convention, naturally, has not fared any better than did the previous one. Only in one instance, as far as Africa is concerned, has there been a return of objects reported, and that was by the Belgian government to Zaire in 1970, three years *before* President Mobutu made his appeal to the UN General Assembly (Van Geluwe 1979:35). Various reasons have been advanced by the West to explain why they cannot implement the provisions of this convention, and I shall return to them later after I look at specific problems in Ghana, Mali, and Nigeria.

Ghana: Asante War Booty

On February 4, 1874, the British government attacked the tiny gold-rich African Kingdom of the Asante (Ashanti) in Ghana, ruled by Asantehene Kofi Kakari. His palace was sacked, and items looted included a *mponponsua* (gold sword) used in the installation of subchiefs, seven gold masks, gold nuggets, and beaded jewelry. Sir Garnet Wolseley (1833–1913), the leader of the invading forces, also demanded from the king an indemnity of 50,000 ounces of gold, of which only 1,040 ounces were available. Asantehene Kakari was, of course, deposed. Two years later, when Asantehene Prempeh I, Kofi Kakari's successor, could not produce the remaining ounces of gold, the British threatened to double the indemnity, and Prehpeh, his wife, the queen mother, and several chiefs were taken prisoner. More items were confiscated, auctioned on the spot, and auctioned by the Crown agents in London to defray the costs incurred by the British government during the war.

On the centenary of the loss of these sacred objects in 1974, the Ghanaians organized memorial services and seminars, sang or wept funeral dirges, and petitioned the British government for the return of these priceless items (Robinson 1976:69). The British government's response to the request by the Ghanaians was to offer them a long-term loan of small batches of the looted items, while the British retained ownership. The British government claimed that the gold items were war booty and part of the indemnity that the Asante had to pay for a war they neither started nor won. The brilliant rhetoric of Viscount Castlereagh on Napoleon's loot—which canonized the notion that scientific and artistic collections cannot be expatriated because they are destined to meet the permanent intellectual needs of their country of origin—was conveniently forgotten; and what was good for the goose was now bad to the gander.

Mali: Djenné Terra-cotta Figurines

For some 30 years now, Mali has been losing to illicit diggers of tombs hundreds of terra-cotta figurines belonging to an ancient civilization that has yet to be properly studied and understood. The Malian case is instructive in the sense that the argument has often been advanced that the black market arises when no legitimate alternative exists for either buyer or seller. The Malian export law allows for the legal exportation of a few items per person at a time. But it happens that one may legally take a few items out as many times as one comes back and may do so *ad infinitum*. For this reason, there are probably 100 times more Malian terra-cotta figurines outside of Mali than there are inside; worse still, the scientific and historical contexts of these objects have forever been wiped out because diggings are carried out illegally and without attention being paid to scientific aspects of the objects.

Nigeria: Benin City

The government of Nigeria decided in the late 1960s to build a national museum in Benin City to depict the history of this city, a city that has contributed so much to the artistic heritage of mankind. The power of Benin as a kingdom was broken in 1897 when the city was sacked by the British Royal Marines, and more than 2,000 pieces of artwork in bronze, ivory, and wood were removed to London (Figure 12.1). Some of these objects were sold to defray the cost of the sack, and some were put into one of the world's most famous museums: the British Museum. Benin

Figure 12.1   British marines and looted treasures of ancient Benin in 1897. Photograph courtesy of British Museum Trustees, London.

pieces have since also been dispersed around the world, ranging from London to St. Petersburg (Leningrad) to Los Angeles. They are also found in Australia and South America.

When construction of the National Museum in Benin City was completed, there arose the problem of furnishing it. Only a few third-rate objects were left in the minor shrines of the Benin chieftains. Although the Nigerian government had brought back several items from England and elsewhere over the years and had placed them on display in the National Museum in Lagos, it was difficult to make any sensible display at Benin City to befit the status of a city that had produced so much material for other world museums.

Faced with this situation, the Nigerian delegation to the General Assembly of the International Council of Museums (ICOM) at Grenoble, France, in 1973 submitted a resolution specifically requesting donations to the new Benin City National Museum of one or two Benin items from museums and collectors who had sympathy for the looting of Benin treasures by the British in 1897. The Resolution Committee of the General Assembly thought that the request was too specific and watered it down to an appeal to those who had items belonging to other countries to return them. This, of course, was useless for the Nigerian purpose, and, predictably, not a single response was received from any individual or institution. Consequently, the National Museum in Benin City opened to the public with photographs and replicas of the art objects that have become the pride of other nations and institutions (Eyo 1979:21).

During the second world Black and African Festival of Arts and Culture (FESTAC), when the representatives of the Black peoples of the world assembled in Nigeria in 1977 to assert themselves, a Benin ivory mask possessed by the British Museum was adopted as its symbol. A request was made to the British Museum for the release of this object to Nigeria, but it was refused with the explanation that the mask was too fragile to travel and could break up in the climate where it was made 400 years earlier. Some sections of the Nigerian press published stories that the British government required about $3 million (U.S.) as an indemnity in case anything happened to the mask (Robinson 1977:B7). In the face of such a ridiculous situation, a replica was carved by a contemporary Benin sculptor who used photographs of the original. The replica was used as the symbol of the world's Black population, while the original mask was stored away in a box in the basement of the British Museum.

Nigeria: Second Exodus of Benin Bronzes

Nigeria resorted to begging at the ICOM General Conference at Grenoble in 1973 because it could not afford the high prices that Benin works were commanding at the international auction houses. However, in 1980–1981, when there was oil money, the Nigerian government was able to spend about $1 million (U.S.) for the purchase of a half dozen Benin pieces to improve the National Museum's holdings. Shortly after this, a tragedy struck the National Museum in Lagos.

Some Benin bronzes, which had been bought back by Nigeria and stored in Lagos, were reported to be on sale in New York City. With the help of the Pace Gallery in New York and the U.S. Federal Bureau of Investigation, Nigeria was able to recover most of them (*International Foundation for Art Research of Stolen Art* 1982:1–2). Investigations in Lagos revealed that one or several of the museum staff had gained access to the Lagos National Museum storeroom by making manholes in the ceiling to fish out the items. This situation arose, unfortunately, because in the United States an exhibition, "Treasures of Ancient Nigeria: Legacy of 2,000 Years," had aroused the attention of dealers in African art more than ever before. Authorities suspect that the staff of the Lagos museum must have come under strong pressure to steal from the museums' storage.

I have made this point to underline the fact that, no matter what laws a country passes to protect its heritage, as long as outside demands exist, these regulations will be ineffective. Nigeria's extensive borders and the demand for its art inhibit the effective functioning of its internal laws; hence, some of these objects of great beauty and cultural importance, which were first looted in 1897 and then bought back, were again stolen and sold abroad. It was only through luck that some of the items were brought back the second time.

Nigeria: Ife

In 1979, Christie's in New York announced the sale of an Ife terra-cotta head (ca. 12th century A.D.) (*African Arts* 1979:10). As soon as the advertisement came to the attention of the Nigerian National Museum, Christie's was informed that the head had been illegally exported from Nigeria. The piece was graciously withdrawn from sale and returned to the "owner," who immediately offered it to Nigeria for $100,000 (U.S.) The "owner" went on to suggest that, if Nigeria could not find the money, it should consider allowing it to be purchased by a respectable museum. He or she warned that, if Nigeria could do neither, the piece might go underground and might never be seen again.

The impossibility of raising that amount is quite apart from the question of the appropriateness of having to find money to pay for an item known to have been illicitly removed from Nigeria. Nigeria felt that paying for the object would encourage and sustain the illegal traffic in stolen property.

Nigeria: Nok

In the wake of the success of the 1980–1981 Nigerian art exhibition in North America, some dealers went to the Glenbow Museum in Calgary, Canada, where the exhibition was being held to sell them a Nok head (ca. 900 B.C.-A.D. 200). The object was said to have been previously in circulation in France and Switzerland. Upon arrival of the dealers in Calgary, the head was impounded by the Royal Canadian Mounted Police, and the matter was taken to court.

Canada is a signatory to the 1970 UNESCO Convention and spent a great deal of money to obtain a court ruling to return the Nok head to Nigeria. The noble part played in this matter by the Canadian government through the director of the Glenbow Museum, Duncan Cameron, deserves high commendation. However, attention must be drawn to the protracted procedure and to the expenses involved in pursuing the implementation of the convention, a procedure that failed in the end. The head was never returned to Nigeria.

During the first phase of the case, the Nigerian delegation, including an attorney, traveled several times between Lagos and Calgary, that is, halfway around the world. The case was first thrown out of court on a technicality, but the Canadian government was convinced that they could win the second round and started preparing for it. Nigeria, on the other hand, was meanwhile experiencing financial problems and changes in government and, as a result, its interest in the protracted case was waning. It took more than four years' time and money to pursue this case, which failed because of the complexities of the UNESCO Convention and the legal system of the implementing country.

Nigeria: Jebba

Ten bronzes of a very unique, if enigmatic, nature were located in certain villages along the Lower Niger Valley in Nigeria. Eight of them were removed to the safety of the National Museum in Lagos. One of them had been stolen before Nigeria's independence in 1960, and the other, the tallest bronze figure in Africa, was stolen in 1972 (Figure 12.2). Bonnie Burnam has given a detailed and impressive account of the loss of this item in her book *The Art Crisis* (1975). She wrote that an African runner, here called "Abudu," had taken the bronze figure first to the Accra Museum in Ghana for evaluation, and from there, he took it to Belgium, France, and Switzerland. "Abudu" maintains luxurious apartments in both Paris and New York and lives in grand style.

The Department of Antiquities was unaware of the loss of this sculpture from Nigeria because it had been located in a village in Jebba, far from any museum. The bronze figure was still an object of veneration for the people of the island. The Department of Antiquities only knew about its loss when a cable was received from the director of the Tervueren Museum in Brussels saying that the piece was being offered for sale. When contacted, the director of Tervueren said that the piece had left for Paris and added that he never knew the location in Paris or the vendor. All of the museums that had been offered the object kept quiet about the issue; perhaps they thought it would ruin their chances of being shown other items by the same vendor.

Nigeria: Ife Bronze Rings

Important artworks often turn up accidentally and, if archaeologists are present, such sites are investigated. At other times, the sites are dug up by robbers who destroy their scientific contexts. In the past decade, a hoard of bronze rings was illegally removed from Nigeria. Where exactly they were found is unknown, but they have since been purchased by some of the world's most important art museums and collectors, and they have been displayed for the delight of the public. It is now left to

Figure 12.2   Female figure, bronze, Jebba, Nigeria. Photograph courtesy of Frank Willett.

scholars to try to figure out what these rings represent, where they came from, and what dates can be assigned to them. This is the case with some of the bronze rings that appeared in Europe and North America whose context inevitably became the subject of speculation (Vogel 1983). Had these rings been properly excavated, much relevant scientific and cultural information would have been gathered. Perhaps some thorny problems of the Benin-Ife relationship in the art history of Nigeria would have been illuminated. As it is, scientific and contextual evidence of these objects is lost, probably forever.

As an archaeologist, I was taught that the context in which an object is found is as important as the object itself. Nonetheless, major museums of the world are proud to collect and display objects that they know have been illegally stripped of their contextual value.

Nigeria: Jos Museum Loot

As recently as December 1986, the Jos Museum suffered a major theft. Nine Ife, Igbo Ukwu, and Benin objects were fished out of the clerestory window of the museum (Kerri 1987: 22–3). Only one item, an early Benin memorial head, which turned up in an auction room in Zurich in 1991, has since been found and returned to Nigeria (Obayemi and Pemberton 1991).

Museums and their Acquisition Programs

Makaminan Makagiansar, the assistant deputy director general of culture for UNESCO, estimated that the industrialized countries of the world with 15.6% of the population have 66.5% of the world's museums, while the nonindustrialized countries with 52.7% of the population have only 3.1% of the existing museums (Makagiansar 1984). In the United States, there are already at least 5,000 museums, containing about 1 billion objects (American Association of Museums 1984:17).

A study of the origins of museums reveals that they arose out of the collections of such kings, popes, and rich merchants as Charles I of England, Peter and Catherine the Great of czarist Russia, Popes Sixtus IV and Julius II, the Medici of Florence, and the Tradescants of England. Most of the largest museums in the world were formed around the collections of compulsive collectors and organizations that had both economic and political power. Examples include the Pio-Clementine Museum, formed around the Vatican treasures in Rome in 1773; the Uffizi Palace Museum in Florence, which arose out of the Medici collections in 1743; the Ashmolean Museum in Oxford, England, which stemmed from the Tradescants' collections in 1683; the British Museum, which originated with the collection of Sir Hans Sloane in 1759; the Hermitage, which was begun in 1767 and contains the collections of the czars of Russia; the Louvre, which opened in 1793 and contains artworks from French royalty; and the Metropolitan Museum of Art in New York City, which in part sprang up in 1869 from the collections of General Luigi P. di Cesnola (Alexander 1982:22–24, 31–33).

Many of these great institutions may indeed have preserved what in some cases may have been lost in the past, but the passion for collecting on the part of those who used their positions as controllers of power and wealth has been adopted by present-day museum directors. Museum directors play a vital role in determining the movements of art objects, both in public sales and in private deals. Because of the fierce competition among them, the prices of objects are now beyond the reach of many countries and museums—even in the industrialized world.

A museum director's tenure is often determined by the growth percentage of the collections. The director, must therefore, raise the money to buy art and must also woo individuals into bequeathing part or all of their collections to the museum, without considering how the collections were assembled in the first place. Such an acquisitions policy has the unwholesome effect of causing the politically and economically weak to part easily with objects of cultural identity and veneration. Museum directors today have used the misfortunes of the politically and economically weaker nations of the world for the glorification of their galleries and vaults, in contradiction to the injunction of Polybius of ancient Greece.

The United States and the Ethics of Acquisition

I am aware that before UNESCO adopted the two conventions on the *Illicit Transfer of Cultural Property* and the *Restitution of Cultural Property to Their Countries of Origin*, a group of museums in the United States had already adopted the joint *Professional Policy on Museum Acquisitions*, which enjoins museums not to "acquire through purchase, gift, or bequest cultural property imported in violation of the laws obtaining in the countries of origin." Various organizations, including the American Association of Museums (AAM), are signatories to the *Statement of Ethics of Acquisition*. However, only a few museums have actually put the contents of this declaration into practice. I am aware also that some museums are dead set against it. Let us look at two examples that illustrate the two ends of the acquisitions spectrum. At one end is the rich institution and at the other is the poor museum.

In 1973, Dr. Robert Goldwater, the late, distinguished director of the Museum of Primitive Art in New York City, talked to Bonnie Burnam about the dilemma posed by illicit trade in antiquities. Goldwater recalled an offer made to him of a private collection of Precolumbian works that, if seen in the context of the AAM's acquisitions policy, would have presented a problem. He knew that the Mexican government could not afford to buy the collection; and, if he himself bought it, the Mexican authorities would not permit its export. He suspected that the best pieces would as a result go underground and be smuggled out to American collectors and dealers, and the Museum of Primitive Art might never see any of these objects again. Furthermore, Goldwater contended that collectors who bought the objects and wanted to give them to the museum someday would still be acting in conflict with the contents of the AAM's declaration (Burnam 1975:139).

But, in answer to another question by Burnam, whether he felt that a good relationship between the United States and Mexico would facilitate legal exports of antiquities from the latter country, Goldwater answered in the negative. And, in Africa, he said,

> More than half of what we pay for fine African objects is paid in bribes to government officials. . . . We pay because everyone pays. This is an accepted way to obtain an object. . . . It's not the serious professionals you're fighting in these countries, it's the system. [Burnam 1975:140]

To some extent, Dr. Goldwater, speaking from a great wealth of experience, was right. However, what he forgot to add is that, as long as there is a strong demand for these objects and fierce competition among directors to purchase them, that situation is inevitable. His explanation, "we pay because everyone pays", underscores the compulsive and acquisitive nature of museum directors. I suggest that Dr. Goldwater, like the Medici of Florence, paid because he had the purchasing power.

At the other end of the spectrum, Dr. Gladys Weinberg, assistant director at the University of Missouri Art and Archaeology Museum, contends that the underprivileged museum cannot compete for objects with the richer ones, that they experience considerable difficulty in obtaining legal export permits from most countries. Still, they need to collect for teaching purposes. For her, therefore, to sign the AAM's declaration would be a "death warrant." Consequently, she believes that a declaration forbidding the illegal import of antiquities into the United States is unnecessary, adding that, once an object has illegally left its country of origin, its final resting place is irrelevant. She concludes,

> The most essential matters are controlled by the countries which possess the antiquities and willingness on their part to realize that we live in one world, not simply a collection of nations whose boundaries are frequently changing. Nearly all of us in the United States have origins elsewhere; why should we not have a share in the cultural heritage which belongs to all of us? [Burnam 1975:141]

I sympathize with the small, financially handicapped museums of the world. I myself used to work in such a place in Nigeria. We are all disadvantaged in comparison with the large, financially stronger museums. But just because small museums cannot afford to compete with the larger ones, should they encourage and support illicit traffic in cultural property? Must they resort to unprofessional, unethical practices to stay in the profession? A university museum ought to be the last institution to support the destruction of scientific evidence that occurs when things are torn out of their original contexts. To say that, when such objects have been illegally exported, it does not matter where they come to rest can only mean that we do not mind if our museums are turned into storehouses for stolen goods.

Dr. Weinberg's point—"we live in one world, not simply a collection of nations. . . . why should we not have a share in the cultural heritage which belongs to all of us?"—is good rhetoric. It is in line with the UNESCO and ICOM proposals for the democratization of culture and the accessibility of cultural artifacts to all the world. The proposal aims to spread knowledge about other peoples and other cultures, with a view toward creating understanding and harmony and eliminating mutual suspicion among the peoples of the world. The only thing wrong with this point of view is its actualization.

In my experience, cultural artifacts seem to flow in only one direction: from the "peripheries of the world" (Meaning the underdeveloped and underprivileged countries) toward the "center" (meaning the politically strong and economically powerful nations of Europe and North America) and not vice versa. As Thurstan C. Shaw has pointed out,

> Can you imagine the British Magna Carta or the American Declaration of Independence in Nigeria?—the French Eiffel Tower or the American Statue of Liberty in Abidjan, Ivory Coast, or Accra, Ghana?—the British Crown Jewels or the American Liberty Bell being held in Mexico City or New Delhi? [1986:47]

When you have imagined all of these, you will have an elementary insight into the feelings and the plight of the less-privileged nations whose objects of national identification and pride are housed in other lands.

Benin bronze memorial heads, for example, adorn some homes and museums in the Western world, but they have no other meaning in these places than as artworks. These heads represent various kings who founded and ruled the Kingdom of Benin; they occupy particular niches in the history of the Benin empire. Their absence from their city of origin creates serious gaps in the Benin people's visual history. Likewise, what is the Golden Sword of the Asante doing in the British Museum, when it should be used in installing chiefs of the Asante nation?

The common excuse given to justify the one-way flow of the world's heritage to the "center" is that they are safer and more accessible there. It is often argued that more tourists go to these "centers," and, consequently, the artifacts will be seen by a greater number of people— though whether the poor from a nation whose objects are in another country can travel to see them is rarely addressed. This actually means that cultural artifacts from the developing world enrich the economically well-off; while the poor countries become poorer, both economically and spiritually. (As for the safety of the objects, I hope it is not too callous to say that, with the development of nuclear weapons, the "center" of the world is probably the most unsafe place of all for human beings and artworks.)

Cultural Property and Restitution

In closing, I would like to congratulate the government of the United States for joining, however late, with other nations of the world in the international effort to reduce illicit traffic in cultural property by ratifying the 1970 UNESCO Convention (UNESCO 1970; U.S. Government Printing Office 1983). This law has established a mechanism whereby the president may enter into bilateral or multilateral agreements or take unilateral emergency action to protect archaeological or ethnological materials that are part of a country's cultural patrimony and in danger of pillage. As one involved at every state of the making of this convention, I wish to commend the United States for its action, which has been seen by concerned countries, UNESCO, and ICOM as a major breakthrough in the war against illicit trade in cultural property. Each of us hopes that all Western countries will follow suit, if only as a token of their disapproval of this illicit trade.

However, whether the mere signing of the convention by the United States or any other Western power will cause any significant check on the flow of illicit art trade remains to be seen. In Nigeria, the enthusiasm generated by the United States' action was greatly dampened by events in Canada. The implementation of the convention may not be much more successful in the United States. The maze of laws, costs, and procedures could well be enough to discourage similar attempts. My experience has taught me that laws or conventions are merely statements of what is respected; the real implementation will come with genuine moral conviction by museum directors that illicit traffic in cultural property is unethical.

I do not believe that any law can work properly unless those involved are convinced of its moral content and necessity. As Dr. Goldwater pointed out, most of the cases brought by developing countries cannot stand up in foreign courts of law because of conflicting legal systems and laws. What developing country will then spend money on litigation that cannot be won? But, those museum directors who acquire cultural property, knowing full well that they were illicitly removed from their countries of origin, should ask themselves one simple question: "Is there any dignity in owning what does not morally belong to you or is illegally acquired by you?" It might be better to revive the apparently moribund AAM *Ethics of Acquisition*. I am sure that the force of moral conviction will be more effective as a deterrent against illicit art trade.

The AAM recently observed that

> by the end of the century only 20% of the world's population will live in what we now consider the developed world—the United States, Canada, Europe, the Soviet Union, Japan, Australia, and New Zealand. This fraction of the world's people now controls more than three-quarters of the world's wealth and consumes 85% of its resources. In the tropics, on the other hand, a third of the people are unable to obtain enough food for themselves and their families to avoid starvation. The effects of such alarming imbalances impose new challenges for all social institutions in the developed world, including museums. [AAM 1984:22–3]

I would like to seize on this observation to make some suggestions to museum directors for tackling the problem of imbalance between the developed world and the developing world. They may thus be able, I hope, to check the uncontrolled exodus of cultural property from the underdeveloped to the developed worlds.

First, as mentioned in the *Report of the Commission on Museums for a New Century*, museums need to make available inventories of their holdings. Such action would surprise us by revealing how much has been locked away in museum vaults that could instead be shared with other museums. In other words, were museum directors to cultivate the habit of sharing with sister institutions, we would move a long way toward both eliminating the fierce competition among museums and making study collections available to smaller museums.

Second, if museums are to maintain their integrity and respectability, acceptance of gifts and bequests must be carefully reconsidered. Contamination of collections with known stolen property can discredit the rest of the collection. If a stolen object could no longer find a resting place in the museum world, collectors would be more careful about what they bought, and this would in turn change the dealers' buying habits. As a consequence, runners would be less important: legitimate exchanges, trade, and sharing could take place openly between parties, countries, and museums.

Third, to build legitimate collections, developing and developed countries could set up joint field expeditions under preconditions of mutual benefit to both sides.

Fourth, since we are discussing the heritage of humankind belonging to one world, could we not begin now to think about setting up world museums in Africa and other parts of the developing world?

These proposals could set us on a course toward stopping museums from continuing to be legalized institutions for housing stolen property. Museum directors would then depart from their conventional practice of acquiring and displaying at all costs. Indeed, Dr. F. K. Keppel, president of the Carnegie Corporation, in his annual report in 1937, called attention to the need "to upset conventions in order to close the gap between what museums are doing and what the world expects them to do" (1937:v). So be it.

References

African Arts
    1979 Christie's for Fine Tribal Art. *African Arts* 12(2):10.
Alexander, Edward P.
    1982 *Museums in Motion: An Introduction to the History and Functions of Museums*. 3rd ed. Nashville: American Association for State and Local History.
American Association of Museums
    1984 *Report of the Commission on Museums for a New Century*. Joel M. Bloomm and Earl A. Power III, eds. Washington, D.C.: American Association for Museums.
Burnam, Bonnie
    1975 *The Art Crisis*. London: Collins.
Eyo, Ekpo
    1979 Return and Restitution of Cultural Property: Nigeria. *Museum Quarterly Review* 31(1): 18–22.
Hall, Judith Vidal
    1982 The Spoils of Empire—Laying Down the Law: Art Treasures, Getting the Heritage Home. *South: Third World Magazine* January: 37–39.
International Foundation for Art Research of Stolen Art
    1982 Nigerian Museum Recovery and Further Caveats. 3(5): 1–20.

Keppel, F.P.
    1937 Annual Report to the Carnegie Corporation. In Alma S. Witlin 1949
        Museum: the History and Its Task in Education, v.
Kerri, Helen
    1987 Report on Significant Objects Stolen from the Nigerian National
        Museum in Jos. In *ICOM News* 40(1): 22–30.
Makagiansar, Makaminan
    1984 Museums for Today and Tomorrow: A Cultural and Educational
        Mission. *Museum Quarterly Review* 141: 3–7.
Monreal, Luis
    1979 Return and Restitution of Cultural Property: Problems and
        Possibilities in Recovery of Dispersed Cultural Heritages. *Museum:
        Quarterly Review* 31(1): 49–57.
Obayemi, Ade, and John Pemberton
    1991 The Recovery of a Benin Bronze Head. *African Arts* 24(3): 8–12.
Robinson, Alma
    1976 The Seized Treasures of Asante. *New Society* 24: 69–71.
    1977 The Controversial Mask of Benin. *The Washington Post*. February 11,
        1977, p. 7, Section B. Washington, D.C.
Rollet-Andriane, Louise-Jacques
    1979 Return and Restitution of Cultural Property: Precedents. *Museum
        Quarterly Review* 31(1) 1–9.
Shaw, Thurstan C.
    1986 Restitution of Cultural Property: Whose Heritage? *Museum Quarterly
        Review* XXXVIII(149): 46–48.
UNESCO
    1970 *Convention on the Means of Prohibiting the Illicit Import, Export and
        Transfer of Cultural Property*. Paris.
U.S. Government Printing Office
    1983 Implementation of Convention on Cultural Property. Public Law 97–
        446. January 12, 1983. Senate Committee on Finance, No. 97–564;
        House of Representatives Ways and Means Committee, No, 97–257;
        Committee of Conferences No. 97–989.
Van Geluwe, Huguette
    1979 Return and Restitution of Cultural Property: Belgium's Contribution
        to the Zairian Cultural Heritage. *Museum Quarterly Review* 31(1): 32–
        37.
Vogel, Susan
    1983 Rapacious Birds and Severed Heads: Early Bronze Rings from
        Nigeria. *The Art Institute of Chicago Centennial Lectures, Museum Studies*
        10: 331–357.

13 The Case for Wampum: Repatriation from the Museum of the American Indian to the Six Nations Confederacy, Brantford, Ontario, Canada

George H. J. Abrams

The issue of repatriation in the field of museum work has become one of the most controversial and contentious areas of relations between the museum professionals, American Indians, and anthropologists.[1] In the case presented here, I examine the repatriation in 1988 of a collection of 11 Canadian Iroquois wampum belts, which had come into the ownership of the Museum of the American Indian-Heye Foundation, New York City, now the National Museum of the American Indian, Smithsonian Institution. The belts that comprise this collection were originally derived from individual representatives of the Iroquois Confederacy in Canada. Their disposition, an example of repatriation, demonstrates the complexity of interwoven legal, political, cultural, and other issues that face decision makers in the amicable resolution of these kinds of cases. The story of this unique event has previously been related by one of the former museum trustees, Dr. William N. Fenton (1989), and bears repeating with elaboration. The case I present here is a further account of the events surrounding this momentous episode in the ongoing history of repatriation. I hope that in the future other direct participants in these instances will also add their interpretations of this procedure as they apply to the Iroquois and other American Indians.

Wampum

"Wampum" a contraction of a New England Algonquian Indian term, are cylindrical beads manufactured from the central column of several varieties of whelk shells (*Buccinum undatum, B. busycon*) to produce a white-colored variety and from the violet-colored areas of the quahog shell (*Mercenaria mercenaria*) to form the so-called black variety. These beads were strung on bast, hemp, or sinew into geometrically patterned "belts" of varying widths and lengths, although they are generally not believed to have been articles of clothing. It has been suggested by one scholar that they may have been used as actual belts at some point in the past (Tooker, pers, comm.). In some cases, the pictographic designs of the belts served as mnemonic devices for those individuals who periodically "read" the belts at ceremonial occasions. Some experts, however, question the strict pictographic interpretation and mnemonic use of the belts (Tooker, pers. comm.; Shimony, pers. comm.).

Other wampum were strung to form a number of individual and distinctively decorated strings and served to identify the duly authorized representatives of the individual tribes. Wampum shells continue to be used in personal adornment, as they were in much earlier times, for earrings and necklaces. Contrary to popular belief, wampum were not regarded by the Indians as money (Tooker 1978: 422–424).

Wampum were not restricted to the Iroquois, being used by tribes in the American South and Far West. The use of various forms of wampum by the Indians in Northeast North America is of considerable antiquity, although its use by the Iroquois is not in evidence in the archaeological record prior to the colonial period. Archaeologists have demonstrated the presence of wampum in the Northeast as early as the Middle Woodland period, an archaeological culture that derives from the tradition of the western Hopewell, 300 B.C. to A.D. 1000 (Fitting 1978). The first description of the manufacture of wampum, in this case among the coastal Algonquian-speaking tribes, was made by Marc Lescarbot about 1606 (1928:211–212). However, it was not until the early colonial period that wampum manufacture proliferated and became prominent, culturally and economically, among the various tribes of the Northeast, including individual tribes of the Iroquois Confederacy. (Figure 13.1)

The manufacture of wampum by white colonists on the southern

Figure 13.1   TEE YEE NEEN HO GA ROW, or Hendrick (c. 1680–1755), a Mohawk. One of the four Indian "Kings" who had their portraits painted by John Verelst during their visit to England in 1710. He holds a wampum belt. Photograph courtesy of the National Archives of Canada, Ottawa, Neg. C-92415.

coast of New England, New York, and New Jersey was well established by 1643. The prehistoric manufacture of wampum involved laborious and time-consuming methods of abrasion that were quickly replaced by new colonial technology, including metal tools and machines specifically designed to produce wampum. These made possible the rapid production of large quantities of wampum for the Indian trade, for tribute, and as a medium of intercolonial currency in the place of European money, which was scarce (Ceci 1983; Hewitt 1912).

Nation and Confederacy

The Iroquois Confederacy was originally composed of five Northern-Iroquois-speaking tribes occupying the area that was later to become the colony of new York. These matrilineal and horticultural tribes, distributed from east to west across New York, from the Hudson River to the Genesee River, were the Mohawk, the Oneida, the Onondaga, the Cayuga, and the Seneca. Later, about 1725, the Tuscarora, a Southern-Iroguois-speaking tribe from North Carolina, was adopted into the Confederacy under the sponsorship of the Oneida, following the dislocation of the Tuscarora from their homeland in the South. Thereafter, the Iroquois Confederacy was known as the Six Nations.

Each of the constituent tribes, or nations, of the Iroquois Confederacy considers itself to be independent and sovereign, separate and distinct from the others, and independent of other nation-states around them, just as are Canada and the United States. The bases for these claims reside in the treaties that the individual tribes, the groups of tribes, or the constituent tribes united in the confederacy entered into with the colonial powers, Canada, and the United States. The Indians hold that the treaties guaranteed to them certain special rights, powers, and privileges in exchange for cession of portions of Indian lands to foreign governments. In effect, the Iroquois gave lands to the various national governments in exchange for reservations, defined by them as reserved lands from their original territories. This understanding is in contrast with the oft-heard statement that the governments gave reservations to the Indians. The national governments, in most cases, did not give reservations to the Iroquois. Quite the reverse was true: the Iroquois gave lands to the national governments in exchange for the aforementioned guarantees. It was, at the conclusion of treaty negotiations, traditional for there to be an exchange of wampum belts, which symbolized the event and customarily represented the recognition of equal standing between the parties. Court rulings in cases that have challenged the sovereignty issue of the American Indian have generally been seen as, or have characterized federally recognized tribes as "semisovereign" or "dependent" nations.

It is commonly believed by the Iroquois that the confederacy came into being hundreds of years ago, if not thousands—long before the coming of the first Europeans. Most scholars of the Iroquois do not subscribe to this belief and think that the formation of the confederacy was a response to the appearance of the Europeans and the various factors that were then introduced or that it perhaps came about only a short time before the appearance of the white man.

Traditional belief among the Iroquois holds that some of the wampum belts date from the period when the confederacy was initially formed and that the use of wampum originated with the cultural hero Hiawatha (fl. ca. 1570), one of the founders of the confederacy. The uncertain translation of the name Hiawatha is sometimes given as "seeker after wampum" or as "he who combs," the latter name referring to his role of combing snakes from the Medusa-like head of Tadadaho, another major figure associated with the origin of the confederacy (Trigger 1978: x–xi).

The organization of the Iroquois Confederacy, whenever it occurred, designated the centrally located Onondaga as the "keeper of the fire" and as the locality where official meetings of the confederacy were to be conducted. Also, it was the Onondaga who were to be the official repository for the wampum collection that related to political organization for the confederacy. One of the 50 chiefs of the confederacy held the chiefly title "keeper of the wampum."

Because the powerful and fearsome Tadadaho of the Onondaga had traditionally been the individual who continued to resist the efforts of Hiawatha and Deganawida (Dekanawidah) to form the confederacy, his name became the major title of both the Onondaga and the confederacy. This title, along with most, if not all, of the chiefly titles, was to become contested at one time or another from the early 1800s and into the 20th century. At one point, there were two individuals claiming the title of Tadadaho, one among the Canadian Onondaga, another among the

United States Onondaga. In addition, there were two simultaneous American Tadadahos contesting the title in the 20th century.

The traditional importance of the Iroquois wampum belts was that, among other uses, they were the tangible reminders and markers of major treaties, alliances, and historical events. To the historic and to the contemporary Iroquois, the wampum was and is the manifestation of their sovereignty as distinct nations and as political equals among other nations. The historical record demonstrates that Superintendent of Northern Indian Affairs Sir William Johnson (1715–1774) was well acquainted with the cultural significance of wampum, using both belts and strings of wampum in the appropriate diplomatic manner throughout his extensive political dealings with the Iroquois.

It does appear that at least some of the names currently attached to individual belts were probably acquired in relatively recent times. One of the repatriated belts from the collection of the Museum of the American Indian (MAI), the so-called Captain Brant Belt, named for Mohawk Chief Joseph Brant (1742–1807), is dated to 1750. Although now culturally identified with Brant, it is virtually impossible for this to have been the original attribution of the belt, since Brant would have been a young child in that year (Figure 13.2). An alternative explanation that has been suggested is that this belt might have initially been attributed, or named, for Chief Brant's grandfather, the Brant that was one of the four "Kings" who had their portraits painted in England in 1710 (Bond 1952).[2]

We do know that belts changed or lost meaning through time and even become personal identifiers of major chiefs when their original meanings lost significance to the confederacy. Belts were broken apart and divided, restrung, redesigned, and altered over the years. In some later cases, glass beads acquired through trade with the Europeans were occasionally added to the design of restrung wampum belts. Other belts became grave goods and have been recovered archaeologically.

Today, several interpreters, or readers, of the belts maintain that the esoteric knowledge of the consistent and ancient meaning of an individual wampum belt has descended to them from ancestors of antiquity. The belts and strings are ideally to be "read" (I.E., the story and the significance behind a belt is ceremonially and solemnly recited annually on a cloudless day. It is said that, if a cloud appears, a belt is covered and put away until the following year.).

A recent reading of the Friendship Belt and the Two Rows (or Roads

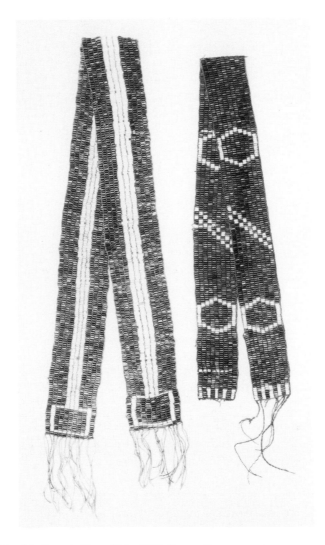

Figure 13.2 *left*: Captain Brant Belt, 1750. Reputedly represents one square as English territory, or England, and the other square the Mohawk territory. The joining white line supposedly designates his repeated diplomatic trips to England. Photograph courtesy of the National Museum of the American Indian, Smithsonian Institution, Neg. #21636. *right*: The Smith Wampum Belt. Presented to Mrs. Erminie Smith by the Mohawks in 1884. This belt was given to the Museum of the American Indian by Harmon Hendricks and accessioned into the collection in 1919. The Smith belt was not part of the repatriated (so-called) Roddy Collection. Photograph courtesy of the National Museum of the American Indian, Smithsonian Institution, Neg. #21636.

or Paths) Belt was conducted by Cayuga Chief Jacob E. Thomas, a multilingual Iroquois from the Six Nations Reserve. This reading was recorded by Dr. Michael K. Foster in 1977 for the National Museum of Man, Ottawa, Canada, in the anticipation that, among other possibilities, data would be derived on how treaty councils were conducted, that verification would be made of agreements from the colonial period, and that continuing reliable oral tradition would be demonstrated. It was also hoped that the analysis would be able to establish the foundation for such data being accepted as legal documents in courts of law (Foster 1978). This research is still ongoing.

It is worth noting that the Seneca wampum belts from the New York State Museum, Albany, now in the custody of the Seneca-Iroquois National Museum on the Allegany Reservation, have not been read in the 15-years since they were moved there. In this instance, many believe that any initial story attached to these belts has been totally or largely forgotten. The less charitable have privately indicated that most of the information currently being related by readers of the Iroquois belts and strings is, at best, wishful thinking. Even if this is the case, it does not minimize the contemporary-Iroquois' emotional attachment to the belts.

Iroquois Historical Background

The American Revolution resulted in the fracturing of the Iroquois Confederacy. Although officially urged by the British and the rebel colonists to remain aloof from this "white man's war," both sides, recognizing the great influence that the Indians would have on the ultimate outcome of the war, surreptitiously sought to bring the confederacy into the conflict. Faced with the issue of the war itself and with which side to support, the Iroquois Confederacy symbolically covered its central fire at Onondaga, indicating that the issue could not be officially resolved by the ideal method of unanimity. Each tribe was to choose its own course. The Oneida and Tuscarora decided to support the Americans, and the other confederacy tribes, the Mohawk, Onondaga, Cayuga, and Seneca, generally supported the British. The ultimate results of the war were politically, economically, and culturally disastrous for all of the constituent tribes and for the confederacy, and all of the tribes suffered.

General George Washington (1732–1799) ordered the formation of the Sullivan-Clinton-Brodhead military expedition in 1779 into the Iroquois homeland to punish the loyalist Iroquois for their part in the Revolution. Iroquois villages, orchards, and farm animals were destroyed by the American invasion into central and western New York. This invasion, which reached deep into westernmost Seneca territory on the Genesee River, drove the Iroquois to the protection of their allies, the British at Fort Niagara, and later into a series of tribal settlements along Buffalo Creek, now generally the area south and east of Buffalo, New York, on Lake Erie.

Chief Joseph Brant decided to lead the loyalist faction of the Iroquois into exile in Canada, having been promised he could keep a large reserve to resettle his people along the banks of the Grand River. It was at this point that the confederacy's corpus of wampum belts was divided between the Canadian Iroquois and the Iroquois who chose to continue residence in what was to become the United States. Because of continuing hostilities with the Americans, a large segment of the American branch of the Iroquois settled at aforementioned Buffalo Creek, where a sizable Seneca reservation, the Buffalo Creek Reservation, was officially established in 1797. This reservation provided a temporary refuge for the Iroquois rather than forcing them to return to their original individual tribal homelands further east.

In 1784, the Six Nations Reserve was established on the Grand River; and it was there that Joseph Brant revived the confederacy's council fire (Figure 13.3). According to oral accounts of the revival of the Confederacy at the Six Nations Reserve, the individual lineages present who carried the traditional titles initiated the revival. However, it was not until some 60 years later (1847) that the American portion of the divided confederacy's wampum belts, those that remained in Onondaga possession at Buffalo Creek, were returned to the Onondaga Reservation in central New York and the American council fire of the Iroquois Confederacy rekindled.

Momentous historical events in Iroquois history continued to occur between the American Revolution and the mid-1800s that directly affected the role that the wampum belts were to have in the traditional culture of the Iroquois by the latter part of the 19th century. A continuing series of treaties was negotiated between the confederacy or its individual members and the new New York State and federal

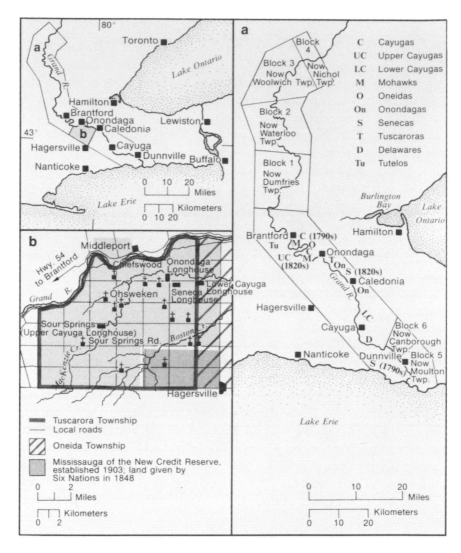

Figure 13.3   A series of maps of the Six Nations Reserve, Grand River, Ontario, Canada, showing the original extent of the Reserve, surrounding communities, and the various locations of tribal settlements. Maps by Judith Crawley Wojcik, Cartographer, handbook project. From *Northeast*, Vol. 15, *Handbook of North American Indians*, Smithsonian Institution, 1978, p. 526.

governments. Ultimately, these treaties resulted in an accelerating reduction of Iroquois lands within the state, until the various tribes were left with only a small fraction of land they had originally owned. In fact, the Cayuga were completely landless by the end of the 18th century and sought refuge on other Iroquois reservations. The treaty process temporarily resulted in the Seneca having a dozen reservations in the early 19th century. Many of the treaties with the Iroquois were fraudulent, initiating protracted and generally unsuccessful legal battles in attempting to reclaim these lands. Some of these efforts continued well into the 20th century; some are still ongoing. (Figure 13.4).

Crisis of Culture Change

One of the ultimate results of the continuing reduction of tribal land bases was a growing dissatisfaction among the Iroquois with the traditional system, which was increasingly seen as being unable to deal with their rapidly changing circumstances. The traditional ideas and the tribal governmental system were being continually challenged by swift culture change over which the Iroquois had little control. New Christian religions were introduced to the Iroquois, as were new ways of farming; bark longhouses and villages were being abandoned for disbursed single-family log homes. The idea of individual ownership of real property was now being accepted, contrary to the communal-ownership principles that had previously governed landownership. Sex roles were changing, with males now beginning to accept agriculture as an appropriate male endeavor, abandoning the old form of female horticulture. Nascent class distinctions were being formed, with the chiefly class beginning to amass relative economic advantages, in contradiction to the older cultural expectations and role models. The disastrous effects of the introduction of alcohol, new diseases, and epidemics increased wide-scale disruption of the traditional social system and challenged the usual methods of dealing with the familiar.

A prophet had appeared among the Seneca, although earlier and less-successful messianic individuals had also arisen among the Mohawks and the Onondaga, in addition to other prophets among the Seneca. Preaching a message and philosophy of hope, salvation, and rejection of new ideas and material culture of the white man, Handsome Lake (1735–

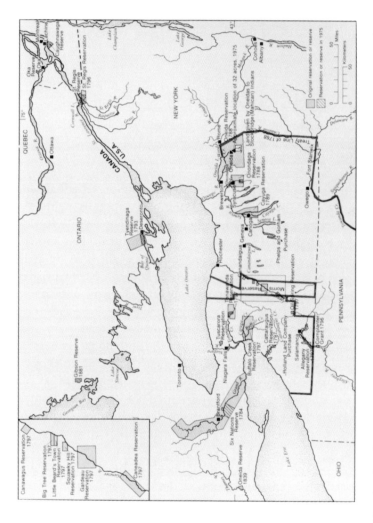

Figure 13.4 Map showing the eastern Iroquois reservations and reserves in the United States and Canada, excluding reservations in Wisconsin and Oklahoma, and a reserve in the Canadian province of Alberta. Dates indicate time of establishment of reservations, and the cross hatching current reservations. Smaller map indicates the former Seneca reservations in the Genesee Valley. Maps by Judith Crawley Wojcik, Cartographer, handbook project. From *Northeast*, vol. 15, *Handbook of North American Indians*, Smithsonian Institution, 1978, p. 450.

1815), the Seneca prophet, brought the possibility of revitalization to the Iroquois during his ministry, 1799–1815. Called the *gai-wiio* (good news, good message), this new syncretized religion has become the traditional, or longhouse, religion of a minority of the modern Iroquois (Parker 1913). Some contemporary Iroquois reservations and tribal groups have not established longhouses in their communities, while others only relatively recently adopted the religion.

The major question of possible forced or voluntary removal from New York became a great factional issue for the Iroquois beginning in the early 1800s. The increasing encroachment and press of whites on the lands and resources of the Iroquois resulted in many Iroquois supporting the possible removal to new lands away from white settlement and negative influence, where the Iroquois would be able to reestablish their traditional culture. Other Iroquois resisted any attempt at or consideration of possible removal, wishing instead to cling to the ancient territory. President Andrew Jackson (1767–1845) encouraged the relocation of relatively small segments of the Iroquois in the 1800s to Ohio, Wisconsin, Kansas, and the Indian Territory (later Oklahoma), where some Iroquois enclaves continue to exist today. The Indian Removal Act in 1830 was passed during his administration. At least in the case of the Ohio Iroquois, they formally relinquished their wampum to tribal groups remaining behind in New York before they began their journey westward.

Eight years later (1838), the disastrous and fraudulent Treaty of Buffalo Creek sold all remaining Iroquois lands in New York State. Although immediately challenged, it was not until 1842 that the Compromise Treaty at Buffalo Creek was negotiated, whereby the Buffalo Creek Reservation was lost, as were the Tonawanda Reservation and a string of Seneca reservations along the Genesee River, but other Seneca reservations were returned. Eventually, through the efforts of Chief Eli S. Parker (1828–1895) of the Tonawanda Senecas, Lewis Henry Morgan (1818–1881), a Rochester, New York, attorney, and the Quakers, the Tonawanda Senecas were able to buy back a portion of their former reservation in 1857.[3]

The various Iroquois tribes that had settled at Buffalo Creek gradually began to move to the tribal reservations that remained to them. It was at this point that the Onondaga returned to their reservation in central New York and rekindled their fire (1847). At least as early as these treaties, the question began to be raised about who legitimately represented the various tribes as chiefs, subchiefs, clan mothers, and so forth, a question that continues to the present day in many Iroquois communities (Shimony 1991).

Governmental Changes at Six Nations Reserve

These events resulted in further dissatisfaction with and distrust of the state of tribal government. In 1848, three of the four Seneca reservations in western New York State overthrew the traditional tribal government by chiefs and established the tripartite government of the Seneca Nation of Indians, with a constitution and elected officials, including a president. However, the establishment of the Seneca republic was not the first Iroquois experiment with a tribal-government reform movement. The Mohawks at Akwesasne (St. Regis) Reservation on the Canadian border had earlier established a shadow government opposed to the traditional chiefs.

Later, in 1861, following decades of dissatisfaction with the traditional political system, there was on the Six Nations Reserve in Canada an abortive attempt to overthrow the hereditary chiefs. Although unsuccessful, this did not end continuing turmoil at the Six Nations Reserve. Adding to the political confusion, by federal statute in 1869 the Canadian government imposed the rule of patrilineality on the matrilineal Iroquois, making this the legal requirement for tribal affiliation and recognition as an Indian in Canada. This act further disrupted the designation of chiefs through the traditional methods of identifying such exemplary individuals who were members of certain lineages within specific clans and their nomination by clan mothers. Between 1875 and 1890, there were other attempts at internal political reform among the Iroquois at Six Nations. Among the reformers was Seth Newhouse (c. 1842–1921), an Onondaga. Newhouse wrote a version of the traditional epic in 1885 describing the establishment of the Great Peace of the Iroquois, the origin of the confederacy, and a constitution for the Five Nations, which was rejected by Seneca Chief John Arthur Gibson (1848–1912).

It was not until 1924 that constitutional government finally arrived at the Six Nations Reserve, with the unilateral passage of the Canadian Indian Act. This legislation established an elected tribal council and decreed that Canada would not officially recognize the traditional chiefs system. The majority of the residents of the Six Nations Reserve objected to the imposition of the legislation, seeing this intrusion into their internal affairs as another instance of substantial erosion of tribal sovereignty and independence. Other, more progressive Iroquois residents welcomed the long-awaited change: they saw the old system of chiefs as outmoded, ineffectual, and corrupt. The new government election was enforced by the presence of Royal Canadian Mounted Police on the reserve. It is interesting to note that this was the same year in which the United States Congress unilaterally conferred citizenship on all Indians within its boundaries, a move that was also officially opposed by Iroquois governments in New York State.

The official creation of a new form of tribal government at the Six Nations Reserve, in opposition to the traditional chiefs, certainly did not end the influence of the chiefs, who vociferously objected to the domineering role taken by the Canadian government. Today, it is generally conceded that the traditional chiefs once again command greater influence of and support by the people on the reserve. In addition, it now appears that there may be an attempt at some form of accommodation, which may be arrived at in the restructuring of tribal government at Six Nations. At the time of the negotiations for the repatriation of the wampum belts, however, only the elected council was officially recognized as the government that was legally constituted to represent the interests of the people. Who officially and legally represented the interests involved in the repatriation request was an important question posed by the Trustees' Collections Committee of the MAI Board of Trustees.

As the confusion of multiple governments continued at the Six Nations Reserve, the question of chiefly titles became equally confounded. The latter half of the 19th century saw a reduction in the importance attached to and role of the traditional chiefs as on-site non-Indian bureaucrats assumed growing influence and responsibility in the administration of the Six Nations Reserve. Although many of the chiefly titles on the reserve continued to pass to succeeding generations, some became vacant and others of only ceremonial or nominal importance. One, the important traditional title of keeper of the wampum of the Six Nations, was assumed by Chief David Skye in 1883 the year that he became a chief (Figure 13.5). Throughout this period, a duplicate title of

Figure 13.5 Photograph of Six Nations Reserve Chiefs in Council House, c.a. 1910, attributed to Arthur C. Parker. Chief David Skye, mentioned in the text, is front left, holding cane. David John, Sr., is holding wampum, front center. Photograph courtesy of the Rochester Museum and Science Center, Rochester, New York, #RM 1355.

keeper of the wampum was also held by the Onondaga in New York State. However, at least in the case of Chief Skye, the assumption of the name was only a formal designation, with few duties actually attached to the title. In reality, Chief John Skanawati Buck, an Onondaga who had become a chief in 1859, functioned as the keeper of the wampum, a position he maintained for some 50 years.

It was during this period that many of those who filled the traditional functions associated with chiefly titles, both in Canada and the United States, including the keeper of the wampum, began to be disregarded or only sporadically enforced. The keepers of the wampum, concerned about the declining interest in the belts among their people, began to consider how they might best protect the objects for the future. They began to consider the release or sale of the belts to others who could guarantee their safekeeping. The heartfelt concern for the prospective fate of the belts and the future of the Iroquois was perhaps best expressed in a quote attributed to Chief John Arthur Gibson: "Another generation and there will be no custom; still another generation and there will be no memory" (Goldenweiser 1912:692).

The Sale of the Belts

"Gleaners," persons who periodically traveled through the reservations collecting ethnographic items for private patrons and for institutions, were often successful in purchasing wampum belts and other materials from individuals who felt it within their rights to sell. It was by this process that the major Iroquois wampum-belt collections of the MAI and the New York State Museum ultimately came into being. Both of these institutions have since repatriated portions of their collections, the Onondaga collection of wampum belts from the New York State Museum having been repatriated in accordance with an agreement signed by confederacy chiefs on October 13, 1989 (Snow 1989).[4]

In 1888, five years after Chief Skye assumed the title keeper of the wampum, J. N. B. Hewitt (1859–1937), an anthropologist of Tuscarora descent, collected ethnographic data on eight of the wampum belts that were in the possession of Chief Buck. Later, in 1892, Harriett Maxwell Converse (1836–1903) recorded 22 belts in Chief Buck's possession. It is likely that Mrs. Converse purchased one of the belts at this time.

When Chief Buck died in 1893, his immediate family, considering the collection of wampum belts as personal, family property, refused a request to relinquish custody of the remaining belts to the Committee of Chiefs Council. The chiefs viewed the belts as national property being held in the custody of the keeper of the wampum. The following year, David Boyle (1842–1913), a private collector and archaeologist, was approached by the committee and was talked into turning over to the chiefs four of the belts that he had obtained from the Buck family. In February 1895, the chiefs appeared to have possession of only these four belts, which were deposited in a safe in Ohsweken, the political and administrative center of the Six Nations Reserve. William M. Beauchamp (1830–1925) photographed six national belts in the possession of the chiefs in 1899. In that same year, Thomas R. Roddy bought a collection of 11 belts from Joshua Buck, son of Chief Buck, and Joshua's brother-in-law, James Jamieson, a Cayuga chief.[5] It was this collection of 11 belts that was ultimately to come into the possession of the MAI.

In February 1900, Mrs. Converse wrote to Superintendent E. D. Cameron of the Department of Indian Affairs at Brantford, Ontario, complaining about Roddy's purchase of 11 of 22 belts that had been shown to her in Chief Buck's possession in 1892 and mentioning that Roddy had attempted to sell the belts to the Buffalo Historical Society. Knowing of the clouds that surrounded the belts, Arthur C. Parker (1881–1955), state archaeologist for New York and director of the Rochester Municipal Museum (now the Rochester Museum and Science Center), himself of part-Seneca ancestry, broadcast to major museums an alert, which resulted in the majority of museums refusing to consider purchase of the items. Cameron began an aggressive although unsuccessful effort to have the belts returned to the Iroquois. Mrs. Converse died in 1903, before she was able to press the issue of the alienation of the belts. A photograph of the Roddy belts appeared in a major publication on the subject of wampum that was published at the turn of the century (Beauchamp 1901:321–480).

From January 1904 to November 1906, Roddy employed George A. Dorsey (1868–1931) of the Field Museum, Chicago, Illinois, as a broker in unsuccessful attempts to dispose of the belts. Later, from August 1908 to November 1909, the belts were fortunately housed at the State Historical Society of Wisconsin Museum in another unsuccessful attempt to sell them. While at the museum, they were cataloged, creating a valuable record of these artifacts. Neither museum could find an "angel" who would be willing to purchase the belts on behalf of the institutions.

It was on December 14, 1909, that William Sandy, a Cayuga chief and member of the Committee of Chiefs at Six Nations, wrote to the governor-general of Canada asking for his aid in the committee's attempts to recover the missing belts. This request initiated a series of letters between the various parties, with the government asking the chiefs to provide evidence of the illegality of the transactions in order to formally proceed against the family of Chief Buck. The chiefs were apparently unwilling to do this since the issues involved might possibly heighten internal factional tensions, demonstrate their own laxity in protecting national property, and reveal their inability to enforce their official decisions in a potentially confrontational contest. In addition, there may have been some reluctance on the part of the chiefs to continue to appeal to an external political authority because this reinforced the perception that they could not govern within their own communities.

Roddy was finally successful, on February 10, 1910, in selling the now-so-called Roddy collection to Willis C. Witte, a representative of the Indian Exhibits Company (later, Indian Trading Company) of New York City. Listed in the sale were the following 11 belts: Red Jacket, Black Hawk, French Mission, French Peace, First William Penn, Captain Brant of 1750, Five Nations War, Six Nations Peace, Two Roads, Governor Denny of 1756, and Old French Fort (Figures 13.6, 13.7). The same year, George Gustav Heye (1874–1957) of New York, a multimillionaire collector of Indian artifacts, purchased the 11 belts from the Indian Trading Company for $2,000. This marks the passage of the belts into the hands of the subsequent founder of the MAI. The belts had now been out of Iroquois hands for some 11 years. It appears to have been several years before some hint of the location of the belts began to become clear. Following Heye's acquisition of the belts, letters of inquiry from Canadian government officials and others began to be sent to Heye; later the letters requested the return of stolen objects.

It was also in 1910 that Roddy revisited Chief James Jamieson and Clara (Buck) Jamieson at the Six Nations Reserve, presumably to attempt to acquire additional ethnographic materials, including any remaining belts in Iroquois possession. He does not seem to have been

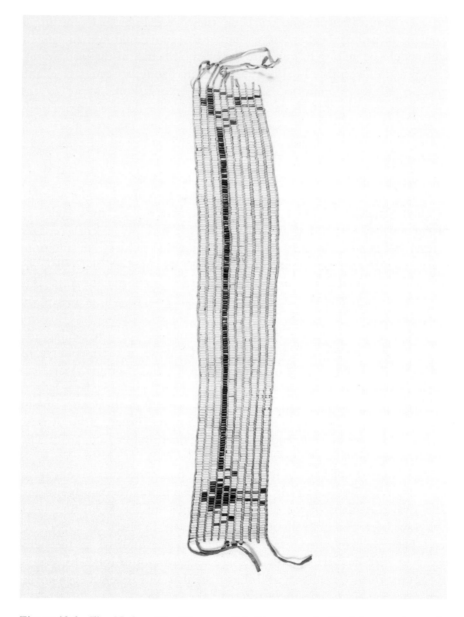

Figure 13.6   Five Nations War Wampum Belt. Represents the Confederacy prior to the incorporation of the Tuscarora. Photograph by Carmelo Guadagno. Photograph courtesy of the National Museum of the American Indian, Smithsonian Institution, Neg. #29163.

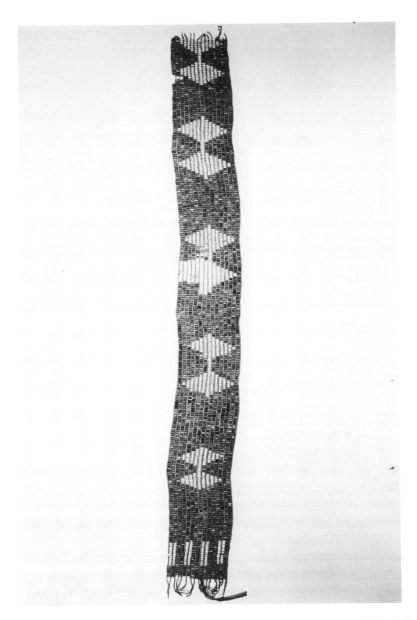

Figure 13.7 Governor Denny 1756 Belt. Represents the invitation to the Ohio Indians to confer with the colonial governor of Pennsylvania in Philadelphia. Photograph by Carmelo Guadagno. Photograph courtesy of the National Museum of the American Indian, Smithsonian Institution, Neg. #39369.

successful. Three years later (1913), however, Joshua Buck attempted to sell Tutelo wampum, which may have come into his possession through his mother, who was of Onondaga-Tutelo ancestry.[6]

Finally, in 1914, government officials, exasperated with the chiefs' claim of sovereignty and their unwillingness to push for prosecution of Joshua Buck in a Canadian court, decided to abandon the effort to recover the belts. Not conceding, the Committee of Chiefs Council, on January 28, 1915, formally resolved that the belts continued to be the property of the Six Nations Indians of Grand River.

It was at this point that both Frank G. Speck (1881–1950), who worked primarily with Algonquian groups, and Edward Sapir (1884–1939), an anthropological linguist, recognizing the questionable circumstances of the alienation of the Iroquois belts, pledged their support in any recovery attempt. Speck, who was affiliated with the Department of Anthropology at the University of Pennsylvania, Philadelphia, had informed Sapir of the situation regarding the Canadian wampum. In turn, Speck contacted Duncan C. Scott, deputy superintendent general of Indian Affairs in Canada, in May 1914, to notify him that the missing belts were now on display in the museum of the University of Pennsylvania as part of the private collection of George Heye. The next month, Scott began a series of letters to Heye attempting to recover the belts. When various individuals questioned the title to the belts, Heye responded with evasion and deception. By the end of 1914, the correspondence had become quite strident; Heye finally responded to Scott's last letter:

> The belts referred to were bought by me in perfectly good faith and I have no proof as to the fact that the were illegally taken from the custody of the Six Nations League, therefore, I see no reason why they do not properly belong to me and naturally I would not hand them over to anyone. [Man-Ah-Atn 1985:7]

In 1916, Heye established the MAI and formally transferred the 11 Canadian Iroquois wampum belts into the permanent collection of the museum. From the very beginning, and until he died in 1957, Heye personally controlled the operations of his museum.

Resurgence

With the rise of Indian nationalism and social activism in the 1960s, the Iroquois began to renew this press for the return of religious and culturally significant objects from museums, both in the United States and in Canada. Several proclamations were issued and widely distributed to museums by the American Iroquois Confederacy demanding the return of these objects from those major institutions holding significant Iroquois collections. The proclamations listed such a wide variety of objects that the museums felt they would decimate their collections. Of major concern to the Iroquois were the collections of skeletal materials and associated grave goods that museums had collected through archaeological excavations, extending back into the 1800s. Much of this material constituted the basis of formal osteological and archaeological study, which the Iroquois viewed as desecration of their former villages in their old homelands. They were becoming increasingly insistent and vocal that this data be reburied.

Faith versus Science

One issue perhaps insolvable, is the question that generally places the Indians on one side—as advocates of religious interpretation or belief—and the scholars and museum people on the other—on behalf of demonstrable science. Some of the Iroquois of a more extreme view contend that many or most of the objects in museum collections are of religious origins. These items include wampum belts; masks; costumes or outfits, which are to be worn only on ceremonial occasions; sports equipment, associated with games, which were given as gifts from the Great Spirit; baskets; ladles; corn pounders and pestles; mortars, used to process corn, beans, and squash (the "Three Sisters" of Iroquois mythology), which are also gifts from the Creator; all grave goods; and other classes of objects. Some contend that there is inherent, potentially malevolent, supernatural power residing within the objects themselves. In the case of masks and wampum, only the annointed should be allowed to touch them. They feel that these items should never have left the possession of the Indians and that the current deplorable conditions in many Iroquois communities, such as alcoholism, crime, drug abuse, family disintegration, substandard health care, poor housing, political dissension, and so on, are punishments being visited on the tribes for having lost these religious items and having strayed from the "right path."

Privately, the more cynical have said that, while there are some sincerely religious individuals who believe that the loss of some classes of objects, especially wampum and masks, has caused divine retribution, many Iroquois politicians are generally using the repatriation fight as a convenient and safe issue to gain widespread Indian support—and considerable uniformed, liberal, politically far-left non-Indian support, as well—in a controversy that will ensure continuing high-profile publicity as they "Mau Mau" the museums. Some also believe that, by focusing on societal problems as the fault of external entities, individuals, or institutions, the Iroquois politicians cannot be held directly responsible for failing to undertake real efforts at correcting conditions in their home communities. In addition, some feel that this new Iroquois religious extremism, or fundamentalism, is symptomatic of an identical religious movement in the United States, but from heightened tribal and racial nationalism, which is increasing the general sense of Indian identity, especially among the young. Parallels are drawn in seeing newfound identities and pride in "Indianness" among individuals who had previously rejected or minimized their Indian roots and who are now taking more radical positions in politics, culture and religion. Many Iroquois also maintain that defining *which* classes of objects may or may not be religious should not be left to the "anthros," historians, museum professionals, or others, that it is, after all, their religion, that they should know what is religious and what is not. They believe that their religion is not compartmentalized, as they think religion to be among the whites and others. For the Iroquois, religion is present throughout the entire culture; no one can understand any single portion of their culture without understanding the interrelationships of all parts of Iroquois culture. Because of this belief, all objects are manifestly religious.

Questions have been raised about the educational value of those wampum belts that continue to reside in museums. There have been instances in which, in the view of some Indian people, misinterpretations, misinformation, and inadequate data have been presented in exhibitions of wampum. They question whether the general public really begins to understand what wampum, in its various forms, means to a segment of the contemporary Indian community. On one hand, the complaint is that the wampum items are in the possession of museums and are being inappropriately presented to the public, resulting in the public having little educational benefit from the efforts of museums. The Indians feel that, if the wampum are going to continue to be part of the educational efforts of museums, Indians should be hired to interpret and approve their continuing role in those museums. On the other hand, there are those who feel that museums are unwilling and, in fact, unable to utilize the wampum in a manner that could possibly be appropriate and that museums generally keep the belts away from the appropriate Iroquois ritualists. Therefore, wampum and other objects should be removed from public exhibition and returned to their original communities.

Other Iroquois do greatly appreciate the role that museums have played in the preservation and protection of their material culture and are quite laudatory of the exhibitions and interpretive efforts that various institutions have made in presentations of their life and culture, both past and present. They express some concern that the current repatriation efforts may jeopardize the availability of the objects to all people; they are concerned that, in the future, the items will once again leave Indian hands and perhaps be lost forever.

Scientists too have expressed concerned about the ultimate fate of the wampum belts not only because of their fragility and of possible damage through handling but also because they might be destroyed through carelessness, fire, or in some other way. It has been pointed out that, once the belts pass from possession by a museum to legal ownership by the Canadian Iroquois, they would no longer be the official concern of scientists or museum personnel. There has also been a fear that they would be misused or not readily available to the scientific community for legitimate research in the future. Later in negotiations between the MAI and the Iroquois, the Iroquois assured the MAI that all of these concerns would be addressed.

Repatriation

The story of the repatriation of the 11 Iroquois belts from Canada began to be revived in early 1977, following the reorganization of the MAI, an organization change that included the formation of a new Board of Trustees. In the entire history of the MAI, this was the first instance of Indians being recruited for the board. Also during this period, an interim director was hired while a search was begun for a new permanent director. These actions had been prompted by the intervention of the New York State attorney general following charges of illegality and misconduct on the part of the immediately preceding MAI administration and board and the loss and alienation of objects from the MAI's permanent collection. One of the positive results of the intervention was that the attorney general required that the collection of the MAI be computerized to determine the extent of the museum's collection and, presumably, to document the extent of suspected losses. Negative publicity involved the irregularities that extended over the years prior to the formal reorganization of the museum.

On March 17 1977, the chairman of the board, the late Curt Muser, received a letter from Paul Williams, an Onondaga lawyer from Toronto, Canada, the legal representative of the Union of Ontario Indians. The museum was asked to identify, enumerate, and provide relevant information on the wampum collection currently in its possession. The renewed interest in the belts in question had, in part, been prompted by the attendant publicity about the losses at the MAI and concern that the Iroquois belts may have been involved. James F. O'Rourke, vice chairman of the board, responded to the rather broad request by saying that the museum could not possibly undertake such a large project, given the understaffing and the ongoing inventory. The wampum collection of the MAI was one of the largest in the world and included various forms of wampum from many tribes across the United States and Canada. The research time that would have been necessary involving only the Iroquois belts made it impossible for the museum to comply.

The chairman of the board requested one of the members, Dr. William N. Fenton, chairman of the Trustees' Collections Committee, to begin an investigation of the organization represented by Paul Williams, the Union of Ontario Indians. In addition, Fenton was to compile and organize already-completed research on the Canadian wampum. Fenton submitted his information and analysis in a letter to the board on July 17 of that year. He had determined that the union was composed primarily of Anishanabe (Chippewa, Ojibwa) and Algonquian groups and had no formal connection with the legally recognized, elected government at the Six Nations Reserve. However, the union was working with the Iroquois chiefs to reinstate the traditional chief system of government at the reserve. The trustees, of course, felt it imperative to deal only with the legitimate government in this delicate situation. When informed that the MAI could not respond to Williams' request, continuing charges of deliberate obfuscation on the part of the museum were, once again, raised.

During this period, Dr. Fenton was a major contributor to an important ethnohistorical undertaking by the Newberry Library, Chicago. This effort, the "Documentary History of the Iroquois Project," naturally involved the consideration of the importance of wampum and resulted in extensive data being compiled on the subject. As a consequence of Fenton's involvement with the project, a copy of his letter to the chairman of the Board of Trustees of the MAI had become a part of the research files of the Newberry.

Throughout this time, the Union of Ontario Indians was conducting its own research, including a visit to the facilities at the Newberry Library. Following a visit by representatives of the union, library personnel discovered that a series of documents, including Fenton's letter to the MAI board, was missing. The staff and administration of the library were appalled and dismayed. After some increasingly strained interactions between the library and the union to recover the documents for the Newberry Library, the late Dr. Lawrence W. Towner, the president of the Newberry, demanded and received Fenton's letter. Later, the information contained in Fenton's letter to the board was included in an anonymous legal brief received by the chairman of the board in April 1981.

By May 1985, Williams could now claim officially to represent the Six Nations Confederacy chiefs. In that capacity, Williams requested a meeting with the MAI trustees on the issue of the 11 stolen belts, which had been illegally taken from the Six Nations Reserve. Williams also maintained that George Heye had been fully aware of the nefarious circumstances of their alienation from the Iroquois and questioned the legal title of the MAI to the belts. Once again, the board confirmed that Williams did represent the chief in the issue of the belts. However, the trustees still were concerned about whether or not the Canadian government would recognize Williams' representation of the confederacy chiefs, a political organization that had no official standing in the eyes of Canada.

It became apparent that the Canadian government would be cooperative in repatriation questions since they were also dealing with these issues relative to their own museums. The notorious confiscation of potlatch material by the Canadian government and its subsequent repatriation to Northwest Coast tribes had made the Canadians even more sensitive to relations with the Iroquois at Six Nations.

When a majority of the board indicated that the belts would most likely be returned, there was brief consideration of the possibility of the museum's availing itself of the Canadian compensation program, whereby repatriated items would be reimbursed to the MAI by the Canadian government for all or part of their worth. Equally brief was the discussion of the possibility of providing replicas of the belts for the Iroquois while retaining the originals. They knew that replicas of belts were currently in existence and were being used for various instructional purposes by the Iroquois. An early version of the repatriation agreement between the MAI and the Iroquois included a provision whereby, once the belts had been given, no further claims or demands would be made on the collections of the MAI, an acknowledgment that early Iroquois repatriation demands had also included a long list of categories of ethnographic material, including masks. These ideas were finally rejected as possibly unseemly and not in the spirit of the proceedings.

The elected government of the Six Nations Reserve indicated that they would not interfere in the process of having the Committee of Chiefs Council negotiate the return of the belts, thus eliminating one of the major stumbling blocks in the prospective transfer of the belts. During the time that discussions were being held, legal advisers had told the trustees that, if the issue were to be tested in court, the MAI would probably win. For the trustees, the issue became one of ethical not legal grounds for their decision to return the 11 belts. Finally, the trustees voted in favor of returning the belts to the Canadian Iroquois chiefs. This vote of the board preceded by several months the unprecedented and amicable meeting in February 1986 in New York of the chiefs' delegation of representatives (both Canadian and American Iroquois Confederacy members) and the MAI board.

The repatriation of the 11 wampum belts occurred on May 8, 1988, at the Onondaga Longhouse on the Six Nations Reserve. A delegation from the MAI attended the ceremony, including Dr. Roland Force, director, and his wife, Maryanne; the late Dr. James G. E. Smith, chief curator; and Dr. William N. Fenton of the board. The belts were ceremoniously unwrapped from their cloth covers and laid out on a table under a canopy. All of those attending, variously estimated at between 500 and 1,000, were able to pass by the table to view and touch the belts, an emotional experience for many of the Iroquois. Also attending was William Montour, chief councillor of the elected government, who presented seven strings of wampum that had been in the possession of the elected government. Chief Jacob E. Thomas, using plastic reproductions, read first the Friendship Belt and then the Two Rows (or Paths) Belt. As a traditional part of major events among the Iroquois, recitations of formal speeches were given, and a feast was offered for all attendants. The event provided a convivial and harmonious conclusion to the tortuous journey of the 11 Canadian Iroquois wampum belts in a successful case of repatriation (Green 1988).

For approximately nine months following the repatriation of the 11 belts from the MAI to the chiefs at the Six Nations Reserve, the belts were on public display at the Woodland Indian Cultural Education Centre, at Brantford, Ontario, adjacent to the Reserve. They have since been removed from the center and are now safely in the care of the chiefs on the reserve. It is presently being suggested that, in fact, none of the Roddy belts are national belts. Of course, this iconoclastic conclusion would be contrary to the basic argument that has been made for repatriation of the collection.

A postscript was provided on January 5, 1991. An additional instance of repatriation occurred when three wampum belts were returned to the Six Nations Reserve chiefs by the Canadian government. These three— the Mohawk Nation, the Three Sisters, and the Covenant Circle—were sold in 1931 by Chief William Loft of the Mohawks to Canadian anthropologist Diamond Jenness (1886–1969). Jenness made the purchase on behalf of the National Museum of Canada (later, the Canadian Museum of Civilization) of which he was an employee. Although Chief Loft had not been the keeper of the wampum, it is now believed that he had wished to avoid possible confiscation of the wampum and possible prosecution for violating Canadian federal laws outlawing the performance of native ceremonies.

It was through the efforts of Dr. Michael K. Foster, a respected

Iroquoianist who enjoys the confidence and support of the Six Nations chiefs, and Paul Williams, a Toronto attorney, that the three belts were returned to the chiefs after 60 years in the care of the museum. Dr. Foster, at that time an employee of the museum, was pursuing his deep interest in Iroquois speeches and oral tradition at the reserve and began to advocate within the museum for the repatriation of those wampum in their care. The continuing role of Williams as an aggressive advocate for and legal representative of the chiefs ensured that the effort would be pressed. The trustees of the National Museum of Canada underwent the same processes that the MAI board had endured, including discussion of possible sale of the belts back to the chiefs. The eventual decision by the trustees in favor of repatriation was based primarily on their determination that the method of acquisition by the museum was apparently illegal and their examination of the circumstances of the repatriation by the MAI (Wiles 1991a, 1991b).

Notes

1. I have deliberately chosen the term "American Indian" over the many other terms that have been in vogue through the years, including the now-popular, and perhaps more politically correct, "Native Americans." There has never been an appropriate generic term invented that adequately applies to all of the original people of the hemisphere; each of the various tribal groups have a term by which they refer to themselves. I am of the opinion that there is somewhat less ambiguity in the use of the term "American Indian" than in any other.

2. The sister of Chief Joseph Brant, Molly (or Mary) Brant was the "wife" of Sir William Johnson. Their numerous descendants are now found among the Mohawks of the Six Nations Reserve and among the Allegany and Tonawanda Senecas of western New York State.

3. Lewis Henry Morgan, considered the founder of American anthropology, published the first ethnographic monograph of an American Indian group, *The League of the Ho-De-No-Sau-Nee, or Iroquois* (1851), which focused primarily on the Seneca. This work presented an idealized view and a somewhat romantic portrait of the Iroquois, already a greatly changed people from those encountered by the first Europeans. However, Morgan's publication has become a deservedly respected classic in the field of anthropology and is found on the shelves of all well-read Iroquois people. Morgan's major "informant" was Eli S. Parker, an important Seneca confederacy chief from the Tonawanda Reservation. Parker was

later to be a Union brigadier general during the American Civil War, and he was the granduncle (patrilineal grandfather's brother) of Arthur C. Parker, who was to play a role in attempting to recover the 11 wampum belts.

4. At one early point in the repatriation negotiations for the American Onondaga wampum belts, an Iroquois professional artist working as an administrator in an Indian museum objected to the use of the term "artifact" in reference to Indian materials, stating that there was a connotation to the word that somehow denegrated the objects. This unique interpretation of a previously culture-free term is now generally defined as any object that has been created or fashioned by the hand of human beings. Nevertheless, several institutions have apparently been convinced and have eliminated the term from labels and catalogs on the basis of recommendations from this Iroquois consultant.

5. Thomas R. Roddy (1857–1924) was born in Peoria, Illinois, probably in the 1850s, of Irish immigrant parents, Patrick and Margaret (Beatty) Roddy. He was the last of their seven children. When Thomas was a boy the Roddy family moved to Black River Falls, Wisconsin, where his father established a general store and became a trader with the local Indians. As a youth Thomas became an employee of the railroad, and, sometime before the death of his father in 1907, also became a full-time Indian trader being especially interested in mink pelts, deriving one his names, "The Mink King," from this trade. Beginning with his childhood association with the local Winnebago Indians, Roddy learned their language as well as a number of other Indian languages, according to one report. He translated the Bible into the Winnebago language, and also served as an advisor to them on a number of occasions. At one point Roddy unsuccessfully attempted to bring peace to the traditional and ongoing conflict between the Winnebago and Chippewa. It seems that Roddy was generally held in high esteem by the Winnebago Indians. However, there appears to have been at least one conflict with the Winnebago that was the case of agitation among one group of the tribe. At some time just before the turn of the century, probably in the mid-1890s, at the deathbed of Chief Blackhawk, Roddy was chosen by the chief to be named "Chief White Buffalo." Roddy assumed the disputed title in the face of growing agitation from Tom Thunder who claimed that title by virtue of descent and the strong support of his followers. Although probably apocryphal, Thunder challenged Roddy to a duel which was prevented by the intervention of the authorities and the failure of Roddy to appear at the proposed site. Afterwards, Thunder assumed the chiefly title, although Roddy also continued to use the title for the rest of his life. His family home in Black River Falls, last used by Roddy in 1906 and informally called the home of "White Buffalo", has recently been renovated by the current owners. It was through his association with the various local

Indian tribes that Roddy was able to organize and recruit Indians for an Indian show that traveled to state fairs and other events. Roddy's Indian performers were a major Midway attraction during the 1893 World's Fair in Chicago. He also obtained local Indians for the Buffalo Bill (William Cody) Wild West Show, and he enlisted Indians from six tribes that had lived in the Chicago area for the centennial celebration in Lincoln Park, Chicago, in 1903. In his profession as Indian trader, Mr. Roddy acquired many valuable ethnographic and archaeological items, acting as a "gleaner" who occasionally swept through Indians reservations and communities in the mid-West as well as in Canada among the Iroquois and other tribes. Most of these items were later sold to the Smithsonian, the Field Museum in Chicago, and to other individuals and companies, although some artifacts remained in the possession of his family after his death. About 1911, Roddy moved his family to Pawhuska, Oklahoma, Osage Indian country, where he established, along with one of his sons, a very successful Indian artifact business. He may have also dealt in Osage oil leases and real estate during this period, the height of the Osage oil boom. It was in Pawhuska that Roddy died of pneumonia on January 18, 1924.

6.   The Tutelo Indians, originally an Eastern-Siouan-speaking group from the tidewater area of Virginia, gradually drifted north and ultimately became affiliated with the Six Nations Reserve, where they have merged into the general population.

Acknowledgements

I would like to thank the following individuals and institutions for their invaluable assistance in the formulation of various data that went into the composition of this article. To others who have also been of help, I also extend my thanks. However, I must absolve any of the following for the conclusions and consequences of this chapter. Ms. Sharon Dean, Assistant Curator, Photography, National Museum of the American Indian, Smithsonian Institution, New York; Dr. William N. Fenton, Guilderlands, New York; Dr. Michael K. Foster, Ottawa, Ontario, Canada; Mr. Charles Hayes III, Director of Research, Rochester Museum and Science Center, Rochester, New York; the late Mr. Richard Johnny John, Faithkeeper, Allegany Indian Reservation, Salamanca, New York; Prof. Flora S. Kaplan, Museum Studies, New York University, New York; Ms. Nancy Rosoff, Assistant Curator, National Museum of the American Indian, Smithsonian Institution, New York;

Ms. Ann Romeril, Documentary Art and Photography Division, Historical Resources Branch, National Archives of Canada, Ottawa; Dr. William C. Sturtevant, Curator, Department of Anthropology, National Museum of Natural History, Smithsonian Institution, Washington, D.C., and Editor-in-Chief, *Handbook of North American Indians*, National Museum of Natural History, Smithsonian Institution, Washington, D.C.; Prof. Elizabeth Tooker, Department of Anthropology, Temple University, Philadelphia; Mrs. Judith Crawley Wojcik, Cartographer, National Museum of Natural History, Smithsonian Institution, Washington, D.C.; Ms. Leatrice M. Kemp, Librarian and Curator, Prints, Rochester Museum and Science Center, Rochester, New York; Ms. Karen Ackoff, Scientific Illustrator, Smithsonian Institution, Washington, D.C.; Dr. Garrick Bailey, Department of Anthropology, University of Tulsa, Tulsa, Oklahoma; Dr. Nancy O. Lurie, Department of Anthropology, Milwaukee Public Museum, Milwaukee, Wisconsin; Ms. Pearl B. Porath, Black River Falls, Wisconsin; Mr. and Mrs. Raymond and Waltina Redcorn, Pawhuska, Oklahoma; Dr. Annamarie Shimony, Department of Anthropology, Wellesley College, Wellesley, Massachusetts; The late Chief Corbett Sundown, Tonawanda Indian Reservation, Akron, New York.

References

Abrams, George H. J.
   1976 *The Seneca People*. Indian Tribal Series, Phoenix, Arizona.
Beauchamp, William M.
   1901 Wampum and Shell Articles Used by the New York Indians. *New York State Museum, Bulletin 41*. pp. 319–480. Albany.
Bond, Richmond P.
   1952 *Queen Anne's American Kings*. Cambridge: Cambridge University Press.
Ceci, Lynn
   1983 The Value of Wampum Among the New York Iroquois: A Case Study in Artifact Analysis. *Journal of Anthropological Research* 38:97–107.
Fenton, William N.
   1989 Return of Eleven Wampum Belts to the Six Nations Iroquois Confederacy on Grand River, Canada. *Ethnohistory* 36(4): 393–410.
Fitting, James E.
   1978 Regional Cultural Development, 300 B.C. to A.D. 1000. *Handbook of*

North American Indians: Northeast. Vol. 15. W.C. Sturtevant, general ed. 44–57. Washington, D.C.: Smithsonian Institution.

Foster, Michael K.
1978 The Recovery and Translation of Native Speeches Accompanying Ancient Iroquois-White Treaties. *Canadian Studies Report* 1–4.

Goldenweiser, Alexander A.
1912 The Death of Chief John A. Gibson. *American Anthropologist* 4: pp. 692–694.

Green, Richard G.
1988 Sacred Wampums Returned! *Turtle Quarterly* :24–5, 28–31.

Hewitt, J. N. B.
1912 Wampum. *Handbook of American Indians North of Mexico.* E. W. Hodge, ed. Part 2. pp. 904–909.

Lescarbot, Marc
1928 *Nova Francia, or a Description of Acadia* [1606]. P. Bigger, ed. pp. 211–212. London: Routledge and Sons.

Man-Ah-Atn
1985 The Keeper of the Sacred Wampum. *American Indian Community House Publication*: 2–9.

Parker, Arthur C.
1913 The Code of Handsome Lake, the Seneca Prophet. *New York State Museum, Bulletin 163.* Albany.

Shimony, Annemarie A.
1991 Current Status of the Traditional Political System at Six Nations Reserve, Canada. Paper presented at the 90th Annual Meeting of the American Anthropological Association, Chicago.

Snow, Dean
1989 Wampum Belts Returned to the Onondaga Nation. *Man in the Northeast* (38): 109–117.

Tooker, Elisabeth
1978 The League of the Iroquois: Its History, Politics, and Ritual. *Handbook of North American Indians: Northeast.* Vol. 15. W.C. Sturtevant, general ed. pp. 418–441 Washington D.C.: Smithsonian Institution.

Trigger, Bruce G. (ed.)
1978 Technical Alphabet. *Handbook of North American Indians: Northeast.* Vol. 15, pp. x–xi, Washington, D.C.: Smithsonian Institution.

Wiles, Brian
1991a An Interview with Dr. Carpentier, Assistant Director of Collections and Research, Canadian Museum of Civilization, Ottawa. *Akwesasne Notes* 23(2): 12–13, 27.
1991b Sacred Wampums Returned to Haudenosaunee Confederacy. *Akwesasne Notes* 23(2): 11.

14 Anthropology and the *Kistapi Waksin* Syndrome: Distortions in Interpreting Subsistence Patterns among Mississippian State, Coast Salish, and Haida Complex Societies and Other Simpler Societies in North America

Howard D. Winters

Subsistence economies are a common theme in museum exhibits, and we are all accustomed to dioramas that portray the hunting of bison or deer or the growing of maize or a variety of other domesticated plants. More frequently, there are exhibits that display the technology associated with those subsistence activities. In the present chapter, I point out that such presentations provide a very superficial view of the roles of plant and animal foods. In so doing, I discuss a number of analytic errors on the part of anthropologists that have long distorted our understanding of subsistence economies, past and present. For the present purpose, I use both hunters and gatherers and complex agricultural societies in North America, although the distortions are quite as rampant elsewhere in the complex societies typified by cities and states. As a rubric, I appropriate the Blackfoot term *kistapi waksin* (nothing food) and enlarge its meaning to cover distortions introduced into the ethnological records through inadequate understanding of the economies of hunters and gatherers. The sources of these misunderstandings include failure to evaluate gender differences as they are expressed in statuses and roles, often reflecting the biases of informants, and the uncritical acceptance of data linked to those biases by the field anthropologists. Errors also derive from failure to place subsistence data in an adequate cultural context and from misplaced emphasis, as well as from failure to consider the ecological relationships of the various subsistence resources among the plant and animal populations of the biome. Also germane to problems of this sort is the simple fact that anthropologists are all too frequently unfamiliar with species that are or have been important to the subsistence economies in non-Western cultures.

Of course, outstanding examples of the *kistapi waksin* syndrome have been contributed by archaeologists for many decades. Even now, screening of midden deposits and feature contents remains desultory at best in many areas; and all too often, where screening has been employed, the mesh is much too coarse to ensure adequate recovery of fish, bird, and small-mammal bones (Shaffer 1992). Furthermore, while there are notable examples of proper screening and flotation of midden and feature samples in the Old World, flotation still remains a rarity in the vast area of Eurasia and Africa, thus ensuring that little or nothing in the way of plant remains will be encountered, to say nothing of the small bones that are a by-product of the flotation procedure. It is little wonder that "big-game hunting" has remained a standard rubric and diorama model for characterizing the subsistence economies of so many early societies of hunters and gatherers, with gathering practically excluded as a significant component of these economies because of inadequate recovery techniques. Conversely, the often-important roles of wild plants and game, large and small, have all too often been ignored in the analyses of the economies of complex, agriculturally based societies. Rare is the archaeological sample from excavations prior to 1965 that can be even remotely considered an adequate sample of prehistoric subsistence economies, even when preservation conditions are ideal.

The Background

First of all, some background for this present topic, which was a by-product of the investigation of a very puzzling problem in interpreting the adaptive systems of early populations (9000–6000 B.C.) in the Prairie Peninsula of the Midwest. It had become apparent that the early Amerindians of that region were living in an area that had been assumed by archaeologists to have been unutilized by prehistoric peoples, namely the interior uplands between the larger river systems, such as the

Kaskaskia, the Illinois, and the Rock. Logically, it seemed that these earliest settlers should have been avoiding the interfluves, which were covered by tallgrass prairie in historic times, an area that was generally shunned by historic Indians, with the exception of an occasional band fleeing from the marauding of their Indian or Euro-American enemies. The reasons for such avoidance are not hard to perceive, since it was a region of devastating prairie fires that swept through grasslands that grew to heights of six feet or more. Even if the risk of recurrent incineration were ignored, making a living would have been a generally depressing experience for even the most optimistic hunters and gatherers. There were very few plant foods suitable for human consumption in these upland prairie areas and a dearth of large mammals. Even bison appeared only briefly in this midwestern region, dating from ca. A.D. 1300 to 1800, the normal habitat of bison being the shortgrass prairie of the western Plains (McDonald 1981; Winters n.d.c). (The late appearance and the abrupt disappearance of bison are interesting problems in their own right but not within the scope of this chapter.) Nor was the region generally suitable for agriculture without the aid of a steel plow that could cut through the dense mat of interlocking grass rootlets. So for historic times, the region may be described as having been depauperate in both plant and animal species useful to humans and as having been hazardous in the extreme as a living area.

Fieldwork over the past 10 years has forced upon us the realization that, for some three millennia in early Holocene times, the interior uplands were not only being heavily utilized but were preferred to the larger river valleys of the Prairie Peninsula and their immediate environs, these latter having few sites dating between 9000 and 6000 B.C., quite in contrast to the valley terraces in the oak-hickory forest arcas of southern Illinois, where Paleo-Indian and Early Archaic artifacts are common on the terrace surfaces, as well as occurring abundantly in the uplands. It also became apparent that most of this favoured upland area in the Prairie Peninsula was abandoned around 6000 B.C., never to be reoccupied in any substantial way by later prehistoric populations, with most localities producing no later materials whatsoever.

So we are faced with two problems: what made the upland areas of the Prairie Peninsula so attractive prior to 6000 B.C.; and why were they shunned thereafter? The first question is the only one relevant to my topic, and the answer to the second will be found in a monograph on the Laws Farm site, Montgomery County, Illinois, awaiting publication (Winters n.d.a).

Two lines of evidence have been pursued in determining why the interior uplands were favoured over the valleys of large rivers during this early portion of the Holocene: the relevance of major geological changes that were taking place at the end of the Pleistocene; and the plant and animal communities that were characteristic of the uplands during this time period.

One factor that would have served to focus attention on upland areas rather than on river valleys derives from events that occurred in the Mississippi Valley around 13,300 B.P. (Hajic 1990; Styles 1985; Wiant and Winters 1991). At that time, the Mississippi River built enormous aggradation barriers that impounded the waters of the Illinois River and those of the other major tributaries, such as the Rock, Kaskaskia, Big Muddy, and Cache (Willman and Frye 1970: Figure 9), thus creating such enormous lakes as Lake Calhoun, which covered the entire floor of the Lower Illinois Valley. Subsequently, lake margins lowered and raised, with the small Keach School Lake appearing around 10,000 B.P. Even when lake levels were low, large expanses of the flanking lake plains were covered by smaller lakes and marshes. Thus, while there is some evidence of utilization of the Illinois Valley during Paleo-Indian and Early Archaic times (ca. 11,000–9,000 B.P.), much of the valley was in an unstable condition and not conducive to substantial representation of economically important plant and animal populations. The more stable environments of the interior interfluves could have been of considerably greater interest to earlier groups of humans.

Examination of the pollen data available (Winters n.d.a) indicated that prior to 6000 B.C. the area of historic tallgrass prairie may well have been oak savanna (i.e., a region in which grass species were dominant, with a consistent association of widely spaced oaks and occasional clusters of mixed deciduous trees in widely separated prairie groves (Curtis 1959:325–338). Oak savannas at first glance seemed to be scarcely more promising than tallgrass prairie, with acorns being the only obvious plant food available, although probably not in significant or reliable quantity.

That plant foods were of extraordinary importance at Early Archaic sites, such as the Laws Farm site, was evident. This upland savanna site has produced more than 300 manos and metates from knolls adjacent to Laws Lake, particularly notable data given that the pebbles and boulders utilized as manos and metates had to have been transported to the sites from considerable distances, such rocks not having been available locally in the thick blanket of wind-transported Pleistocene loesses that mantled the glacial tills of the interior uplands (Winters n.d.a).

A visit to surviving lakes and marshy areas in the upland regions of the former savannas led to the observation that only one plant was present in abundance, namely, the cattail (*Typha latifolia*, with local replacement by another genus, *Sagittaria* sp.—arrowhead, duck potato). A search of 19th-century descriptive reports and photographs also revealed that the cattail was a common species bordering the numerous shallow lakes and marshes that dotted the upland areas prior to their drainage for agricultural purposes in the 19th and 20th centuries, these lakes and marshes having been present in that region since late third-glacial times (cf., Illinoian) or in excess of 100,000 years. Perforce, we were led to an examination of a species that we had previously viewed only as providing something suitable for inclusion in winter bouquets (Figures 14.1 and 14.2). The results were intriguing. First of all, one might note that this species has a contemporary range from the Plains of southern Canada to the Deep South and that it is present in pollen profiles dating from later Pleistocene times to the present. There is an abundant literature documenting cattail's considerable potential as a food item, as a raw material, as a pharmaceutical, and as an adjunct of various Amerindians' rituals (Morton 1975). Furthermore, its economic roles can be documented not only from North America but from South America, Europe, Africa, Asia, Australia, and New Zealand as well.

Without digressing lengthily on the virtues of cattails, a testimonial from H. D. Harrington (1968:220–221), an authority on edible wild plants in the Rocky Mountain area, will suffice:

> This is probably the most famous of all the edible plants in the Northern Hemisphere. It has been called an "outdoor pantry." The Boy Scouts of this area have a saying, "You name it, we'll make it with cattails." Certainly no one should starve or even go hungry in an area where cattails are abundant. They were favorite plants with the Indians, who used them as food throughout most of the year.

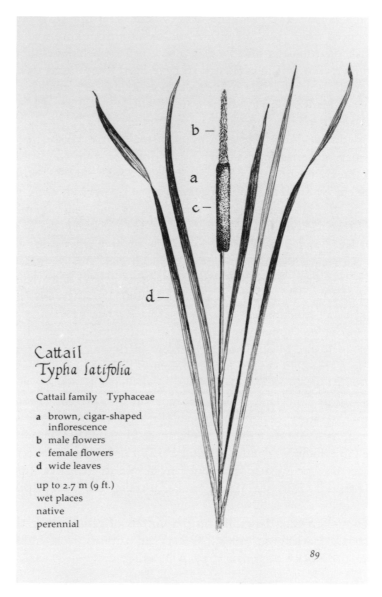

Figure 14.1   Cattail, *Typha latifolia*, a plant that has been important economically to prehistoric and historic populations in the Eastern and Western Hemispheres, although virtually ignored by anthropologists in their field studies. Drawing by Lauren Brown. From Lauren Brown, *Grasses: An Identification Guide*, Boston: Houghton Mifflin Co. 1979. P. 89. Book Courtesy of Glenn Horowitz, Bookseller, East Hampton, New York.

Figure 14.2 Cattails at the shoreline, Amwell Lake Wildlife Management Area, New Jersey. The cattail grows in dense stands in marshes and shallow lakes. In addition to other economic benefits, cattails can yield more than 2.5 tons of nutritious flour per acre in unimproved stands. Photograph by Greg Johnson. Courtesy of the New Jersey Department of Environmental Protection and Energy.

As a source of food, cattails can be used from top to bottom: the roots as a baked vegetable, as a jelly, or as a source of flour equivalent nutritionally to maize or rice flour; the young stalks as a succulent vegetable; the pollen as a basic material for bread; and the seeds as another source for flour.

Research at Cornell University in Ithaca, New York, and at the Cattail Research Center of Syracuse University (New York) has shown that unimproved stands of cattail will produce 2.5 or more tons of flour per acre (Morton 1975:21, 23; see also Lovering 1956). Testing of the flour at the Sheffield Laboratory of Physiological Chemistry at Yale University, New Haven, Connecticut, first using mice and then Yale students, gave satisfactory nutritional results (Fernald and Kinsey

1958:83). Professor P. W. Claasen's experiments with the flour at Cornell University provided evidence of its palatability as an ingredient in breads, biscuits, and puddings (Claasen 1919:185). Quite understandably, the cattail has been recommended as an addition to the roster of plants that could be sources of commercially produced flours.

The young shoots, pollen, and seeds are of lesser importance as food sources but were frequently noted as a consistent item in the diets of groups ranging from the Don Cossacks of Russia to the Paiutes of the Great Basin of Utah. In fact, in many parts of Europe and North America, the cattail was referred to as Cossack asparagus. Fernald and Kinsey (1958:83–84) cite an interesting comment by an early-19th-century traveler on the role of cattails among the Don Cossack:

> He found the people devouring it raw; "with a degree of avidity as though it had been a religious observance." It was to be seen in all the streets and in every house. . . . "They peel off the outer rind and find a tender, white part of the stem, which . . . affords a crisp, cooling, and very pleasant article of food."

However, Fernald and Kinsey also note the somewhat chauvinistic views of Don Cossack officers who have traveled extensively that, "It is fit food only when it grows in the marshes of the Don" (1958:84).

Of course, the disparaging remarks of some earlier commentators on plant foods, such as cattails, might well have deterred systematic investigation of these plants. For example, James A. Teit (Steedman 1930:482) in discussing the ethnobotany of the Thomson Indians of British Columbia remarked of the cattail, "The farinaceous rootstock forms an important part of the Indian's diet. It is seldom eaten by the White man." And Edward L. Sturtevant (Hedrick 1919:582) noted that in Virginia the roots were consumed by the poorer settlers, who were very fond of their sweetish taste. Both observations contain elements of ethnic and economic biases that probably reflect the general tendency to consign the foods of Indians and poor-white settlers to inferior categories. One must also keep in mind, however, that Indians themselves frequently classified plant foods as inferior to such foods as the meat of the larger mammals, which was procured by adult males engaged in the high-prestige activities associated with hunting.

Technologically, the cattail has played roles from the cradle to the grave, having been used as diapers by Amerindians and as dressing for wounds in 19th-century French and American hospitals; as construction material for houses, furniture, and rafts in various prehistoric and historic societies; as a favored material for the weaving of mats; as filling for mattresses and baseballs; as lighting for theatrical productions; as a commercial source of alcohol; and as shrouds and in funerary masks for the burial of the dead (Johnson and Ready 1992; Morton 1975). But in spite of the abundant evidence of its economic potential, the cattail remains inadequately exploited in Western societies, and the roles of the cattail have never been noted in any systematic way by anthropologists. Perhaps something of the nature of this lack of attention to what we have come to call the "shmoo plant" (with apologies to Al Capp and Li'l Abner) is contained within the remarks of Euell Gibbons (1962:55–56), an outstanding 20th-century forager:

> For the number of different kinds of food it produces there is no plant, wild or domesticated, which tops the common cattail. . . . Whenever I recite the virtues of the cattail, the first question that I encounter is always, "Then why aren't they used?" Why will a European go hungry rather than eat the tender green corn growing in his fields, when we consider it the finest delicacy the garden produces? Why was the tomato regarded solely as an ornamental for two hundred years before anyone discovered it was good to eat? Human food prejudices are not related to logic or reason.

One might question the final remark, but the point is made.

A check of ethnographic sources on the utilization of the cattail as food by North American Indians certainly can be used to document the statements of Gibbons and Harrington, but at the same time I must note that the documentation was obtained only by laborious unearthing of brief remarks scattered through dozens of sources, including an intriguing remark by A. F. Whiting (1939:64), which was given without comment or explanation, that the Hopi had introduced cattails into Oraibi Wash from near Tuba City, Arizona. On the other hand, volumes on the hunting of bison, antelope, deer, and rabbits could be obtained with little effort. Both the informants and the anthropologists seem to have been preoccupied with the hunting activities of males, with female gathering activities being noted frequently only in passing. And it was in checking a report on the ethnobotany of the Blackfoot for references to the cattail that I encountered two terms that seem to have utility as rubrics for this type of bias, which so frequently distorts the nature of subsistence activities of both hunters and gatherers and agriculturalists. The Blackfoot have two terms for food, *natapi waksin* and *kistapi waksin* (Johnston 1970:301), the former meaning "real food" and referring only to meat, the latter meaning "nothing foods" that is those that were not meat, although the latter group was clearly a major component of the Blackfoot diet. Thus, real food was the product of male activities, nothing foods generally the contribution of females.

The *Kistapi Waksin* Syndrome

Examples of what I have come to call the *kistapi waksin* syndrome, which I have redefined for my own purposes as referring to serious distortions in the reporting and analysis of the contents of subsistence systems, whether they be plant or animal, are rife in both the ethnographic and the archaeological literature. However, the *kistapi waksin* syndrome is most often associated with the role of plant foods. A few examples will suffice to illustrate the point.

One is reminded that the importance of plant foods was masked among the ¡Kung San by the emphasis on hunting and its products as pertaining to a sphere of high-prestige male activities, while the quantitatively more significant contribution from the low-prestige gathering of plant foods by females was accorded scant attention by earlier ethnographers beyond casual observations on some of the species of plants and associated technical details (Lee 1968:33). I suspect that there was little commentary from local ¡Kung informants that would have encouraged the naive ethnographer to examine the role of plant foods more intensively or to assess the economic roles of women in an adequate fashion.

In North America, examples of various Plains tribes, such as the Cheyenne and the Dakota, are particularly interesting since ethnographies provide reams of material on all aspects of bison hunting but append only a few lines to the effect that women also gathered nuts and berries. A recent survey of edible wild plants of the western prairie documents the importance of a variety of plant species to the bison hunters of the Plains (Kindscher 1987). At least for their sedentary neighbors, such as the Mandan, Hidatsa, and the Arikara, who were also bison hunters, the archaeological evidence indicates that considerable quantities of plant foods were gathered besides the harvesting of such domesticated species as maize. Even more interesting is the failure of ethnographers and archaeologists to consider the economic import of the dominant position of the former tribes in respect to trading relationships with the sedentary valley farmers, who perforce provided maize and beans in exchange for bison products. Perhaps of greater interest is the failure to consider the theoretical implications deriving from the contention that several of the bison-hunting tribes had probably lived in areas to the east as farmers with mixed economies that included the gathering of considerable quantities of wild plant foods. Perhaps one could just as easily refer to the Cheyenne and Dakota as farmers once removed, both literally and figuratively. But no one has really undertaken an adequate study of the role of corn, beans, and squash in their dietary and economic systems. The role of wild plant species has been treated in an even more perfunctory way. But, clearly, it simply will not do to continue forcing the Dakota and equivalent Plains groups into the classificatory straitjacket of hunters and gatherers, with unbalanced emphasis on the former (Figure 14.3).

Another classic example of the role of the *kistapi waksin* syndrome can be found within the reports of anthropologists on the various Northwest Coast tribes of Washington, British Columbia, and southwestern Alaska. Helen H. Norton (1981), who investigated the utilization of plant foods by the Kaigani Haida in southeastern Alaska, summarizes the role of plant foods among the Haida and among other Northwest Coast groups quite well (1981:436, 446–447).

> While the economy of the pre-contact Kaigani Haida is most frequently described as one dependent on marine resources, actually the economy depended on the knowledge of the properties of local plant resources for the production of their material goods. Similarly, the diet of the Haida (and the rest of the people on the Northwest Coast) is most often described as consisting of fish, marine mammals, and mollusks. Even though plant foods have been discounted as unimportant in the precontact diet, the memory of their use, methods of preparation and storage, and terms have been retained by older Haida, especially the women. Their ability to identify these plants, some of which have not been collected for many years, both in their fertile and dormant stages, is an indication of the cultural importance of these resources in the past. During the winter months the people depended almost exclusively upon stored foods (dried

Figure 14.3   Painted elkhide robe with design of Sun Dance Ceremony and showing buffalo hunt. By George Washakie, Shoshone, Wyoming, circa 1900. Bison hunting is generally presented as the *single important* food-procurement activity for various nonsedentary Plains tribes; it is possible to view some of these groups as farmers once removed. Photograph by Carmelo Guadagno. Courtesy of the National Museum of the American Indian, Smithsonian Institution. Negative #39962.

salmon and berries) for subsistence. . . . Since dried salmon does not supply iron or vitamin C, the dried berries and preserved sprouts used by the Haida must have fulfilled these nutritional needs. Nutritional analyses have shown that some of the berries and sprouts used by the Haida are good sources of the vitamins and minerals necessary for good nutrition as well as sources of the fiber so important in the human diet. In addition, precontact preservation methods appear to maximize vitamin retention. . . . Thus plant foods can be seen as important elements in the precontact diet, both for supplementing the marine foods and for maintaining good health. . . . Today the root plants have been supplanted by Euro-American foods, but berries and other fruits remain important in the diet, with some greens and sprouts eaten on occasion.

Similar documentation can be provided for the Coast Salish and other groups to the south. For example, for coastal British Columbia, Turner and Bell (1971, 1973) provide an inventory of almost 100 plant foods that were used traditionally. And Turner and Kuhnlein (1982) discuss at length the importance of *Trifolium wormskoldii* (springbank clover) and *Potentilla anserina* ssp. *pacifica* (Pacific silverweed) as root crops for immediate consumption and as stored food for use in the winter. These authors also cite evidence of the cultivation by the Bella Coola of springbank clover in gardens. As an addendum, one might note that *Potentilla* spp. were important foods in other parts of the world, and the authors cite evidence of the cultivation of this plant in the Hebrides in the British Isles until it was replaced by the introduction of the potato (1982:418).

Our biased interpretation of Northwest Coast subsistence patterns probably stems from a variety of factors: (1) earlier studies were largely the work of male anthropologists, who apparently received little information from female informants; (2) a tendency for anthropologists to emphasize activities accorded high prestige value and to ignore segments of the social system that were regarded as more mundane by their informants, particularly those that were related to gathering and to women's activities; (3) observations of Northwest Coast societies when they were already undergoing substantial changes from traditional lifeways; and (4) an ethnocentric bias that tended to relegate plant species that were unfamiliar or dissimilar to those that were important to middle-class Western economies to positions of trivial significance in the economies of hunters and gatherers (Figure 14.4).

Figure 14.4   Detail of diorama showing American Indian boat building. Numerous studies document economies based on the exploitation of marine resources, but recent studies indicate that such interpretations may often be distortions of reality. Courtesy of the National Museum of the American Indian, Smithsonian Institution. Negative #13870.

More recently, Walens (1981:49–50) in his important work on the Kwakiutl discusses meals and feasting at length but mentions only one plant food, dogwood, the fruits of which are owned by important males. Women are hired to collect the berries, the final distribution of which is regulated by the size of the containers: the large and medium baskets are the property of the male owners; the women may keep the contents of the smallest baskets. Once again, one receives the impression of an insignificant role for plant foods and for the association of women with such resources.

Equally intriguing are references to the Chinook buying wapato (*Sagittaria*) and camas roots (Kehoe 1981:418, 429) and the switch by the Tlingit around 1820 from cultivating native roots to commercially growing potatoes for sale to the Russians in New Archangel (Sitka, Alaska) (110,000 kg in 1845; 17,000 kg in 1847), along with other seasonal plant foods. Were some of the precontact Northwest Coast tribes growing such root crops as well?

Similarly, the significance of the intake of plant foods among north Alaskan Eskimos has long been masked by reporting biases of informants and by ethnographers who have acquiesced in equating general recognition of prestige-linked activities, such as caribou hunting and sealing, with the overall importance of such foods in the diet and the relegating of plant foods to a role of virtual irrelevance. Nickerson et al. (1973:23) observe that

> the casual use of plants is far more important in the Eskimo diet than their quantity or regularity of use would indicate. Several plant foods were definitely present at each of the village sites we visited, in spite of the fact that these plants are seldom mentioned as food sources by *other authors or by the Eskimos themselves.* [Emphasis added]

Particularly important was the preservation of plant parts in seal oil and the pounding of blueberries and cranberries into caribou meat, which was also frozen and stored. Such practices do much to explain how vitamin-C levels were maintained in the Arctic, with many additional vitamins, minerals, and fiber being obtained through the consumption of lichens fermented in the rumen of caribou. The latter practice is somewhat better known to anthropologists than the practice of storing plants in "frozen food lockers" (i.e., underground storage pits), perhaps because the practice is associated with a high-prestige activity, the hunting of caribou by males, and by virtue of the rather exotic nature of an adaptive mechanism that is quite alien to us. In any case, the misunderstanding on the roles of plants among both the Northwest Coast tribes and the Eskimos would seem to be classic examples of the *kistapi waksin* syndrome, with both ethnographers and the native informants having contributed shares toward relegating plant foods to a more trivial role than they should have been accorded. It is amazing, however, that well-educated anthropologists should be so willing to accept nutritionally improbable diets that are based almost entirely on the intake of animal protein and fat.

Sometimes the *kistapi waksin* syndrome is more subtly manifested. For example, Rozaire (1963) in discussing specialized prehistoric lakeside adaptive systems in the Great Basin notes the intensive utilization of plant materials, particularly tule (*Scirpus lacustris*), but his subsequent discussion is limited almost entirely to the roles of fish and waterfowl and to the artifacts associated with the exploitation thereof. The net effect is to impress upon the reader the importance of fish in particular and to leave only a vague recollection that plant foods had been mentioned earlier in the text. In fact, Rozaire implies (1963:73) that shifts to nonfish sources of food would have been during "off-seasons" and as lake sizes diminished with concomitant reductions in the fish populations. In other words, plant foods are less desirable, fish more desirable, and hence more important. Such might even have been the overt view of the prehistoric occupants of the lakeside sites in the Great Basin, but it does not necessarily correspond to the covert realities of the actual dietary system as it functioned on a continuous basis during the occupation of these sites. One should not take as axiomatic that which needs to be rigorously examined.

Parenthetically, certain artifacts associated with the processing of plant materials, such as pebble manos, have been consistently under-represented in museum collections. For example, pebble manos are often discarded by archaeologists in the field because of their numbers and weight. Many are misclassified as hammerstones because of the battering of end surfaces, the result of crushing seeds or other foodstuffs prior to grinding with the mano.

There are other notable and elegant examples of the *kistapi waksin* syndrome in the archaeological literature, including a statement by

Mason and Irwin (1960:55) that also incorporates elements of "technological determinism" and the "self-proving hypothesis":

> Because Eden, Scottsbluff, Plainview, Angostura, and such point assemblages exhibit a markedly similar stone-working tradition with the fluted point complexes and likewise shared a similar mode of life, we suggest that they should all be classified as Paleo-Indian. . . . Numerous discoveries have related this highly specialized stone-working tradition with the specific life-way of big-game hunting. . . . It seems the most reasonable course to infer that all these groups sharing a fundamentally similar economy and technology also shared a similar social system, one appropriate to the predominance of the male role in food getting.

Thus, once one has identified the attributes associated with the manufacture of a spearpoint and its style, one apparently need know nothing else to ascertain the organization and structure of a prehistoric society. It is indeed regrettable that we have spent the past two decades pursuing exotic methodologies and convoluted theories, when all that we need to have been doing was refining our typologies of projectile points.

The merits of the big-game-hunting model for interpreting the lifeways of Paleo-Indians and Early Archaic peoples in eastern North America continue to be rather more uncertain, however. While it is true that mammoths and a few other now-extinct species were hunted in the Southwest and Great Plains, so far there is not a single instance of the taking of mammoth, mastodon, giant sloth, giant beaver, or any of the other giant, now-extinct forms east of the Mississippi River during this time period. And it should be noted that the publications dealing with the recovery of these species in eastern North America run into the hundreds, with more than 80 mastodons and 30 mammoths having been published for Illinois alone (Winters n.d.c), as well as the records of mastodons for Ontario, Michigan, Ohio, and Indiana that run into the hundreds (Griffin 1968:128). Unhappily for the big-game-hunting model, the only site to have produced adequate data on the subsistence activities of Paleo-Indians east of the Mississippi River is Shawnee-Minisink in the Delaware Valley, where the food remains consisted of seeds, fruits, and fish (Kauffman and Dent 1982:10), with no evidence of even the smallest of mammals. I have proposed elsewhere that a mastodon, the most common of the giant species in North America, would never have been hunted as a food item, given that a diet heavy in conifers would have resulted in meat that tasted like turpentine (Winters n.d.c). But makers of dioramas and pictorial interpretations doggedly persist in incorporating proboscideans that were, at best, rarely hunted.

A slightly different type of bias, the "biggest is the most important" bias, arises from the interpretation of lists of faunal remains. While the presentation of such data has become increasingly sophisticated through the years, analyses still remain quite primitive. We have seen a progression from reports that merely enumerated a few of the most obvious species, principally large mammals, to the quantification by genus and species and even the reporting of the exact bones represented. And reporting of minimum numbers of individuals (MNI) and estimated meat weights is common today. The relevance of the latter to the interpretation of prehistoric economies is not always clear given the many unresolved problems of taphonomy and anastasionomy (the processes through which materials leave the biosphere to enter the lithosphere, or conversely to return to the biosphere), as well as the problem of seasonally fluctuating body weights. And, indeed, some 25 years ago, our own preliminary excursions into more rigorous treatment of bone counts led to dismaying results. An analysis of Opal Skaggs' bone counts for Indian Knoll in Kentucky (Webb 1946:330–340) led to the conclusion that something on the order of one-half deer per 100 people per year was available to the inhabitants of that site. That should have been a powerful incentive for the Indian Knollers to sit down on the spot and invent agriculture, although the question as to whether they would have had sufficient energy to do anything about their cerebral breakthrough remains unresolved.

Even today, a typical interpretation of faunal remains will stop essentially with the observation that deer, or sometimes fish, was the only important item of fauna for the economy, other species being regarded only as sources for minor percentages of protein and fat or as variety in an otherwise monotonous diet. Such interpretations are generally drawn from tables of the following type (hypothetical):

	N	MNI	Weight
Deer	15,573	700	7500 lbs
Raccoon	2,253	75	300 lbs
Squirrel	791	45	75 lbs
Muskrat	37	4	5 lbs

Figure 14.5 Muskrat. The muskrat, active all winter in his water world under the ice, stores and eats the roots of water plants, such as the cattail and duck potato. While generally treated by archaeologists as a minor and insignificant component in subsistence systems, ecological studies suggest that they have a more complex role in human-plant-animal ecosystems. Photograph by M. C. Dickerson. Courtesy of the Department of Library Services, American Museum of Natural History. Negative #102902.

Rabbit	94	15	3 lbs
Meadowlark	7	1	3 oz

There are, however, other ways of looking at faunal data. As mentioned earlier, our present interest has centered on constructing a model to explain the adaptations of Paleo-Indians and Early Archaic populations to the oak savannas in the interior uplands of the Prairie Peninsula prior to 6000 B.C. And as mentioned earlier, the cattail is a good candidate as the major plant food in the innumerable marshes and lakes that dotted the Springfield and Galesburg Plains until a few decades ago. The ecology of a marsh or shallow lake is very complex, with muskrat being the prime competitor for the cattail as a preferred food (Figure 14.5). So that, other things being equal, as muskrats increase, cattails decrease and are replaced by *Sagittaria* in many localities (Curtis 1959:392). Thus judicious thinning of the numbers of muskrat around a marsh will improve cattail yields (and muskrat was historically a delicacy for groups as diverse as the Seneca Indians and the Euro-American settlers of western Kentucky) (Figure 14.6). If restraint is used and the muskrat population is not decimated, an additional dividend can accrue. The disadvantages of the replacement species, *Sagittaria*, lie in their having smaller roots and in their being at some distance from the stems and foliage, thus necessitating grubbing in the muck in the vicinity of the plant. Muskrats quite frequently harvest *Sagittaria* roots and store them in their burrows as a winter food supply, a fact well known to historic Indians (Bellrose 1951:304–305; Errington 1961:15–17; Fernald and Kinsey 1958:89). In addition, muskrat houses often contain quantities of edible portions of cattails and *Sagittaria* as construction materials. In short, the consumption of minor quantities of muskrats can have a drastic effect on the availability of plant food, and the judicious harvesting of the muskrats, their winter food supplies, and their houses can serve as an example of what I have termed a "you can have your cake and eat it too" system. At any rate, muskrats may provide only a meager amount of meat but have much larger importance when viewed as part of a system involving human beings and the plant resources of savanna marshes and lakes.

A comparable example can be derived from a study of the utilization of birds in four New Mexican Pueblos (Emslie 1981), in which it was concluded that the great diversity of avian species resulted from prehistoric agricultural practices that created artificial habitats with quantities of plant foods attractive to birds, such habitats as ecotones at field edges, a breaking down of natural habitat barriers, and an environment favorable to the proliferation of the insects upon which some predatory species feed, along with a concomitant increase in avian predators occupying a higher trophic level. In discussing the prehistoric roles of birds, Emslie (1981:323–325) notes their consistent utilization as food and suggests that the species involved may have ranged from the turkey, Canada goose, and sandhill crane to the mourning dove, robin, blackbird, and horned lark. The quantities of bone do not, however, indicate that the yields of protein and other nutrients would have been a substantial contribution to the subsistence base. More importantly, Emslie (1981:323, Table 2) remarks,

Figure 14.6   Man hunting muskrat in winter, Bannock, Lemhi Reservation, Idaho. Although virtually unknown to urbanites as food, the muskrat is regarded as a delicacy for special occasions by groups ranging from Amerindians to 20th-century residents of the Midsouth. Photograph by De Cost Smith, 1904. Courtesy of the National Museum of the American Indian, Smithsonian Institution. Negative #22409.

Thus although the avifauna from the four Pueblo sites represent extreme diversity of habitat and ecology, classifying them into procurement categories suggests the possibility that most species were field hunted or trapped near the pueblos and were attracted to the large prehistoric agricultural fields.

I suggest that the consistent removal of the seed-eating species may have had an important effect through the increase in agricultural productivity and that one cannot assess the economic importance of small birds in the economy simply by citing raw data on their contribution to the subsistence base in general. Of course, the problem is complex, and one might well raise a question about the negative effects of removing birds that prey on the insects that decrease agricultural yields.

Still, the point stands: prehistoric populations, whether they were hunters and gatherers or sedentary agriculturalists, were involved in complex networks with the plants and animals that were being exploited. And it follows that a truly ecological approach is essential to anthropologists for interpreting prehistoric economic systems, rather than presenting the simple statements on environmental settings that have often been labeled as ecological studies.

Similarly, harvesting rabbits can have a drastic effect on the economic potential of the shrubby fringes that characterize Illinois prairie groves, which contain a rich food supply (hazelnuts and other seeds, roots, and fruits), at least if one can extrapolate experimental data from Wisconsin fens that show that the growth of a number of plant species is severely impeded in rabbit-infested areas in comparison to areas where rabbit populations were excluded (Curtis 1959:364). So again, I suggest that the inclusion of rabbit in the diet need not be viewed only from the standpoint of pounds of meat but can also be seen as having larger implications in terms of the productivity of potentially important plant species.

Neumann (1984) provides examples of a similar nature, pointing out the relationship between opossum and yields of persimmons and the effects on the availability of nuts and mast-feeding competitors, such as white-tailed deer, turkey, raccoon, and gray fox squirrel. Squirrels certainly could not have contributed much in the way of meat to the total diet, but reductions in their numbers, particularly if taken before the arrival of the spring litters, could have had a disproportionate effect on the subsequent availability of nuts in the fall. In discussing these examples, Neumann remarks (1984:298):

> Humans played two roles within the prehistoric plant-game food web: (1) they were competitors with other creatures for plant foods, primarily tree nuts and, later, maize; and (2) they were general predators. The apparent concentration on the major nut competitors as prey was not only a case of preferential predation . . . it was also, by definition a case of keystone predation. . . . By preying on a set of mutual competitors a predator effectively prevents any one of the competitors from dominating or monopolizing a finite resource. . . . Prehistoric people not only were in competition for the mast crop, they also hunted their competitors for that food. Thus, from the vantage of the human population a captured grey squirrel would, in effect, represent not only its meat but also those nuts that it would otherwise conceal or consume in the fall.

Certainly, the quantity of meat contributed by rabbits, muskrats, opossums, and small birds was probably never very important in the Midwest, but what was important was the effect on the local flora, especially in such areas as the interior uplands. In other words, faunal analyses should go beyond pounds of meat and consider the data within the contexts of ecological systems and not simply dismiss species that can contribute only insignificant quantities of meat as uninteresting. At present, interpretation in archaeology rarely goes beyond consideration of the local environment, not reaching the analytic stage of developing ecological interpretations.

Misplaced emphasis as an example of the *kistapi waksin* syndrome can be found in an analysis of the nutritional value of shellfish (Parmalee and Klippel 1974:421–434). The authors concluded quite reasonably that shellfish are an inferior food in comparison to deer and other large mammals. But there is another way of viewing the nutritional role of shellfish. Generally, in the economies in which shellfish are quantitatively important, this resource can be interpreted as an item providing an essential daily margin of protein, vitamins, and minerals that evens out periodic deficiencies arising from uncertainties of success in the hunt. The foregoing certainly does not imply that the practitioners of this mixed economy understood such a strategy in nutritional terms. But it was a very successful solution since a diet emphasizing deer, nuts, and shellfish is replete with essential nutrients, lacking only adequate vitamin C and fiber (Winters n.d.b). Again, I emphasize the importance of interpreting data within the context of the systems of which they are a part rather than solely as isolated variables.

To digress a bit at this point, one must note that there is another problem in evaluating the effects of including substantial quantities of shellfish in the diet on a daily basis. Shellfish, as well as several species of fish, contain substantial amounts of thiaminase, an enzyme that acts specifically to destroy thiamine, or vitamin B-1 (Jensen 1953:107), a deficiency of which can lead to beriberi and serious damage to the nervous and cardiovascular systems. However, cooking destroys thiaminase, mitigating the deleterious effects of vitamin B-1 deficiency that would be induced by large intakes of thiaminase. I defy anyone to find adequate discussions of the mode of utilization of shellfish in archaeological reports, my own included, aside from an occasional illustration of shellfish in a baking pit or descriptions of selected features containing shellfish.

Cui Bono?

As a final point, I consider the question of the relevancy of better interpretation of prehistoric and historic subsistence patterns. In the long run, does it really matter whether we correctly assess the roles of plant foods, small mammals, and shellfish, beyond noting their existence? In answering this question, I use as an example the demise of the complex Mississippian urbanized societies that had flourished in the Prairie Peninsula area of the Midwest between ca. A.D. 1000 and 1450 (Figure 14.7). A number of factors probably contributed to the precipitous decline and disappearance of these societies, including an agricultural system that was disastrously maladaptive in the Prairie Peninsula area, culturally induced environmental deterioration, population expansion, rebellion, disease (both endemic and epidemic), starvation, warfare, and collapse of a trading network that might have provided adequate food supplements for the rapidly expanding populations in the cities, towns, hamlets, and farmsteads that characterized these societies.

While intensive agriculture is generally presented as a beneficent component of the Mississippian subsistence system, the larger reality would argue that there is a baneful aspect. Malnutrition may have been a

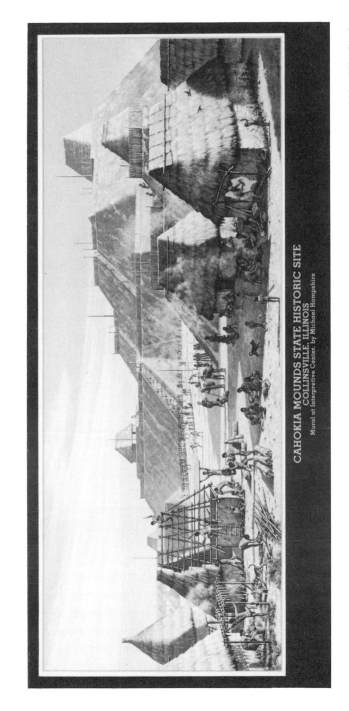

CAHOKIA MOUNDS STATE HISTORIC SITE
COLLINSVILLE, ILLINOIS
Mural at Interpretive Center, by Michael Hampshire

Figure 14.7 Cahokia, Madison County, Illinois. One of the larger cities of the world during the few centuries (A.D. 900–1350) that it was occupied. Even such urban centers of prehistoric civilizations manifested aspects of the *kistapi waksin* syndrome.

possible additional factor, given that recent studies have indicated that for many Mississippian populations maize may have contributed as much as 60% of the diet. Such heavy reliance on maize can create serious problems, especially for infants and children fed large quantities of corn gruel or other corn products. These dietary problems included lysine deficiency, pellagra, scurvy, zinc deficiency, and iron-deficiency anemia (El-Najjar 1977; Schindler et al. 1981; Wing and Brown 1979).[1]

Compounding the problems deriving from maize agriculture is evidence of the presence of blastomycosis (a debilitating fungal infection caused by spores in the soil) or tuberculosis as endemic factors among farming populations. The evidence somewhat favors tuberculosis rather than blastomycosis as the source of the lesions found on bones (Buikstra 1977:316–328).

In reaching a deeper level of interpretation of Mississippian nutrition, we should consider the role of the *kistapi waksin* syndrome in these complex societies as well. Emphasis has consistently been placed on the roles of agricultural products, although there is abundant evidence that fish, migratory birds, a variety of small and large mammals, and wild plant foods, particularly nuts, are consistently present in Mississippian sites, even to the point that at some sites wild plant foods are quantitatively considerably more important than maize (Kline and Crites 1979). The importance of the former subsistence items is rarely considered beyond statements noting their presence.

In summary, no one factor can be singled out to explain the collapse of the spectacular Mississippian societies. But the decline was in part linked to the introduction of an agricultural system that was initially quite rewarding but that led to malnutrition, declining crop yields, and perhaps ultimately to starvation in many instances. As the general health of the population slowly deteriorated, productivity and social stability would also have been affected. And environmental degradation from agricultural practices and the considerable demands for timber would have ultimately progressed to the point that it could no longer be controlled by the simple technology of the Mississippians. When we consider as well the probable effects of inadequate distribution systems and question whether levy and exchange were adequate for supplying the larger communities, adding to these the political and economic havoc of warfare, one might well begin to wonder how the Mississippian political units survived as long as they did. We may eventually find that Mississippian societies could cope more effectively with some of the factors than we realize, but equally it would seem that the Mississippians could not solve their pyramiding problems, including chronic malnutrition, with the effects of each disastrous change reinforcing other deleterious shifts in the economic and political stability of the Mississippian states.

Conclusion

To conclude, unless the errors that accrue from the biases of the *kistapi waksin* syndrome, which permeate so much of the ethnological and archaeological literature, are rectified, there are many facets of anthropological problems that can never be examined or interpreted adequately.

In respect to the world of the museum, the foregoing discussion of the varieties of distortion that give rise to the *kistapi waksin* syndrome might form the basis for rethinking museum strategies. Instead of dioramas devoted to the bison hunt of the Dakota or the farming of the Arikara, one might propose a broader perspective in which the complex interactions of these groups are brought together, with the roles of the sexes being given better definition for each. Such an approach would not be without its perils since it is unlikely that even the most intrepid museum director would be willing to provide the depth of interpretation that would include some of the mechanisms by which the Dakota ensured that the transfer of maize and other plant foods by the Arikara in exchange for bison meat and hides would continue on a regular basis.

There is also a wistful longing on my part that museums begin to move in the direction of meaningful content. Today, we routinely find exhibits that are aesthetically pleasing and technically correct but with a vapidity of content that is often disquieting. Perhaps we should explore paths that lead us away from Disneyland.

Note

1. The following comments are derived from Wing and Brown (1979) and other authors as noted.

Lysine Deficiency: The essential amino acid lysine is deficient in maize, leading to growth disorders. Lysine deficiency can be counteracted in several ways. (1) A regular supplement of beans, which are high in lysine. While domesticated beans first appear in Mississippian sites shortly before A.D. 1000, they seem to remain quite rare. Perhaps they do not preserve as well as maize, which is common in Mississippian sites. A more commonly occurring native bean, *Strophostyles*, occurs consistently in Archaic and Woodland sites, but whether they were quantitatively significant in any regular fashion and whether they were also lysine rich are variables for which we lack data. (2) Treatment of maize with CaOH (lime), which makes lysine that is present more available to the body. But there is no evidence to suggest such treatment either prehistorically or historically in the Midwest. (3) Heavier intake of meat. In the initial stage of slash-and-burn agriculture, clearing of land may have led to an explosive increase in deer populations, as was the case in the 19th century (Hofmeister 1972:202), but in the Prairie Peninsula such initial gains may have been wiped out by the encroachment of prairie grasses in the cleared upland areas, and deer are browsers not grazers. On the other hand, there is some evidence that upper-class Mississippians were better nourished than the lower classes, with a diet higher in meat content.

Pellagra: (Wing and Brown 1979:38) caused by inadequate nicotinic acid (niacin) and tryptophan, an amino acid that can be converted into niacin. Has been endemic in corn-eating populations for well over 200 years (1979:59). General symptoms: (a) weight loss, (b) gastrointestinal disturbances, (c) mental disturbances, (d)skin lesions (sores). Chronic stage: degenerative changes in nervous system (disturbances in sensation and muscle paralysis). Can be remedied in part by lime treatment, with an increase in available tryptophan, the amino acid precursor of niacin. But as mentioned previously there is nothing to suggest that CaOH was used in this fashion in the Midwest.

Scurvy: (1979:38) lack of vitamin C. The body is unable to maintain connective tissues; there are pathological changes in the bones and teeth; teeth become loose; growth is impeded; hematoma develops, from rupture of capillaries.

Zinc Deficiency: (1979:43) Retards growth in children and development of male genitals.

Iron-Deficiency Anemia: Symptoms range from lassitude to inadequate cardiac function. Maize itself may be iron deficient, and high-starch diets critically inhibit iron absorption (El-Najjar 1977:334). At Dickson Mounds, Illinois, indications of iron-deficiency anemia increase from 13.6% in Late Woodland times to 51.5% in Mississippian times, with bone lesions increasing from 27% to 81% (Schindler et al. 1981:241).

References

Bellrose, Frank C.
   1950 The Relationship of Muskrat Populations to Various Marsh and Aquatic Plants. *Journal of Wildlife Management* 14(3): 299–315.
Brown, Lauren
   1979 *Grasses: An Identification Guide.* Boston: Houghton Mifflin.
Buikstra, Jane E.
   1977 Differential Diagnosis: An Epidemiological Model. John Buettner-Janusch, ed. *Yearbook of Physical Anthropology* (1976), Yearbook Series 20:315–328. Washington, D.C.: American Association of Physical Anthropologists.
Claasen, P. W.
   1919 A Possible New Source of Food Supply. *Scientific Monthly* 9:179–185.
Curtis, John T.
   1959 *The Vegetation of Wisconsin.* Madison: University of Wisconsin Press.
El-Najjar, Mahmoud Y.
   1977 Maize, Malaria, and the Anemias in the Pre-Columbian New World. John Buettner-Janusch, ed. *Yearbook of Physical Anthropology* (1976), Yearbook Series 20:329–37. Washington, D.C.: American Association of Physical Anthropologists.
Emslie, Steven D.
   1981 Birds and Prehistoric Agriculture: The New Mexican Pueblos. *Human Ecology* 19(3):305–329.
Errington, Paul L.
   1961 *Muskrats and Marsh Management.* Lincoln: University of Nebraska Press.
Fernald, Merritt Lyndon, and Alfred Charles Kinsey
   1958 *Edible Wild Plants of North America.* (Rev. ed. by Reed C. Rollins.) New York: Harper and Row.
Gibbons, Euell
   1962 *Stalking the Wild Asparagus.* (Field Guide) New York: David McKay.
Griffin, James B.
   1968 Observations on Illinois Prehistory in Late Pleistocene and Early Recent Times. Robert E. Bergstrom, ed. *The Quaternary of Illinois.* Special Publication 14:125–137. Urbana: College of Agriculture, University of Illinois.
Hajic, Edwin R.
   1990 *Koster Site Archeology I: Stratigraphy and Landscape Evolution.* Research Series, 8. Kampsville, Illinois: Kampsville Archaeological Center.
Harrington, Harold David
   1968 *Edible Native Plants of the Rocky Mountains.* Albuquerque: University of New Mexico Press.

Hedrick, U. P., ed.
   1919 Sturtevant's Notes on Edible Plants. *Annual Report*, New York State
      Department of Agriculture 27:582.
Hofmeister, Donald G., and Carl O. Mohr
   1972 *Fieldbook of Illinois Mammals*. New York: Dover Publications, Inc.
Jensen, Lloyd B.
   1953 *Man's Foods: Nutrition and Environments in Food Gathering and Food
      Producing Times*. Champaign, Illinois: Garrard Press.
Johnson, Eldon, and Tim Ready
   1992 Ceramic Funerary Masks from McKinstry Mound 2. *Midcontinental
      Journal of Archaeology* 17(1):16–45.
Johnston, Alex
   1970 Blackfoot Indian Utilization of the Flora of the Northwestern Great
      Plains. *Economic Botany*, 24(3):301–324.
Kauffman, Barbara E., and Richard J. Dent
   1982 Preliminary Floral and Faunal Recovery and Analysis at the
      Shawnee-Minisink Site (36 R 43). Roger W. Moeller, ed. *Practicing
      Environmental Archaeology: Methods and Interpretations*. Occasional Paper
      3. Washington, Connecticut: American Indian Archaeological
      Institute.
Kehoe, Alice B.
   1981 *North American Indians*. Englewood, New Jersey: Prentice-Hall, Inc.
Kindscher, Kelly
   1987 *Edible Wild Plants of the Prairie*. Lawrence: University Press of
      Kansas.
Kline, Gerald, W., and Gary D. Crites
   1979 Paleoethnobotany of the Ducks Nest Site: Early Mississippian Plant
      Utilization in the Eastern Highland Rim. *Tennessee Anthropologist*
      4(1):82–99.
Lee, Richard B.
   1968 What Hunters Do for a Living, or How to Make Out on Scarce
      Resources. In *Man the Hunter*. Richard B. Lee and Irven De Vore, eds.
      Pp. 30–48. Chicago: Aldine Press.
Lovering, F. W.
   1956 Scientists Say Cattail a Potential Goldmine. *Florida Grower and Rancher*.
      Pp. 11–12, 14.
Mason, Ronald J., and Carol Irwin
   1960 An Eden-Scottsbluff Burial in Northeastern Wisconsin. *American
      Antiquity* 26(1):43–57.
McDonald, Jerry N.
   1981 *North American Bison*. Berkeley: University of California Press.
Morton, Julia B.
   1975 Cattails (*Typha spp.*)—Weed Problem or Potential Crop. *Economic
      Botany* 29(1):7–28.

Neumann, Thomas W.
  1984 The Opossum Problem, Implications for Human-Wildlife Competition over Plant Foods. *North American Archaeologist* 5(4):287–313.
Nickerson, N. H., N. H. Rowe, and E. A. Richter
  1973 Native Plants in the Diets of North Alaskan Eskimos. In *Man and His Foods.* C. Earle Smith, ed. Pp. 3–27. University: University of Alabama Press.
Norton, Helen H.
  1981 Plant Use in Kaigani Haida Culture, Correction of an Ethnohistorical Oversight. *Economic Botany* 35(4):434–449.
Parmalee, Paul W., and Walter E. Klippel
  1974 Freshwater Mussels as a Prehistoric Food Resource. *American Antiquity* 39(3):421–434.
Rozaire, Charles E.
  1963 Lake-side Cultural Specializations in the Great Basin. *Anthropological Papers* 9:72–77. Carson City: Nevada State Museum.
Schindler, D. L., G. J. Armelagos, and M. P. Bumstead
  1981 Biocultural Adaptations: New Directions in Northeastern Anthropology. In *Foundations of Northeast Archaeology.* Dean R. Snow, ed. Pp. 229–59. New York: Academic Press.
Shaffer, Brian S.
  1992 Quarter-Inch Screening: Understanding Biases in Recovery of Vertebrate Faunal Remains. *American Antiquity* 57(1):129–136.
Steedman, Elsie Viault
  1930 Ethnobotany of the Thompson Indians of British Columbia: Based on Field Notes by James A. Teit. *Annual Report of the Bureau of American Ethnology*, Washington, D.C.: U.S. Government Printing Office.
Styles, Thomas R.
  1985 *Holocene and Late Pleistocene Geology of the Napoleon Hollow Site in the Lower Illinois Valley.* Research Series 5. Kampsville, Illinois: Center for American Archeology.
Turner, Nancy Chapman, and Marcus A. M. Bell
  1971 The Ethnobotany of the Coast Salish Indians of Vancouver Island. *Economic Botany* 25(1):63–104.
  1973 The Ethnobotany of the Southern Kwakiutl Indians of British Columbia. *Economic Botany* 27(3):257–310.
Turner, Nancy Chapman, and Harriet V. Kuhnlein
  1982 Two Important Root Foods of the Northwest Coast Indians: Springbank Clover (*Trifolium wormskoldii*) and Pacific Silverweed (*Potentilla anserina ssp. pacifica*). *Economic Botany* 36(4):411–433.
Walens, Stanley
  1981 *Feasting with Cannibals.* Princeton, New Jersey: Princeton University Press.

Webb, William S.
  1946 Indian Knoll. *Reports in Anthropology and Archaeology*. Vol 4, no. 3, pt. 1. Department of Anthropology and Archaeology. Lexington: University of Kentucky.
Whiting, A. F.
  1939 Ethnobotany of the Hopi Indians. *Bulletin* 15. Flagstaff: Museum of Northern Arizona.
Wiant, Michael D., and Howard D. Winters
  1991 The Lincoln Hills Site. Paper presented at the 56th Annual Meeting of the Society for American Archaeology, New Orleans, Louisiana.
Willman, H. B., and John C. Frye
  1970 Pleistocene Stratigraphy of Illinois. *Bulletin* 94. Urbana: Illinois State Geological Survey.
Wing, Elizabeth S., and Antoinette B. Brown
  1979 *Paleonutrition: Method and Theory in Prehistorical Foodways*. New York: Academic Press.
Winters, Howard D.
  n.d.a The Early Archaic of the Oak Savanna: The Laws Farm Site, Montgomery County, Illinois. Ms. on file, Department of Anthropology. New York: New York University.
  n.d.b The Nutritional Potential of the Narrow Spectrum Economy of the Late Archaic Riverton Culture. Ms. on file, Department of Anthropology. New York: New York University.
  n.d.c Paleo-Indian Settlement Patterns in the Oak Savanna and Oak-hickory Forest Regions of Illinois. Ms. on file, Department of Anthropology. New York: New York University.

Index

Note: Page numbers in **bold** type refer to **figures**. Page numbers in *italic* type refer to *tables*. Alphabetical arrangement is word-by-word. Museums are listed under 'museums', 'national museums' and by category e.g. historical museums